Scalia's Court

SCALIA'S COURT

A Legacy of Landmark Opinions and Dissents

WITH EDITS AND COMMENTARY BY
KEVIN A. RING

REGNERY
PUBLISHING
A Division of Salem Media Group

Regnery® is a registered trademark of Salem Communications Holding Corporation

Portions of this book were originally published in 2004 under the title *Scalia Dissents: Writings of the Supreme Court's Wittiest, Most Outspoken Justice* (ISBN 978-0-89526-053-6)

This edition ISBN 978-1-62157-522-1

Cataloging-in-Publication Data on file with the Library of Congress

Published in the United States by
Regnery Publishing
A Division of Salem Media Group
300 New Jersey Ave NW
Washington, DC 20001
www.Regnery.com

Manufactured in the United States of America

10 9 8 7 6 5 4 3 2 1

Books are available in quantity for promotional or premium use. For information on discounts and terms, please visit our website: www.Regnery.com.

Distributed to the trade by
Perseus Distribution
250 West 57th Street
New York, NY 10107

FOR KILEY AND AUDREY

CONTENTS

Introduction ix

Chapter One   Scalia's Philosophy   1

Chapter Two   Interpreting Laws   21

Chapter Three   Separation of Powers   41

Chapter Four   Race   73

Chapter Five   Abortion   91

Chapter Six   Gun Rights   131

Chapter Seven   Death Penalty   175

Chapter Eight   Rights of the Accused   227

Chapter Nine   Religious Freedom   275

Chapter Ten   Illegal Immigration   327

Chapter Eleven   Homosexuality   353

Chapter Twelve   Sexual Equality   403

Chapter Thirteen   Free Speech   443

Chapter Fourteen   Non-Speech and Un-Free Speech   475

Chapter Fifteen   Obamacare   497

Chapter Sixteen   Other "Rights"   525

Epilogue   Scalia's Legacy   541

Acknowledgments   545

Notes   547

Bibliography   553

Index   561

INTRODUCTION

~✦~

SHORTLY AFTER THE PRESS reported Supreme Court Associate Justice Antonin Scalia's death on February 13, 2016, tributes began pouring in from longtime allies and adversaries alike. Many noted his towering intellect and praised his consistent approach to interpreting cases. Some spoke of his love of the law and his larger-than-life personality. Others were impressed that his strongly held views did not prevent him from establishing warm friendships with those who disagreed with him.

One trait that nearly everyone praised was Scalia's brilliant literary style. His "gift for analysis and words," one progressive law professor said, made him "the best judicial stylist since Oliver Wendell Holmes. Through his opinions, he exerted gravitational pull on the law, even when he lost."[1] Indeed, during his nearly thirty years on the Court, Scalia was its premier conservative, intellectual gladiator, and wordsmith.

To be sure, many important and influential conservative jurists have served on the High Court, and there remain today others who share Scalia's textualist and originalist philosophy. Yet it was Scalia who gave life to Aristotle's injunction that "it is not enough to know what to say—one must know how to say it."[2]

His words could be pointed. "Today's opinion has no foundation in American constitutional law, and barely pretends to," he charged in one case.[3] He famously dismissed colleagues' arguments as "legalistic argle-bargle"[4] and "pure applesauce."[5]

Scalia's opinions could also be remarkably witty and humorous. Explaining why he did not think the Court should try to create a standard for defining "literary or artistic value" in an obscenity case, Scalia said, "... in my view it is quite impossible to come to an objective assessment of (at least) literary or artistic value, there being many accomplished people who found literature in Dada and art in the replication of a soup can."[6] In another decision, he explained why the Court could comfortably rely on the testimony of witnesses who saw the face of an alleged killer: "Facial features are the _primary means_ by which human beings recognize one another. That is why police departments distribute "mug" shots of wanted felons, rather than Ivy-League-type posture pictures; it is why bank robbers wear stockings over their faces instead of floor-length capes over their shoulders; it is why the Lone Ranger wears a mask instead of a poncho; and it is why a criminal defense lawyer who seeks to destroy an identifying witness by asking 'You admit that you saw only the killer's face?' will be laughed out of the courtroom."[7]

His humor was often subtle. Consider his explanation of the proper meaning of the term, "modify." " 'Modify,' in our view, connotes moderate change. It might be good English to say that the French Revolution 'modified' the status of the French nobility—but only because there is a figure of speech called understatement and a literary device known as sarcasm."[8]

Scalia could conjure up vivid images to communicate his arguments. In one case, rather than simply admonish the Court for its selective use of the often criticized *Lemon* test, which was created to identify government action that violates the religious Establishment Clause (see chapter nine), Scalia wrote, "Like some ghoul in a late-night horror movie that repeatedly sits up in his grave and shuffles abroad, after being repeatedly killed and buried, *Lemon* stalks our Establishment Clause jurisprudence once again, frightening the little children and school attorneys of Center Moriches Union Free School District."[9]

Decrying the Court's refusal to reconsider its controversial decision in *Roe v. Wade* despite agreement among the majority of the Court that the decision was flawed, Scalia said, "It thus appears the mansion of constitutionalized abortion law, constructed overnight in *Roe v. Wade*, must be disassembled doorjamb by doorjamb, and never entirely brought down, no matter how wrong it might be."[10]

In addition, Scalia had a special ability to put complex arguments about fundamental principles in easy-to-understand terms. Slicing through the various First Amendment analyses that might be applied to determine the speech rights of the religious, Scalia concluded, "A priest has as much liberty to proselytize as a patriot."[11] In another case, while arguing for freedom of political parties to set their own rules of organization, Scalia wrote, "A freedom of political association that must await the Government's favorable response to a 'Mother, may I?' is not freedom of political association at all."[12]

As even casual followers of the Supreme Court recognized, Scalia's words could reveal his outrage at the decisions reached and lack of judicial restraint demonstrated by his colleagues on the High Court. Scalia concluded one opinion, "The Court must be living in another world. Day by day, case by case, it is busy designing a Constitution for a country I do not recognize."[13] And in another: "This Court seems incapable of admitting that some matters—*any* matters—are none of its business."[14]

Finally, Scalia could use language to humanize his argument, to let the reader inside his life and mind, a frequently useful step toward persuasion. "Some there are—many, perhaps—who are offended by public displays of religion," Scalia wrote in a 2014 opinion. "Religion, they believe, is a personal matter; if it must be given external manifestation, that should not occur in public places where others may be offended. I can understand that attitude: It parallels my own toward the playing in public of rock music or Stravinsky. And I too am especially annoyed when the intrusion upon my inner peace occurs while I am part of a captive audience, as on a municipal bus or in the waiting room of a public agency."[15] Scalia's "portrait of a Supreme Court Justice stuck at the DMV" is not what one expects to find in a judicial opinion.

Scalia's way with words is what makes this book possible. His opinions—though full of legal arguments and analyses only a lawyer could love—employ metaphors, stories, and emotion in ways that frequently carry legal writing into the realm of belles-lettres. His entertaining writing style made it easier to understand and remember his arguments. It made some of the most mundane areas of the law seem interesting.

The opinions chosen for this book are not necessarily Scalia's most important but those that I believe are the most interesting to read. Most are dissenting opinions, in which Scalia was not burdened by having to speak for others and in which his passionate views could be set forth with all the fury and righteousness he could muster. His abortion dissent in *Casey* (chapter five) burns on the page. Other opinions, like his majority for the Court in *Heller* (chapter six), upholding an individual right to bear arms, demonstrate his method of interpretation.

Together, the opinions in this collection show Scalia's judicial philosophy in practice, reveal his skill at argumentation, demonstrate his ability to foresee future controversies, and showcase his compelling writing style. In every opinion, a combination of these factors is at work. Before each opinion, I provide information to give the reader background on the case: the relevant text of the Constitution, its historical interpretation, Scalia's general view of the text, the Court's previous decisions in the area, the relevant facts that led to the case, and the opinions of the Court and other Justices.

For the sake of readability, I have eliminated many citations and almost all footnotes. Legal opinions are usually full of references to other cases or materials in order to support the arguments made therein. If a reader wishes to dig deeper into one or more opinions, he should consult an unedited version of the opinions.

The simple goal of this book is to share some of the most powerful, colorful, and entertaining opinions ever written by an American jurist. So after devoting the first chapter to a brief overview of Justice Scalia's judicial philosophy and record, I try to get out of the way and let readers enjoy the great justice in his own words.

SCALIA'S PHILOSOPHY

~✦~

JUSTICE ANTONIN SCALIA was a verbal craftsman. His mastery of language and respect for words carried over into his judicial philosophy. That philosophy was fairly simple and straightforward, and Scalia explained and championed it in his opinions, public speeches, and even a couple of books. As with his memorable opinions, the basis of Scalia's philosophy was that words matter.

Scalia was a self-proclaimed "textualist." He believed laws—and especially that supreme law known as the Constitution of the United States—say what they mean and mean what they say. In short, when interpreting the Constitution, Scalia thought judges should focus on the text. If someone claims he is being denied the exercise of a right or if the government asserts it has authority to take a given action, courts must make certain there is specific textual support for each assertion.

If the proper meaning of the text is clear, judges should then determine whether it provides support for the claimed individual right or governmental authority. If so, the claim is valid; if not, it should be rejected. The analysis is complete.

If the text is ambiguous or not dispositive, however, Scalia said courts should look for support for the claimed right or authority in the legal and social traditions of the United States. If an agency of government had been exercising a certain authority since the Constitution was adopted and it had been accepted by law or custom, it should stand. Conversely, if an asserted individual liberty had been restricted or eliminated by the states throughout history, the claim for constitutional protection should fail. Scalia used the lack of textual and historical support to oppose recognition of, among others, the "right" to abortion (chapter five) and the "right" to die (chapter sixteen).

Scalia also advocated adoption and adherence to general and clear rules when interpreting the Constitution. For instance, with regard to the Fourth Amendment's prohibition of unreasonable searches and seizures, Scalia noted that it was not always clear what constitutes a seizure.[1] Of course an individual has been seized if he has been physically forced into the back of a police car, but what if a suspect were being chased by police on foot? He certainly does not have freedom of movement at that point, but has he been seized for constitutional purposes? Scalia said that questions like this should be answered whenever possible with clear general rules. In a case involving these very facts, he joined an opinion that argued that police conduct does not constitute a seizure until it has had "a restraining effect." Such a rule, if adopted by the Court, would help to define what constitutes a seizure for all future related cases.

In Scalia's view, general rules are beneficial because they provide notice and certainty to the public that is expected to obey the law.[2] They also ensure that the American people will receive equal and consistent treatment and not be subjected to the predilections of the current justices on the Court or to shifting popular opinion.

Consistent with his textualism and preference for clear lines, Scalia argued for a strict separation of powers between the executive, legislative, and judicial branches of the federal government. In his view, each branch of government had the authority granted to it by the Constitution. No more, no less. None of the branches could give up its power or exercise authority given to another branch, even if consent was explicit and the goal was more efficient government. Scalia contended the Constitution's structural designs—separation of powers (division of power among three federal branches) and federalism (division of power between federal government and states)—were more important to safeguarding individual liberties than the Bill of Rights (chapter three).[3]

Nevertheless, the Bill of Rights was not unimportant in Scalia's philosophy. He believed the freedoms enumerated in the Bill of Rights were nonnegotiable and deserved the highest level of protection, even when competing interests seemed convincing. For example, the Confrontation Clause of the Sixth Amendment guarantees criminal defendants the right "to be confronted with the witnesses against him." The clause does not say defendants shall have that right "sometimes" or "often" and it does not cover "some" witnesses. All the time, all witnesses. Yet a majority of the Supreme Court had held that in light of modern psychology's concerns about the impact on youthful accusers and witnesses, especially those alleging sexual abuse, use of closed-circuit television does not abridge a defendant's confrontation right. Scalia opposed the Court's decision and said the Sixth Amendment should not be watered down to avoid potential harm to child witnesses.[4] The text is clear. The right is guaranteed.

These are the types of difficult cases, Scalia believed, for which the Framers designed a Constitution and gave the justices of the

Supreme Court the benefit of life tenure—to prevent society from changing the law in ways that violate the enduring values the nation enshrined in the text of the Constitution. After all, Scalia argued, a democratic nation does not need a written constitution to reflect current values.[5] Elections do that. A written constitution is needed to protect values *against* prevailing wisdom.

For example, the First Amendment to the United States Constitution prohibits the suppression of free expression. The Framers wanted to create an environment in which all ideas would be heard and debated and the best would prevail. They understood that for a self-governing people this freedom had to include the right to criticize the government.

Nearly two hundred years later, a substantial majority of the American public seemed willing to forfeit some of that freedom to curb a form of political protest that offended it: burning the American flag. The Congress, being a political body, responded by passing the Flag Protection Act of 1989. Scalia voted with four of his colleagues to strike down the law on the grounds that the act of burning the flag amounted to protected speech.[6] The value enshrined in the First Amendment—freedom of speech, especially political speech—must trump popular opinion, however strongly held, or the First Amendment's guarantee is meaningless (see chapter thirteen).

Scalia contended that the nation's founding charter is flexible enough—as written—to deal with most challenges presented by modernity. The same guarantee of freedom of "the press," which covered early American printing presses, applies with equal force today to the online press, even though the Framers could not have foreseen computers, much less the Internet. When ruling on the legality of a police department's use of thermal imaging to search a suspected drug dealer's house for contraband without a warrant, Scalia did not find the Constitution lacking, even though it was written before sheriffs had cars, let alone thermal imaging technology. Scalia wrote for the Court's majority that the Fourth Amendment's prohibition against unreasonable searches protected Americans against this modern law enforcement practice.[7]

Finally, Scalia's fidelity to the Constitution did not lead him to conclude that the document could not be changed. He simply argued that it should be amended only according to the procedures set forth in the charter itself. The Constitution's amendment process was followed when the American people wanted to make structural changes to their government, as when they ratified the Seventeenth Amendment to provide for direct election of United States Senators. And, he pointed out, it was used when Americans wished to create additional individual rights, such as when the Nineteenth Amendment was ratified to guarantee women the right to vote.[8]

Some might believe changes such as women's suffrage were long overdue and should have been incorporated into the Constitution by a more generous interpretation of another provision, such as the Equal Protection Clause. Yet the Supreme Court in those days did not feel empowered to establish new rights without textual or, at least, historical support. As important and overdue as women's right to vote was, its legitimacy was established by its adoption—as required by the Constitution—by a two-thirds vote of the Congress and ratification by 75 percent of the states. This legitimacy stands in stark contrast to the way rights are added to the Constitution by activist judges today.

Scalia's judicial philosophy and methodology for constitutional interpretation were fairly simple to describe but not always easy to apply. Scalia admitted as much.[9] But he said that adherence to his approach would help to steer judges clear of policymaking roles. Further, Scalia said you can't beat his methodology with no methodology.[10]

PHILOSOPHY IN PRACTICE

In applying his unique judicial philosophy, Scalia bucked some modern trends in constitutional interpretation. Chief among those theories was that of a "living" Constitution. The idea is that the document's meaning changes from age to age to accommodate the evolving values of the American people.[11] This view of constitutional interpretation, which is shared to some extent by nearly all liberal legal scholars, gives judges tremendous power. After all, it is the judge who gets to decide which rights and responsibilities are valued by the public and which ones can be discarded. The obvious danger in such an approach is that the rule of law becomes rule by lawyers.

With bracing political incorrectness, Scalia said he likes his Constitution "dead."[12] He argued that only a fixed and enduring charter could keep judges from reading new fads into the Constitution and less popular mandates out. He pointed to the death penalty, ironically, as a good example of the dangers of a "living" Constitution.[13] Although the text of the Constitution specifically contemplates capital punishment, no fewer than four members of the Supreme Court during Scalia's tenure asserted it was unconstitutional in all situations (see chapter seven). In their view, government-administered execution is no longer in synch with "evolving standards of decency." Still other judges have limited states' use of capital punishment against certain classes of convicted criminals after deciding, in their view, that it is now "cruel and unusual."

As breezily as advocates of a "living" Constitution write the death penalty out of the Constitution, they also read new rights into the nation's charter. Whether one believes same-sex marriage should or should not be recognized, neither the federal government nor any of the states thought it a constitutional right for the 135 years following ratification of the Fourteenth Amendment. States could allow it, states could deny it; it was their choice. No one thought it a federal constitutional matter because same-sex marriage was not protected by an explicit provision of the Constitution or by long-standing tradition. Consequently, the voters of each state were free to choose.

In 2015, however, this question was removed from democratic debate when, in Scalia's words, a majority of the Supreme Court, in *Obergefell v. Hodges*, "discovered in the Fourteenth Amendment a 'fundamental right' overlooked by every person alive at the time of ratification, and almost everyone else in the time since." The living Constitution apparently "matured," and a new right to same-sex marriage emerged that could not be limited by the states.

For textualists like Scalia, the results should not change unless the law, that is, the text, changes. Thus, neither same-sex marriage nor any other favored activity can become a constitutional right without passage of a constitutional amendment. But as Scalia wrote, for the advocates of the "living" Constitution every issue is open to new and changing interpretations.[14]

Though not to the degree it conflicts with the living Constitution theory, Scalia's approach also differed from a couple of modes of interpretation that were fashionable in conservative legal camps before he joined the High Court. While nearly all judicial conservatives agreed that the text should control, they diverged over how to interpret ambiguous text or how to apply it to unforeseen circumstances. Some judicial conservatives suggested the proper interpretation can be discerned by examining the "original intent" of the Framers. They searched the historical record in an attempt to figure out what James Madison or another drafter of the Constitution intended a particular provision—the Establishment Clause, for example—to accomplish. But this mode of interpretation suffered from its reliance on something that was often unknowable. To continue the example, if a search of the historical record revealed that James Madison intended the Establishment Clause to prevent only the declaration of a national religion, while every other Framer who supported its adoption intended the clause to prohibit any manifestation of government support for religion generally, whose intent should be determinative?

For this reason, among others, Scalia did not find intent authoritative. Instead, he urged judges to search for "original meaning," which he defined as the original understanding of the text at the time it was drafted and ratified. This theory of interpretation is known as "originalism," and it is distinct from "original intent." Scalia said an originalist would look to many of the same historical sources that a proponent of original intent does—for example, the record of debates regarding the Constitution's ratification and the writings of the Framers. Scalia used these sources not to determine the drafters' intent but to gain insight into what the most informed people of the time understood the words of the Constitution to mean.

Scalia's reliance on context when interpreting the text of the Constitution also distinguished him from those judicial conservatives, known as "strict constructionists," who believed all words should be interpreted narrowly. For example, where a strict constructionist might see the First Amendment as protecting "speech" and "press" and only activities that fit into one of those categories, Scalia would say the First Amendment covers communication more generally. Thus, while a handwritten letter might not fall under "speech" or "press" for strict constructionists, he believed such a letter is undoubtedly protected by the First Amendment.[15]

Scalia's textualism (informed by originalism) was a unique judicial philosophy when he joined the Supreme Court in 1986. Moreover, Scalia was unique simply because he had articulated a coherent judicial philosophy that he applied to all cases. Some justices he served with seemed to agree with parts of Scalia's methodology and disagree with others, but no other justice had put forward a comprehensive theory of constitutional interpretation to rival Scalia's.

The coherence of Scalia's philosophy—and the fidelity with which he adhered to it—alone did not explain his cult-like following among many conservatives. After all, there had been other conservatives in government who had pressed the Right's view of the world. Even on the current Supreme Court, Justice Clarence Thomas has argued for greater fidelity to the Constitution and against judicial activism. What set Scalia apart was his ability to communicate the conservative judicial philosophy in a passionate, persuasive, and entertaining manner.

Scalia's unique communication skills were the product of what even liberal adversaries like the late Senator Edward Kennedy described as a "brilliant" intellect.[16] Indeed, when first appointed to the Court, Scalia was considered to be an "intellectual lodestar who would pull the Court to the right by the force of his brilliance."[17] How bright was he? He graduated first in his high school class at Xavier Military Academy in Manhattan, first in his class at Georgetown University, and magna cum laude at Harvard Law School, where he served as editor of the school's law review.[18] Scalia was so superior academically, said one classmate, that "people just competed for second."[19]

Scalia's brilliance gave him a unique ability to foresee the logical (and often illogical) legal and policy consequences of the Court's decisions. Especially when in dissent, Scalia used this ability to call attention to the flaws in the Court's reasoning, not only because of the result it produced in the case at hand but because of the results it is likely to produce in future cases. Illustrations abound.

In *Morrison v. Olson* (1988), the Supreme Court upheld the constitutionality of the law authorizing appointment of independent counsels. The law created a new office to prosecute alleged crimes of certain executive branch officials. In order to give the new prosecutor additional independence, the law limited the president's ability to appoint or terminate a counsel. Scalia wrote a memorable solo dissenting opinion in which he not only set forth the Constitution's structural incompatibility with the independent counsel law but also foresaw the real-world problems the law posed (see chapter three). Scalia said that having a prosecutor who is not part of the executive branch (as the Constitution requires) will lead to unaccountable Inspector Javerts running wild in order to "get" someone.

Republicans acknowledged Scalia's prescience after watching the independent counsel Lawrence Walsh announce the indictment of President George H. W. Bush's defense secretary a mere week before the 1992 election. Democrats did not appreciate Scalia's insight until the independent counsel Kenneth Starr's investigation of President Bill Clinton culminated in his impeachment in 1998. Senate Democratic whip Harry Reid, for one, took to the Senate floor to extol "the very articulate, brilliant Supreme Court Justice Antonin Scalia,"[20] who in his "visionary" *Morrison* dissent "predicted what we are now witnessing."[21] With each side's ox gored, Republicans and Democrats in the Congress both agreed to let the independent counsel statute expire in 1999.

In *Lee v. Weisman* (1992), the Supreme Court held that making students listen to non-ecumenical invocations and benedictions at public high school graduation ceremonies amounted to coercion and breached the wall of separation between church and state required by the First Amendment's Establishment Clause. Scalia, in dissent, argued that whatever level of uneasiness nonbelieving adults feel when listening to prayers, it does not amount to an establishment of religion (see chapter nine). During the course of his argument, Scalia said if simply hearing a prayer amounts to impermissible coercion, then the Court was likely to find recitation of the Pledge of Allegiance at high school ceremonies unconstitutional. He noted that the Pledge had since 1954 included the words "under God." Scalia proved to be prophetic. In 2003, the Ninth Circuit Court of Appeals held that recitation of the Pledge in grade-school classrooms violated the Establishment Clause. The Supreme Court in 2004 reversed the decision on procedural grounds, but the Pledge controversy is likely to return at some point in the future.

Finally, in *Lawrence v. Texas*, the 2003 Court decision declaring homosexual sodomy a constitutionally protected right, Scalia warned that the Court's reasoning would undermine state laws against same-sex marriages (see chapter eleven). He was right. Eight months later, the Massachusetts Supreme Judicial Court struck down the Bay State's ban on such marriages. Eleven years after that, the U.S. Supreme Court voided all state laws prohibiting same-sex marriage.

THE CRITICS

While they often conceded that Scalia possessed a potent intellect, his critics devoted a great deal of energy and ink to highlighting what they deemed the flaws in his performance on the Court. Their criticism of Scalia almost always included one of three points: (1) he did not apply his judicial philosophy consistently; (2) despite his complaints about activist judges, he himself was a judicial activist; and (3) he failed to win majorities on the issues he cared about most deeply.

First, critics said that while Scalia loved to crow about his textualist methodology, he did not always apply it consistently. This criticism usually included the charge that he would desert his methodology whenever it conflicted with a politically conservative agenda. His critics usually pointed to one or two of his several hundred opinions and argued that they are out of synch with one facet or another of his approach.

For example, a few critics attacked Scalia's interpretation of the Equal Protection Clause of the Fourteenth Amendment as inconsistent with his professed allegiance to the Constitution's original meaning.[22] These critics argued that the Fourteenth Amendment was originally understood to benefit black Americans. They also made note of the historical evidence that affirmative action existed at the time the Equal Protection Clause was adopted. From these facts, they concluded that in invoking the Fourteenth Amendment against affirmative action programs, Scalia ignored his originalist approach.

What this and related criticisms miss, however, is that Scalia was first and always a textualist. Originalism informed his understanding of the text, especially when the words were unclear, but the plain text was the law for Scalia. When he interpreted the Equal Protection Clause of the Fourteenth Amendment—"no state...shall deny to any person within its jurisdiction the equal protection of the laws"—he read "any person" to mean, as it says, any person. Black, white, brown—Americans of every color—deserve equal treatment according to the text. This interpretation of the Equal Protection Clause was not a case of Scalia's ignoring his philosophy; it was a compelling example of his application of it.

The decisions and votes his critics did not point to were far more illuminating than the ones they did. For if his critics were right that Scalia disregarded his philosophy when it led to results that did not match his politically conservative ideology, it should be difficult to find in Scalia's jurisprudence opinions that produced results diametrically opposed to the goals of a political conservative. Yet even a cursory review of his record reveals numerous such examples.

In *Employment Division of Oregon v. Smith* (1990), for example, Scalia wrote a majority opinion for the Court that was assailed almost universally by faith-driven conservatives for insufficiently protecting religious freedom. The case involved ceremonial use of peyote, an illegal drug in the State of Oregon, by Native Americans. Scalia, a strong proponent of legislative accommodation of religious exercise, said the Constitution protects religion only from attacks by a law or government policy. Oregon's law, by contrast, prohibited any and all uses of peyote and did not target the Native Americans' rituals. Faithful to his philosophy, he refused to allow the Court to enter the business of crafting religious accommodations. That job should be left to the legislature, Scalia argued.

Scalia's commitment to textualism in some cases involving so-called substantive due process rights also produced results out of step with the political conservative agenda. He never acceded to the creation of "rights" favored by political conservatives (or liberals, for that matter). In *Troxel v. Granville* (2000), for example, the issue of parental rights came before the Court (see chapter sixteen). A plurality of the justices held that a mother had a constitutionally protected liberty to restrict the visitation privileges of her child's grandparents.

While it is hard to imagine that Antonin Scalia, the proud Catholic father of nine children, was hostile to the idea that parents should have the freedom to raise their children as they see fit, he did not let any personal sympathy subordinate his view that rights not contained in the Constitution should not be added by judges. In his dissenting opinion, Scalia acknowledged that the Supreme Court in the 1920s created a constitutional right of parents "to direct the upbringing of their children." He argued, however, that this "right" had no basis in the text of the Constitution and thus should not be maintained, much less broadened. Any issue not specifically addressed by the text or by tradition should be left to the American people to decide through democratic means.

Finally, Scalia provided the fifth and deciding vote to invalidate the aforementioned federal law prohibiting flag burning. Although later admitting in a speech that he does not care for "scruffy, bearded, sandal-wearing people who go around burning the United States flag,"[23] in *United States v. Eichman* (1990), Scalia agreed with a majority of the Court that an act of Congress criminalizing destruction of the American flag violated the Free Speech Clause of the First Amendment.

These and numerous other examples illustrate plainly that Scalia followed his philosophy and not his personal predilections. Some critics charged that these "contrarian" opinions were simply convenient props that allowed Scalia to tout his neutral philosophy and record.[24]

It is an impossible charge to rebut. Nor does one need to, since it serves only to endorse the original contention that Scalia's philosophy was not result-oriented.

Second, some critics asserted that while Scalia decried judicial activism, he was an activist himself because he often voted to strike down laws and overturn Court precedents, especially when those laws and precedents conflicted with what the critics believed to be his policy preferences.[25] These critics charged that while Scalia argued that judges should show restraint and yield to the informed judgment of legislatures, he was quick to overturn legislative enactments when they conflicted with his notions of good policy.

There are really two parts to this charge. The first—Scalia was an activist because he voted to invalidate popular enacted laws and to reverse Court precedents—seems premised on a mistaken understanding of the true vice of activism. Judicial activism is not considered objectionable simply because some Court precedents are overturned or popular laws are found unconstitutional; most Americans seem to accept that a major part of the Supreme Court's job, at least since *Marbury v. Madison* (1803), is to determine whether acts of Congress are faithful to the Constitution. Activism becomes problematic when the Court strikes down laws for reasons that have no grounding in the Constitution—as the Court did to President Franklin Roosevelt's New Deal programs in the 1930s, angering the Left, and then again when it invalidated state laws restricting abortion in the 1970s, provoking the Right.

Scalia was not a judicial activist, as that term is properly understood, because when he voted to strike down acts of Congress, he relied solely on the text and structure of the Constitution. Similarly, when he ignored the doctrine of *stare decisis*—the following of Court precedent—he did so because the Court's previous holdings had no foundation in constitutional text or American legal or social traditions. Thus, Scalia sought to *deactivate* the Court's previous activism. That task sometimes required reversing precedents as well as invalidating laws that relied on unconstitutional precedents.

The second part of the activist criticism is that Scalia was more apt to strike down laws and reverse prior rulings when they conflicted with his personal policy preferences. This charge, however, resembles the first criticism—namely, that he jettisoned his textualist philosophy when it conflicted with his personal ideology. The examples mentioned above amply demonstrate otherwise. Still another decision reveals that Scalia refrained from substituting his notion of good policy even when doing so would *not* disrupt popularly enacted laws or long-standing precedents.

In *BMW v. Gore* (1996), the Supreme Court voted to overturn a state court's award of $2 million in punitive damages on the grounds that it was "grossly excessive." The Court's decision fitted nicely with the effort by many Republicans in Congress at the time who had been trying to legislate curbs on the size of the verdicts juries could award—to some extent because they feared the effect of enormous awards on the economy, but also because the trial lawyers who take a cut of the awards helped to bankroll the Democratic Party.

Scalia remained true to his principles and dissented from the Court's decision. He wrote that "no matter how much in need of correction" the system that produces excessive punitive damage awards may be, the Constitution does not give the federal government any authority to second-guess a state court's determination of what level of damages is "reasonable." If Scalia had truly been an activist—no matter how that term is defined—he would have joined the Court's decision (which merely overturned a state court award) to fix a broken system (whose political beneficiaries are not conservatives). But he wasn't, and so he didn't.

In reality, the essence of Scalia's philosophy for constitutional and statutory interpretation was a response to and repudiation of judicial activism. By urging courts to adhere to the text and its original meaning, Scalia sought to box judges in so they were not tempted to impose their values through the law.

The final criticism frequently leveled at Scalia was that he failed to pull the Court in his direction, especially because of his inability to build majority support for his opinions.[26] It was said that he even disappointed conservatives who had hoped he would be able to move the Court and the law rightward.[27] This is damning criticism. It is also sheer fiction. One would be hard-pressed to find a conservative who actually feels that way. Conservatives loved and appreciated Scalia because he was unwilling to moderate his views in order to gain a majority. His defeats simply reminded conservatives how much better off the Court would have been with five Scalias rather than one.

To be sure, there have been justices who viewed their roles differently from Scalia. The late Justice William Brennan, the Court's leading liberal for many years, seemed to think the job of Supreme Court justice was similar to that of Senate majority leader. Brennan famously remarked, "You can do anything around here with five votes." But Scalia did not want to do "anything," he wanted the Court to do the right thing.

More specifically, the charge that Scalia failed to move the Court rightward is misguided for a few reasons. First, it is premised on the shaky assumption that having a discernible influence is likely, let alone possible. Yet whatever one thinks of the justices of the Supreme

Court, they are not sheep. They arrive at the bench with their own views. If an intelligent man like Justice Anthony Kennedy truly believed that the Constitution of the United States prohibits states from restricting an individual's "right to define" his own "concept of the universe, and of the mystery of human life,"[28] Scalia's chances of seducing him away from that view with something as finite and terrestrial as the text of the Constitution were, at best, remote.

This criticism was buttressed by the more specific charge that Scalia could not attract a majority because his sharp pen and biting comments alienated so many of his colleagues.[29] This was a dicey accusation for—if it was to have any meaning whatsoever—it implied that some of his benchmates voted against Scalia *even when they thought he was right*. There were justices of the United States Supreme Court, in other words, who were voting not in accordance with the Constitution as required by their oaths but out of anger or hurt feelings. This criticism was insulting, but not to Scalia.

The truth is that Scalia by any objective measure was an enormously influential Supreme Court justice. First, his position prevailed in many of the most vital constitutional debates of the past three decades. Justice Scalia wrote the majority decision in landmark cases involving religious freedom, the right to bear arms, private property rights, the right of criminal defendants to confront witnesses, the Fourth Amendment's protection against unreasonable searches, and the Eighth Amendment's prohibition on cruel and unusual punishment. Scalia's views prevailed in other high-profile Court decisions protecting core political speech, upholding a ban on partial-birth abortions, and preserving the jury trial guarantee of the Sixth Amendment. Between 1986 and 2014 he was the deciding vote in 342 decisions.[30]

His influence appears even greater if the lens is widened beyond majority votes and opinions. Scalia's methodology for interpreting the Constitution took root in the Court. Although the justices do not always accord the text its proper meaning, they now routinely begin their analysis with consideration of the textual provision at issue. Before she became his colleague on the Supreme Court, Elena Kagan, then the dean of Harvard Law School, said of Justice Scalia, "His views on textualism and originalism, his views on the role of judges in our society, on the practice of judging, have really transformed the legal debate in this country. He is the justice who has had the most important impact over the years on how we think and talk about the law." In fact, one analysis of scanned books found that Justice Scalia was "the most written about jurist in American English" during the last fifteen years of his life.[31]

Clearly, there are many ways to quantify Justice Scalia's influence on the Supreme Court, the law, and the country. And while its full extent might not be known for a generation or longer, his importance is undeniable. For as two of his most thorough critics said while he was still serving on the Court, Scalia's importance "lies in the words and reasoning that constitute his vision, and that vision, when placed in the enduring form of a written opinion, has the potential to shape doctrines and decisions in the near and distant future."[32]

CHAPTER TWO

INTERPRETING LAWS

~✦~

I T IS OFTEN SAID THAT THE UNITED STATES enjoys "a government of laws and not of men." Americans value the rule of law as the best alternative to arbitrary rule by individuals. If the rule of law is to have meaning, however, the public must understand what the law says.

Enter the judiciary. The Supreme Court in its famous decision in *Marbury v. Madison* (1803) said, "[I]t is emphatically the province and duty of the judicial department to say what the law is." Judges, we know, are given authority to interpret not only the Constitution but federal and state statutes and regulations as well. Some might think it is easy to know what the law is; just look it up in the codes of laws kept by the United States or individual states. Yet the task of determining the proper meaning of the law is not so simple.

Consider, for example, a case that reached the Supreme Court in 1993. Congress had passed a law imposing longer prison terms for those who "use" a firearm "during and in relation to" a drug trafficking crime. At issue was whether the tougher sentence should apply to a man who swapped his automatic rifle for cocaine. Six justices on the

Court said the law applied because trading the weapon constituted a "use" of the weapon during a crime. Three justices, led by Scalia, said the law should not apply, arguing that to use an instrument means to use it for its intended purpose. Scalia wrote, "When someone asks, 'Do you use a cane?,' he is not inquiring whether you have your grandfather's silver-handled walking stick on display in the hall; he wants to know whether you walk with a cane."[1]

In cases like this, the debate among the justices focuses on figuring out what the words truly mean. Policy objectives do not seem to be in play. There are some cases, however, in which the Court seems to torture or ignore altogether the meaning of words in order to achieve a result it thinks that Congress likely intended or that reflects, in the view of a majority of justices, good public policy.

In all cases of statutory interpretation, how should the Court figure out what the law is? During his long career, Justice Scalia helped to define, promote, and implement a coherent methodology for answering this question.

Known as textualism, Scalia's methodology first directs judges to focus on the words of a statute or regulation. Unlike some conservative judges, Scalia argued that texts should not be construed "strictly." Nor should they be construed "liberally." Rather, Scalia said, words should be interpreted reasonably, that is, words should be accorded the ordinary meaning that would have made sense to the legislature that passed the law and to the people who would have been subjected to it. At the same time, the Court should ensure the meaning makes sense within the context of the law or code of which it is a part. Where the meaning of a statute was not immediately clear, Scalia relied on certain tools to find the right meaning. He frequently consulted dictionaries from the period in which the law was passed. He would look to see if words were used elsewhere in the statute and, if they were, would give them the same meaning.

Looking for original meaning, also known as originalism, is not the same as looking at the legislature's "intent" as evidenced by a statute's legislative history. Scalia famously objected to reliance on legislative intent for a couple of reasons. First, it is not usually ascertainable.[2] Members of Congress usually have many different reasons (or no reason at all) for voting for a bill, and thus there is no singular intent that can be attributed to the body passing the law. Second, even if intent can somehow be determined, it is an illegitimate source of meaning.[3] Scalia wrote, "We are governed by laws, not the intention of legislators."[4] He railed against the practice of using legislative history—the statements on the floor of the House or Senate by the bill's sponsors or committee reports drafted by staff, for example—to interpret a law's text. These statements and reports are not ratified by Congress and therefore do not have the effect of law. In most cases, they reflect only the intent of the person making the statement or writing the report.

In one classic concurring opinion, Scalia explained the practical reason for his avoidance of legislative history:

> As today's opinion shows, the Court's disposition is required by the text of the statute.... That being so, it is not only (as I think) improper but also quite unnecessary to seek repeated support in the words of a Senate Committee Report—which, as far as we know, not even the full committee, much less the full Senate, much much less the House, and much much much less the President who signed the bill, agreed with.... [B]ecause the statute—the only sure expression of the will of Congress—says what the Court says it says, I join in the judgment.[5]

Finally, Scalia believed that judges should allow even stupid laws to stand. "I do not think...the avoidance of unhappy consequences is adequate basis for interpreting a text," he wrote in one decision.[6] Unless confusion and uncertainty are traceable to scrivener's error, courts should give the law the meaning of its words. If that meaning is nonsensical and not what Congress intended, Congress can go back and change it. In Scalia's view, it was far better for Congress—elected by and accountable to the people—to make the law, rather than unelected, life-tenured judges.

Scalia accused the Court of misusing its authority in order to rewrite the law on many occasions. One of his most memorable examples involved the case of the golfer Casey Martin.

MARTIN v. PGA TOUR, INC. (2001)

This case involved a challenge to the Professional Golf Association's rule prohibiting golfers from using motorized carts during tournaments. The challenge was brought by Casey Martin, a champion golfer. Martin has a degenerative circulatory condition that resulted in the atrophy of his right leg. By the end of his college career, he could no longer walk an eighteen-hole golf course. He sought to compete in the PGA TOUR's qualifying school (known as Q-school) in 1999 and petitioned to use a cart. The tour denied his request. Martin sued, citing the Americans with Disabilities Act.

The Americans with Disabilities Act of 1990 (ADA) prohibits discrimination against disabled individuals at places of public accommodation. As defined by the Act, the law protects disabled persons seeking "enjoyment of the goods, services, facilities, privileges, advantages, or accommodations" at public establishments.

The ADA specifically lists a "golf course" as an example of the type of public accommodation at which a disabled person may "exercise or recreate." Businesses are required to make reasonable modifications of "policies, practices, or procedures" as are necessary to ensure that disabled persons have equal access to the same goods, services, and privileges that others enjoy. But the Act does not require places of public accommodation to make "modifications [that] would fundamentally alter the nature" of the benefits sought.

In 2001, a seven-justice majority of the Supreme Court held that PGA TOUR events fit within the Act's definition of "public accommodation" and that Martin was likewise covered as an individual who deserved the "full and equal enjoyment of the . . . privileges" of the courses used by the tour during its events. In response to the PGA TOUR's argument that the Act covers only "clients and customers" of the tour, the Court said Martin qualifies as a customer because he paid a fee to compete in the qualifying school (Q-School) as required. Finally, the Court said that allowing Martin to use a cart would not "fundamentally alter" the game.

Scalia, joined by Justice Thomas, said the Court's decision reflected "benevolent compassion" but was unfaithful to the text and meaning of the ADA. He argued that "a professional sport" is not a place of public accommodation and that a professional athlete who plays a sport to provide entertainment for others is not a "customer." By torturing the text in these ways, Scalia said, the Court then is forced to answer the "incredibly difficult and incredibly silly question" of whether walking is essential to the game of golf. The Court's answer of "no" was unsatisfactory to Scalia and not simply, he said, because many consider walking to be "the central feature" of the game. Rather, he argued that because the rules of sports are entirely arbitrary, it is impossible to say that any are "essential."

Scalia admitted he was not convinced the PGA TOUR should not make an exception for Martin. But he said that decision belonged with the PGA

TOUR, which could amend its rules, or with Congress, which could extend the Act to explicitly cover this and similar situations. The Court should not, according to Scalia, rewrite the law to promote "what this Court sententiously decrees to be 'decent, tolerant, [and] progressive.'"

~◦◦◦~

JUSTICE SCALIA, WITH WHOM
JUSTICE THOMAS JOINS, DISSENTING.

In my view today's opinion exercises a benevolent compassion that the law does not place it within our power to impose. The judgment distorts the text of Title III, the structure of the ADA, and common sense. I respectfully dissent.

I

The Court holds that a professional sport is a place of public accommodation and that respondent is a "custome[r]" of "competition" when he practices his profession. It finds that this strange conclusion is compelled by the "literal text" of Title III of the Americans with Disabilities Act of 1990 (ADA), by the "expansive purpose" of the ADA, and by the fact that Title II of the Civil Rights Act of 1964 has been applied to an amusement park and public golf courses. I disagree.

The ADA has three separate titles: Title I covers employment discrimination, Title II covers discrimination by government entities, and Title III covers discrimination by places of public accommodation. Title II is irrelevant to this case. Title I protects only "employees" of employers who have 15 or more employees. It does not protect independent contractors. Respondent claimed employment discrimination under Title I, but the District Court found him to be an independent contractor rather than an employee.

Respondent also claimed protection under § 12182 of Title III. That section applies only to particular places and persons. The place must be a "place of public accommodation," and the person must be an "individual" seeking "enjoyment of the goods, services, facilities, privileges, advantages, or accommodations" of the covered place. Of course a court indiscriminately invoking the "sweeping" and "expansive" purposes of the ADA could argue that when a place of public accommodation denied *any* "individual," on the basis of his disability, *anything* that might be called a "privileg[e]," the individual has a valid Title III claim. On such an interpretation, the employees and independent contractors of every place of public accommodation come within Title III: The employee enjoys the "privilege" of employment, the contractor the "privilege" of the contract.

For many reasons, Title III will not bear such an interpretation. The provision of Title III at issue here is a public-accommodation law, and it is the traditional understanding of public-accommodation laws that they provide rights for *customers*. "At common law, innkeepers, smiths, and others who made profession of a public employment, were prohibited from refusing, without good reason, to serve a customer." *Hurley v. Irish-American Gay, Lesbian and Bisexual Group of Boston, Inc.* (1995). This understanding is clearly reflected in the text of Title III itself. Section 12181(7) lists 12 specific types of entities that qualify as "public accommodations," with a follow-on expansion that makes it clear what the "enjoyment of the goods, services, etc." of those entities consists of—and it plainly envisions that the person "enjoying" the "public accommodation" will be a *customer*. For example, Title III is said to cover an "auditorium" or "other place of public gathering." Thus, "gathering" is the distinctive enjoyment derived from an auditorium; the persons "gathering" at an auditorium are presumably covered by Title III, but those contracting to clean the auditorium are not. Title III is said to cover a "zoo" or "other place of recreation." The persons "recreat[ing]" at a "zoo" are presumably covered, but the animal handlers bringing in the latest panda are not. The one place where Title III specifically addresses discrimination by places of public accommodation through "contractual" arrangements, it makes clear that discrimination against the other party to the contract is not covered, but only discrimination against "clients or customers of the covered public accommodation that enters into the contractual, licensing or other arrangement." And finally, the regulations promulgated by the Department of Justice reinforce the conclusion that Title III's protections extend only to customers. "The purpose of the ADA's public accommodations requirements," they say, "is to ensure accessibility to the goods offered by a public accommodation." Surely this has nothing to do with employees and independent contractors.

If there were any doubt left that § 12182 covers only clients and customers of places of public accommodation, it is eliminated by the fact that a contrary interpretation would make a muddle of the ADA as a whole. The words of Title III must be read "in their context and with a view to their place in the overall statutory scheme." *Davis v. Michigan Dept. of Treasury* (1989). Congress expressly excluded employers of fewer than 15 employees from Title I. The mom-and-pop grocery store or laundromat need not worry about altering the nonpublic areas of its place of business to accommodate handicapped employees—or about the litigation that failure to do so will invite. Similarly, since independent contractors are not covered by Title I, the small business (or the large one, for that matter) need not worry about making special accommodations for the painters, electricians, and other independent workers whose services are contracted for from time to time. It is an entirely unreasonable interpretation of the statute to say that these exemptions so carefully crafted in Title I are entirely eliminated by Title III (for the many businesses that are places of public accommodation) because employees and independent contractors "enjoy" the employment and contracting that such places provide. The only *distinctive* feature of places of public accommodation is that they accommodate the *public*, and Congress could have no conceivable reason for according the employees and independent contractors of such businesses protections that employees and independent contractors of other businesses do not enjoy.

The United States apparently agrees that employee claims are not cognizable under Title III, but despite the implications of its own regulations, appears to believe (though it does not explicitly state) that claims of independent contractors are cognizable. In a discussion littered with entirely vague statements from the legislative history, the United States argues that Congress presumably wanted independent contractors with private entities covered under Title III because independent contractors with governmental entities are covered by Title II—a line of reasoning that does not commend itself to the untutored intellect. But since the United States does not provide (and I cannot conceive of) any possible construction of the *terms* of Title III that will exclude employees while simultaneously covering independent contractors, its concession regarding employees effectively concedes independent contractors as well. Title III applies only to customers.

The Court, for its part, assumes that conclusion for the sake of argument, but pronounces respondent to be a "customer" of the PGA TOUR or of the golf courses on which it is played. That seems to me quite incredible. The PGA TOUR is a professional sporting event, staged for the entertainment of a live and TV audience, the receipts from whom (the TV audience's admission price is paid by advertisers) pay the expenses of the tour, including the cash prizes for the winning golfers. The professional golfers on the tour are no more "enjoying" (the statutory term) the entertainment that the tour provides, or the facilities of the golf courses on which it is held, than professional baseball players "enjoy" the baseball games in which they play or the facilities of Yankee Stadium. To be sure, professional ballplayers *participate* in the games, and *use* the ballfields, but no one in his right mind would think that they are *customers* of the American League or of Yankee Stadium. They are themselves the entertainment that the customers pay to watch. And professional golfers are no different. It makes not a bit of difference, insofar as their "customer" status is concerned, that the remuneration for their performance (unlike most of the remuneration for ballplayers) is not fixed but contingent—viz., the purses for the winners in the various events, and the compensation from product endorsements that consistent winners are assured. The compensation of *many* independent contractors is contingent upon their success—real estate brokers, for example, or insurance salesmen.

> *The professional golfers on the tour are no more "enjoying" (the statutory term) the entertainment that the tour provides, or the facilities of the golf courses on which it is held, than professional baseball players "enjoy" the baseball games in which they play or the facilities of Yankee Stadium.*

As the Court points out, the ADA specifically identifies golf courses as one of the covered places of public accommodation. See § 12181(7) (L) ("a gymnasium, health spa, bowling alley, golf course, or other place of exercise or recreation"); and the distinctive "goo[d], servic[e], facilit[y], privileg[e], advantag[e], or accommodatio[n]" identified by that provision as distinctive to that category of place of public accommodation is "exercise or recreation." Respondent did not seek to "exercise" or "recreate" at the PGA TOUR events; he sought to make money (which is why he is called a *professional* golfer). He was not a customer *buying* recreation or entertainment; he was a professional athlete *selling* it. That is the reason (among others) the Court's reliance upon Civil Rights Act cases like *Daniel v. Paul* (1969) is misplaced. A professional golfer's practicing his profession is not comparable to John Q. Public's frequenting "a 232-acre amusement area with swimming, boating, sun bathing, picnicking, miniature golf, dancing facilities, and a snack bar."

> *But the Q[ualifying] School is no more a "privilege" offered for the general public's "enjoyment" than is the California Bar Exam. It is a competition for entry into the PGA TOUR.*

The Court relies heavily upon the Q-School. It says that petitioner offers the golfing public the "privilege" of "competing in the Q-School and playing in the tours; indeed, the former is a privilege for which thousands of individuals from the general public pay, and the latter is one for which they vie." But the Q-School is no more a "privilege" offered for the general public's "enjoyment" than is the California Bar Exam. It is a competition for entry into the PGA TOUR—an open tryout, no different in principle from open casting for a movie or stage production, or walk-on tryouts for other professional sports, such as baseball. See, *e.g.*, Amateurs Join Pros for New Season of HBO's "Sopranos," *Detroit News*, Dec. 22, 2000, p. 2 (20,000 attend open casting for "The Sopranos"); Bill Zack, Atlanta Braves, *Sporting News*, Feb. 6, 1995 (1,300 would-be players attended an open tryout for the Atlanta Braves). It may well be that some amateur golfers enjoy trying to make the grade, just as some amateur actors may enjoy auditions, and amateur baseball players may enjoy open tryouts (I hesitate to say that amateur lawyers may enjoy taking the California Bar Exam). But the purpose of holding those tryouts is not to provide entertainment; it is to hire. At bottom, open tryouts for performances to be held at a place of public accommodation are no different from open bidding on contracts to cut the grass at a place of public accommodation, or open applications for any job at a place of public accommodation. Those bidding, those applying—and those trying out—are not converted into customers. By the Court's reasoning, a business exists not only to sell goods and services to the public, but to provide the "privilege" of employment to the public; wherefore it follows, like night the day, that everyone who seeks a job is a customer.

II

Having erroneously held that Title III applies to the "customers" of professional golf who consist of its practitioners, the Court then erroneously answers—or to be accurate simply ignores—a second question. The ADA requires covered businesses to make such reasonable modifications of "policies, practices, or procedures" as are necessary to "afford" goods, services, and privileges to individuals with disabilities; but it explicitly does not require "modifications

[that] would fundamentally alter the nature" of the goods, services, and privileges. In other words, disabled individuals must be given *access* to the same goods, services, and privileges that others enjoy. The regulations state that Title III "does not require a public accommodation to alter its inventory to include accessible or special goods with accessibility features that are designed for, or facilitate use by, individuals with disabilities." As one Court of Appeals has explained:

> The common sense of the statute is that the content of the goods or services offered by a place of public accommodation is not regulated. A camera store may not refuse to sell cameras to a disabled person, but it is not required to stock cameras specially designed for such persons. Had Congress purposed to impose so enormous a burden on the retail sector of the economy and so vast a supervisory responsibility on the federal courts, we think it would have made its intention clearer and would at least have imposed some standards. It is hardly a feasible judicial function to decide whether shoestores should sell single shoes to one-legged persons and if so at what price, or how many Braille books the Borders or Barnes and Noble bookstore chains should stock in each of their stores.
>
> DOE v. MUTUAL OF OMAHA INS. CO. (CA7 1999)

It is as irrelevant to the PGA TOUR's compliance with the statute whether walking is essential to the game of golf as it is to the shoe store's compliance whether "pairness" is essential to the nature of shoes. If a shoe store wishes to sell shoes only in pairs it may; and if a golf tour (or a golf course) wishes to provide only walk-around golf, it may.

Since this is so, even if respondent here is a consumer of the "privilege" of the PGA TOUR competition, I see no basis for considering whether the rules of that competition must be altered. It is as
irrelevant to the PGA TOUR's compliance with the statute whether
walking is essential to the game of golf as it is to the shoe store's compliance whether "pairness" is essential to the nature of shoes. If a shoe
store wishes to sell shoes only in pairs it may; and if a golf tour (or
a golf course) wishes to provide only walk-around golf, it may. The
PGA TOUR cannot deny respondent *access* to that game because of
his disability, but it need not provide him a game different (whether in
its essentials or in its details) from that offered to everyone else.

Since it has held (or assumed) professional golfers to be customers
"enjoying" the "privilege" that consists of PGA TOUR golf; and
since it inexplicably regards the rules of PGA TOUR golf as merely
"policies, practices, or procedures" by which access to PGA TOUR
golf is provided, the Court must then confront the question whether
respondent's requested modification of the supposed policy, practice,
or procedure of walking would "fundamentally alter the nature" of
the PGA TOUR game. The Court attacks this "fundamental alteration" analysis by asking two questions: first, whether the "essence" or
an "essential aspect" of the sport of golf has been altered; and second,
whether the change, even if not essential to the game, would give the
disabled player an advantage over others and thereby "fundamentally
alter the character of the competition." It answers no to both.

Before considering the Court's answer to the first question, it is
worth pointing out that the assumption which underlies that question is
false. Nowhere is it writ that PGA TOUR golf must be classic "essential" golf. Why cannot the PGA TOUR, if it wishes, promote a new
game, with distinctive rules (much as the American League promotes a
game of baseball in which the pitcher's turn at the plate can be taken by

a "designated hitter")? If members of the public do not like the new rules—if they feel that these rules do not truly test the individual's skill at "real golf" (or the team's skill at "real baseball") they can withdraw their patronage. But the rules are the rules. They are (as in all games) entirely arbitrary, and there is no basis on which anyone—not even the Supreme Court of the United States—can pronounce one or another of them to be "nonessential" if the rulemaker (here the PGA TOUR) deems it to be essential.

If one assumes, however, that the PGA TOUR has some legal obligation to play classic, Platonic golf—and if one assumes the correctness of all the other wrong turns the Court has made to get to this point—then we Justices must confront what is indeed an awesome responsibility. It has been rendered the solemn duty of the Supreme Court of the United States, laid upon it by Congress in pursuance of the Federal Government's power "[t]o regulate Commerce with foreign Nations, and among the several States," U. S. Const., Art. I, § 8, cl. 3, to decide What Is Golf. I am sure that the Framers of the Constitution, aware of the 1457 edict of King James II of Scotland prohibiting golf because it interfered with the practice of archery, fully expected that sooner or later the paths of golf and government, the law and the links, would once again cross, and that the

I am sure that the Framers of the Constitution, aware of the 1457 edict of King James II of Scotland prohibiting golf because it interfered with the practice of archery, fully expected that sooner or later the paths of golf and government, the law and the links, would once again cross, and that the judges of this august Court would some day have to wrestle with that age-old jurisprudential question, for which their years of study in the law have so well prepared them: Is someone riding around a golf course from shot to shot really a golfer?

judges of this august Court would some day have to wrestle with that age-old jurisprudential question, for which their years of study in the law have so well prepared them: Is someone riding around a golf course from shot to shot *really* a golfer? The answer, we learn, is yes. The Court ultimately concludes, and it will henceforth be the Law of the Land, that walking is not a "fundamental" aspect of golf.

Either out of humility or out of self-respect (one or the other) the Court should decline to answer this incredibly difficult and incredibly silly question. To say that something is "essential" is ordinarily to say that it is necessary to the achievement of a certain object. But since it is the very nature of a game to have no object except amusement (that is what distinguishes games from productive activity), it is quite impossible to say that any of a game's arbitrary rules is "essential." Eighteen-hole golf courses, 10-foot-high basketball hoops, 90-foot baselines, 100-yard football fields—all are arbitrary and none is essential. The only support for any of them is tradition and (in more modern times) insistence by what has come to be regarded as the ruling body of the sport—both of which factors support the PGA TOUR's position in the present case. (Many, indeed, consider walking to be *the central feature* of the game of golf—hence Mark Twain's classic criticism of the sport: "a good walk spoiled.") I suppose there is some point at which the rules of a well-known game are changed to such a degree that no reasonable person would call it the same game. If the PGA TOUR competitors were required to dribble a large, inflated ball and put it through a round hoop, the game could no longer reasonably be called golf. But this criterion—destroying recognizability as the same generic game—is surely not the test of "essentialness" or "fundamentalness" that the Court applies, since it apparently thinks that merely changing the diameter of the *cup* might "fundamentally alter" the game of golf.

Having concluded that dispensing with the walking rule would not violate federal-Platonic "golf" (and, implicitly, that it is federal-Platonic golf, and no other, that the PGA TOUR can insist upon) the Court moves on to the second part of its test: the competitive effects of waiving this nonessential rule. In this part of its analysis, the Court first finds that the effects of the change are "mitigated" by the fact that in the game of golf weather, a "lucky bounce," and "pure chance" provide different conditions for each competitor and individual ability may not "be the sole determinant of the outcome." I guess that is why those who follow professional golfing consider Jack Nicklaus the *luckiest* golfer of all time, only to be challenged of late by the phenomenal *luck* of Tiger Woods. The Court's empiricism is unpersuasive. "Pure chance" is randomly distributed among the players, but allowing respondent to use a cart gives him a "lucky" break every time he plays. Pure chance also only matters at the margin—a stroke here or there; the cart substantially improves this respondent's competitive prospects beyond a couple of strokes. But even granting that there are significant nonhuman variables affecting competition, that fact does not justify adding another variable that always favors one player.

In an apparent effort to make its opinion as narrow as possible, the Court relies upon the District Court's finding that even with a cart, respondent will be at least as fatigued as everyone else. This, the Court says, *proves* that competition will not be affected. Far from thinking that reliance on this finding cabins the effect of today's opinion, I think it will prove to be its most expansive and destructive feature. Because step one of the Court's two-part inquiry into whether a requested change in a sport will "fundamentally alter [its] nature" consists of an utterly unprincipled ontology of sports (pursuant to which the Court is not even sure whether golf's "essence" requires a 3-inch hole), there is every reason to think that in future cases involving requests for special treatment by would-be athletes the second step of the analysis will be determinative. In resolving that second step—determining whether waiver of the "nonessential" rule will have an impermissible "competitive effect"—by measuring the athletic capacity of the requesting individual, and asking whether the special dispensation would do no more than place him on a par (so to speak) with other competitors, the Court guarantees that future cases of this sort will have to be decided on the basis of individualized factual findings. Which means that future cases of this sort will be numerous, and a rich source of lucrative litigation. One can envision the parents of a Little League player with attention deficit disorder trying to convince a judge that their son's disability makes it at least 25% more difficult to hit a pitched ball. (If they are successful, the only thing that could prevent a court order giving the kid four strikes would be a judicial determination that, in baseball, three strikes are metaphysically necessary, which is quite absurd.)

The statute, of course, provides no basis for this individualized analysis that is the Court's last step on a long and misguided journey. The statute seeks to assure that a disabled person's disability will not deny him *equal access* to (among other things) competitive sporting events—not that his disability will not deny him an *equal chance to win* competitive sporting events. The latter is quite impossible, since the very *nature* of competitive sport is the measurement, by uniform rules, of unevenly distributed excellence. This unequal distribution is precisely what determines the winners and losers—and artificially to "even out" that distribution, by giving one or another player exemption from a rule that emphasizes his particular weakness, is to destroy the game. That is why the "handicaps" that are customary in social games of golf—which, by adding strokes to the scores of the good players and subtracting them from scores of the bad ones, "even out" the varying abilities—are *not* used in professional golf. In the Court's world, there is one set of rules that is "fair with respect to the able-bodied" but "individualized" rules, mandated by the ADA, for "talented but disabled athletes." The ADA mandates no such ridiculous thing. Agility, strength, speed, balance, quickness of mind, steadiness of nerves, intensity of concentration—these talents are not evenly distributed. No wild-eyed dreamer has ever suggested that the managing bodies of the competitive sports that test precisely these qualities should try to take account of the uneven distribution of God-given gifts when writing and enforcing the rules of competition. And I have no doubt Congress did not authorize misty-eyed judicial supervision of such a revolution.

My belief that today's judgment is clearly in error should not be mistaken for a belief that the PGA TOUR clearly *ought not* allow respondent to use a golf cart. *That* is a close question, on which even those who compete in the PGA TOUR are apparently divided; but it is a *different* question from the one before the Court. Just as it is a different question whether the Little League *ought* to give disabled youngsters a fourth strike, or some other waiver from the rules that makes up for their disabilities. In both cases, whether they *ought* to do so depends upon (1) how central to the game that they have organized (and over whose rules they are the master) they deem the waived provision to be, and (2) how competitive—how strict a test of raw athletic ability in all aspects of the competition—they want their game to be. But whether Congress has said they *must* do so depends upon the answers to the legal questions I have discussed above—not upon what this Court sententiously decrees to be "decent, tolerant, [and] progressive."

And it should not be assumed that today's decent, tolerant, and progressive judgment will, in the long run, accrue to the benefit of sports competitors with disabilities. Now that it is clear courts will review the rules of sports for "fundamentalness," organizations that value their autonomy have every incentive to defend vigorously the necessity of every regulation. They may still be second-guessed in the end as to the Platonic requirements of the sport, but they will *assuredly* lose if they have at all wavered in their enforcement. The lesson the PGA TOUR and other sports organizations should take from this case is to make sure that the same written rules are set forth for all levels of play, and never voluntarily to grant any modifications. The second lesson is to end open tryouts. I doubt that, in the long run, even disabled athletes will be well served by these incentives that the Court has created.

Complaints about this case are not "properly directed to Congress." They are properly directed to this Court's Kafkaesque determination that professional sports organizations, and the fields they rent for their exhibitions, are "places of public accommodation" to the competing athletes, and the athletes themselves "customers" of the organization that pays them; its Alice in Wonderland determination that there are such things as judicially determinable "essential" and "nonessential" rules of a made-up game; and its Animal Farm determination that fairness and the ADA mean that everyone gets to play by individualized rules which will assure that no one's lack of ability (or at least no one's lack of ability so pronounced that it amounts to a disability) will be a handicap. The year was 2001, and "everybody was finally equal." K. Vonnegut, Harrison Bergeron, in Animal Farm and Related Readings (1997).

CHAPTER THREE

SEPARATION OF POWERS

~⊰⊙⊹⊙⊱~

T HE CONSTITUTION OF THE UNITED STATES established three
distinct branches of the federal government—the executive, the
legislative, and the judicial. With this clear division of power between
the branches in place, and fortified by the division of power between
the federal government and states (a.k.a. federalism), "a double security arises," James Madison wrote, for the vital purpose of protecting
"the rights of the people."[1] Far from serving as a simple housekeeping
list of functions of the three branches, the Constitution's separation of
powers is necessary to protect individual liberty by keeping the power
of government in check.

Many judges today approach separation of powers questions from a
practical standpoint. These judges, sometimes referred to as "function-
alists," look at the overall balance of federal power before determining
whether one branch has usurped too much power.[2] For example, the
Court ruled in 1989 that creation of the U.S. Sentencing Commission—an entity in which federal judges are authorized to act in an
executive policymaking capacity—did not violate the independent
authority of the judiciary under Article III of the Constitution.[3]

Justice Scalia dissented from the Court's decision in that case and squarely rejected the functional approach to separation-of-powers questions. Instead, he tried to maintain clear lines. In his view, the Constitution did not allow for the branches to "share" authority specifically given to one branch. Not a little, not at all. His separation-of-powers opinions tended to be long, filled with references to the Framers' objectives in dividing power as they did, and sprinkled with pointed warnings about the harmful consequences of allowing power to be commingled.

Scalia's passionate views in this area were not fueled by a naïve belief in the wisdom of one or all of the branches; he was not, for example, adamantly opposed to the exercise of lawmaking power by executive agencies because he had high regard for the Congress. Rather, he believed first that the text of the Constitution demands clear separation (Article I grants "all" legislative power to Congress, not "some" or even "most"). Equally important to Scalia, it seemed, were the practical reasons for dividing power cleanly and evenly; he recognized and feared that any one of the branches, if not strictly limited, would seek greater power. In Scalia's view, as in that of Madison and the other Framers, the concentration of power in any one branch posed a threat to individual liberty.

Scalia believed the rigid separation of powers set forth in the Constitution is the most important bulwark against government tyranny, even more important than the Bill of Rights. For support, he pointed out that the bills of rights of many foreign nations, including the Soviet Union—patterned on and even more extensive than our own—were of little use without the right structure of government.[4] Moreover, Scalia noted that the original Constitution of the United States did not even contain a Bill of Rights. The Framers thought liberty could be protected through a firm separation of powers that did not allow any single branch to grow too powerful.

Convinced that the separation of powers was essential for the protection of cherished liberties and mindful of the tendency for power to be usurped gradually over time, Scalia sought to maintain bright lines between the branches. He once wrote, "Separation of powers, a distinctively American political doctrine, profits from the advice authored by a distinctively American poet: Good fences make good neighbors."[5] Viewed in this context, it is easier to understand why seemingly arcane, structure-of-government cases prompted Scalia to write opinions as spirited and eloquent as one would expect to find in cases involving hot-button social issues like the death penalty or abortion.

MORRISON v. OLSON (1988)

In 1978, Congress passed the Ethics in Government Act. The new law provided for appointment of an independent counsel by a special court upon a recommendation by the U.S. attorney general. Up to that point, investigations into wrongdoing by executive officials had been carried out by special prosecutors appointed directly by the attorney general. In the wake of the Watergate scandal, however, in which the attorney general himself was implicated, Congress thought an independent prosecutor was needed to restore public confidence. Unlike a special prosecutor, who was terminable at will, an independent counsel could be removed only by the attorney general upon a showing of "good cause."

Article II, section 1, of the Constitution vests the executive power in the president of the United States. That power extends to the appointment and removal of "inferior Officers." Before *Morrison v. Olson*, the Supreme Court had reviewed the scope of the president's power to remove executive branch officials in order to determine whether the official exercised "purely executive" authority or if he also exercised "quasi-legislative" or "quasi-judicial" authority. Under this formalist approach, if an official exercised "purely executive" duties, the president had absolute authority to remove him. If the official exercised other powers, Congress could place restrictions on the president's removal authority.

In *Morrison*, the Court moved away from its formal approach and examined whether, on the whole, limiting his removal authority by requiring "good cause" impeded the president's ability to perform his constitutional duty. The Court concluded it did not. The majority found that the independent counsel was an "inferior" official with limited jurisdiction, tenure, and authority who could be terminated for misconduct. As a result, the president's control over the executive power was not unreasonably impaired by the new law and its creation of a new criminal prosecutor.

Justice Scalia, in a long solo dissenting opinion, strongly objected to the Court's adoption of a functional approach. By focusing on the "technical details" of the Appointments Clause and removal power rather than the Constitution's structural imperative to keep power strictly separated, Scalia said, the majority opinion missed the forest while staring at the trees. In his analysis, the independent counsel law had to be struck down because (1) criminal prosecution is an exercise of "purely executive power" and (2) the law deprived the president of "exclusive control" of that power.

What makes Scalia's opinion so noteworthy is his prediction of how the independent counsel law might be abused in practice. He noted that normal prosecutions had a political brake in place; specifically, blame for the egregious conduct of an out-of-control Justice Department prosecutor could be put on the president who appointed or retained him. But no such protection existed against an independent counsel run amok under the law. Scalia wrote, "How frightening it must be to have your own independent counsel and staff appointed, with nothing else to do but to investigate you until investigation is no longer worthwhile."

Four years after the Court's decision in *Morrison*, many right-leaning Americans began to share Justice Scalia's concern about the dangers of a runaway independent counsel. Conservatives were outraged when Lawrence Walsh announced the re-indictment of former defense secretary Caspar Weinberger four days before the 1992 election on charges relating to the so-called Iran-Contra affair. Worse yet, they sensed dirty politics when Walsh's office leaked a note suggesting that President Bush, who was running for re-election, lied when he said he was "out of the loop" on Iran-Contra decisions.

Most left-leaning Americans did not appreciate Scalia's foresight until independent counsel Kenneth Starr and his staff spent more than four years and $40 million investigating President Bill Clinton's land deals and extramarital relationships. Though Clinton was impeached by the House of Representatives, many thought the investigation was plagued by partisanship.

In his *Morrison* dissent, Scalia wrote, "I fear the Court has permanently encumbered the Republic with an institution that will do it great harm." Because so many came to share Scalia's fear, Congress let the law expire in 1999.

～❦～

JUSTICE SCALIA, DISSENTING.

It is the proud boast of our democracy that we have "a government of laws and not of men." Many Americans are familiar with that phrase;

not many know its derivation. It comes from Part the First, Article XXX, of the Massachusetts Constitution of 1780, which reads in full as follows:

> In the government of this Commonwealth, the legislative department shall never exercise the executive and judicial powers, or either of them: The executive shall never exercise the legislative and judicial powers, or either of them: The judicial shall never exercise the legislative and executive powers, or either of them: to the end it may be a government of laws and not of men.

The Framers of the Federal Constitution similarly viewed the principle of separation of powers as the absolutely central guarantee of a just Government. In No. 47 of The Federalist, Madison wrote that "[n]o political truth is certainly of greater intrinsic value, or is stamped with the authority of more enlightened patrons of liberty." Without a secure structure of separated powers, our Bill of Rights would be worthless, as are the bills of rights of many nations of the world that have adopted, or even improved upon, the mere words of ours.

The principle of separation of powers is expressed in our Constitution in the first section of each of the first three Articles. Article I, 1, provides that "[a]ll legislative Powers herein granted shall be vested in a Congress of the United States, which shall consist of a Senate and House of Representatives." Article III, 1, provides that "[t]he judicial Power of the United States, shall be vested in one supreme Court, and in such inferior Courts as the Congress may from time to time ordain and establish." And the provision at issue here, Art. II, 1, cl. 1, provides that "[t]he executive Power shall be vested in a President of the United States of America."

But just as the mere words of a Bill of Rights are not self-effectuating, the Framers recognized "[t]he insufficiency of a mere parchment delineation of the boundaries" to achieve the separation of powers. Federalist No. 73 (A. Hamilton). "[T]he great security," wrote Madison, "against a gradual concentration of the several powers in the same department consists in giving to those who administer each department the necessary constitutional means and personal motives to resist encroachments of the others. The provision for defense must in this, as in all other cases, be made commensurate to the danger of attack." Federalist No. 51. Madison continued:

> But it is not possible to give to each department an equal power of self-defense. In republican government, the legislative authority necessarily predominates. The remedy for this inconveniency is to divide the legislature into different branches; and to render them, by different modes of election and different principles of action, as little connected with each other as the nature of their common functions and their common dependence on the society will admit.... As the weight of the legislative authority requires that it should be thus divided, the weakness of the executive may require, on the other hand, that it should be fortified.

The major "fortification" provided, of course, was the veto power. But in addition to providing fortification, the Founders conspicuously and very consciously declined to sap the Executive's strength in the same way they had weakened the Legislature: by dividing the executive power. Proposals to have multiple executives, or a council of advisers with separate authority were rejected. Thus, while "[a]ll legislative Powers herein granted shall be vested in a Congress of the United States, which shall consist of a Senate *and* House of Representatives," U.S. Const., Art. I, 1 (emphasis added), "[t]he executive Power shall be vested in *a President of the United States*," Art. II, 1, cl. 1 (emphasis added).

Frequently an issue of this sort will come before the Court clad, so to speak, in sheep's clothing. . . . But this wolf comes as a wolf.

That is what this suit is about. Power. The allocation of power among Congress, the President, and the courts in such fashion as to preserve the equilibrium the Constitution sought to establish—so that "a gradual concentration of the several powers in the same department," Federalist No. 51 (J. Madison), can effectively be resisted. Frequently an issue of this sort will come before the Court clad, so to speak, in sheep's clothing: the potential of the asserted principle to effect important change in the equilibrium of power is not immediately evident, and must be discerned by a careful and perceptive analysis. But this wolf comes as a wolf.

I

The present case began when the Legislative and Executive Branches became "embroiled in a dispute concerning the scope of the congressional investigatory power," *United States v. House of Representatives of United States* (DC 1983), which—as is often the case with such interbranch conflicts—became quite acrimonious. In the course of oversight hearings into the administration of the Superfund by the Environmental Protection Agency (EPA), two Subcommittees of the

House of Representatives requested and then subpoenaed numerous internal EPA documents. The President responded by personally directing the EPA Administrator not to turn over certain of the documents and by having the Attorney General notify the congressional Subcommittees of this assertion of executive privilege. In his decision to assert executive privilege, the President was counseled by appellee Olson, who was then Assistant Attorney General of the Department of Justice for the Office of Legal Counsel, a post that has traditionally had responsibility for providing legal advice to the President (subject to approval of the Attorney General). The House's response was to pass a resolution citing the EPA Administrator, who had possession of the documents, for contempt. Contempt of Congress is a criminal offense. The United States Attorney, however, a member of the Executive Branch, initially took no steps to prosecute the contempt citation. Instead, the Executive Branch sought the immediate assistance of the Third Branch by filing a civil action asking the District Court to declare that the EPA Administrator had acted lawfully in withholding the documents under a claim of executive privilege. The District Court declined (in my view correctly) to get involved in the controversy, and urged the other two branches to try "[c]ompromise and cooperation, rather than confrontation." After further haggling, the two branches eventually reached an agreement giving the House Subcommittees limited access to the contested documents.

Congress did not, however, leave things there. Certain Members of the House remained angered by the confrontation, particularly by the role played by the Department of Justice. Specifically, the Judiciary Committee remained disturbed by the possibility that the Department had persuaded the President to assert executive privilege despite reservations by the EPA; that the Department had "deliberately and unnecessarily precipitated a constitutional confrontation with Congress"; that the Department had not properly reviewed and selected the documents as to which executive privilege was asserted; that the Department had directed the United States Attorney not to present the contempt certification involving the EPA Administrator to a grand jury for prosecution; that the Department had made the decision to sue the House of Representatives; and that the Department had not adequately advised and represented the President, the EPA, and the EPA Administrator. Accordingly, staff counsel of the House Judiciary Committee were commissioned (apparently without the knowledge of many of the Committee's members) to investigate the Justice Department's role in the controversy. That investigation lasted 2½ years, and produced a 3,000-page report issued by the Committee over the vigorous dissent of all but one of its minority-party members. That report, which among other charges questioned the truthfulness of certain statements made by Assistant Attorney General Olson during testimony in front of the Committee during the early stages of its investigation, was sent to the Attorney General along with a formal request that he appoint an independent counsel to investigate Mr. Olson and others.

As a general matter, the Act before us here requires the Attorney General to apply for the appointment of an independent counsel within 90 days after receiving a request to do so, unless he determines within that period that "there are no reasonable grounds to believe that further investigation or prosecution is warranted." As a practical matter, it would be surprising if the Attorney General had any choice (assuming this statute is constitutional) but to seek appointment of an independent counsel to pursue the charges against the principal object of the congressional request, Mr. Olson. Merely the political consequences (to him and the President) of seeming to break the law by refusing to do so would have been substantial. How could it not be, the public would ask, that a 3,000-page indictment drawn by our representatives over 2½ years does not even establish "reasonable grounds to believe" that further investigation or prosecution is warranted with respect to at least the principal alleged culprit? But the Act establishes more than just practical compulsion. Although the Court's opinion asserts that the Attorney General had "no duty to comply with the [congressional] request" that is not entirely accurate. He had a duty to comply unless he could conclude that there were "*no reasonable grounds to believe*," not that prosecution was warranted, but merely that "*further investigation*" was warranted (emphasis added) after a 90-day investigation in which he was prohibited from using such routine investigative techniques as grand juries, plea bargaining, grants of immunity, or even subpoenas. The Court also makes much of the fact that "the courts are specifically prevented from reviewing the Attorney General's decision not to seek appointment." Yes, but Congress is not prevented from reviewing it. The context of this statute is acrid with the smell of threatened impeachment. Where, as here, a request for appointment of an independent counsel has come from the Judiciary Committee of either House of Congress, the Attorney General must, if he decides not to seek appointment, explain to that Committee why.

> *The context of this statute is acrid with the smell of threatened impeachment.*

Thus, by the application of this statute in the present case, Congress has effectively compelled a criminal investigation of a high-level appointee of the President in connection with his actions arising out of a bitter power dispute between the President and the Legislative Branch. Mr. Olson may or may not be guilty of a crime; we do not

know. But we do know that the investigation of him has been com-
menced, not necessarily because the President or his authorized subordinates believe it is in the interest of the United States, in the sense
that it warrants the diversion of resources from other efforts, and is
worth the cost in money and in possible damage to other governmental interests; and not even, leaving aside those normally considered
factors, because the President or his authorized subordinates necessarily believe that an investigation is likely to unearth a violation worth
prosecuting; but only because the Attorney General cannot affirm, as
Congress demands, that there are no reasonable grounds to believe
that further investigation is warranted. The
decisions regarding the scope of that further
investigation, its duration, and, finally, whether
or not prosecution should ensue, are likewise
beyond the control of the President and his
subordinates.

*If to describe this case
is not to decide it, the
concept of a government
of separate and coordinate
powers no longer has
meaning.*

II

If to describe this case is not to decide it, the
concept of a government of separate and coordinate powers no longer has meaning. The Court devotes most of
its attention to such relatively technical details as the Appointments
Clause and the removal power, addressing briefly and only at the end
of its opinion the separation of powers. As my prologue suggests, I
think that has it backwards. Our opinions are full of the recognition
that it is the principle of separation of powers, and the inseparable
corollary that each department's "defense must . . . be made commensurate to the danger of attack," Federalist No. 51 (J. Madison),
which gives comprehensible content to the Appointments Clause,

and determines the appropriate scope of the removal power. Thus, while I will subsequently discuss why our appointments and removal jurisprudence does not support today's holding, I begin with a consideration of the fountainhead of that jurisprudence, the separation and equilibration of powers.

First, however, I think it well to call to mind an important and unusual premise that underlies our deliberations, a premise not expressly contradicted by the Court's opinion, but in my view not faithfully observed. It is rare in a case dealing, as this one does, with the constitutionality of a statute passed by the Congress of the United States, not to find anywhere in the Court's opinion the usual, almost formulary caution that we owe great deference to Congress' view that what it has done is constitutional and that we will decline to apply the statute only if the presumption of constitutionality can be overcome. That caution is not recited by the Court in the present case because it does not apply. Where a private citizen challenges action of the Government on grounds unrelated to separation of powers, harmonious functioning of the system demands that we ordinarily give some deference, or a presumption of validity, to the actions of the political branches in what is agreed, between themselves at least, to be within their respective spheres. But where the issue pertains to separation of powers, and the political branches are (as here) in disagreement, neither can be presumed correct. The reason is stated concisely by Madison: "The several departments being perfectly co-ordinate by the terms of their common commission, neither of them, it is evident, can pretend to an exclusive or superior right of settling the boundaries between their respective powers...." Federalist No. 49. The playing field for the present case, in other words, is a level one. As one of the interested and coordinate parties to the underlying constitutional dispute, Congress, no more than the President, is entitled to the benefit of the doubt. To repeat, Article II, 1, cl. 1, of the Constitution provides:

> The executive Power shall be vested in a President of the United States.

As I described at the outset of this opinion, this does not mean some of the executive power, but all of the executive power. It seems to me, therefore, that the decision of the Court of Appeals invalidating the present statute must be upheld on fundamental separation-of-powers principles if the following two questions are answered affirmatively: (1) Is the conduct of a criminal prosecution (and of an investigation to decide whether to prosecute) the exercise of purely executive power? (2) Does the statute deprive the President of the United States of exclusive control over the exercise of that power? Surprising to say, the Court appears to concede an affirmative answer to both questions, but seeks to avoid the inevitable conclusion that since the statute vests some purely executive power in a person who is not the President of the United States it is void.

The Court concedes that "[t]here is no real dispute that the functions performed by the independent counsel are 'executive'," though it qualifies that concession by adding "in the sense that they are law enforcement functions that typically have been undertaken by officials within the Executive Branch." The qualifier adds nothing but atmosphere. In what other sense can one identify "the executive Power" that is supposed to be vested in the President (unless it includes everything the Executive Branch is given to do) except by reference to what has always and everywhere—if conducted by government at all—been conducted never by the legislature, never by the courts, and always by the executive. There is no possible doubt that the independent counsel's functions fit this description. She is vested with the "full power and independent authority to exercise all *investigative and prosecutorial* functions and powers of the Department of Justice [and] the Attorney General." (emphasis added). Governmental investigation and prosecution of crimes is a quintessentially executive function.

As for the second question, whether the statute before us deprives the President of exclusive control over that quintessentially executive activity: The Court does not, and could not possibly, assert that it does not. That is indeed the whole object of the statute. Instead, the Court points out that the President, through his Attorney General, has at least some control. That concession is alone enough to invalidate the statute, but I cannot refrain from pointing out that the Court greatly exaggerates the extent of that "some" Presidential control. "Most importan[t]" among these controls, the Court asserts, is the Attorney General's "power to remove the counsel for 'good cause.'" This is somewhat like referring to shackles as an effective means of locomotion. As we recognized in *Humphrey's Executor v. United States* (1935)—indeed, what *Humphrey's Executor* was all about—limiting removal power to "good cause" is an impediment to, not an effective grant of, Presidential control. We said that limitation was necessary with respect to members of the Federal Trade Commission, which we found to be "an agency of the legislative and judicial departments," and "wholly disconnected from the executive department" because "it is quite evident that one who holds his office only during the pleasure of another, cannot be depended upon to maintain an attitude of independence against the latter's will." What

> *This is somewhat like referring to shackles as an effective means of locomotion.*

we in *Humphrey's Executor* found to be a means of eliminating Presidential control, the Court today considers the "most importan[t]" means of assuring Presidential control. Congress, of course, operated under no such illusion when it enacted this statute, describing the "good cause" limitation as "protecting the independent counsel's ability to act independently of the President's direct control" since it permits removal only for "misconduct."

Moving on to the presumably "less important" controls that the President retains, the Court notes that no independent counsel may be appointed without a specific request from the Attorney General. As I have discussed above, the condition that renders such a request mandatory (inability to find "no reasonable grounds to believe" that further investigation is warranted) is so insubstantial that the Attorney General's discretion is severely confined. And once the referral is made, it is for the Special Division to determine the scope and duration of the investigation. And in any event, the limited power over referral is irrelevant to the question whether, once appointed, the independent counsel exercises executive power free from the President's control. Finally, the Court points out that the Act directs the independent counsel to abide by general Justice Department policy, except when not "possible." The exception alone shows this to be an empty promise. Even without that, however, one would be hard put to come up with many investigative or prosecutorial "policies" (other than those imposed by the Constitution or by Congress through law) that are absolute. Almost all investigative and prosecutorial decisions—including the ultimate decision whether, after a technical violation of the law has been found, prosecution is warranted—involve the balancing of innumerable legal and practical considerations. Indeed, even political considerations (in the nonpartisan sense) must be considered, as exemplified by the recent decision of an independent counsel to subpoena the former Ambassador of Canada, producing considerable tension in our relations with that country. Another pre-eminently political decision is whether getting a conviction in a particular case is worth the disclosure of national security information that would be necessary. The Justice Department and our intelligence agencies are often in disagreement on this point, and the Justice Department does not always win. The present Act even goes so far as specifically to take the resolution of that dispute away from the President and give it to the independent counsel. In sum, the balancing of various legal, practical, and political considerations, none of which is absolute, is the very essence of prosecutorial discretion. To take this away is to remove the core of the prosecutorial function, and not merely "some" Presidential control.

As I have said, however, it is ultimately irrelevant how much the statute reduces Presidential control. The case is over when the Court acknowledges, as it must, that "[i]t is undeniable that the Act reduces the amount of control or supervision that the Attorney General and, through him, the President exercises over the investigation and prosecution of a certain class of alleged criminal activity." It effects a revolution in our constitutional jurisprudence for the Court, once it has determined that (1) purely executive functions are at issue here, and (2) those functions have been given to a person whose actions are not fully within the supervision and control of the President, nonetheless to proceed further to sit in judgment of whether "the President's need to control the exercise of [the independent counsel's] discretion is *so central* to the functioning of the Executive Branch" as to require complete control (emphasis added), whether the conferral of his powers upon someone else "*sufficiently* deprives the President of control over the independent counsel to interfere impermissibly with [his] constitutional obligation to ensure the faithful execution of the laws" (emphasis added), and whether "the Act give[s] the Executive Branch *sufficient* control over the independent counsel to ensure that the President is able to perform his constitutionally assigned duties" (emphasis added). It is not for us to determine, and we have never presumed to determine, how much of the purely executive powers of government must be within the full control of the President. The Constitution prescribes that they all are.

The utter incompatibility of the Court's approach with our constitutional traditions can be made more clear, perhaps, by applying it to the powers of the other two branches. Is it conceivable that if Congress passed a statute depriving itself of less than full and entire control over some insignificant area of legislation, we would inquire whether the matter was "so central to the functioning of the Legislative Branch" as really to require complete control, or whether the statute gives Congress "sufficient control over the surrogate legislator to ensure that Congress is able to perform its constitutionally assigned duties"? Of course we would have none of that. Once we determined that a purely legislative power was at issue we would require it to be exercised, wholly and entirely, by Congress. Or to bring the point closer to home, consider a statute giving to non–Article III judges just a tiny bit of purely judicial power in a relatively insignificant field, with substantial control, though not total control, in the courts—perhaps "clear error" review, which would be a fair judicial equivalent of the Attorney General's "for cause" removal power here. Is there any doubt that we would not pause to inquire whether the matter was "so central to the functioning of the Judicial Branch" as really to require complete control, or whether we retained "sufficient control over the matters to be decided that we are able to perform our constitutionally assigned duties"? We would say that our "constitutionally assigned duties" include complete control over all exercises of the judicial power—or, as the plurality opinion said in *Northern Pipeline Construction Co. v. Marathon Pipe Line Co.* (1982): "The inexorable command of [Article III] is clear and definite: The judicial power of the United States must be exercised by courts having the attributes prescribed in Art. III." We should say here that the President's constitutionally assigned duties include complete control over investigation and prosecution of violations of the law, and that the inexorable command of Article II is clear and definite: the executive power must be vested in the President of the United States.

Is it unthinkable that the President should have such exclusive power, even when alleged crimes by him or his close associates are at issue? No more so than that Congress should have the exclusive power of legislation, even when what is at issue is its own exemption from the burdens of certain laws. See Civil Rights Act of 1964, Title VII (prohibiting "employers," not defined to include the United States, from discriminating on the basis of race, color, religion, sex, or national origin). No more so than that this Court should have the exclusive power to pronounce the final decision on justiciable cases and controversies, even those pertaining to the constitutionality of a statute reducing the salaries of the Justices. A system of separate and coordinate powers necessarily involves an acceptance of exclusive power that can theoretically be abused. As we reiterate this very day, "[i]t is a truism that constitutional protections have costs." *Coy v. Iowa* (1988). While the separation of powers may prevent us from righting every wrong, it does so in order to ensure that we do not lose liberty. The checks against any branch's abuse of its exclusive powers are twofold: First, retaliation by one of the other branch's use of its exclusive powers: Congress, for example, can impeach the executive who willfully fails to enforce the laws; the executive can decline to prosecute under unconstitutional statutes; and the courts can dismiss malicious prosecutions. Second, and ultimately, there is the political check that the people will replace those in the political branches (the branches more "dangerous to the political rights of the Constitution," Federalist No. 78) who are guilty of abuse. Political pressures produced special prosecutors—for Teapot Dome and for Watergate, for example—long before this statute created the independent counsel.

Evidently, the governing standard is to be what might be called the unfettered wisdom of a majority of this Court, revealed to an obedient people on a case-by-case basis.

The Court has, nonetheless, replaced the clear constitutional prescription that the executive power belongs to the President with a "balancing test." What are the standards to determine how the balance is to be struck, that is, how much removal of Presidential power is too much? Many countries of the world get along with an executive that is much weaker than ours—in fact, entirely dependent upon the continued support of the legislature. Once we depart from the text of the Constitution, just where short of that do we stop? The most amazing feature of the Court's opinion is that it does not even purport to give an answer. It simply announces, with no analysis, that the ability to control the decision whether to investigate and prosecute the President's closest advisers, and indeed the President himself, is not "so central to the functioning of the Executive Branch" as to be constitutionally required to be within the President's control. Apparently that is so because we say it is so. Having abandoned as the basis for our deci-sionmaking the text of Article II that "the executive Power" must be vested in the President, the Court does not even attempt to craft a substitute criterion—a "justiciable standard," however remote from the Constitution—that today governs, and in the future will govern, the decision of such questions. Evidently, the governing standard is to be what might be called the unfettered wisdom of a majority of this Court, revealed to an obedient people on a case-by-case basis. This is not only not the government of laws that the Constitution estab-lished; it is not a government of laws at all.

In my view, moreover, even as an ad hoc, standardless judgment the Court's conclusion must be wrong. Before this statute was passed, the President, in taking action disagreeable to the Congress, or an executive officer giving advice to the President or testifying before Congress concerning one of those many matters on which the two branches are from time to time at odds, could be assured that his acts and motives would be adjudged—insofar as the decision whether to conduct a criminal investigation and to prosecute is concerned—in the Executive Branch, that is, in a forum attuned to the interests and the policies of the Presidency. That was one of the natural advantages the Constitution gave to the Presidency, just as it gave members of Congress (and their staffs) the advantage of not being prosecutable for anything said or done in their legislative capacities. It is the very object of this legislation to eliminate that assurance of a sympathetic forum. Unless it can honestly be said that there are "no reasonable grounds to believe" that further investigation is warranted, further investigation must ensure; and the conduct of the investigation, and determination of whether to prosecute, will be given to a person neither selected by nor subject to the control of the President—who will in turn assemble a staff by finding out, presumably, who is willing to put aside whatever else they are doing, for an indeterminate period of time, in order to investigate and prosecute the President or a particular named individual in his administration. The prospect is frightening (as I will discuss at some greater length at the conclusion of this opinion) even outside the context of a bitter, interbranch political dispute. Perhaps the boldness of the President himself will not be affected—though I am not even sure of that. (How much easier it is for Congress, instead of accepting the political damage attendant to the commencement of impeachment proceedings against the President on trivial grounds— or, for that matter, how easy it is for one of the President's political foes outside of Congress—simply to trigger a debilitating criminal investigation of the Chief Executive under this law.) But as for the President's high-level assistants, who typically have no political base of support, it is as utterly unrealistic to think that they will not be intimidated by this prospect, and that their advice to him and their advocacy of his interests before a hostile Congress will not be affected, as it would be to think that the Members of Congress and their staffs would be unaffected by replacing the Speech or Debate Clause with a similar provision. It deeply wounds the President, by substantially reducing the President's ability to protect himself and his staff. That is the whole object of the law, of course, and I cannot imagine why the Court believes it does not succeed.

Besides weakening the Presidency by reducing the zeal of his staff, it must also be obvious that the institution of the independent counsel enfeebles him more directly in his constant confrontations with Congress, by eroding his public support. Nothing is so politically effective as the ability to charge that one's opponent and his associates are not merely wrongheaded, naive, ineffective, but, in all probability, "crooks." And nothing so effectively gives an appearance of validity to such charges as a Justice Department investigation and, even better, prosecution. The present statute provides ample means for that sort of attack, assuring that massive and lengthy investigations will occur, not merely when the Justice Department in the application of its usual standards believes they are called for, but whenever it cannot be said that there are "no reasonable grounds to believe" they are called for. The statute's highly visible procedures assure, moreover, that unlike most investigations these will be widely known and prominently displayed. Thus, in the 10 years since the institution of the independent counsel was established by law, there have been nine highly publicized investigations, a source of constant political damage to two administrations. That they could not remotely be described as merely the application of "normal" investigatory and prosecutory standards is demonstrated by, in addition to the language of the statute ("no reasonable grounds to believe"), the following facts: Congress appropriates approximately $50 million annually for general legal activities, salaries, and expenses of the Criminal Division of the Department of Justice. This money is used to support "[f]ederal appellate activity," "[o]rganized crime prosecution," "[p]ublic integrity" and "[f]raud" matters, "[n]arcotic & dangerous drug prosecution," "[i]nternal security," "[g]eneral litigation and legal advice," "special investigations," "[p]rosecution support," "[o]rganized crime drug enforcement," and "[m]anagement & administration." By comparison, between May 1986 and August 1987, four independent counsels (not all of whom

Nothing is so politically effective as the ability to charge that one's opponent and his associates are not merely wrongheaded, naive, ineffective, but, in all probability, "crooks."

were operating for that entire period of time) spent almost $5 million (one-tenth of the amount annually appropriated to the entire Criminal Division), spending almost $1 million in the month of August 1987 alone. For fiscal year 1989, the Department of Justice has requested $52 million for the entire Criminal Division and $7 million to support the activities of independent counsel.

In sum, this statute does deprive the President of substantial control over the prosecutory functions performed by the independent counsel, and it does substantially affect the balance of powers. That the Court could possibly conclude otherwise demonstrates both the wisdom of our former constitutional system, in which the degree of reduced control and political impairment were irrelevant, since all purely executive power had to be in the President; and the folly of the new system of standardless judicial allocation of powers we adopt today.

. . .

V

The purpose of the separation and equilibration of powers in general, and of the unitary Executive in particular, was not merely to assure effective government but to preserve individual freedom. Those who hold or have held offices covered by the Ethics in Government Act are entitled to that protection as much as the rest of us, and I conclude my discussion by considering the effect of the Act upon the fairness of the process they receive.

Only someone who has worked in the field of law enforcement can fully appreciate the vast power and the immense discretion that are placed in the hands of a prosecutor with respect to the objects of his investigation. Justice Robert Jackson, when he was Attorney

General under President Franklin Roosevelt, described it in a memorable speech to United States Attorneys, as follows:

> There is a most important reason why the prosecutor should have, as nearly as possible, a detached and impartial view of all groups in his community. Law enforcement is not automatic. It isn't blind. One of the greatest difficulties of the position of prosecutor is that he must pick his cases, because no prosecutor can even investigate all of the cases in which he receives complaints. If the Department of Justice were to make even a pretense of reaching every probable violation of federal law, ten times its present staff will be inadequate. We know that no local police force can strictly enforce the traffic laws, or it would arrest half the driving population on any given morning. What every prosecutor is practically required to do is to select the cases for prosecution and to select those in which the offense is the most flagrant, the public harm the greatest, and the proof the most certain.
>
> If the prosecutor is obliged to choose his case, it follows that he can choose his defendants. Therein is the most dangerous power of the prosecutor: that he will pick people that he thinks he should get, rather than cases that need to be prosecuted. With the law books filled with a great assortment of crimes, a prosecutor stands a fair chance of finding at least a technical violation of some act on the part of almost anyone. In such a case, it is not a question of discovering the commission of a crime and then looking for the man who has committed it, it is a question of picking the man and then searching the law books, or putting investigators to work, to pin some offense on him.

It is in this realm—in which the prosecutor picks some person whom he dislikes or desires to embarrass, or selects some group of unpopular persons and then looks for an offense, that the greatest danger of abuse of prosecuting power lies. It is here that law enforcement becomes personal, and the real crime becomes that of being unpopular with the predominant or governing group, being attached to the wrong political views, or being personally obnoxious to or in the way of the prosecutor himself.

R. JACKSON, THE FEDERAL PROSECUTOR

ADDRESS DELIVERED AT THE SECOND ANNUAL CONFERENCE

OF UNITED STATES ATTORNEYS, APRIL 1, 1940

Under our system of government, the primary check against prosecutorial abuse is a political one. The prosecutors who exercise this awesome discretion are selected and can be removed by a President, whom the people have trusted enough to elect. Moreover, when crimes are not investigated and prosecuted fairly, nonselectively, with a reasonable sense of proportion, the President pays the cost in political damage to his administration. If federal prosecutors "pick people that [they] thin[k] [they] should get, rather than cases that need to be prosecuted," if they amass many more resources against a particular prominent individual, or against a particular class of political protesters, or against members of a particular political party, than the gravity of the alleged offenses or the record of successful prosecutions seems to warrant, the unfairness will come home to roost in the Oval Office. I leave it to the reader to recall the examples of this in recent years. That result, of course, was precisely what the Founders had in mind when they provided that all executive powers would be exercised by a single Chief Executive. As Hamilton put it, "[t]he ingredients which constitute safety in the republican sense are a due dependence on the people, and a due responsibility." Federalist No. 70. The President is directly dependent on the people, and since there is only one President, he is responsible. The people know whom to blame, whereas "one of the weightiest objections to a plurality in the executive ... is that it tends to conceal faults and destroy responsibility."

That is the system of justice the rest of us are entitled to, but what of that select class consisting of present or former high-level Executive Branch officials? If an allegation is made against them of any violation of any federal criminal law (except Class B or C misdemeanors or infractions) the Attorney General must give it his attention. That in itself is not objectionable. But if, after a 90-day investigation without the benefit of normal investigatory tools, the Attorney General is unable to say that there are "no reasonable grounds to believe" that further investigation is warranted, a process is set in motion that is not in the full control of persons "dependent on the people," and whose flaws cannot be blamed on the President. An independent counsel is selected, and the scope of his or her authority prescribed, by a panel of judges. What if they are politically partisan, as judges have been known to be, and select a prosecutor antagonistic to the administration, or even to the particular individual who has been selected for this special treatment? There is no remedy for that, not even a political one. Judges, after all, have life tenure, and appointing a surefire enthusiastic prosecutor could hardly be considered an impeachable offense. So if there is anything wrong with the selection, there is effectively no one to blame. The independent counsel thus selected proceeds to assemble a staff. As I observed earlier, in the nature of things this has to be done by finding lawyers who are willing to lay aside their current careers for an indeterminate amount of time, to take on a job that has no prospect of permanence and little prospect for promotion. One thing is certain, however: it involves investigating and perhaps prosecuting a particular individual. Can one imagine a less equitable manner of fulfilling the executive responsibility to investigate and prosecute? What would be the reaction if, in an area not covered by this statute, the Justice Department posted a public notice inviting applicants to assist in an investigation and possible prosecution of a certain prominent person? Does this not invite what Justice Jackson described as "picking the man and then searching the law books, or putting investigators to work, to pin some offense on him"? To be sure, the investigation must relate to the area of criminal offense specified by the life-tenured judges. But that has often been (and nothing prevents it from being) very broad—and should the independent counsel or his or her staff come up with something beyond that scope, nothing prevents him or her from asking the judges to expand his or her authority or, if that does not work, referring it to the Attorney General, whereupon the whole process would recommence and, if there was "reasonable basis to believe" that further investigation was warranted, that new offense would be referred to the Special Division, which would in all likelihood assign it to the same independent counsel. It seems to me not conducive to fairness. But even if it were entirely evident that unfairness was in fact the result—the judges hostile to the administration, the independent counsel an old foe of the President, the staff refugees from the recently defeated administration—there would be no one accountable to the public to whom the blame could be assigned.

I do not mean to suggest that anything of this sort (other than the inevitable self-selection of the prosecutory staff) occurred in the present case. I know and have the highest regard for the judges on the

Special Division, and the independent counsel herself is a woman of accomplishment, impartiality, and integrity. But the fairness of a process must be adjudged on the basis of what it permits to happen, not what it produced in a particular case. It is true, of course, that a similar list of horribles could be attributed to an ordinary Justice Department prosecution—a vindictive prosecutor, an antagonistic staff, etc. But the difference is the difference that the Founders envisioned when they established a single Chief Executive accountable to the people: the blame can be assigned to someone who can be punished.

The above described possibilities of irresponsible conduct must, as I say, be considered in judging the constitutional acceptability of this process. But they will rarely occur, and in the average case the threat to fairness is quite different. As described in the brief filed on behalf of three ex–Attorneys General from each of the last three administrations:

> The problem is less spectacular but much more worrisome. It is that the institutional environment of the Independent Counsel—specifically, her isolation from the Executive Branch and the internal checks and balances it supplies—is designed to heighten, not to check, all of the occupational hazards of the dedicated prosecutor; the danger of too narrow a focus, of the loss of perspective, of preoccupation with the pursuit of one alleged suspect to the exclusion of other interests.
>
> BRIEF FOR EDWARD H. LEVI, GRIFFIN B. BELL, AND
> WILLIAM FRENCH SMITH AS AMICI CURIAE

It is, in other words, an additional advantage of the unitary Executive that it can achieve a more uniform application of the law. Perhaps

How frightening it must be to have your own independent counsel and staff appointed, with nothing else to do but to investigate you until investigation is no longer worthwhile.

that is not always achieved, but the mechanism to achieve it is there. The mini-Executive that is the independent counsel, however, operating in an area where so little is law and so much is discretion, is intentionally cut off from the unifying influence of the Justice Department, and from the perspective that multiple responsibilities provide. What would normally be regarded as a technical violation (there are no rules defining such things), may in his or her small world assume the proportions of an indictable offense. What would normally be regarded as an investigation that has reached the level of pursuing such picayune matters that it should be concluded, may to him or her be an investigation that ought to go on for another year. How frightening it must be to have your own independent counsel and staff appointed, with nothing else to do but to investigate you until investigation is no longer worthwhile—with whether it is worthwhile not depending upon what such judgments usually hinge on, competing responsibilities. And to have that counsel and staff decide, with no basis for comparison, whether what you have done is bad enough, willful enough, and provable enough, to warrant an indictment. How admirable the constitutional system that provides the means to avoid such a distortion. And how unfortunate the judicial decision that has permitted it.

The notion that every violation of law should be prosecuted, including—indeed, especially—every violation by those in high places, is an attractive one, and it would be risky to argue in an election campaign

that that is not an absolutely overriding value. *Fiat justitia, ruat coelum.*
Let justice be done, though the heavens may fall. The reality is, however, that it is not an absolutely overriding value, and it was with the
hope that we would be able to acknowledge and apply such realities
that the Constitution spared us, by life tenure, the necessity of election campaigns. I cannot imagine that there are not many thoughtful
men and women in Congress who realize that the benefits of this
legislation are far outweighed by its harmful effect upon our system
of government, and even upon the nature of justice received by those
men and women who agree to serve in the Executive Branch. But it is
difficult to vote not to enact, and even more difficult to vote to repeal,
a statute called, appropriately enough, the Ethics in Government Act.
If Congress is controlled by the party other than the one to which the
President belongs, it has little incentive to repeal it; if it is controlled
by the same party, it dare not. By its shortsighted action today, I fear
the Court has permanently encumbered the Republic with an institution that will do it great harm.

Worse than what it has done, however, is the manner in which it has
done it. A government of laws means a government of rules. Today's
decision on the basic issue of fragmentation of executive power is
ungoverned by rule, and hence ungoverned by law. It extends into the
very heart of our most significant constitutional function the "totality
of the circumstances" mode of analysis that this Court has in recent
years become fond of. Taking all things into account, we conclude
that the power taken away from the President here is not really too
much. The next time executive power is assigned to someone other
than the President we may conclude, taking all things into account,
that it is too much. That opinion, like this one, will not be confined
by any rule. We will describe, as we have today (though I hope more

accurately) the effects of the provision in question, and will author-
itatively announce: "The President's need to control the exercise of
the [subject officer's] discretion is so central to the functioning of the
Executive Branch as to require complete control." This is not analysis;
it is ad hoc judgment. And it fails to explain why it is not true that—as
the text of the Constitution seems to require, as the Founders seemed
to expect, and as our past cases have uniformly assumed—all purely
executive power must be under the control of the President.

The ad hoc approach to constitutional adjudication has real attraction, even apart from its work-saving potential. It is guaranteed to
produce a result, in every case, that will make a majority of the Court
happy with the law. The law is, by definition, precisely what the
majority thinks, taking all things into account, it ought to be. I prefer to rely upon the judgment of the wise men who constructed our
system, and of the people who approved it, and of two centuries of
history that have shown it to be sound. Like it or not, that judgment
says, quite plainly, that "[t]he executive Power shall be vested in a
President of the United States."

CHAPTER FOUR

RACE

T HE FOURTEENTH AMENDMENT to the Constitution states that "[n]o State shall make or enforce any law which shall...deny any person within its jurisdiction the equal protection of the laws." The amendment was ratified after the Civil War with the purpose of ensuring equal treatment of ex-slaves by the states. But it has been interpreted by the Supreme Court over the years to protect women, ethnic minorities, homosexuals, and other classes of people.

While the Fourteenth Amendment speaks only of the states, the Supreme Court has held since 1954 that the federal government is subject to the same duty of nondiscrimination (under the Due Process Clause of the Fifth Amendment).[1] Thus, although the Court has struggled with the issue, the current analysis for determining whether a class of persons has suffered from unequal treatment is the same regardless of whether it is an act of Congress or of a particular state.

The Equal Protection guarantee is commonly invoked when an individual or group is treated differently because of an identifiable trait, for example, race, age, and sexuality. Not all classifications give rise to constitutional violations. In most cases, the states have wide latitude to treat groups differently so long as they have a "rational basis" for doing so. In cases involving legislative classifications based on race and national origin, however, courts will require the government to demonstrate that the classification is narrowly tailored to achieve a compelling government interest. This very demanding level of review—known as strict scrutiny—usually results in the courts' invalidating the law making the classification. That is why the standard is sometimes called "strict in theory, but fatal in fact."[2]

When Justice Scalia joined the Supreme Court in 1986, the Court had held that legislative classifications designed to overcome past racial discrimination by favoring minorities were permissible and not subject to strict scrutiny under the Equal Protection Clause. The prevailing wisdom was that Congress and the states had the authority to take concrete steps to rectify any inequities caused by racial prejudice and bigotry. In short, they were free to try to "level the playing field."

Justice Scalia argued that such "benign" racial classifications were no more constitutional than distinctions rooted in prejudice. In *Richmond v. J. A. Croson Co.* (1989), the Court agreed with Scalia and held that all racial classifications would thereafter be subject to strict scrutiny. To Justice Scalia, application of this new standard meant the end was near for any and all government-sponsored racial distinctions. In his view, the government simply could never have a compelling interest in discriminating based on race.

Specifically, he argued that the Equal Protection Clause applied to individuals and therefore government could not unfairly discriminate against any individual in order to give an advantage to another individual who was a member of a group that had been historically disadvantaged. His opinions on race were brief but eloquent.

RICHMOND v. J.A. CROSON CO. (1989)

The City of Richmond, Virginia, enacted a plan to help minority-owned businesses by requiring that prime contractors on city construction projects subcontract at least 30 percent of the contract to one or more minority business enterprises. To be considered a minority business enterprise, a business had to be at least 51 percent owned by minority group members. The City Council designed the plan to overcome the effects of past discrimination against African Americans in the Richmond area. As such, it was deemed a modest remedial effort to right past wrongs.

The Supreme Court deemed the Richmond plan unconstitutional because the city did not provide direct evidence of prior discrimination against minorities in the construction business, nor did the city show that race-neutral plans could not have helped the city to achieve its objective of increasing minority-business participation. The opinion marked the first time that the Supreme Court applied "strict-scrutiny" review to a racial classification designed to benefit minorities. This new application of the strict-scrutiny standard angered the Court's liberal members, who believed the government should be free to take steps to undo the effects of past racism. The majority argued that application of the tougher standard of review would not doom all government efforts to eradicate racism. Writing for the Court, Justice O'Connor said cities such as Richmond had a compelling interest in reversing the effects of past racism and were free to do so as long as they proved that racism had indeed existed and that their use of reverse discrimination was necessary to remedy the harmful effects or the past racism.

Writing separately, Justice Scalia agreed with the majority that courts should apply strict scrutiny to any attempt by the government to use racial classifications. But he disagreed with the majority's assertion that government can use "benign" racial discrimination in favor of a race that has been the subject of discrimination in the past. Scalia advised that the government must be especially vigilant about combating discrimination at the local level, since the smaller numbers needed to create a ruling majority there increased the incidence of discrimination. Finally, Scalia argued that the government has options for ameliorating the effects of past discrimination without resorting to further race-based classifications. For example, it can enact laws that provide government assistance to disadvantaged individuals (including blacks) rather than to blacks (some of whom might be disadvantaged).

⚜

JUSTICE SCALIA, CONCURRING IN THE JUDGMENT.

I agree with much of the Court's opinion, and, in particular, with Justice O'Connor's conclusion that strict scrutiny must be applied to all governmental classification by race, whether or not its asserted purpose is "remedial" or "benign." I do not agree, however, with Justice O'Connor's dictum suggesting that, despite the Fourteenth Amendment, state and local governments may in some circumstances discriminate on the basis of race in order (in a broad sense) "to ameliorate the effects of past discrimination." The benign purpose of compensating for social disadvantages, whether they have been acquired by reason of prior discrimination or otherwise, can no more be pursued by the illegitimate means of racial discrimination than can other assertedly benign purposes we have repeatedly rejected. The difficulty of overcoming the effects of past discrimination is as nothing compared with the difficulty of eradicating from our society the source of those effects, which is the tendency—fatal to a Nation such as ours—to classify and judge men and women on the basis of their country of origin or the color of their skin. A solution to the first problem that aggravates the second is no solution at all. I share the view expressed by Alexander Bickel that "[t]he lesson of the great decisions of the Supreme Court and the lesson of contemporary history have been the same for at least a generation: discrimination on the basis of race is illegal, immoral, unconstitutional, inherently wrong, and destructive of democratic society." A. Bickel, *The Morality of Consent* (1975). At least where state or local action is at issue, only a social emergency rising to the level of imminent danger to life and limb—for example, a prison race riot, requiring temporary segregation of inmates—can justify an exception to the principle embodied in the Fourteenth Amendment that "[o]ur Constitution is colorblind, and neither knows nor tolerates classes among citizens," *Plessy v. Ferguson* (1896) (Harlan, J., dissenting).

We have in some contexts approved the use of racial classifications by the Federal Government to remedy the effects of past discrimination. I do not believe that we must or should extend those holdings to the States. In *Fullilove* v. *Klutznick* (1980), we upheld legislative action by Congress similar in its asserted purpose to that at issue here. And we have permitted federal courts to prescribe quite severe, race-conscious remedies when confronted with egregious and persistent unlawful discrimination. As Justice O'Connor acknowledges, however, it is one thing to permit racially based conduct by the Federal Government—whose legislative powers concerning matters of race were explicitly enhanced by the Fourteenth Amendment—and quite another to permit it by the precise entities against whose conduct in matters of race that Amendment was specifically directed. As we said in *Ex parte Virginia*, the Civil War Amendments were designed to "take away all possibility of oppression by law because of race or color" and "to be ... limitations on the power of the States and enlargements of the power of Congress." Thus, without revisiting what we held in *Fullilove* (or trying to derive a rationale from the three separate opinions supporting the judgment, none of which commanded more than three votes), I do not believe our decision in that case controls the one before us here.

A sound distinction between federal and state (or local) action based on race rests not only upon the substance of the Civil War Amendments, but upon social reality and governmental theory. It is a simple fact that what Justice Stewart described in *Fullilove* as "the dispassionate objectivity [and] the flexibility that are needed to mold a race-conscious remedy around the single objective of eliminating the effects of past or present discrimination"—political qualities already to be doubted in a national legislature—are substantially less likely to exist at the state or local level. The struggle for racial justice has historically been a struggle by the national society against oppression in the individual States. And the struggle retains that character in modern times. Not all of that struggle has involved discrimination against blacks and not all of it has been in the Old South. What the record shows, in other words, is that racial discrimination against any group finds a more ready expression at the state and local than at the federal level. To the children of the Founding Fathers, this should come as no surprise. An acute awareness of the heightened danger of oppression from political factions in small, rather than large, political units dates to the very beginning of our national history. As James Madison observed in support of the proposed Constitution's enhancement of national powers:

The smaller the society, the fewer probably will be the distinct parties and interests composing it; the fewer the distinct parties and interests, the more frequently will a majority be found of the same party; and the smaller the number of individuals composing a majority, and the smaller the compass within which they are placed, the more easily will they concert and execute their plan of oppression. Extend the sphere and you take in a greater variety of parties and interests; you make it less probable that a majority of the whole will have a common motive to invade the rights of other citizens; or if such a common motive exists, it will be more difficult for all who feel it to discover their own strength and to act in unison with each other.

THE FEDERALIST NO. 10

The prophe[c]y of these words came to fruition in Richmond in the enactment of a set-aside clearly and directly beneficial to the dominant political group, which happens also to be the dominant racial group. The same thing has no doubt happened before in other cities (though the racial basis of the preference has rarely been made textually explicit)—and blacks have often been on the receiving end of the injustice. Where injustice is the game, however, turnabout is not fair play.

Where injustice is the game, however, turnabout is not fair play.

In my view there is only one circumstance in which the States may act by race to "undo the effects of past discrimination": where that is necessary to eliminate their own maintenance of a system of unlawful racial classification. If, for example, a state agency has a discriminatory pay scale compensating black employees in all positions at 20% less than their nonblack counterparts, it may assuredly promulgate an order raising the salaries of "all black employees" to

eliminate the differential. This distinction explains our school deseg-
regation cases, in which we have made plain that States and locali-
ties sometimes have an obligation to adopt race-conscious remedies.
While there is no doubt that those cases have taken into account the
continuing "effects" of previously mandated racial school assignment,
we have held those effects to justify a race-conscious remedy only
because we have concluded, in that context, that they perpetuate a
"dual school system." We have stressed each school district's constitutional "duty to dismantle its dual system," and have found that "[e]
ach instance of a failure or refusal to fulfill this affirmative duty *continues the violation* of the Fourteenth Amendment." *Columbus Board of
Education v. Penick* (1979) (emphasis added). Concluding in this context that race-neutral efforts at "dismantling the state-imposed dual
system" were so ineffective that they might "indicate a lack of good
faith," *Green v. New Kent County School Board* (1968), we have permitted, as part of the local authorities' "affirmative duty to disestablish
the dual school system[s]," such voluntary (that is, noncourt-ordered)
measures as attendance zones drawn to achieve greater racial balance,
and out-of-zone assignment by race for the same purpose. While
thus permitting the use of race to declassify racially classified students,
teachers, and educational resources, however, we have also made it
clear that the remedial power extends no further than the scope of the
continuing constitutional violation. And it is implicit in our cases that
after the dual school system has been completely disestablished, the
States may no longer assign students by race.

Our analysis in *Bazemore v. Friday* reflected our unwillingness to
conclude, outside the context of school assignment, that the continuing effects of prior discrimination can be equated with state maintenance of a discriminatory system. There we found both that the

government's adoption of "wholly neutral admissions" policies for 4-H and Homemaker Clubs sufficed to remedy its prior constitutional violation of maintaining segregated admissions, and that there was no further obligation to use racial reassignments to eliminate continuing effects—that is, any remaining all-black and all-white clubs. "[However sound *Green [v. New Kent County School Board]* may have been in the context of the public schools," we said, "it has no application to this wholly different milieu." The same is so here.

A State can, of course, act "to undo the effects of past discrimination" in many permissible ways that do not involve classification by race. In the particular field of state contracting, for example, it may adopt a preference for small businesses, or even for new businesses—which would make it easier for those previously excluded by discrimination to enter the field. Such programs may well have racially disproportionate impact, but they are not based on race. And, of course, a State may "undo the effects of past discrimination" in the sense of giving the identified victim of state discrimination that which it wrongfully denied him—for example, giving to a previously rejected black applicant the job that, by reason of discrimination, had been awarded to a white applicant, even if this means terminating the latter's employment. In such a context, the white jobholder is not being selected for disadvantageous treatment because of his race, but because he was wrongfully awarded a job to which another is entitled. That is worlds apart from the system here, in which those to be disadvantaged are identified solely by race.

I agree with the Court's dictum that a fundamental distinction must be drawn between the effects of "societal" discrimination and the effects of "identified" discrimination, and that the situation would be different if Richmond's plan were "tailored" to identify those particular bidders who "suffered from the effects of past discrimination by the city or prime contractors." In my view, however, the reason that would make a difference is not, as the Court states, that it would justify race-conscious action . . . but rather that it would enable race-neutral remediation. Nothing prevents Richmond from according a contracting preference to identified victims of discrimination. While most of the beneficiaries might be black, neither the beneficiaries nor those disadvantaged by the preference would be identified on the basis of their race. In other words, far from justifying racial classification, identification of actual victims of discrimination makes it less supportable than ever, because more obviously unneeded.

In this final book, Professor Bickel wrote:

[A] racial quota derogates the human dignity and individuality of all to whom it is applied; it is invidious in principle as well as in practice. Moreover, it can easily be turned against those it purports to help. The history of the racial quota is a history of subjugation, not beneficence. Its evil lies not in its name, but in its effects: a quota is a divider of society, a creator of castes, and it is all the worse for its racial base, especially in a society desperately striving for an equality that will make race irrelevant.

BICKEL, *THE MORALITY OF CONSENT*

Those statements are true and increasingly prophetic. Apart from their societal effects, however, which are "in the aggregate disastrous," *id.*, it is important not to lose sight of the fact that even "benign" racial quotas have individual victims, whose very real injustice we ignore whenever we deny them enforcement of their right not to be disadvantaged on the basis of race. As Justice Douglas observed:

"A DeFunis who is white is entitled to no advantage by virtue of that fact; nor is he subject to any disability, no matter what his race or color. Whatever his race, he had a constitutional right to have his application considered on its individual merits in a racially neutral manner." *DeFunis v. Odegaard* (1974) (dissenting opinion). When we depart from this American principle we play with fire, and much more than an occasional DeFunis, Johnson, or Croson burns.

It is plainly true that in our society blacks have suffered discrimination immeasurably greater than any directed at other racial groups. But those who believe that racial preferences can help to "even the score" display, and reinforce, a manner of thinking by race that was the source of the injustice and that will, if it endures within our society, be the source of more injustice still. The relevant proposition is not that it was blacks, or Jews, or Irish who were discriminated against, but that it was individual men and women, "created equal," who were discriminated against. And the relevant resolve is that that should never happen again. Racial preferences appear to "even the score" (in some small degree) only if one embraces the proposition that our society is appropriately viewed as divided into races, making it right that an injustice rendered in the past to a black man should be compensated for by discriminating against a white. Nothing is worth that embrace. Since blacks have been disproportionately disadvantaged by racial discrimination, any race-neutral remedial program aimed at the disadvantaged as such will have a disproportionately beneficial impact

Those who believe that racial preferences can help to "even the score" display, and reinforce, a manner of thinking by race that was the source of the injustice and that will, if it endures within our society, be the source of more injustice still.

on blacks. Only such a program, and not one that operates on the basis of race, is in accord with the letter and the spirit of our Constitution.

Since I believe that the appellee here had a constitutional right to have its bid succeed or fail under a decisionmaking process uninfected with racial bias, I concur in the judgment of the Court.

ADARAND CONSTRUCTORS, INC. v. PENA (1995)

Six years after *Croson*, the Supreme Court extended its decision to apply strict scrutiny to federal affirmative action plans. At issue in *Adarand* was a federal program to provide financial incentives to government contractors who hired small businesses controlled by "socially and economically disadvantaged" individuals. Lower courts upheld the program, but a closely divided Supreme Court sent the case back for review with instruction to apply strict scrutiny to the federal contracting program.

Justice Scalia filed a very short opinion agreeing with the Court's decision. In a concise manner, Scalia explained that the Constitution's guarantee of equal protection applies to individuals, not races.

⧏⊰⊙⊹⊙⊱⧐

JUSTICE SCALIA, CONCURRING IN
PART AND CONCURRING IN THE JUDGMENT.

I join the opinion of the Court...except insofar as it may be inconsistent with the following: In my view, government can never have a "compelling interest" in discriminating on the basis of race in order to "make up" for past racial discrimination in the opposite direction.

Individuals who have been wronged by unlawful racial discrimination should be made whole; but under our Constitution there can be no such thing as either a creditor or a debtor race. That concept is alien to the Constitution's focus upon the individual, see Amdt. 14, § 1 ("[N]or shall any State...deny to *any person*" the equal protection of the laws) (emphasis added), and its rejection of dispositions based on race, see Amdt. 15, § 1 (prohibiting abridgment of the right to vote "on account of race"), or based on

> *Under our Constitution there can be no such thing as either a creditor or a debtor race. . . . In the eyes of government, we are just one race here. It is American.*

blood, see Art. III, § 3 ("[N]o Attainder of Treason shall work Corruption of Blood"); Art. I, § 9 ("No Title of Nobility shall be granted by the United States"). To pursue the concept of racial entitlement—even for the most admirable and benign of purposes—is to reinforce and preserve for future mischief the way of thinking that produced race slavery, race privilege and race hatred. In the eyes of government, we are just one race here. It is American.

It is unlikely, if not impossible, that the challenged program would survive under this understanding of strict scrutiny, but I am content to leave that to be decided on remand.

GRUTTER v. BOLLINGER (2003)

In 2003, the Supreme Court heard two affirmative action cases involving admissions policies at the University of Michigan. In *Grutter v. Bollinger*, the Court was asked to decide if the University of Michigan Law School's admissions policy violated the Equal Protection Clause of the Fourteenth Amendment. The controversy arose after a white applicant with high test scores was denied admission. She claimed her denial was due to the reverse discrimination she suffered as a result of the law school's race-conscious admissions policy.

The law school admitted to using race as a factor in assessing applicants but justified its practice on the ground that "achieving diversity among the student body" is a compelling government interest. Specifically, the school said it sought to attain a "critical mass" of underrepresented minority students in order to produce "educational benefits" such as "cross-racial understanding" and breaking down of racial stereotypes. The school contended the scheme did not amount to an unlawful quota system as demonstrated by the fact that minority population fluctuated from year to year. The policy was "narrowly tailored," the school argued, to meet its goal of diversity since no other means existed to advance its interest without reducing the academic quality of the school.

In a 5–4 decision written by Justice O'Connor, the Court upheld the law school's admissions policy. The Court not only agreed with the school that obtaining a diverse student body was a compelling government interest, but it held that its program of considering race along with many other factors that may contribute to diversity was an appropriately narrow way to further that interest.

In the other University of Michigan affirmative action case decided that day, the Supreme Court in *Gratz v. Bollinger* struck down the undergraduate school's admissions program. The undergraduate school attempted to increase diversity on campus by granting twenty points, or one-fifth of the points needed to gain admission, to every "underrepresented minority" applicant. The Court ruled that, although diversity might represent a compelling government interest, the awarding of points based solely on race was not narrowly tailored to achieving the asserted interest in fostering diversity.

Justice Scalia voted against both affirmative action programs. In *Grutter*, Scalia wrote an opinion in which he reiterated his argument that government can never have a compelling interest in classifying people on the basis of race. Scalia then questioned the importance of the "educational benefits" the law school alleged would flow from a racially diverse student body. Finally, he predicted that rather than settling the issue of affirmative action on America's campuses, the Court's unprincipled "split doubleheader"—upholding the law school's race-conscious policy, while striking down the undergraduate school's program—would precipitate more lawsuits.

⤙⤛❊⤚⤜

JUSTICE SCALIA, WITH WHOM JUSTICE THOMAS JOINS, CONCURRING IN PART AND DISSENTING IN PART.

I join the opinion of The Chief Justice. As he demonstrates, the University of Michigan Law School's mystical "critical mass" justification for its discrimination by race challenges even the most gullible mind. The admissions statistics show it to be a sham to cover a scheme of racially proportionate admissions.

I also join Parts I through VII of Justice Thomas's opinion. I find particularly unanswerable his central point: that the allegedly "compelling state interest" at issue here is not the incremental "educational benefit" that emanates from the fabled "critical mass" of minority students, but rather Michigan's interest in maintaining a "prestige" law school whose normal admissions standards disproportionately exclude blacks and other minorities. If that is a compelling state interest, everything is.

> *This is not an "educational benefit" on which students will be graded on their Law School transcript (Works and Plays Well with Others: B⁺) or tested by the bar examiners (Q: Describe in 500 words or less your cross-racial understanding).*

I add the following: The "educational benefit" that the University of Michigan seeks to achieve by racial discrimination consists, according to the Court, of "'cross-racial understanding'" and "'better prepar[ation of] students for an increasingly diverse workforce and society,'" all of which is necessary not only for work, but also for good "citizenship." This is not, of course, an "educational benefit" on which students will be graded on their Law School transcript (Works and Plays Well with Others: B⁺) or tested by the bar examiners (Q: Describe in 500 words or less your cross-racial understanding). For it is a lesson of life rather than law—essentially the same lesson taught to (or rather learned by, for it cannot be "taught" in the usual sense) people three feet shorter and twenty years younger than the full-grown adults at the University of Michigan Law School, in institutions ranging from Boy Scout troops to public-school kindergartens. If properly considered an "educational benefit" at all, it is surely not one that is either uniquely relevant to law school or uniquely "teachable" in a formal educational setting. *And therefore:* If it is appropriate for the University of Michigan Law School to use racial discrimination for the purpose of putting together a "critical mass" that will convey generic lessons in socialization and good citizenship, surely it is no less appropriate—indeed, *particularly* appropriate—for the civil service system of the State of Michigan to do so. There, also, those exposed to "critical masses" of certain races will presumably become better Americans, better Michiganders, better civil servants. And surely private employers cannot be criticized—indeed, should be praised—if they also "teach" good citizenship to their adult employees through a patriotic, all-American system of racial discrimination in hiring. The nonminority individuals who are deprived of a legal education, a civil service job, or any job at all by reason of their skin color will surely understand.

Unlike a clear constitutional holding that racial preferences in state educational institutions are impermissible, or even a clear anticonstitutional holding that racial preferences in state educational institutions are OK, today's *Grutter-Gratz* split double header seems perversely designed to prolong the controversy and the litigation. Some future lawsuits will presumably focus on whether the discriminatory scheme in question contains enough evaluation of the applicant "as an individual" and sufficiently avoids "separate admissions tracks" to fall under *Grutter* rather than *Gratz*. Some will focus on whether a university has gone beyond the bounds of a "'good faith effort'" and has so zealously pursued its "critical mass" as to make it an unconstitutional *de facto* quota system, rather than merely "'a permissible goal.'" Other lawsuits may focus on whether, in the particular setting at issue, any educational benefits flow from racial diversity. (That issue was not contested in *Grutter*; and while the opinion accords "a

> *Tempting targets, one would suppose, will be those universities that talk the talk of multiculturalism and racial diversity in the courts but walk the walk of tribalism and racial segregation on their campuses.*

degree of deference to a university's academic decisions," "deference does not imply abandonment or abdication of judicial review," *Miller-El v. Cockrell* (2003).) Still other suits may challenge the bona fides of the institution's expressed commitment to the educational benefits of diversity that immunize the discriminatory scheme in *Grutter*. (Tempting targets, one would suppose, will be those universities that talk the talk of multiculturalism and racial diversity in the courts but walk the walk of tribalism and racial segregation on their campuses—through minority-only student organizations, separate minority housing opportunities, separate minority student centers, even separate minority-only graduation ceremonies.) And still other suits may claim that the institution's racial preferences have gone below or above the mystical *Grutter*-approved "critical mass." Finally, litigation can be expected on behalf of minority groups intentionally short changed in the institution's composition of its generic minority "critical mass." I do not look forward to any of these cases. The Constitution proscribes government discrimination on the basis of race, and state-provided education is no exception.

CHAPTER FIVE

ABORTION

~&⊙⦂⊙&~

THE CONSTITUTION OF THE UNITED STATES does not contain a provision stating, "Congress shall make no law abridging the right of privacy." Nor does it mention the word "abortion." During the past fifty years, however, the Supreme Court has decreed that certain "private" activities, including abortion, should be considered "fundamental rights" under the Constitution. These newly discovered rights receive the same high level of constitutional protection as those in the Bill of Rights, including the freedoms of speech and religion.

The theory that the Court relies upon to protect these "rights" is called substantive due process. Under this theory, the Fourteenth Amendment's protection of "liberty" includes substantive rights that one will not find anywhere in the Constitution. For example, in 1965, the Court found married persons had a fundamental right to use contraceptives.[1] In 1966, the right was extended to all persons, married or not.[2] And then, in its 1973 decision in *Roe v. Wade*, the Court declared abortion a constitutional right.

During his three decades on the Supreme Court, Justice Scalia was by far the most passionate and persistent critic of the view that the Constitution contains a right to end the natural development of an unborn child. He did not believe judges should have free rein to create rights as they see fit; instead, he believed they should employ a standard that is rooted in the Constitution and American history and that cannot be altered or manipulated by future court majorities. First, the Court should look to the text of the Constitution to determine if there is specific language justifying protection for the asserted right. If there is no such text, the Court should inquire whether "the long-standing traditions of American society" have protected the asserted right. If neither of these conditions is met, no fundamental right can be said to exist.

Scalia pointed out in several opinions that the text of the Constitution is completely and undeniably silent on the subject of abortion. In addition, procurement of an abortion was not protected by any long-standing tradition since many states enacted laws limiting abortion before *Roe v. Wade*. Therefore, abortion cannot be considered a "fundamental right" worthy of constitutional protection.

In the absence of text and tradition, Scalia maintained the Supreme Court had nothing to guide its decisions on abortion. The result, he argued, is constant confusion and inconsistency. In a 1990 case involving Minnesota's law requiring minors to obtain parental consent before having an abortion,[3] Justice Scalia noted that at the time, the justices on the Court had applied various legal standards (and even applied the same standards differently) to state abortion restrictions. Scalia concluded, "The random and unpredictable results of our consequently unchanneled individual views make it increasingly evident, term after term, that the tools for this job are not to be found in the lawyer's—and hence not in the judge's—work-box. I continue to dissent from this enterprise of devising an Abortion Code, and from the illusion that we have authority to do so."[4]

Instead, Justice Scalia contended that issues involving the circumstances in which a state could lawfully regulate abortion were policy questions. They should be resolved by legislatures, in which the majority of citizens could express their will through their elected representatives. In advocating that the Court get out of what he called the "abortion-umpiring" business, Scalia did not suggest that abortion will (or even should) become illegal. Rather, as with all issues not addressed by the Constitution, he believed that the matter should be decided by the people. Thus, while abortion might be outlawed or severely restricted in some states, it would likely maintain strong legal protection in many other states.

Finally, Justice Scalia expressed great concern that the Court's continued involvement in the abortion issue has undermined its credibility as a neutral interpreter of laws. By creating a right to abortion without textual support and then constantly shifting the standards it used to decide abortion-related cases, the Court, Scalia said, was guilty of swapping its judicial role for policymaking and, as a result, inviting political lobbying efforts designed to influence not only its abortion decisions but also who should be nominated and confirmed to serve on the Supreme Court. He lamented that our nation's highest court—set up by our Founders to be insulated from public opinion—had become a magnet for mass public demonstration every time a case involving abortion went before the Court.

WEBSTER v. REPRODUCTIVE HEALTH SERVICES (1989)

In 1986, Missouri passed a law requiring doctors perform certain medical tests before performing an abortion on any fetus they believe to be at least twenty weeks old to determine whether the fetus is "viable." The statute also prohibited the use of public funds to perform or assist abortions that are not necessary to save the life of the mother. Finally, the law barred use of state funds for encouraging or counseling a woman to have an abortion unless the abortion was deemed necessary to save the life of the mother.

At the time of the decision, *Roe v. Wade* was still the law of the land. Thus, judges considering the constitutionality of legislative proposals to regulate abortion had to use the *Roe* Court's trimester analysis to determine whether a regulation was too restrictive. In short, the Court in *Roe* said that women had an unrestricted right to choose abortion during the first three months of pregnancy. In the second trimester, the government could regulate abortion if it was doing so to protect the health of the mother. In the final trimester of pregnancy, the *Roe* majority ruled that the government's interest in protecting the potential life of the unborn child was great enough to warrant significant restrictions on abortion.

Several post-*Roe* decisions upheld legislative attempts to regulate abortion. For example, the Supreme Court in 1980 declared constitutional federal legislation prohibiting the use of Medicaid funds to pay for nontherapeutic abortions. But strict constructionists and antiabortion advocates never accepted the *Roe* decision as legitimate and hoped a future Court would have the opportunity to overturn it. In 1989, after President Reagan had added Justices Sandra Day O'Connor, Scalia, and Anthony Kennedy to the high court, *Roe*'s critics sensed that such an opportunity had arrived with the *Webster* case.

To the clear disappointment of Justice Scalia, Justice O'Connor demurred. She filed a separate opinion agreeing with the plurality to uphold the Missouri law's restrictions on abortion but declining to reexamine *Roe*. O'Connor said she did not believe the viability testing requirement conflicted with *Roe* or any other abortion-related decision. The Court had a practice of not deciding a constitutional question unless it was absolutely essential to resolving the case before it. Applying that practice in this case, she said, *Roe* need not be reconsidered because the case could be decided without doing so.

O'Connor agreed with the Court that Missouri's restrictions did not violate the Constitution. In order to make that determination, she employed a standard that asked whether the state regulations imposed an "undue burden" on a woman's decision to seek an abortion. O'Connor had used the "undue burden" language in a dissent she had written six years earlier, in which she said the "*Roe* framework... is clearly on a collision course with itself."[5] In *Webster*, she found that none of the Missouri restrictions constituted an undue burden.

Scalia's frustration with Justice O'Connor's decision to sidestep *Roe* was at full boil. In a separate concurrence, he attacked nearly every point of her opinion. Whereas O'Connor cautioned against devising a broader rule of constitutional law than she felt was required to decide the case, Justice Scalia cited decisions from earlier in the same term in which O'Connor authored or joined opinions that did exactly that. He then dismissed the "undue burden" for providing no guidance to the Court on how to resolve abortion-related questions. Finally, Scalia charged that, by ducking *Roe* altogether, the Court made the "least responsible" decision.

⚜

JUSTICE SCALIA, CONCURRING IN PART AND CONCURRING IN THE JUDGMENT.

...As to Part II-D [regarding viability testing], I share Justice Black-mun's view that it effectively would overrule *Roe v. Wade*. I think that should be done, but would do it more explicitly. Since today we contrive to avoid doing it, and indeed avoid almost any decision of national import, I need not set forth my reasons, some of which have been well recited in dissents of my colleagues in other cases.

The outcome of today's case will doubtless be heralded as a tri-umph of judicial statesmanship. It is not that, unless it is statesmanlike needlessly to prolong this Court's self-awarded sovereignty over a field where it has little proper business since the answers to most of the cruel questions posed are political and not juridicial—a sover-eignty which therefore quite properly, but to the great damage of the Court, makes it the object of the sort of organized public pressure that political institutions in a democracy ought to receive.

Justice O'Connor's assertion, that a "fundamental rule of judicial restraint" requires us to avoid reconsidering *Roe*, cannot be taken seri-ously. By finessing *Roe* we do not, as she suggests, adhere to the strict and venerable rule that we should avoid "decid[ing] questions of a con-stitutional nature." We have not disposed of this case on some stat-utory or procedural ground, but have decided, and could not avoid deciding, whether the Missouri statute meets the requirements of the United States Constitution. The only choice available is whether, in deciding that constitutional question, we should use *Roe v. Wade* as the benchmark, or something else. What is involved, therefore, is not the rule of avoiding constitutional questions where possible, but the quite separate principle that we will not "'formulate a rule of constitutional law broader than is required by the precise facts to which it is applied.'" The latter is a sound general principle, but one often departed from when good reason exists. Just this Term, for example, in an opinion authored by Justice O'Connor, despite the fact that we had already held a racially based set-aside unconstitutional because unsupported by evidence of identified discrimination, which was all that was needed to decide the case, we went on to outline the criteria for properly tailoring race-based remedies in cases where such evidence is present. Also this Term, in an opinion joined by Justice O'Connor, we announced the constitutional rule that deprivation of the right to confer with counsel during trial violates the Sixth Amendment even if no prejudice can be shown, despite our finding that there had been no such deprivation on the facts before us—which was all that was needed to decide that case....

It would be wrong, in any decision, to ignore the reality that our policy not to "formulate a rule of constitutional law broader than is required by the precise facts" has a frequently applied good-cause exception. But it seems particularly perverse to convert the policy into an absolute in the present case, in order to place beyond reach the inexpressibly "broader-than-was-required-by-the-precise-facts" structure established by *Roe v. Wade.*

The real question, then, is whether there are valid reasons to go beyond the most stingy possible holding today. It seems to me there are not only valid but compelling ones. Ordinarily, speaking no more broadly than is absolutely required avoids throwing settled law into confusion; doing so today preserves a chaos that is evident to anyone

We can now look forward to at least another term with carts full of mail from the public, and the streets full of demonstrators, urging us—their unelected and life-tenured judges who have been awarded those extraordinary, undemocratic characteristics precisely in order that we might follow the law despite popular will—to follow the popular will.

who can read and count. Alone sufficient to justify a broad holding is the fact that our retaining control, through *Roe*, of what I believe to be, and many of our citizens recognize to be, a political issue, continuously distorts the public perception of the role of this Court. We can now look forward to at least another Term with carts full of mail from the public, and the streets full of demonstrators, urging us—their unelected and life-tenured judges who have been awarded those extraordinary, undemocratic characteristics precisely in order that we might follow the law despite popular will—to follow the popular will. Indeed, I expect we can look forward to even more of that than before, given our indecisive decision today. And if these reasons for taking the unexceptional course of reaching a broader holding are not enough, then consider the nature of the constitutional question we avoid: In most cases, we do not harm by not speaking more broadly than the decision requires. Anyone affected by the conduct that the avoided holding would have prohibited will be able to challenge it himself and have his day in court to make the argument. Not so with respect to the harm that many States believed, pre-*Roe*, and many may continue to believe, is caused by largely unrestricted abortion. That will continue to occur if the States have the constitutional power to prohibit it, and would do so, but we skillfully avoid telling them so. Perhaps those abortions cannot constitutionally be proscribed. That is surely an arguable question, the question that reconsideration of *Roe v. Wade* entails. But what is not at all arguable, it seems to me, is that we should decide now and not insist that we be run into a corner before we grudgingly yield up our judgment. The only sound reason for the latter course is to prevent a change in the law—but to think that desirable begs the question to be decided.

It was an arguable question today whether...the Missouri law contravened this Court's understanding of *Roe v. Wade*, and I would have examined *Roe* rather than examining this contravention. Given the Court's newly contracted abstemiousness, what will it take, one must wonder, to permit us to reach that fundamental question? The result of our vote today is that will not reconsider that prior opinion, even if most of the Justices think it is wrong, unless we have a statute before us that in fact contradicts it—and even then (under our newly discovered "no-broader-then-necessary" requirement) only minor problematic aspects of *Roe* will be reconsidered, unless one expects state legislatures to adopt provisions whose compliance with *Roe* cannot even be argued with a straight face. It thus appears that the mansion of constitutionalized abortion law, constructed overnight in *Roe v. Wade*, must be disassembled doorjamb by doorjamb, and never entirely brought down, no matter how wrong it might be....

It thus appears that the mansion of constitutionalized abortion law, constructed overnight in Roe v. Wade, must be disassembled doorjamb by doorjamb, and never entirely brought down, no matter how wrong it might be.

[Footnote]...Justice O'Connor would nevertheless uphold the law because it "does not impose an undue burden on a woman's abortion decision." This conclusion is supported by the observation that the required tests impose only a marginal cost on the abortion procedure, far less of an increase than the cost-doubling hospitalization requirement invalidated in *Akron v. Akron Center for Reproductive Health, Inc.* The fact that the challenged regulation is less costly than what we struck down in *Akron* tells us only that we cannot decide the present case on the basis of that earlier decision. It does not tell us whether the present requirement is an "undue burden," and I know of no basis for determining that this particular burden (or any other for that matter) is "due." One could with equal justification conclude that it is not. To avoid the question of *Roe v. Wade*'s validity, with the attendant costs that this will have for the Court and for the principles of self-governance, on the basis of a standard that offers "no guide but the Court's own discretion" merely adds to the irrationality of what we do today.

Similarly irrational is the new concept that Justice O'Connor introduces into the law in order to achieve her result, the notion of a State's "interest in potential life when viability is possible." Since "viability" means the mere possibility (not the certainty) of survivability outside the womb, "possible viability" must mean the possibility of a possibility of survivability outside the womb. Perhaps our next opinion will expand the third trimester into the second even further, by approving state action designed to take account of "the chance of possible viability."

Of the four courses we might have chosen today—to reaffirm *Roe*, to overrule it explicitly, to overrule it sub silentio, or to avoid the question—the last is the least responsible. On the question of the constitutionality of § 188.029 [viability testing requirement], I concur in the judgment of the Court and strongly dissent from the manner in which it has been reached.

PLANNED PARENTHOOD OF SOUTHEASTERN PENNSYLVANIA v. CASEY (1992)

Three years after *Webster*, the Court was asked to determine the constitutionality of five provisions of Pennsylvania's abortion law. These provisions required a woman seeking an abortion to give her informed consent; mandated the consent of one parent for a minor seeking an abortion (with provision for judicial approval where parental consent could not be obtained); required a woman to obtain the written approval of her husband before seeking an abortion (with exceptions); imposed certain reporting requirements on facilities that perform abortions; and, finally, set forth a definition of "medical emergency" that would alleviate the need to comply with the other requirements.

The Court's decision was noteworthy—and controversial—not because it upheld four of the five restrictions (only the spousal consent law was struck down) but because the Court threw aside *Roe*'s trimester analysis yet preserved its "central holding" that abortion is a constitutionally protected right.

Since its *Webster* decision, the composition of the Court had changed with the addition of Justices David Souter and Clarence Thomas, who had been appointed by Republican President George H. W. Bush. Souter and Thomas gave antiabortion forces renewed hope that *Roe v. Wade* might be overturned, a fanciful thought in hindsight as Souter quickly emerged as one of the Court's most reliably liberal votes.

Souter joined Justices O'Connor and Kennedy to draft the Court's main opinion in *Casey*. Although public opinion polls at the time showed the country almost evenly divided on abortion, the three Republican appointees chose to preserve *Roe* on the grounds that its creation of a constitutional right to abortion had established a rule of law that was accepted by most Americans. The plurality said that *stare decisis*—the practice of adhering to precedent—was especially important in this case because the issue was divisive and because so many people had come to rely on the legality of abortion. According to the joint opinion, the Court's legitimacy was at stake, and any decision to overturn *Roe* would be perceived as succumbing to political pressure. Thus, the justices wrote that, notwithstanding the doubts they had about *Roe*, it was important to preserve its central holding. The opinion did not rely solely on the justices' concern for the Court's legitimacy. In often grandiloquent language, the joint authors reaffirmed abortion's protection within the fundamental right to privacy. In trying to define this right, they wrote, "At the heart of liberty is the right to define one's own concept of existence, of meaning, of the universe, and of the mystery of human life."

The joint opinion—long on lofty rhetoric about things such as the "mystery of human life" and short on traditional constitutional interpretation— prompted Justice Scalia to pen one of the most caustic opinions ever written by a justice of the Supreme Court. At the outset, Scalia set forth in clear terms the standard he used to determine whether a right deserves constitutional protection before finding that abortion fell short of this standard. He expressed contempt for the joint opinion's reliance on *stare decisis* to overcome its authors' admitted reservations about *Roe*, concluding, "The notion that we would decide a case differently from the way we otherwise would have in order to show that we can stand firm against public disapproval is frightening." He also chastised the three justices for adopting the "undue burden" standard, "as doubtful in its application as it is unprincipled in its origin." Scalia also took the joint opinion authors to task for pretending to save *Roe* when, in fact, they abandoned the trimester analysis—the only thing most people remember about that decision.

Lastly, Scalia challenged the joint opinion for claiming that *Roe* helped to settle the "national controversy" over abortion. He observed that the abortion debate grew even more intense in the wake of *Roe* as the question was elevated from the state to the national level. Scalia concluded the joint opinion would only provoke greater passion on both sides of the abortion divide.

⌘

Justice Scalia, with whom the Chief Justice, Justice White, and Justice Thomas join, concurring in the judgment in part and dissenting in part.

My views on this matter are unchanged from those I set forth in my separate opinions in *Webster v. Reproductive Health Services* and *Ohio v. Akron Center for Reproductive Health*. The States may, if they wish, permit abortion on demand, but the Constitution does not *require* them to do so. The permissibility of abortion, and the limitations upon it, are to be resolved like most important questions in our democracy: by citizens trying to persuade one another and then voting. As the Court acknowledges, "where reasonable people disagree the government can adopt one position or the other." The Court is correct in adding the qualification that this "assumes a state of affairs in which the choice does not intrude upon a protected liberty," but the crucial part of that qualification is the penultimate word. A State's choice between two positions on which reasonable people can disagree is constitutional even when (as is often the case) it intrudes upon a "liberty" in the absolute sense. Laws against bigamy, for example—with which entire societies of reasonable people disagree—intrude upon men and women's liberty to marry and live with one another. But bigamy happens not to be a liberty specially "protected" by the Constitution.

That is, quite simply, the issue in this case: not whether the power of a woman to abort her unborn child is a "liberty" in the absolute sense; or even whether it is a liberty of great importance to many women. Of course it is both. The issue is whether it is a liberty protected by the Constitution of the United States. I am sure it is not. I reach that conclusion not because of anything so exalted as my views concerning the "concept of existence, of meaning, of the universe, and of the mystery of human life." Rather, I reach it for the same reason I reach the conclusion that bigamy is not constitutionally protected—because of two simple facts: (1) the Constitution says absolutely nothing about it, and (2) the long-standing traditions of American society have permitted it to be legally proscribed.

No government official is "tempted" to place restraints upon his own freedom of action, which is why Lord Acton did not say "Power tends to purify."

The Court destroys the proposition, evidently meant to represent my position, that "liberty" includes "only those practices, defined at the most specific level, that were protected against government interference by other rules of law when the Fourteenth Amendment was ratified" (citing *Michael H. v. Gerald D.* (1989)). That is not, however, what *Michael H.* says; it merely observes that, in defining "liberty," we may not disregard a specific, "relevant tradition protecting, or denying protection to, the asserted right." But the Court does not wish to be fettered by any such limitations on its preferences. The Court's statement that it is "tempting" to acknowledge the authoritativeness of tradition in order to "cur[b] the discretion of federal judges" is, of course, rhetoric rather than reality; no government official is "tempted" to place restraints upon his own freedom of action, which is why Lord Acton did not say "Power tends to purify." The Court's temptation is in the quite opposite and more natural direction—towards systematically eliminating checks upon its own power; and it succumbs.

Beyond that brief summary of the essence of my position, I will not swell the United States Reports with repetition of what I have said before; and applying the rational basis test, I would uphold the Pennsylvania statute in its entirety. I must, however, respond to a few of the more outrageous arguments in today's opinion, which it is beyond human nature to leave unanswered. I shall discuss each of them under a quotation from the Court's opinion to which they pertain.

> The inescapable fact is that adjudication of substantive due process claims may call upon the Court, in interpreting the Constitution, to exercise that same capacity which, by tradition, courts always have exercised: reasoned judgment.

Assuming that the question before us is to be resolved at such a level of philosophical abstraction, in such isolation from the traditions of American society, as by simply applying "reasoned judgment," I do not see how that could possibly have produced the answer the Court arrived at in *Roe v. Wade.* Today's opinion describes the methodology of *Roe,* quite accurately, as weighing against the woman's interest the State's "'important and legitimate interest in protecting the potentiality of human life.'" (quoting *Roe*). But "reasoned judgment" does not begin by begging the question, as *Roe* and subsequent cases unquestionably did by assuming that what the State is protecting is the mere "potentiality of human life." The

whole argument of abortion opponents is that what the Court calls
the fetus and what others call the unborn child *is a human life*. Thus,
whatever answer *Roe* came up with after conducting its "balancing"
is bound to be wrong, unless it is correct that the human fetus is in
some critical sense merely potentially human. There is of course no
way to determine that as a legal matter; it is,
in fact, a value judgment. Some societies have
considered newborn children not yet human,
or the incompetent elderly no longer so.

The best the Court can do to explain how it is that the word "liberty" must be thought to include the right to destroy human fetuses is to rattle off a collection of adjectives that simply decorate a value judgment and conceal a political choice.

The authors of the joint opinion, of course,
do not squarely contend that *Roe v. Wade* was
a *correct* application of "reasoned judgment";
merely that it must be followed, because of
stare decisis. But in their exhaustive discussion
of all the factors that go into the determination
of when *stare decisis* should be observed and
when disregarded, they never mention "how
wrong was the decision on its face?" Surely,
if "[t]he Court's power lies...in its legitimacy, a product of substance and perception,"
the "substance" part of the equation demands that plain error be
acknowledged and eliminated. *Roe* was plainly wrong—even on the
Court's methodology of "reasoned judgment," and even more so (of
course) if the proper criteria of text and tradition are applied.

The emptiness of the "reasoned judgment" that produced *Roe* is
displayed in plain view by the fact that, after more than 19 years of
effort by some of the brightest (and most determined) legal minds in
the country, after more than 10 cases upholding abortion rights in this
Court, and after dozens upon dozens of *amicus* briefs submitted in this

and other cases, the best the Court can do to explain how it is that the word "liberty" *must* be thought to include the right to destroy human fetuses is to rattle off a collection of adjectives that simply decorate a value judgment and conceal a political choice. The right to abort, we are told, inheres in "liberty" because it is among "a person's most basic decisions"; it involves a "most intimate and personal choic[e]"; it is "central to personal dignity and autonomy"; it "originate[s] within the zone of conscience and belief"; it is "too intimate and personal" for state interference; it reflects "intimate views" of a "deep, personal character"; it involves "intimate relationships" and notions of "personal autonomy and bodily integrity"; and it concerns a particularly "'important decisio[n].'" But it is obvious to anyone applying "reasoned judgment" that the same adjectives can be applied to many forms of conduct that this Court (including one of the Justices in today's majority) has held are *not* entitled to constitutional protection—because, like abortion, they are forms of conduct that have long been criminalized in American society. Those adjectives might be applied, for example, to homosexual sodomy, polygamy, adult incest, and suicide, all of which are equally "intimate" and "deep[ly] personal" decisions involving "personal autonomy and bodily integrity," and all of which can constitutionally be proscribed because it is our unquestionable constitutional tradition that they are proscribable. It is not reasoned judgment that supports the Court's decision; only personal predilection. Justice Curtis' warning is as timely today as it was 135 years ago:

[W]hen a strict interpretation of the Constitution, according to the fixed rules which govern the interpretation of laws, is abandoned, and the theoretical opinions of individuals are allowed to control its meaning, we have no longer a Constitution; we are under the government of individual men, who for the time being have power to declare what the Constitution is, according to their own views of what it ought to mean.

DRED SCOTT v. SANDFORD, (1857)

Liberty finds no refuge in a jurisprudence of doubt.

One might have feared to encounter this august and sonorous phrase in an opinion defending the real *Roe v. Wade,* rather than the revised version fabricated today by the authors of the joint opinion. The shortcomings of *Roe* did not include lack of clarity: virtually all regulation of abortion before the third trimester was invalid. But to come across this phrase in the joint opinion—which calls upon federal district judges to apply an "undue burden" standard as doubtful in application as it is unprincipled in origin—is really more than one should have to bear.

The joint opinion frankly concedes that the amorphous concept of "undue burden" has been inconsistently applied by the Members of this Court in the few brief years since that "test" was first explicitly propounded by Justice O'Connor in her dissent in *Akron I.* Because the three Justices now wish to "set forth a standard of general application," the joint opinion announces that "it is important to clarify what is meant by an undue burden." I certainly agree with that, but I do not agree that the joint opinion succeeds in the announced endeavor. To the contrary, its efforts at clarification make clear only that the standard is inherently manipulable, and will prove hopelessly unworkable in practice.

The joint opinion explains that a state regulation imposes an "undue burden" if it "has the purpose or effect of placing a substantial obstacle in the path of a woman seeking an abortion of a nonviable fetus." An obstacle is "substantial," we are told, if it is "calculated[,] [not] to inform the woman's free choice, [but to] hinder it." This latter statement cannot possibly mean what it says. *Any* regulation of abortion that is intended to advance what the joint opinion concedes is the State's "substantial" interest in protecting unborn life will be "calculated [to] hinder" a decision to have an abortion. It thus seems more accurate to say that the joint opinion would uphold abortion regulations only if they do not *unduly* hinder the woman's decision. That, of course, brings us right back to square one: Defining an "undue burden" as an "undue hindrance" (or a "substantial obstacle") hardly "clarifies" the test. Consciously or not, the joint opinion's verbal shell game will conceal raw judicial policy choices concerning what is "appropriate" abortion legislation.

The ultimately standardless nature of the "undue burden" inquiry is a reflection of the underlying fact that the concept has no principled or coherent legal basis. As The Chief Justice points out, *Roe*'s strict-scrutiny standard "at least had a recognized basis in constitutional law at the time *Roe* was decided," while "[t]he same cannot be said for the 'undue burden' standard, which is created largely out of whole cloth by the authors of the joint opinion." The joint opinion is flatly wrong in asserting that "our jurisprudence relating to all liberties save perhaps abortion has recognized" the permissibility of laws that do not impose an "undue burden." It argues that the abortion right is similar to other rights in that a law "not designed to strike at the right itself, [but which] has the incidental effect of making it more difficult or more expensive to [exercise the right,]" is not invalid. I agree, indeed I have forcefully urged, that a law of general applicability which places only an incidental burden on a fundamental right does not infringe that right, but that principle does not establish the quite different (and quite dangerous) proposition that a law which *directly* regulates a fundamental right will not be found to violate the Constitution unless it imposes an "undue burden." It is that, of course, which is at issue here: Pennsylvania has *consciously and directly* regulated conduct that our cases have held is constitutionally protected. The appropriate analogy, therefore, is that of a state law requiring purchasers of religious books to endure a 24-hour waiting period, or to pay a nominal additional tax of 1¢. The joint opinion cannot possibly be correct in suggesting that we would uphold such legislation on the ground that it does not impose a "substantial obstacle" to the exercise of First Amendment rights. The "undue burden" standard is not at all the generally applicable principle the joint opinion pretends it to be; rather, it is a unique concept created specially for this case, to preserve some judicial foothold in this ill-gotten territory. In claiming otherwise, the three Justices show their willingness to place all constitutional rights at risk in an effort to preserve what they deem the "central holding in *Roe*."

It is difficult to maintain the illusion that we are interpreting a Constitution rather than inventing one, when we amend its provisions so breezily.

The rootless nature of the "undue burden" standard, a phrase plucked out of context from our earlier abortion decisions, is further reflected in the fact that the joint opinion finds it necessary expressly to repudiate the more narrow formulations used in Justice O'Connor's earlier opinions. Those opinions stated that a statute imposes an "undue burden" if it imposes "*absolute* obstacles or *severe* limitations on the abortion decision," *Akron I* (dissenting opinion) (emphasis added). Those strong adjectives are conspicuously missing from the joint opinion, whose authors have for some unexplained reason now determined that a burden is "undue" if it merely imposes a "substantial" obstacle to abortion decisions. Justice O'Connor has also abandoned (again without explanation) the view she expressed in *Planned Parenthood Assn. of Kansas City, Mo., Inc.* v. *Ashcroft* that a medical regulation which imposes an "undue burden" could nevertheless be upheld if it "reasonably relate[s] to the preservation and protection of maternal health." In today's version, even health measures will be upheld only *"if they do not constitute an undue burden"* (emphasis added). Gone too is Justice O'Connor's statement that "the State possesses *compelling* interests in the protection of potential human life . . . throughout pregnancy," *Akron I* (emphasis added); instead, the State's interest in unborn human life is stealthily downgraded to a merely "substantial" or "profound" interest. (That had to be done, of course, since designating the interest as "compelling" throughout pregnancy would have been, shall we say, a "substantial obstacle" to the joint opinion's determined effort to reaffirm what it views as the "central holding" of *Roe*.) And "viability" is no longer the "arbitrary" dividing line previously decried by Justice O'Connor in *Akron I*; the Court now announces that "the attainment of viability may continue to serve as the critical fact." It is difficult to maintain the illusion that we are interpreting a Constitution rather than inventing one, when we amend its provisions so breezily.

Because the portion of the joint opinion adopting and describing the undue burden test provides no more useful guidance than the empty phrases discussed above, one must turn to the 23 pages applying that standard to the present facts for further guidance. In evaluating Pennsylvania's abortion law, the joint opinion relies extensively on the factual findings of the District Court, and repeatedly qualifies its conclusions by noting that they are contingent upon the record developed in these cases. Thus, the joint opinion would uphold the 24-hour waiting period contained in the Pennsylvania statute's informed consent provision because "the record evidence shows that, in the vast majority of cases, a 24-hour delay does not create any appreciable health risk." The three Justices therefore conclude that, "on the record before us, ... we are not convinced that the 24-hour waiting period constitutes an undue burden." The requirement that a doctor provide the information pertinent to informed consent would also be upheld because "there is no evidence on this record that [this requirement] would amount in practical terms to a substantial obstacle to a woman seeking an abortion." Similarly, the joint opinion would uphold the reporting requirements of the Act because "there is no ... showing on the record before us" that these requirements constitute a "substantial obstacle" to abortion decisions. But at the same time the opinion pointedly observes that these reporting requirements may increase the costs of abortions, and that "at some point, [that fact] could become a substantial obstacle." Most significantly, the joint opinion's conclusion that the spousal notice requirement of the Act imposes an "undue burden" is based in large measure on the District Court's "detailed findings of fact," which the joint opinion sets out at great length.

I do not, of course, have any objection to the notion that, in applying legal principles, one should rely only upon the facts that are contained in the record or that are properly subject to judicial notice. But what is remarkable about the joint opinion's fact-intensive analysis is that it does not result in any measurable clarification of the "undue burden" standard. Rather, the approach of the joint opinion is, for the most part, simply to highlight certain facts in the record that apparently strike the three Justices as particularly significant in establishing (or refuting) the existence of an undue burden; after describing these facts, the opinion then simply announces that the provision either does or does not impose a "substantial obstacle" or an "undue burden." We do not know whether the same conclusions could have been reached on a different record, or in what respects the record would have had to differ before an opposite conclusion would have been appropriate. The inherently standardless nature of this inquiry invites the district judge to give effect to his personal preferences about abortion. By finding and relying upon the right facts, he can invalidate, it would seem, almost any abortion restriction that strikes him as "undue"—subject, of course, to the possibility of being reversed by a court of appeals or Supreme Court that is as unconstrained in reviewing his decision as he was in making it.

To the extent I can discern *any* meaningful content in the "undue burden" standard as applied in the joint opinion, it appears to be that a State may not regulate abortion in such a way as to reduce significantly its incidence. The joint opinion repeatedly emphasizes that an important factor in the "undue burden" analysis is whether the regulation "prevent[s] a significant number of women from obtaining an abortion;" whether a "significant number of women . . . are likely to be deterred from procuring an abortion" and whether the regulation often "deters" women from seeking abortions. We are not told, however, what forms of "deterrence" are impermissible or what degree of success in deterrence is too much to be tolerated. If, for example, a State required a woman to read a pamphlet describing, with illustrations, the facts of fetal development before she could obtain an abortion, the effect of such legislation might be to "deter" a "significant number of women" from procuring abortions, thereby seemingly allowing a district judge to invalidate it as an undue burden. Thus, despite flowery rhetoric about the State's "substantial" and "profound" interest in "potential human life," and criticism of *Roe* for undervaluing that interest, the joint opinion permits the State to pursue that interest only so long as it is not too successful. As Justice Blackmun recognizes (with evident hope), the "undue burden" standard may ultimately require the invalidation of each provision upheld today if it can be shown, on a better record, that the State is too effectively "express[ing] a preference for childbirth over abortion." Reason finds no refuge in this jurisprudence of confusion.

> *It seems to me that* stare decisis *ought to be applied even to the doctrine of* stare decisis, *and I confess never to have heard of this new, keep-what-you-want-and-throw-away-the-rest version.*

While we appreciate the weight of the arguments...that *Roe* should be overruled, the reservations any of us may have in reaffirming the central holding of *Roe* are outweighed by the explication of individual liberty we have given combined with the force of *stare decisis.*

The Court's reliance upon *stare decisis* can best be described as contrived. It insists upon the necessity of adhering not to all of *Roe,* but only to what it calls the "central holding." It seems to me that *stare decisis* ought to be applied even to the doctrine of *stare decisis,* and I confess never to have heard of this new, keep-what-you-want-and-throw-away-the-rest version. I wonder whether, as applied to *Marbury v. Madison*, for example, the new version of *stare decisis* would be satisfied if we allowed courts to review the constitutionality of only those statutes that (like the one in *Marbury*) pertain to the jurisdiction of the courts.

I am certainly not in a good position to dispute that the Court *has saved* the "central holding" of *Roe* since to do that effectively I would have to know what the Court has saved, which in turn would require me to understand (as I do not) what the "undue burden" test means. I must confess, however, that I have always thought, and I think a lot of other people have always thought, that the arbitrary trimester framework, which the Court today discards, was quite as central to *Roe* as the arbitrary viability test, which the Court today retains. It seems particularly ungrateful to carve the trimester framework out of the core of *Roe,* since its very rigidity (in sharp contrast to the utter indeterminability of the "undue burden" test) is probably the only reason the Court is able to say, in urging *stare decisis,* that *Roe* "has in no sense proven 'unworkable.'" I suppose the Court is entitled to call a "central holding" whatever it wants to call a "central holding"—which is, come to think of it, perhaps one of the difficulties with this modified version of *stare decisis*. I thought I might note, however, that the following portions of *Roe* have not been saved:

— Under *Roe,* requiring that a woman seeking an abortion be provided truthful information about abortion before giving informed written consent is unconstitutional if the information is designed to influence her choice. Under the joint opinion's "undue burden" regime (as applied today, at least) such a requirement is constitutional.

— Under *Roe,* requiring that information be provided by a doctor, rather than by nonphysician counselors, is unconstitutional. Under the "undue burden" regime (as applied today, at least) it is not.

— Under *Roe,* requiring a 24-hour waiting period between the time the woman gives her informed consent and the time of the abortion is unconstitutional. Under the "undue burden" regime (as applied today, at least) it is not.

— Under *Roe,* requiring detailed reports that include demographic data about each woman who seeks an abortion and various information about each abortion is unconstitutional. Under the "undue burden" regime (as applied today, at least) it generally is not.

To portray Roe *as the statesmanlike "settlement" of a divisive issue, a jurisprudential Peace of Westphalia that is worth preserving, is nothing less than Orwellian.*

Where, in the performance of its judicial duties, the Court decides a case in such a way as to resolve the sort of intensely divisive controversy reflected in *Roe*...its decision has a dimension that the resolution of the normal case does not carry. It is the dimension present whenever the Court's interpretation of the Constitution calls the contending sides of a national controversy to end their national division by accepting a common mandate rooted in the Constitution.

The Court's description of the place of *Roe* in the social history of the United States is unrecognizable. Not only did *Roe* not, as the Court suggests, *resolve* the deeply divisive issue of abortion; it did more than anything else to nourish it, by elevating it to the national level, where it is infinitely more difficult to resolve. National politics were not plagued by abortion protests, national abortion lobbying, or abortion marches on Congress, before *Roe v. Wade* was decided. Profound disagreement existed among our citizens over the issue—as it does over other issues, such as the death penalty—but that disagreement was being worked out at the state level. As with many other issues, the division of sentiment within each State was not as closely balanced as it was among the population of the Nation as a whole, meaning not only that more people would be satisfied with the results of state-by-state resolution, but also that those results would be more stable. Pre-*Roe,* moreover, political compromise was possible.

Roe's mandate for abortion on demand destroyed the compromises of the past, rendered compromise impossible for the future, and required the entire issue to be resolved uniformly, at the national level. At the same time, *Roe* created a vast new class of abortion consumers and abortion proponents by eliminating the moral opprobrium that had attached to the act. ("If the Constitution *guarantees* abortion, how can it be bad?"—not an accurate line of thought, but a natural one.) Many favor all of those developments, and it is not for me to say that they are wrong. But to portray *Roe* as the statesmanlike "settlement" of a divisive issue, a jurisprudential Peace of Westphalia that is worth preserving, is nothing less than Orwellian. *Roe* fanned into life an issue that has inflamed our national politics in general, and has obscured with its smoke the selection of Justices to this Court, in particular, ever since. And by keeping us in the abortion-umpiring business, it is the perpetuation of that disruption, rather than of any *Pax Roeana* that the Court's new majority decrees.

[T]o overrule under fire . . . would subvert the Court's legitimacy. . . .

. . . To all those who will be . . . tested by following, the Court
implicitly undertakes to remain steadfast. . . . The promise of
constancy, once given, binds its maker for as long as the power
to stand by the decision survives and . . . the commitment [is not]
obsolete. . . .

[The American people's] belief in themselves as . . . a people
[who aspire to live according to the rule of law] is not readily
separable from their understanding of the Court invested with
the authority to decide their constitutional cases and speak
before all others for their constitutional ideals. If the Court's
legitimacy should be undermined, then so would the country be in its very ability to see itself through its constitutional
ideals.

The Imperial Judiciary lives. It is instructive to compare this Nietzs-
chean vision of us unelected, life-tenured judges—leading a Volk who
will be "tested by following," and whose very "belief in themselves" is
mystically bound up in their "understanding" of a Court that "speak[s]
before all others for their constitutional ideals"—with the somewhat
more modest role envisioned for these lawyers by the Founders.

The judiciary . . . has . . . no direction either of the strength or
of the wealth of the society, and can take no active resolution
whatever. It may truly be said to have neither Force nor Will,
but merely judgment. . . .

THE FEDERALIST NO. 78

Or, again, to compare this ecstasy of a Supreme Court in which there is, especially on controversial matters, no shadow of change or hint of alteration ("There is a limit to the amount of error that can plausibly be imputed to prior courts"), with the more democratic views of a more humble man:

> [T]he candid citizen must confess that if the policy of the Government upon vital questions affecting the whole people is to be irrevocably fixed by decisions of the Supreme Court, ... the people will have ceased to be their own rulers, having to that extent practically resigned their Government into the hands of that eminent tribunal.
>
> A. LINCOLN, FIRST INAUGURAL ADDRESS (MAR. 4, 1861)

It is particularly difficult, in the circumstances of the present decision, to sit still for the Court's lengthy lecture upon the virtues of "constancy," of "remain[ing] steadfast," and adhering to "principle." Among the five Justices who purportedly adhere to *Roe,* at most three agree upon the *principle* that constitutes adherence (the joint opinion's "undue burden" standard)—and that principle is inconsistent with *Roe.* To make matters worse, two of the three, in order thus to remain steadfast, had to abandon previously stated positions. It is beyond me how the Court expects these accommodations to be accepted "as grounded truly in principle, not as compromises with social and political pressures having, as such, no bearing on the principled choices that the Court is obliged to make." The only principle the Court "adheres" to, it seems to me, is the principle that the Court must be seen as standing by *Roe.* That is not a principle of law (which is what I thought the Court was talking about), but a principle of *Realpolitik*—and a wrong one at that.

I cannot agree with, indeed I am appalled by, the Court's suggestion that the decision whether to stand by an erroneous constitutional decision must be strongly influenced—*against* overruling, no less—by the substantial and continuing public opposition the decision has generated. The Court's judgment that any other course would "subvert the Court's legitimacy" must be another consequence of reading the error-filled history book that described the deeply divided country brought together by *Roe*. In my history book, the Court was covered with dishonor and deprived of legitimacy by *Dred Scott v. Sandford*, an erroneous (and widely opposed) opinion that it did not abandon, rather than by *West Coast Hotel Co. v. Parrish*, which produced the famous "switch in time" from the Court's erroneous (and widely opposed) constitutional opposition to the social measures of the New Deal. (Both *Dred Scott* and one line of the cases resisting the New Deal rested upon the concept of "substantive due process" that the Court praises and employs today....)

But whether it would "subvert the Court's legitimacy" or not, the notion that we would decide a case differently from the way we otherwise would have in order to show that we can stand firm against public disapproval is frightening. It is a bad enough idea, even in the head of someone like me, who believes that the text of the Constitution, and our traditions, say what they say and there is no fiddling with them. But when it is in the mind of a Court that believes the Constitution has an evolving meaning; that the Ninth Amendment's reference to "othe[r]" rights is not a disclaimer, but a charter for action; and that the function of this Court is to "speak before all others for [the people's] constitutional ideals" unrestrained by meaningful text or tradition—then the notion that the Court must adhere to a decision for as long as the decision faces "great opposition" and the Court is "under fire" acquires a character of almost czarist arrogance. We are offended by these marchers who descend upon us, every year on the anniversary of *Roe,* to protest our saying that the Constitution requires what our society has never thought the Constitution requires. These people who refuse to be "tested by following" must be taught a lesson. We have no Cossacks, but at least we can stubbornly refuse to abandon an erroneous opinion that we might otherwise change—to show how little they intimidate us.

Of course, as The Chief Justice points out, we have been subjected to what the Court calls "political pressure" by *both* sides of this issue. Maybe today's decision *not* to overrule *Roe* will be seen as buckling to pressure from *that* direction. Instead of engaging in the hopeless task of predicting public perception—a job not for lawyers but for political campaign managers—the Justices should do what is legally right by asking two questions: (1) Was *Roe* correctly decided? (2) Has *Roe* succeeded in producing a settled body of law? If the answer to both questions is no, *Roe* should undoubtedly be overruled.

In truth, I am as distressed as the Court is—and expressed my distress several years ago—about the "political pressure" directed to the Court: the marches, the mail, the protests aimed at inducing us to change our opinions. How upsetting it is, that so many of our citizens (good people, not lawless ones, on both sides of this abortion issue, and on various sides of other issues as well) think that we Justices should properly take into account their views, as though we were engaged not in ascertaining an objective law, but in determining some kind of social consensus. The Court would profit, I think, from giving less attention to the *fact* of this distressing phenomenon, and more attention to the *cause* of it. That cause permeates today's opinion: a new mode of constitutional adjudication that relies not upon text and traditional practice to determine the law, but upon what the Court calls "reasoned judgment," which turns out to be nothing but philosophical predilection and moral intuition. All manner of "liberties," the Court tells us, inhere in the Constitution and are enforceable by this Court—not just those mentioned in the text or established in the traditions of our society. Why even the Ninth Amendment—which says only that "[t]he enumeration in the Constitution, of certain rights, shall not be construed to deny or disparage others retained by the people"—is, despite our contrary understanding for almost 200 years, a literally boundless source of additional, unnamed, unhinted-at "rights," definable and enforceable by us, through "reasoned judgment."

What makes all this relevant to the bothersome application of "political pressure" against the Court are the twin facts that the American people love democracy and the American people are not fools. As long as this Court thought (and the people thought) that we Justices were doing essentially lawyers' work up here—reading text and discerning our society's traditional understanding of that text—the public pretty much left us alone. Texts and traditions are facts to study, not convictions to demonstrate about. But if in reality our process of constitutional adjudication consists primarily of making *value judgments;* if we can ignore a long and clear tradition clarifying an ambiguous text, as we did, for example, five days ago in declaring unconstitutional invocations and benedictions at public high school graduation ceremonies; if, as I say, our pronouncement of constitutional law rests primarily on value judgments, then a free and intelligent people's attitude towards us can be expected to be (*ought* to be) quite different. The people know that their value judgments are quite as good as those taught in any law school—maybe better. If, indeed, the "liberties" protected by the Constitution are, as the Court says, undefined and unbounded, then the people *should* demonstrate, to protest that we do not implement *their* values instead of *ours*. Not only that, but the confirmation hearings for new Justices *should* deteriorate into question-and-answer sessions in which Senators go through a list of their constituents' most favored and most disfavored alleged constitutional rights, and seek the nominee's commitment to support or oppose them. Value judgments, after all, should be voted on, not dictated; and if our Constitution has somehow accidentally committed them to the Supreme Court, at least we can have a sort of plebiscite each time a new nominee to that body is put forward. . . .

There is a poignant aspect to today's opinion. Its length, and what might be called its epic tone, suggest that its authors believe they are bringing to an end a troublesome era in the history of our Nation, and of our Court. "It is the dimension" of authority, they say, to "cal[l] the contending sides of national controversy to end their national division by accepting a common mandate rooted in the Constitution."

There comes vividly to mind a portrait by Emanuel Leutze that hangs in the Harvard Law School: Roger Brooke Taney, painted in 1859, the 82nd year of his life, the 24th of his Chief Justiceship, the second after his opinion in *Dred Scott*. He is all in black, sitting in a shadowed red armchair, left hand resting upon a pad of paper in his lap, right hand hanging limply, almost lifelessly, beside the inner arm of the chair. He sits facing the viewer, and staring straight out. There seems to be on his face, and in his deep-set eyes, an expression of profound sadness and disillusionment. Perhaps he always looked that way, even when dwelling upon the happiest of thoughts. But those of us who know how the lustre of his great Chief Justiceship came to be eclipsed by *Dred Scott* cannot help believing that he had that case—its already apparent consequences for the Court, and its soon-to-be-played-out consequences for the Nation—burning on his mind. I expect that two years earlier he, too, had thought himself "call[ing] the contending sides of national controversy to end their national division by accepting a common mandate rooted in the Constitution."

It is no more realistic for us in this litigation than it was for him in that, to think that an issue of the sort they both involved—an issue involving life and death, freedom and subjugation—can be "speedily and finally settled" by the Supreme Court, as President James Buchanan, in his inaugural address, said the issue of slavery in the territories would be. Quite to the contrary, by foreclosing all democratic outlet for the deep passions this issue arouses, by banishing the issue from the political forum that gives all participants, even the losers, the satisfaction of a fair hearing and an honest fight, by continuing the imposition of a rigid national rule instead of allowing for regional differences, the Court merely prolongs and intensifies the anguish.

We should get out of this area, where we have no right to be, and where we do neither ourselves nor the country any good by remaining.

STENBERG v. CARHART (2000)

In the mid-1990s, many Americans were shocked to learn of an abortion procedure known as "partial-birth abortion," used to abort fetuses in women who are twenty to thirty-two weeks pregnant. Guided by ultrasound, the doctor reaches into the uterus, grabs the unborn baby's legs with forceps, and pulls the baby into the birth canal, except for the head, which is deliberately kept just inside the womb. The doctor then forces scissors into the back of the baby's skull and spreads the tips of the scissors apart to enlarge the wound. After removing the scissors, a suction catheter is inserted into the skull and the baby's brain is sucked out.

The procedure was so gruesome that many traditionally prochoice legislators—along with upwards of 70 percent of Americans—supported a ban on the practice. The U.S. Congress passed legislation to prohibit doctors from performing the procedure. The ban was vetoed by President Bill Clinton, but a nearly identical version was later signed by President George W. Bush.

Many states, including Nebraska, also passed legislative bans. The Nebraska law stated, "No partial-birth abortion shall be performed in this state, unless such procedure is necessary to save the life of the mother whose life is endangered by a physical disorder, physical illness, or physical injury, including a life-endangering physical condition caused by or arising from the pregnancy itself."

The statute defined partial-birth abortion as "an abortion procedure in which the person performing the abortion partially delivers vaginally a living unborn child before killing the unborn child and completing the delivery. The law further defined the phrase "partially delivers vaginally a living unborn child before killing the unborn child" as "deliberately and intentionally delivering into the vagina a living unborn child, or a substantial portion thereof, for the purpose of performing a procedure that the person performing such procedure knows will kill the unborn child and does kill the unborn child."

Writing for the majority of the Court, Justice Stephen Breyer said that the statute violated the Constitution because it did not allow an exception for the preservation of the health of the mother and because it eliminated this procedure as a choice for a woman, "thereby unduly burdening the right to choose abortion itself."

Scalia did nothing to hide his disdain for the Court's opinion, comparing it to the two decisions many legal scholars consider among the worst in Supreme Court history: *Korematsu v. United States* (1944), which upheld the internment of Japanese Americans during World War II, and *Dred Scott* (1856), the slavery case that precipitated the Civil War. The impassioned language notwithstanding, Scalia wrote that he did not originally intend to deliver a separate dissenting opinion. Rather, he planned to let Justice Clarence Thomas's and Justice Anthony Kennedy's dissenting opinions expose what he viewed as the flaws in the majority's decision. He said, however, he was afraid their opinions might make it seem as though the Court's decision was an aberration. In Scalia's mind, the *Stenberg* case was the foreseeable—albeit regrettable—product of the Court's recent abortion decisions, especially *Casey*. Scalia, in a highly unusual move for any justice, directly implored the Court to overturn *Casey*.

❦

JUSTICE SCALIA, DISSENTING.

I am optimistic enough to believe that, one day, *Stenberg v. Carhart* will be assigned its rightful place in the history of this Court's jurisprudence beside *Korematsu* and *Dred Scott*. The method of killing a human child—one cannot even accurately say an entirely unborn human child—proscribed by this statute is so horrible that the most clinical description of it evokes a shudder of revulsion. And the Court must know (as most state legislatures banning this procedure have concluded) that demanding a "health exception"—which requires the abortionist to assure himself that, in his expert medical judgment, this method is, in the case at hand, marginally safer than others (how can one prove the contrary beyond a reasonable doubt?)—is to give live-birth abortion free rein. The notion that the Constitution of the United States, designed, among other things, "to establish Justice, insure domestic Tranquility, . . . and secure the Blessings of Liberty to ourselves and our Posterity," prohibits the States from simply banning this visibly brutal means of eliminating our half-born posterity is quite simply absurd. . . .

It would be unfortunate, however, if those who disagree with the result were induced to regard it as merely a regrettable misapplication of *Casey*. It is not that, but is *Casey*'s logical and entirely predictable consequence. To be sure, the Court's construction of this statute so as to make it include procedures other than live-birth abortion involves not only a disregard of fair meaning, but an abandonment of the principle that even ambiguous statutes should be interpreted in such a fashion as to render them valid rather than void. *Casey* does not permit that jurisprudential novelty—which must be chalked up to the Court's inclination to bend the rules when any effort to limit abortion, or even to speak in opposition to abortion, is at issue. . . .

But the Court gives a second and independent reason for invalidating this humane (not to say antibarbarian) law: That it fails to allow an exception for the situation in which the abortionist believes that

> *The notion that the Constitution of the United States, designed, among other things, "to establish Justice, insure domestic Tranquility, . . . and secure the Blessings of Liberty to ourselves and our Posterity," prohibits the States from simply banning this visibly brutal means of eliminating our half-born posterity is quite simply absurd.*

the live-birth method of destroying the child might be safer for the woman. (As pointed out by Justice Thomas, and elaborated upon by Justice Kennedy, there is no good reason to believe this is ever the case, but—who knows?—it sometime might be.)

I never put much stock in *Casey's* explication of the inexplicable. In the last analysis, my judgment that *Casey* does not support today's tragic result can be traced to the fact that what I consider to be an "undue burden'" is different from what the majority considers to be an "undue burden"—a conclusion that cannot be demonstrated true or false by factual inquiry or legal reasoning. It is a value judgment, dependent upon how much respects (or believes society ought to respect) the life of a partially delivered fetus, and how much one respects (or believes society ought to respect) the freedom of the woman who gave it life to kill it. Evidently, the five Justices in today's majority value the former less, or the latter more (or both), than the four of us in dissent. Case closed. There is no cause for anyone who believes in *Casey* to feel betrayed by this outcome. It has been arrived at by precisely the process *Casey* promised—a democratic vote by nine lawyers, not on the question whether the text of the Constitution has anything to say about this subject (it obviously does not); not even on the question (also appropriate for lawyers) whether the legal traditions of the American people would have sustained such a limitation upon abortion (they obviously would); but upon the pure policy question whether this limitation upon abortion is "undue"—i.e., goes too far.

In my dissent in *Casey*, I wrote that the "undue burden" test made law by the joint opinion created a standard that was "as doubtful in application as it is unprincipled in origin", "hopelessly unworkable in practice", "ultimately standardless." Today's decision is the proof. As long as we are debating the issue of necessity for a health-of-the-mother exception on the basis of *Casey*, it is really quite impossible for us dissenters to contend that the majority is wrong on the law—any more than it could be said that one is wrong in law to support or oppose the death penalty, or to support or oppose mandatory minimum sentences. The most that we can honestly say is that we disagree with the majority on their policy-judgment-couched-as-law. And those who believe that a 5-to-4 vote on a policy matter by unelected lawyers should not overcome the judgment of 30 state legislatures that have a problem, not with the *application* of *Casey*, but with its *existence*. *Casey* must be overruled.

> *The most that we can honestly say is that we disagree with the majority on their policy-judgment-couched-as-law.*

While I am in an I-told-you-so mood, I must recall my bemusement, in *Casey*, at the joint opinion's expressed belief that *Roe v. Wade* had "call[ed] the contending sides of a national controversy to end their national division by accepting a common mandate rooted in the Constitution," and that the decision in *Casey* would ratify that happy truce. It seemed to me, quite to the contrary, that "*Roe* fanned into life an issue that has inflamed our national politics in general, and has obscured with its smoke the selection of Justices to this Court in particular, ever since"; and that, "by keeping us in the abortion-umpiring business, it is the perpetuation of that disruption, rather than of any *Pax Roeana*, that the Court's new majority decrees." Today's decision, that the Constitution of the United States prevents the prohibition of a horrible mode of abortion, will be greeted by a firestorm of criticism—as well it should. I cannot understand why those who *acknowledge* that, in the opening words of Justice O'Connor's concurrence, "[t]he issue of abortion is one of the most contentious and controversial in contemporary American society," persist in the belief that this Court, armed with neither constitutional text nor accepted tradition, can resolve that contention and controversy rather than be consumed by it. If only for the sake of its own preservation, the Court should return this matter to the people—where the Constitution, by its silence on the subject, left it—and to let *them* decide, State by State, whether this practice should be allowed. *Casey* must be overruled.

～✺✧✺～

Editor's Postscript: In 2003, Congress passed the Partial-Birth Abortion Ban Act. The new federal law was challenged in court, and in 2007, the Supreme Court, with Justice Scalia in the five-to-four majority this time, ruled that the late-term-abortion ban was constitutional. Although the federal statute was nearly identical to the Nebraska law, the Court itself was different. Justice Sandra Day O'Connor, who voted to invalidate the Nebraska law in *Stenberg*, had retired and been replaced by Justice Samuel Alito, who sided with the majority to uphold the federal law.

CHAPTER SIX

GUN RIGHTS

~≈◦⊹◦≈~

THE SECOND AMENDMENT to the U.S. Constitution reads, "A well regulated Militia, being necessary to the security of a free State, the right of the people to keep and bear Arms, shall not be infringed." The admittedly awkward phrasing of this guarantee, along with its limited review by the Supreme Court, has helped to perpetuate a fierce debate about what this right entails and, most important, to whom it belongs. Does the right to bear arms belong to individual Americans or just those who are part of state militias? This question was finally teed up for the Supreme Court to answer in 2008, more than two centuries after the Second Amendment was adopted.

Before 2008, Justice Scalia had not had an opportunity to decide a case involving the Second Amendment. In *A Matter of Interpretation*, however, Scalia made clear his sense of what the Founders thought the Second Amendment protected. In a passage attacking the argument that a "living Constitution" would evolve forever "in the direction of greater personal liberty," Scalia pointed out instances in which proponents of that view seemed content to curtail constitutional freedoms, not expand them. He wrote:

The provision prohibiting impairment of the obligation of contracts, for example, has been gutted. I am sure We the People
agree with that development; we value property rights less than
the Founders did. So also, we value the right to bear arms less
than did the Founders (who thought the right of self-defense to
be absolutely fundamental), and there will be few tears shed if
and when the Second Amendment guarantee is held to guarantee
nothing more than the state National Guard.

Eleven years after writing this, Justice Scalia would write a majority opinion for the Supreme Court that honored the Founders' view.

DISTRICT OF COLUMBIA v. HELLER (2008)

Well known for having some of the strictest gun control laws in the country, the District of Columbia government made it illegal for residents to own
a handgun unless the chief of police issued the resident a one-year license.
D.C. law also required that all firearms be kept unloaded and disassembled
or bound by a trigger lock unless the firearms were located in a place of
business or were being used for legal recreational activities.

A D.C. special police officer named Dick Heller challenged the law.
Heller, who was authorized to carry a handgun while on duty, had applied
for a license to keep his gun at home, but the chief denied his request.
Heller argued that the D.C. law restricting the licensing of handguns and
requiring all licensed guns to be kept disassembled violated his individual
right guaranteed by the Second Amendment to keep and bear arms.

The district court dismissed Heller's complaint, but the U.S. Court of
Appeals for the D.C. Circuit reversed, holding that the Second Amendment

protects the right to keep firearms in the home for the purpose of self-defense. The court ruled that the District's requirement that firearms kept in the home be nonfunctional violated that right.

In a lengthy, history-filled opinion, Justice Scalia argued that the Second Amendment, as understood by those who wrote and ratified it, guaranteed the right of self-defense for individuals. Scalia argued that the amendment has a prefatory clause and an operative clause, and that the prefatory clause's reference to "militia" does not limit the substantive individual right protected by the operative clause. Scalia further noted that the term "militia" referred at the time to all able-bodied men who might be capable of being called into military service. "There seems to us no doubt, on the basis of both text and history, that the Second Amendment conferred an individual right to keep and bear arms," Scalia wrote for the Court.

Scalia stated that the Second Amendment right to keep arms was not unlimited, just as First Amendment rights are not absolute. He said the Court's ruling would not endanger laws prohibiting the possession of firearms, for example, by felons and the mentally ill. In the end, however, Scalia said the right was a fundamental one and could not be abridged without changing the Constitution. He concluded, "Undoubtedly some think that the Second Amendment is outmoded in a society where our standing army is the pride of our Nation, where well-trained police forces provide personal security, and where gun violence is a serious problem. That is perhaps debatable, but what is not debatable is that it is not the role of this Court to pronounce the Second Amendment extinct."

Writing for Justices Souter, Ginsburg, and Breyer, and himself, Justice John Paul Stevens argued in dissent that the most natural reading of the Second Amendment, and the reading supported by history, is that it protects the right to keep and bear arms for certain military purposes, which they viewed in the context of state militias. Justice Stevens argued that the

Second Amendment, unlike some similar state provisions enacted at the time, does not address at all the right to keep firearms for self-defense. Most notable about Justice Stevens's dissent was its appeal to history and the original meaning of the Second Amendment. Though he reached a different conclusion than Scalia, Stevens adopted Scalia's originalist approach.

⋯⋙⊙⊱⋯

Justice Scalia delivered the opinion of the Court, in which Chief Justice Roberts and Justices Kennedy, Thomas, and Alito joined.

We consider whether a District of Columbia prohibition on the possession of usable handguns in the home violates the Second Amendment to the Constitution.

I

The District of Columbia generally prohibits the possession of handguns. It is a crime to carry an unregistered firearm, and the registration of handguns is prohibited. Wholly apart from that prohibition, no person may carry a handgun without a license, but the chief of police may issue licenses for 1-year periods. District of Columbia law also requires residents to keep their lawfully owned firearms, such as registered long guns, "unloaded and dissembled or bound by a trigger lock or similar device" unless they are located in a place of business or are being used for lawful recreational activities.

Respondent Dick Heller is a D.C. special police officer authorized to carry a handgun while on duty at the Federal Judicial Center. He applied for a registration certificate for a handgun that he wished to keep at home, but the District refused. He thereafter filed a lawsuit in the Federal District Court for the District of Columbia seeking, on Second Amendment grounds, to enjoin the city from enforcing the bar on the registration of handguns, the licensing requirement insofar as it prohibits the carrying of a firearm in the home without a license, and the trigger-lock requirement insofar as it prohibits the use of "functional firearms within the home." The District Court dismissed respondent's complaint. The Court of Appeals for the District of Columbia Circuit, construing his complaint as seeking the right to render a firearm operable and carry it about his home in that condition only when necessary for self-defense, reversed. It held that the Second Amendment protects an individual right to possess firearms and that the city's total ban on handguns, as well as its requirement that firearms in the home be kept nonfunctional even when necessary for self-defense, violated that right.

We granted certiorari.

II

We turn first to the meaning of the Second Amendment.

A

The Second Amendment provides: "A well regulated Militia, being necessary to the security of a free State, the right of the people to keep and bear Arms, shall not be infringed." In interpreting this text, we are guided by the principle that "[t]he Constitution was written to be understood by the voters; its words and phrases were used in their normal and ordinary as distinguished from technical meaning." *United States v. Sprague* (1931). Normal meaning may of course include an idiomatic meaning, but it excludes secret or technical meanings that would not have been known to ordinary citizens in the founding generation.

The two sides in this case have set out very different interpretations of the Amendment. Petitioners and today's dissenting Justices believe that it protects only the right to possess and carry a firearm in connection with militia service. Respondent argues that it protects an individual right to possess a firearm unconnected with service in a militia, and to use that arm for traditionally lawful purposes, such as self-defense within the home.

The Second Amendment is naturally divided into two parts: its prefatory clause and its operative clause. The former does not limit the latter grammatically, but rather announces a purpose. The Amendment could be rephrased, "Because a well regulated Militia is necessary to the security of a free State, the right of the people to keep and bear Arms shall not be infringed." Although this structure of the Second Amendment is unique in our Constitution, other legal documents of the founding era, particularly individual-rights provisions of state constitutions, commonly included a prefatory statement of purpose.

Logic demands that there be a link between the stated purpose and the command. The Second Amendment would be nonsensical if it read, "A well regulated Militia, being necessary to the security of a free State, the right of the people to petition for redress of grievances shall not be infringed." That requirement of logical connection may cause a prefatory clause to resolve an ambiguity in the operative clause ("The separation of church and state being an important objective, the teachings of canons shall have no place in our jurisprudence." The preface makes clear that the operative clause refers not to canons of interpretation but to clergymen.) But apart from that clarifying function, a prefatory clause does not limit or expand the scope of the operative clause.... Therefore, while we will begin our textual analysis with the operative clause, we will return to the prefatory clause to ensure that our reading of the operative clause is consistent with the announced purpose.

1. Operative Clause.

a. "Right of the People." The first salient feature of the operative clause is that it codifies a "right of the people." The unamended Constitution and the Bill of Rights use the phrase "right of the people" two other times, in the First Amendment's Assembly-and-Petition Clause and in the Fourth Amendment's Search-and-Seizure Clause. The Ninth Amendment uses very similar terminology ("The enumeration in the Constitution, of certain rights, shall not be construed to deny or disparage others retained by the people"). All three of these instances unambiguously refer to individual rights, not "collective" rights, or rights that may be exercised only through participation in some corporate body.

Nowhere else in the Constitution does a "right" attributed to "the people" refer to anything other than an individual right.

Three provisions of the Constitution refer to "the people" in a context other than "rights"—the famous preamble ("We the people"), § 2 of Article I (providing that "the people" will choose members of the House), and the Tenth Amendment (providing that those powers not given the Federal Government remain with "the States" or "the people"). Those provisions arguably refer to "the people" acting collectively—but they deal with the exercise or reservation of powers, not rights. Nowhere else in the Constitution does a "right" attributed to "the people" refer to anything other than an individual right.

What is more, in all six other provisions of the Constitution that mention "the people," the term unambiguously refers to all members of the political community, not an unspecified subset. As we said in *United States v. Verdugo-Urquidez* (1990):

> " '[T]he people' seems to have been a term of art employed in select parts of the Constitution.... [Its uses] sugges[t] that 'the people' protected by the Fourth Amendment, and by the First and Second Amendments, and to whom rights and powers are reserved in the Ninth and Tenth Amendments, refers to a class of persons who are part of a national community or who have otherwise developed sufficient connection with this country to be considered part of that community."

This contrasts markedly with the phrase "the militia" in the prefatory clause. As we will describe below, the "militia" in colonial America consisted of a subset of "the people"—those who were male, able bodied, and within a certain age range. Reading the Second Amendment as protecting only the right to "keep and bear Arms" in an organized militia therefore fits poorly with the operative clause's description of the holder of that right as "the people."

We start therefore with a strong presumption that the Second Amendment right is exercised individually and belongs to all Americans.

b. "Keep and bear Arms." We move now from the holder of the right—"the people"—to the substance of the right: "to keep and bear Arms."

Before addressing the verbs "keep" and "bear," we interpret their object: "Arms." The 18th-century meaning is no different from the meaning today. The 1773 edition of Samuel Johnson's dictionary defined "arms" as "weapons of offence, or armour of defence." Timothy Cunningham's important 1771 legal dictionary defined "arms" as "any thing that a man wears for his defence, or takes into his hands, or useth in wrath to cast at or strike another."

Some have made the argument, bordering on the frivolous, that only those arms in existence in the 18th century are protected by the Second Amendment. We do not interpret constitutional rights that way.

The term was applied, then as now, to weapons that were not specifically designed for military use and were not employed in a military capacity. For instance, Cunningham's legal dictionary gave as an example of usage: "Servants and labourers shall use bows and arrows on Sundays, &c. and not bear other arms." Although one founding-era thesaurus limited "arms" (as opposed to "weapons") to "instruments of offence generally made use of in war," even that source stated that all firearms constituted "arms."

Some have made the argument, bordering on the frivolous, that only those arms in existence in the 18th century are protected by the Second Amendment. We do not interpret constitutional rights that way. Just as the First Amendment protects modern forms of communications and the Fourth Amendment applies to modern forms of search, the Second Amendment extends, prima facie, to all instruments that constitute bearable arms, even those that were not in existence at the time of the founding.

We turn to the phrases "keep arms" and "bear arms." Johnson defined "keep" as, most relevantly, "[t]o retain; not to lose," and "[t]o have in custody." Webster defined it as "[t]o hold; to retain in one's power or possession." No party has apprised us of an idiomatic meaning of "keep Arms." Thus, the most natural reading of "keep Arms" in the Second Amendment is to "have weapons."

The phrase "keep arms" was not prevalent in the written documents of the founding period that we have found, but there are a few examples, all of which favor viewing the right to "keep Arms" as an individual right unconnected with militia service. William Blackstone, for example, wrote that Catholics convicted of not attending service in the Church of England suffered certain penalties, one of which was that they were not permitted to "keep arms in their houses." Petitioners point to militia laws of the founding period that required militia members to "keep" arms in connection with militia service, and they conclude from this that the phrase "keep Arms" has a militia-related connotation. This is rather like saying that, since there are many statutes that authorize aggrieved employees to "file complaints" with federal agencies, the phrase "file complaints" has an employment-related connotation. "Keep arms" was simply a common way of referring to possessing arms, for militiamen and everyone else.

At the time of the founding, as now, to "bear" meant to "carry." When used with "arms," however, the term has a meaning that refers to carrying for a particular purpose—confrontation. In *Muscarello v. United States* (1998), in the course of analyzing the meaning of "carries a firearm" in a federal criminal statute, Justice Ginsburg wrote that "[s]urely a most familiar meaning is, as the Constitution's Second Amendment...indicate[s]: 'wear, bear, or carry...upon the person or in the clothing or in a pocket, for the purpose...of being armed and ready for offensive or defensive action in a case of conflict with another person.' " We think that Justice Ginsburg accurately captured the natural meaning of "bear arms." Although the phrase implies that the carrying of the weapon is for the purpose of "offensive or defensive action," it in no way connotes participation in a structured military organization.

From our review of founding-era sources, we conclude that this natural meaning was also the meaning that "bear arms" had in the 18th century. In numerous instances, "bear arms" was unambiguously used to refer to the carrying of weapons outside of an organized militia. The most prominent examples are those most relevant to the Second Amendment: Nine state constitutional provisions written in the 18th century or the first two decades of the 19th, which enshrined a right of citizens to "bear arms in defense of themselves and the state" or "bear arms in defense of himself and the state." It is clear from those formulations that "bear arms" did not refer only to carrying a weapon in an organized military unit.

Nine state constitutional provisions written in the 18th century or the first two decades of the 19th, which enshrined a right of citizens to "bear arms in defense of themselves and the state" or "bear arms in defense of himself and the state."

Justice James Wilson interpreted the Pennsylvania Constitution's arms-bearing right, for example, as a recognition of the natural right of defense "of one's person or house"—what he called the law of "self preservation." That was also the interpretation of those state constitutional provisions adopted by pre-Civil War state courts. These provisions demonstrate—again, in the most analogous linguistic context—that "bear arms" was not limited to the carrying of arms in a militia.

The phrase "bear Arms" also had at the time of the founding an idiomatic meaning that was significantly different from its natural meaning: "to serve as a soldier, do military service, fight" or "to wage war." But it unequivocally bore that idiomatic meaning only when followed by the preposition "against," which was in turn followed by the target of the hostilities. Every example given by petitioners' amici for the idiomatic meaning of "bear arms" from the founding period either includes the preposition "against" or is not clearly idiomatic. Without the preposition, "bear arms" normally meant (as it continues to mean today) what Justice Gingsburg's opinion in *Muscarello* said.

In any event, the meaning of "bear arms" that petitioners and Justice Stevens propose is not even the (sometimes) idiomatic meaning. Rather, they manufacture a hybrid definition, whereby "bear arms" connotes the actual carrying of arms (and therefore is not really an idiom) but only in the service of an organized militia. No dictionary has ever adopted that definition, and we have been apprised of no source that indicates that it carried that meaning at the time of the founding. But it is easy to see why petitioners and the dissent are driven to the hybrid definition. Giving "bear Arms" its idiomatic meaning would cause the protected right to consist of the right to be a soldier or to wage war—an absurdity that no commentator has ever endorsed. Worse still, the phrase "keep and bear Arms" would be incoherent. The word "Arms" would have two different meanings at once: "weapons" (as the object of "keep") and (as the object of "bear") one-half of an idiom. It would be rather like saying "He

> *It would be rather like saying "He filled and kicked the bucket" to mean "He filled the bucket and died." Grotesque.*

filled and kicked the bucket" to mean "He filled the bucket and died." Grotesque.

Petitioners justify their limitation of "bear arms" to the military context by pointing out the unremarkable fact that it was often used in that context—the same mistake they made with respect to "keep arms." It is especially unremarkable that the phrase was often used in a military context in the federal legal sources (such as records of congressional debate) that have been the focus of petitioners' inquiry. Those sources would have had little occasion to use it except in discussions about the standing army and the militia. And the phrases used primarily in those military discussions include not only "bear arms" but also "carry arms," "possess arms," and "have arms"—though no one thinks that those other phrases also had special military meanings. The common references to those "fit to bear arms" in congressional discussions about the militia are matched by use of the same phrase in the few nonmilitary federal contexts where the concept would be relevant. Other legal sources frequently used "bear arms" in nonmilitary contexts. Cunningham's legal dictionary, cited above, gave as an example of its usage a sentence unrelated to military affairs ("Servants and labourers shall use bows and arrows on Sundays, &c. and not bear other arms"). And if one looks beyond legal sources, "bear arms" was frequently used in nonmilitary contexts.

Justice Stevens points to a study by amici supposedly showing that the phrase "bear arms" was most frequently used in the military context. Of course, as we have said, the fact that the phrase was commonly used in a particular context does not show that it is limited to that context, and, in any event, we have given many sources where the phrase was used in nonmilitary contexts. Moreover, the study's collection appears to include (who knows how many times) the idiomatic phrase "bear arms against," which is irrelevant. The amici also dismiss examples such as " 'bear arms... for the purpose of killing game' " because those uses are "expressly qualified." Justice Stevens uses the same excuse for dismissing the state constitutional provisions analogous to the Second Amendment that identify private-use purposes for which the individual right can be asserted. That analysis is faulty. A purposive qualifying phrase that contradicts the word or phrase it modifies is unknown this side of the looking glass (except, apparently, in some courses on Linguistics). If "bear arms" means, as we think, simply the carrying of arms, a modifier can limit the purpose of the carriage ("for the purpose of self-defense" or "to make war against the King"). But if "bear arms" means, as the petitioners and the dissent think, the carrying of arms only for military purposes, one simply cannot add "for the purpose of killing game." The right "to carry arms in the militia for the purpose of killing game" is worthy of the mad hatter. Thus, these purposive qualifying phrases positively establish that "to bear arms" is not limited to military use.

Justice Stevens places great weight on James Madison's inclusion of a conscientious-objector clause in his original draft of the Second Amendment: "but no person religiously scrupulous of bearing arms, shall be compelled to render military service in person." He argues that this clause establishes that the drafters of the Second Amendment intended "bear Arms" to refer only to military service. It is always perilous to derive the meaning of an adopted provision from another provision deleted in the drafting process. In any case, what Justice Stevens would conclude from the deleted provision does not follow. It was not meant to exempt from military service those who objected to going to war but had no scruples about personal gunfights. Quakers opposed the use of arms not just for militia service, but for any violent purpose whatsoever—so much so that Quaker frontiersmen were forbidden to use arms to defend their families, even though "[i]n such circumstances the temptation to seize a hunting rifle or knife in self-defense...must sometimes have been almost overwhelming." P. Brock, Pacifism in the United States (1968). The Pennsylvania Militia Act of 1757 exempted from service those "scrupling the use of arms"—a phrase that no one contends had an idiomatic meaning. Thus, the most natural interpretation of Madison's deleted text is that those opposed to carrying weapons for potential violent confrontation would not be "compelled to render military service," in which such carrying would be required.

Finally, Justice Stevens suggests that "keep and bear Arms" was some sort of term of art, presumably akin to "hue and cry" or "cease and desist." (This suggestion usefully evades the problem that there is no evidence whatsoever to support a military reading of "keep arms.") Justice Stevens believes that the unitary meaning of "keep and bear Arms" is established by the Second Amendment's calling it a "right" (singular) rather than "rights" (plural). There is nothing to this. State constitutions of the founding period routinely grouped multiple (related) guarantees under a singular "right," and the First Amendment protects the "right [singular] of the people peaceably to assemble, and to petition the Government for a redress of grievances." And even if "keep and bear Arms" were a unitary phrase, we find no evidence that it bore a military meaning. Although the phrase was not at all common (which would be unusual for a term of art), we have found instances of its use with a clearly nonmilitary connotation. In a 1780 debate in the House of Lords, for example, Lord Richmond described an order to disarm private citizens (not militia members) as "a violation of the constitutional right of

Protestant subjects to keep and bear arms for their own defense."
In response, another member of Parliament referred to "the right
of bearing arms for personal defence," making
clear that no special military meaning for "keep
and bear arms" was intended in the discussion.

> *The very text of the Second Amendment implicitly recognizes the pre-existence of the right and declares only that it "shall not be infringed."*

c. Meaning of the Operative Clause.
Putting all of these textual elements together,
we find that they guarantee the individual right
to possess and carry weapons in case of confrontation. This meaning is strongly confirmed
by the historical background of the Second
Amendment. We look to this because it has
always been widely understood that the Second Amendment, like the
First and Fourth Amendments, codified a pre-existing right. The very
text of the Second Amendment implicitly recognizes the pre-existence
of the right and declares only that it "shall not be infringed." As we
said in *United States v. Cruikshank* (1876), "[t]his is not a right granted
by the Constitution. Neither is it in any manner dependent upon that
instrument for its existence. The Second amendment declares that it
shall not be infringed...."

Between the Restoration and the Glorious Revolution, the Stuart Kings Charles II and James II succeeded in using select militias
loyal to them to suppress political dissidents, in part by disarming
their opponents. Under the auspices of the 1671 Game Act, for
example, the Catholic James II had ordered general disarmaments of
regions home to his Protestant enemies. These experiences caused
Englishmen to be extremely wary of concentrated military forces
run by the state and to be jealous of their arms. They accordingly
obtained an assurance from William and Mary, in the Declaration

of Right (which was codified as the English Bill of Rights), that Protestants would never be disarmed: "That the subjects which are Protestants may have arms for their defense suitable to their condi-

tions and as allowed by law." This right has long been understood to be the predecessor to our Second Amendment. It was clearly an individual right, having nothing whatever to do with service in a militia. To be sure, it was an individual right not available to the whole population, given that it was restricted to Prot- estants, and like all written English rights it was held only against the Crown, not Parliament. But it was secured to them as individuals, according to "libertarian political principles," not as members of a fighting force.

By the time of the founding, the right to have arms had become fundamental for English subjects.

By the time of the founding, the right to have arms had become fundamental for English subjects. Blackstone, whose works, we have said, "constituted the preeminent authority on English law for the founding generation," cited the arms provision of the Bill of Rights as one of the fundamental rights of Englishmen. His description of it cannot possibly be thought to tie it to militia or military service. It was, he said, "the natural right of resistance and self-preservation," and "the right of having and using arms for self-preservation and defence." Other contemporary authorities concurred. Thus, the right secured in 1689 as a result of the Stuarts' abuses was by the time of the founding understood to be an individual right protecting against both public and private violence.

And, of course, what the Stuarts had tried to do to their political enemies, George III had tried to do to the colonists. In the tumul- tuous decades of the 1760's and 1770's, the Crown began to disarm the inhabitants of the most rebellious areas. That provoked polemical reactions by Americans invoking their rights as Englishmen to keep arms. A New York article of April 1769 said that "[i]t is a natural right which the people have reserved to themselves, confirmed by the Bill of Rights, to keep arms for their own defence." They understood the right to enable individuals to defend themselves. As the most important early American edition of Blackstone's Commentaries (by the law professor and former Antifederalist St. George Tucker) made clear in the notes to the description of the arms right, Americans understood the "right of self-preservation" as permitting a citizen to "repe[l] force by force" when "the intervention of society in his behalf, may be too late to prevent an injury."

There seems to us no doubt, on the basis of both text and history, that the Second Amendment conferred an individual right to keep and bear arms. Of course the right was not unlimited, just as the First Amendment's right of free speech was not. Thus, we do not read the Second Amendment to protect the right of citizens to carry arms for any sort of confrontation, just as we do not read the First Amendment to protect the right of citizens to speak for any purpose. Before turning to limitations upon the individual right, however, we must determine whether the prefatory clause of the Second Amendment comports with our interpretation of the operative clause.

2. Prefatory Clause.

The prefatory clause reads: "A well regulated Militia, being necessary to the security of a free State...."

a. "Well-Regulated Militia." In *United States v. Miller* (1939), we explained that "the Militia comprised all males physically capable of acting in concert for the common defense." That definition comports with founding-era sources. See, e.g., Webster ("The militia of a country are the able bodied men organized into companies, regiments and brigades... and required by law to attend military exercises on certain days only, but at other times left to pursue their usual occupations"); The Federalist No. 46 ("near half a million of citizens with arms in their hands"); Letter to Destutt de Tracy (Jan. 26, 1811), in *The Portable Thomas Jefferson* ("[T]he militia of the State, that is to say, of every man in it able to bear arms").

Petitioners take a seemingly narrower view of the militia, stating that "[m]ilitias are the state- and congressionally-regulated military forces described in the Militia Clauses." Although we agree with petitioners' interpretive assumption that "militia" means the same thing in Article I and the Second Amendment, we believe that petitioners identify the wrong thing, namely, the organized militia. Unlike armies and navies, which Congress is given the power to create, the militia is assumed by Article I already to be in existence. Congress is given the power to "provide for calling forth the militia," and the power not to create, but to "organiz[e]" it—and not to organize "a" militia, which is what one would expect if the militia were to be a federal creation, but to organize "the" militia, connoting a body already in existence. This is fully consistent with the ordinary definition of the militia as all able-bodied men. From that pool, Congress has plenary power to organize the units that will make up an effective fighting force. That is what Congress did in the first militia Act, which specified that "each and every free able-bodied white male citizen of the respective states, resident therein, who is or shall be of the age of eighteen years, and under the age of forty-five years (except as is herein after excepted) shall severally and respectively be enrolled in the militia." To be sure, Congress need not conscript every able-bodied man into the militia, because nothing in Article I suggests that in exercising its power to organize, discipline, and arm the militia, Congress must focus upon the entire body. Although the militia consists of all able-bodied men, the federally organized militia may consist of a subset of them.

Finally, the adjective "well-regulated" implies nothing more than the imposition of proper discipline and training.

b. "Security of a Free State." The phrase "security of a free state" meant "security of a free polity," not security of each of the several States as the dissent argued. Joseph Story wrote in his treatise on the Constitution that "the word 'state' is used in various senses [and in] its most enlarged sense, it means the people composing a particular nation or community." It is true that the term "State" elsewhere in the Constitution refers to individual States, but the phrase "security of a free state" and close variations seem to have been terms of art in 18th-century political discourse, meaning a " 'free country' " or free polity. Moreover, the other instances of "state" in the Constitution are typically accompanied by modifiers making clear that the reference is to the several States—"each state," "several states," "any state," "that state," "particular states," "one state," "no state." And the presence of the term "foreign state" in Article I and Article III shows that the word "state" did not have a single meaning in the Constitution.

There are many reasons why the militia was thought to be "necessary to the security of a free state." First, of course, it is useful in repelling invasions and suppressing insurrections. Second, it renders large standing armies unnecessary—an argument that Alexander Hamilton made in favor of federal control over the militia. Third, when the able-bodied men of a nation are trained in arms and organized, they are better able to resist tyranny.

3. Relationship between Prefatory Clause and Operative Clause

We reach the question, then: Does the preface fit with an operative clause that creates an individual right to keep and bear arms? It fits perfectly, once one knows the history that the founding generation knew and that we have described above. That history showed that the way tyrants had eliminated a militia consisting of all the able-bodied men was not by banning the militia but simply by taking away the people's arms, enabling a select militia or standing army to suppress political opponents. This is what had occurred in England that prompted codification of the right to have arms in the English Bill of Rights.

The debate with respect to the right to keep and bear arms, as with other guarantees in the Bill of Rights, was not over whether it was desirable (all agreed that it was) but over whether it needed to be codified in the Constitution. During the 1788 ratification debates, the fear that the federal government would disarm the people in order to impose rule through a standing army or select militia was pervasive in Antifederalist rhetoric. John Smilie, for example, worried not only that Congress's "command of the militia" could be used to create a "select militia," or to have "no militia at all," but also, as a separate concern, that "[w]hen a select militia is formed; the people in general may be disarmed." Federalists responded that because Congress was given no power to abridge the ancient right of individuals to keep and bear arms, such a force

> *The debate with respect to the right to keep and bear arms, as with other guarantees in the Bill of Rights, was not over whether it was desirable (all agreed that it was) but over whether it needed to be codified in the Constitution.*

could never oppress the people. It was understood across the political spectrum that the right helped to secure the ideal of a citizen militia, which might be necessary to oppose an oppressive military force if the constitutional order broke down.

It is therefore entirely sensible that the Second Amendment's prefatory clause announces the purpose for which the right was codified: to prevent elimination of the militia. The prefatory clause does not suggest that preserving the militia was the only reason Americans valued the ancient right; most undoubtedly thought it even more important for self-defense and hunting. But the threat that the new Federal Government would destroy the citizens' militia by taking away their arms was the reason that right—unlike some other English rights—was codified in a written Constitution. . . .

Besides ignoring the historical reality that the Second Amendment was not intended to lay down a "novel principl[e]" but rather codified a right "inherited from our English ancestors," *Robertson v. Baldwin* (1897), petitioners' interpretation does not even achieve the narrower purpose that prompted codification of the right. If, as they believe, the Second Amendment right is no more than the right to keep and use weapons as a member of an organized militia. . .—if, that is, the organized militia is the sole institutional beneficiary of the Second Amendment's guarantee—it does not assure the existence of a "citizens' militia" as a safeguard against tyranny. For Congress retains plenary authority to organize the militia, which must include the authority to say who will belong to the organized force. That is why the first Militia Act's requirement that only whites enroll caused States to amend their militia laws to exclude free blacks. Thus, if petitioners are correct, the Second Amendment protects citizens' right to use a gun in an organization from which Congress has plenary authority to exclude them. It guarantees a select militia of the sort the Stuart kings found useful, but not the people's militia that was the concern of the founding generation.

B

Our interpretation is confirmed by analogous arms-bearing rights in state constitutions that preceded and immediately followed adoption of the Second Amendment. Four States adopted analogues to the Federal Second Amendment in the period between independence and the ratification of the Bill of Rights. Two of them—Pennsylvania and Vermont—clearly adopted individual rights unconnected to militia service. Pennsylvania's Declaration of Rights of 1776 said: "That the people have a right to bear arms for the defence of themselves, and the state...." In 1777, Vermont adopted the identical provision, except for inconsequential differences in punctuation and capitalization.

North Carolina also codified a right to bear arms in 1776: "That the people have a right to bear arms, for the defence of thè State...." This could plausibly be read to support only a right to bear arms in a militia—but that is a peculiar way to make the point in a constitution that elsewhere repeatedly mentions the militia explicitly. Many colonial statutes required individual arms-bearing for public-safety reasons—such as the 1770 Georgia law that "for the security and defence of this province from internal dangers and insurrections" required those men who qualified for militia duty individually "to carry fire arms" "to places of public worship." That broad public-safety understanding was the connotation given to the North Carolina right by that State's Supreme Court in 1843.

The 1780 Massachusetts Constitution presented another variation on the theme: "The people have a right to keep and to bear arms for the common defence...." Once again, if one gives narrow meaning to the phrase "common defence" this can be thought to limit the right to the bearing of arms in a state-organized military force. But once again the State's highest court thought otherwise. Writing for the court in an 1825 libel case, Chief Justice Parker wrote: "The liberty of the press was to be unrestrained, but he who used it was to be responsible in cases of its abuse; like the right to keep fire arms, which does not protect him who uses them for annoyance or destruction." *Commonwealth v. Blanding.* The analogy makes no sense if firearms could not be used for any individual purpose at all.

We therefore believe that the most likely reading of all four of these pre-Second Amendment state constitutional provisions is that they secured an individual right to bear arms for defensive purposes. Other States did not include rights to bear arms in their pre-1789 constitutions—although in Virginia a Second Amendment analogue was proposed (unsuccessfully) by Thomas Jefferson. (It read: "No freeman shall ever be debarred the use of arms [within his own lands or tenements].")

Between 1789 and 1820, nine States adopted Second Amendment analogues. Four of them—Kentucky, Ohio, Indiana, and Missouri—referred to the right of the people to "bear arms in defence of themselves and the State." Another three States—Mississippi, Connecticut, and Alabama—used the even more individualistic phrasing that each citizen has the "right to bear arms in defence of himself and the State." Finally, two States—Tennessee and Maine—used the "common defence" language of Massachusetts. That of the nine state constitutional protections for the right to bear arms enacted immediately after

1789 at least seven unequivocally protected an individual citizen's right to self-defense is strong evidence that that is how the founding generation conceived of the right. And with one possible exception that we discuss in Part II-D-2, 19th-century courts and commentators interpreted these state constitutional provisions to protect an individual right to use arms for self-defense.

The historical narrative that petitioners must endorse would thus treat the Federal Second Amendment as an odd outlier, protecting a right unknown in state constitutions or at English common law, based on little more than an overreading of the prefatory clause.

. . .

D

We now address how the Second Amendment was interpreted from immediately after its ratification through the end of the 19th century. Before proceeding, however, we take issue with Justice Stevens' equating of these sources with postenactment legislative history, a comparison that betrays a fundamental misunderstanding of a court's interpretive task. "Legislative history," of course, refers to the pre-enactment statements of those who drafted or voted for a law; it is considered persuasive by some, not because they reflect the general understanding of the disputed terms, but because the legislators who heard or read those statements presumably voted with that understanding. "Postenactment legislative history," a deprecatory contradiction in terms, refers to statements of those who drafted or voted for the law that are made after its enactment and hence could

As we will show, virtually all interpreters of the Second Amendment in the century after its enactment interpreted the amendment as we do.

have had no effect on the congressional vote. It most certainly does not refer to the examination of a variety of legal and other sources to determine the public understanding of a legal text in the period after its enactment or ratification. That sort of inquiry is a critical tool of constitutional interpretation. As we will show, virtually all interpreters of the Second Amendment in the century after its enactment interpreted the amendment as we do.

1. Post-ratification Commentary

Three important founding-era legal scholars interpreted the Second Amendment in published writings. All three understood it to protect an individual right unconnected with militia service.

St. George Tucker's version of Blackstone's Commentaries, as we explained above, conceived of the Blackstonian arms right as necessary for self-defense. He equated that right, absent the religious and class-based restrictions, with the Second Amendment. In Note D, entitled, "View of the Constitution of the United States," Tucker elaborated on the Second Amendment: "This may be considered as the true palladium of liberty.... The right to self-defence is the first law of nature: in most governments it has been the study of rulers to confine the right within the narrowest limits possible. Wherever standing armies are kept up, and the right of the people to keep and bear arms is, under any colour or pretext whatsoever, prohibited, liberty, if not already annihilated, is on the brink of destruction." He believed that the English game laws had abridged the right by prohibiting "keeping a gun or other engine for the destruction of game." He later grouped the right with some of the individual rights included in the First Amendment and said that if "a law be passed by congress, prohibiting" any of those rights, it would "be the province of the judiciary to pronounce whether any such act were constitutional, or not; and if not, to acquit the accused..." It is unlikely that Tucker was referring to a person's being "accused" of violating a law making it a crime to bear arms in a state militia.

In 1825, William Rawle, a prominent lawyer who had been a member of the Pennsylvania Assembly that ratified the Bill of Rights, published an influential treatise, which analyzed the Second Amendment as follows:

> "The first [principle] is a declaration that a well regulated militia is necessary to the security of a free state; a proposition from which few will dissent....
>
> "The corollary, from the first position is, that the right of the people to keep and bear arms shall not be infringed.
>
> "The prohibition is general. No clause in the constitution could by any rule of construction be conceived to give to congress a power to disarm the people. Such a flagitious attempt could only be made under some general pretence by a state legislature. But if in any blind pursuit of inordinate power, either should attempt it, this amendment may be appealed to as a restraint on both."

Like Tucker, Rawle regarded the English game laws as violating the right codified in the Second Amendment. Rawle clearly differentiated between the people's right to bear arms and their service in a militia: "In a people permitted and accustomed to bear arms, we have the rudiments of a militia, which properly consists of armed citizens, divided into military bands, and instructed at least in part, in the use of arms for the purposes of war." Rawle further said that the Second Amendment right ought not "be abused to the disturbance of the public peace," such as by assembling with other armed individuals "for an unlawful purpose"—statements that make no sense if the right does not extend to any individual purpose.

Joseph Story published his famous Commentaries on the Constitution of the United States in 1833. Justice Stevens suggests that "[t]here is not so much as a whisper" in Story's explanation of the Second Amendment that favors the individual-rights view. That is wrong. Story explained that the English Bill of Rights had also included a "right to bear arms," a right that, as we have discussed, had nothing to do with militia service. He then equated the English right with the Second Amendment:

> "§ 1891. A similar provision [to the Second Amendment] in favour of protestants (for to them it is confined) is to be found in the bill of rights of 1688, it being declared, 'that the subjects, which are protestants, may have arms for their defence suitable to their condition, and as allowed by law.' But under various pretences the effect of this provision has been greatly narrowed; and it is at present in England more nominal than real, as a defensive privilege."

This comparison to the Declaration of Right would not make sense if the Second Amendment right was the right to use a gun in a militia, which was plainly not what the English right protected. As the Tennessee Supreme Court recognized 38 years after Story wrote his Commentaries, "[t]he passage from Story, shows clearly that this right was intended. . . and was guaranteed to, and to be exercised and enjoyed by the citizen as such, and not by him as a soldier, or in defense solely of his political rights." *Andrews v. State* (1871). Story's Commentaries also cite as support Tucker and Rawle, both of whom clearly viewed the right as unconnected to militia service. In addition, in a shorter 1840 work Story wrote: "One of the ordinary modes, by which tyrants accomplish their purposes without resistance, is, by disarming the people, and making it an offence to keep arms, and by substituting a regular army in the stead of a resort to the militia."

Antislavery advocates routinely invoked the right to bear arms for self-defense.

Antislavery advocates routinely invoked the right to bear arms for self-defense. Joel Tiffany, for example, citing Blackstone's description of the right, wrote that "the right to keep and bear arms, also implies the right to use them if necessary in self defence; without this right to use the guaranty would have hardly been worth the paper it consumed." A Treatise on the Unconstitutionality of American Slavery (1849). In his famous Senate speech about the 1856 "Bleeding Kansas" conflict, Charles Sumner proclaimed:

"The rifle has ever been the companion of the pioneer and, under God, his tutelary protector against the red man and the beast of the forest. Never was this efficient weapon more needed in just self-defence, than now in Kansas, and at least one article in our National Constitution must be blotted out, before the complete right to it can in any way be impeached. And yet such is the madness of the hour, that, in defiance of the solemn guarantee, embodied in the Amendments to the Constitution, that 'the right of the people to keep and bear arms shall not be infringed,' the people of Kansas have been arraigned for keeping and bearing them, and the Senator from South Carolina has had the face to say openly, on this floor, that they should be disarmed—of course, that the fanatics of Slavery, his allies and constituents, may meet no impediment." ...

2. Pre-Civil War Case Law

The 19th-century cases that interpreted the Second Amendment universally support an individual right unconnected to militia service. In *Houston v. Moore* (1820), this Court held that States have concurrent power over the militia, at least where not pre-empted by Congress. Agreeing in dissent that States could "organize, discipline, and arm" the militia in the absence of conflicting federal regulation, Justice Story said that the Second Amendment "may not, perhaps, be thought to have any important bearing on this point. If it have, it confirms and illustrates, rather than impugns the reasoning already suggested." Of course, if the Amendment simply "protect[ed] the right of the people of each of the several States to maintain a well-regulated militia," it would have enormous and obvious bearing on the point. But the Court and Story derived the States' power over the militia from the nonexclusive nature of federal power, not from the Second Amendment, whose preamble merely "confirms and illustrates" the importance of the militia. Even clearer was Justice Baldwin. In the famous fugitive-slave case of *Johnson v. Tompkins* (CC Pa. 1833), Baldwin, sitting as a circuit judge, cited both the Second Amendment and the Pennsylvania analogue for his conclusion that a citizen has "a right to carry arms in defence of his property or person, and to use them, if either were assailed with such force, numbers or violence as made it necessary for the protection or safety of either."

Many early 19th-century state cases indicated that the Second Amendment right to bear arms was an individual right unconnected to militia service, though subject to certain restrictions.

Many early 19th-century state cases indicated that the Second Amendment right to bear arms was an individual right unconnected to militia service, though subject to certain restrictions. A Virginia case in 1824 holding that the Constitution did not extend to free blacks explained that "numerous restrictions imposed on [blacks] in our Statute Book, many of which are inconsistent with the letter and spirit of the Constitution, both of this State and of the United States as respects the free whites, demonstrate, that, here, those instruments have not been considered to extend equally to both classes of our population. We will only instance the restriction upon the migration of free blacks into this State, and upon their right to bear arms." *Aldridge v. Commonwealth*. The claim was obviously not that blacks were prevented from carrying guns in the militia. An 1829 decision by the Supreme Court of Michigan said: "The constitution of the United States also grants to the citizen the right to keep and bear arms. But the grant of this privilege cannot be construed into the right in him who keeps a gun to destroy his neighbor. No rights are intended to be granted by the constitution for an unlawful or unjustifiable purpose." *United States v. Sheldon*. It is not possible to read this as discussing anything other than an individual right unconnected to militia service. If it did have to do with militia service, the limitation upon it would not be any "unlawful or unjustifiable purpose," but any nonmilitary purpose whatsoever.

In *Nunn v. State*, 1 Ga. 243, 251 (1846), the Georgia Supreme Court construed the Second Amendment as protecting the "natural right of self-defence" and therefore struck down a ban on carrying pistols openly. Its opinion perfectly captured the way in which the operative clause of the Second Amendment furthers the purpose announced in the prefatory clause, in continuity with the English right:

> "The right of the whole people, old and young, men, women and boys, and not militia only, to keep and bear arms of every description, and not such merely as are used by the militia, shall not be infringed, curtailed, or broken in upon, in the smallest degree; and all this for the important end to be attained: the rearing up and qualifying a well-regulated militia, so vitally necessary to the security of a free State. Our opinion is, that any law, State or Federal, is repugnant to the Constitution, and void, which contravenes this right, originally belonging to our forefathers, trampled under foot by Charles I. and his two wicked sons and successors, re-established by the revolution of 1688, conveyed to this land of liberty by the colonists, and finally incorporated conspicuously in our own Magna Charta!"

Likewise, in *State v. Chandler*, 5 La. Ann. 489, 490 (1850), the Louisiana Supreme Court held that citizens had a right to carry arms openly: "This is the right guaranteed by the Constitution of the United States, and which is calculated to incite men to a manly and noble defence of themselves, if necessary, and of their country, without any tendency to secret advantages and unmanly assassinations."

Those who believe that the Second Amendment preserves only a militia-centered right place great reliance on the Tennessee Supreme Court's 1840 decision in *Aymette v. State*. The case does not stand for that broad proposition; in fact, the case does not mention the word "militia" at all, except in its quoting of the Second Amendment. *Aymette* held that the state constitutional guarantee of the right to "bear" arms did not prohibit the banning of concealed weapons. The opinion first recognized that both the state right and the federal right were descendents of the 1689 English right, but (erroneously, and contrary to virtually all other authorities) read that right to refer only to "protect[ion of] the public liberty" and "keep[ing] in awe those in power." The court then adopted a sort of middle position, whereby citizens were permitted to carry arms openly, unconnected with any service in a formal militia, but were given the right to use them only for the military purpose of banding together to oppose tyranny. This odd reading of the right is, to be sure, not the one we adopt—but it is not petitioners' reading either. More importantly, seven years earlier the Tennessee Supreme Court had treated the state constitutional provision as conferring a right "of all the free citizens of the State to keep and bear arms for their defence," *Simpson*; and 21 years later the court held that the "keep" portion of the state constitutional right included the right to personal self-defense: "[T]he right to keep arms involves, necessarily, the right to use such arms for all the ordinary purposes, and in all the ordinary modes usual in the country, and to which arms are adapted, limited by the duties of a good citizen in times of peace." *Andrews*.

3. Post–Civil War Legislation.

In the aftermath of the Civil War, there was an outpouring of discussion of the Second Amendment in Congress and in public discourse, as people debated whether and how to secure constitutional rights for newly free slaves. Since those discussions took place 75 years after the ratification of the Second Amendment, they do not provide as much insight into its original meaning as earlier sources. Yet those born and educated in the early 19th century faced a widespread effort to limit arms ownership by a large number of citizens;

Blacks were routinely disarmed by Southern States after the Civil War. Those who opposed these injustices frequently stated that they infringed blacks' constitutional right to keep and bear arms.

their understanding of the origins and continuing significance of the Amendment is instructive.

Blacks were routinely disarmed by Southern States after the Civil War. Those who opposed these injustices frequently stated that they infringed blacks' constitutional right to keep and bear arms. Needless to say, the claim was not that blacks were being prohibited from carrying arms in an organized state militia. A Report of the Commission of the Freedmen's Bureau in 1866 stated plainly: "[T]he civil law [of Kentucky] prohibits the colored man from bearing arms.... Their arms are taken from them by the civil authorities.... Thus, the right of the people to keep and bear arms as provided in the Constitution is infringed." A joint congressional Report decried:

"in some parts of [South Carolina], armed parties are, without proper authority, engaged in seizing all fire-arms found in the hands of the freemen. Such conduct is in clear and direct violation of their personal rights as guaranteed by the Constitution of the United States, which declares that 'the right of the people to keep and bear arms shall not be infringed.' The freedmen of South Carolina have shown by their peaceful and orderly conduct that they can safely be trusted with fire-arms, and they need them to kill game for subsistence, and to protect their crops from destruction by birds and animals."

JOINT COMM. ON RECONSTRUCTION,

H. R. REP. NO. 30, 39TH CONG., 1ST SESS. (1866)

The view expressed in these statements was widely reported and was apparently widely held. For example, an editorial in The Loyal Georgian (Augusta) on February 3, 1866, assured blacks that "[a]ll men, without distinction of color, have the right to keep and bear arms to defend their homes, families or themselves."

Congress enacted the Freedmen's Bureau Act on July 16, 1866. Section 14 stated:

> "[T]he right... to have full and equal benefit of all laws and proceedings concerning personal liberty, personal security, and the acquisition, enjoyment, and disposition of estate, real and personal, including the constitutional right to bear arms, shall be secured to and enjoyed by all the citizens... without respect to race or color, or previous condition of slavery...."

The understanding that the Second Amendment gave freed blacks the right to keep and bear arms was reflected in congressional discussion of the bill, with even an opponent of it saying that the founding generation "were for every man bearing his arms about him and keeping them in his house, his castle, for his own defense." Cong. Globe, 39th Cong., 1st Sess.(1866) (Sen. Davis).

Similar discussion attended the passage of the Civil Rights Act of 1871 and the Fourteenth Amendment. For example, Representative Butler said of the Act: "Section eight is intended to enforce the well-known constitutional provision guaranteeing the right of the citizen to 'keep and bear arms,' and provides that whoever shall take away, by force or violence, or by threats and intimidation, the arms and weapons which any person may have for his defense, shall be deemed guilty of larceny of the same." With respect to the proposed Amendment,

It was plainly the understanding in the post-Civil War Congress that the Second Amendment protected an individual right to use arms for self-defense.

Senator Pomeroy described as one of the three "indispensable" "safeguards of liberty...under the Constitution" a man's "right to bear arms for the defense of himself and family and his homestead." Representative Nye thought the Fourteenth Amendment unnecessary because "[a]s citizens of the United States [blacks] have equal right to protection, and to keep and bear arms for self-defense."

It was plainly the understanding in the post-Civil War Congress that the Second Amendment protected an individual right to use arms for self-defense.

4. Post-Civil War Commentators.

Every late-19th-century legal scholar that we have read interpreted the Second Amendment to secure an individual right unconnected with militia service. The most famous was the judge and professor Thomas Cooley, who wrote a massively popular 1868 Treatise on Constitutional Limitations. Concerning the Second Amendment it said:

"Among the other defences to personal liberty should be mentioned the right of the people to keep and bear arms.... The alternative to a standing army is 'a well-regulated militia,' but this cannot exist unless the people are trained to bearing arms. How far it is in the power of the legislature to regulate this right, we shall not undertake to say, as happily there has been very little occasion to discuss that subject by the courts."

That Cooley understood the right not as connected to militia service, but as securing the militia by ensuring a populace familiar with arms, is made even clearer in his 1880 work, *General Principles of Constitutional Law.* The Second Amendment, he said, "was adopted with some modification and enlargement from the English Bill of Rights of 1688, where it stood as a protest against arbitrary action of the overturned dynasty in disarming the people." In a section entitled "The Right in General," he continued:

> "It might be supposed from the phraseology of this provision that the right to keep and bear arms was only guaranteed to the militia; but this would be an interpretation not warranted by the intent. The militia, as has been elsewhere explained, consists of those persons who, under the law, are liable to the performance of military duty, and are officered and enrolled for service when called upon. But the law may make provision for the enrolment of all who are fit to perform military duty, or of a small number only, or it may wholly omit to make any provision at all; and if the right were limited to those enrolled, the purpose of this guaranty might be defeated altogether by the action or neglect to act of the government it was meant to hold in check. The meaning of the provision undoubtedly is, that the people, from whom the militia must be taken, shall have the right to keep and bear arms; and they need no permission or regulation of law for the purpose. But this enables government to have a well-regulated militia; for to bear arms implies something more than the mere keeping; it implies the learning to handle and use them in a way that makes those who keep them ready for their efficient use; in other words, it implies the right to meet for voluntary discipline in arms, observing in doing so the laws of public order."

All other post-Civil War 19th-century sources we have found concurred with Cooley. One example from each decade will convey the general flavor:

"[The purpose of the Second Amendment is] to secure a well-armed militia. . . . But a militia would be useless unless the citizens were enabled to exercise themselves in the use of warlike weapons. To preserve this privilege, and to secure to the people the ability to oppose themselves in military force against the usurpations of government, as well as against enemies from without, that government is forbidden by any law or proceeding to invade or destroy the right to keep and bear arms. . . . The clause is analogous to the one securing the freedom of speech and of the press. Freedom, not license, is secured; the fair use, not the libellous abuse, is protected."

J. POMEROY, *AN INTRODUCTION TO THE CONSTITUTIONAL LAW OF THE*
UNITED STATES (1868)

"As the Constitution of the United States, and the constitutions of several of the states, in terms more or less comprehensive, declare the right of the people to keep and bear arms, it has been a subject of grave discussion, in some of the state courts, whether a statute prohibiting persons, when not on a journey, or as travellers, from wearing or carrying concealed weapons, be constitutional. There has been a great difference of opinion on the question."

J. KENT, *COMMENTARIES ON AMERICAN LAW* (12TH ED. 1873)

"Some general knowledge of firearms is important to the public welfare; because it would be impossible, in case of war, to organize promptly an efficient force of volunteers unless the people had some familiarity with weapons of war. The Constitution secures the right of the people to keep and bear arms. No doubt, a citizen who keeps a gun or pistol under judicious precautions, practices in safe places the use of it, and in due time teaches his sons to do the same, exercises his individual right. No doubt, a person whose residence or duties involve peculiar peril may keep a pistol for prudent self-defence."

B. Abbott, *Judge and Jury: A Popular Explanation of the Leading Topics in the Law of the Land* (1880)

"The right to bear arms has always been the distinctive privilege of freemen. Aside from any necessity of self-protection to the person, it represents among all nations power coupled with the exercise of a certain jurisdiction.... [I]t was not necessary that the right to bear arms should be granted in the Constitution, for it had always existed."

J. Ordronaux, *Constitutional Legislation in the United States* (1891)

. . .

III

Like most rights, the right secured by the Second Amendment is not unlimited. From Blackstone through the 19th-century cases, commentators and courts routinely explained that the right was not a right to keep and carry any weapon whatsoever in any manner whatsoever and for whatever purpose. For example, the majority of the 19th-century courts to consider the question held that prohibitions on carrying concealed weapons were lawful under the Second Amendment or state analogues. Although we do not undertake an exhaustive historical analysis today of the full scope of the Second Amendment, nothing in our opinion should be taken to cast doubt on longstanding prohibitions on the possession of firearms by felons and the mentally ill, or laws forbidding the carrying of firearms in sensitive places such as schools and government buildings, or laws imposing conditions and qualifications on the commercial sale of arms.

We also recognize another important limitation on the right to keep and carry arms. *Miller* said, as we have explained, that the sorts of weapons protected were those "in common use at the time." We think that limitation is fairly supported by the historical tradition of prohibiting the carrying of "dangerous and unusual weapons."

It may be objected that if weapons that are most useful in military service—M-16 rifles and the like—may be banned, then the Second Amendment right is completely detached from the prefatory clause. But as we have said, the conception of the militia at the time of the Second Amendment's ratification was the body of all citizens capable of military service, who would bring the sorts of lawful weapons that they possessed at home to militia duty. It may well be true today that a militia, to be as effective as militias in the 18th century, would require sophisticated arms that are highly unusual in society at large. Indeed, it may be true that no amount of small arms could be useful against modern-day bombers and tanks. But the fact that modern developments have limited the degree of fit between the prefatory clause and the protected right cannot change our interpretation of the right.

IV

We turn finally to the law at issue here. As we have said, the law totally bans handgun possession in the home. It also requires that any lawful firearm in the home be disassembled or bound by a trigger lock at all times, rendering it inoperable.

As the quotations earlier in this opinion demonstrate, the inherent right of self-defense has been central to the Second Amendment right. The handgun ban amounts to a prohibition of an entire class of "arms" that is overwhelmingly chosen by American society for that lawful purpose. The prohibition extends, moreover, to the home, where the need for defense of self, family, and property is most acute. Under any of the standards of scrutiny that we have applied to enumerated constitutional rights, banning from the home "the most preferred firearm in the nation to 'keep' and use for protection of one's home and family" would fail constitutional muster.

Few laws in the history of our Nation have come close to the severe restriction of the District's handgun ban. And some of those few have been struck down. In *Nunn v. State*, the Georgia Supreme Court struck down a prohibition on carrying pistols openly (even though it upheld a prohibition on carrying concealed weapons). In *Andrews v. State*, the Tennessee Supreme Court likewise held that a statute that forbade openly carrying a pistol "publicly or privately, without regard to time or place, or circumstances," violated the state constitutional provision (which the court equated with the Second Amendment). That was so even though the statute did not restrict the carrying of long guns.

It is no answer to say, as petitioners do, that it is permissible to ban the possession of handguns so long as the possession of other firearms (i.e., long guns) is allowed. It is enough to note, as we have observed, that the American people have considered the handgun to be the quintessential self-defense weapon. There are many reasons that a citizen may prefer a handgun for home defense: It is easier to store in

a location that is readily accessible in an emergency; it cannot easily
be redirected or wrestled away by an attacker; it is easier to use for

There are many reasons that a citizen may prefer a handgun for home defense.

those without the upper-body strength to lift
and aim a long gun; it can be pointed at a burglar with one hand while the other hand dials
the police. Whatever the reason, handguns are
the most popular weapon chosen by Americans
for self-defense in the home, and a complete
prohibition of their use is invalid.

We must also address the District's requirement (as applied to
respondent's handgun) that firearms in the home be rendered and
kept inoperable at all times. This makes it impossible for citizens to
use them for the core lawful purpose of self-defense and is hence
unconstitutional. The District argues that we should interpret this
element of the statute to contain an exception for self-defense. But
we think that is precluded by the unequivocal text, and by the
presence of certain other enumerated exceptions: "Except for law
enforcement personnel..., each registrant shall keep any firearm in
his possession unloaded and disassembled or bound by a trigger lock
or similar device unless such firearm is kept at his place of business, or
while being used for lawful recreational purposes within the District
of Columbia." The nonexistence of a self-defense exception is also
suggested by the D. C. Court of Appeals' statement that the statute
forbids residents to use firearms to stop intruders, see *McIntosh v.
Washington* (1978). ...

We are aware of the problem of handgun violence in this country,
and we take seriously the concerns raised by the many amici who
believe that prohibition of handgun ownership is a solution. The
Constitution leaves the District of Columbia a variety of tools for

combating that problem, including some measures regulating handguns. But the enshrinement of constitutional rights necessarily takes certain policy choices off the table. These include the absolute prohibition of handguns held and used for self-defense in the home. Undoubtedly some think that the Second Amendment is outmoded in a society where our standing army is the pride of our Nation, where well-trained police forces provide personal security, and where gun violence is a serious problem. That is perhaps debatable, but what is not debatable is that it is not the role of this Court to pronounce the Second Amendment extinct.

We affirm the judgment of the Court of Appeals.

CHAPTER SEVEN

DEATH PENALTY

T HE CONSTITUTION OF THE UNITED STATES expressly refers to the death penalty. The Due Process Clauses of the Fifth and Fourteenth Amendments state that no person shall be deprived of "life" without due process of law. The Grand Jury Clause of the Fifth Amendment ensures that no person shall be held for a "capital...crime" without a grand jury indictment. These provisions make clear that the constitution allows imposition of the death penalty with due process and after indictment. Among historians, there is no serious doubt as to whether the death penalty was an accepted form of punishment when the Constitution was adopted.

In 1972, however, the Supreme Court effectively suspended use of capital punishment on the grounds that its arbitrary administration violated the Eighth Amendment's prohibition of "cruel and unusual punishments."[1] Although it later affirmed the death penalty's constitutionality, the Court over time added a number of restrictions governing both who could be subject to capital punishment and the discretion juries should have to impose it. The Court said that its determinations about whether imposition of capital (or other severe) punishments is impermissibly "cruel and unusual" are governed by consideration of the "evolving standards of decency that mark the progress of a maturing society."[2]

Justice Scalia was an ardent defender of the government's authority to use the death penalty as it saw fit. He voted to uphold application of capital punishment to fifteen-year-old[3] and mentally retarded convicted criminals. His argument was, not surprisingly, a textual one: capital punishment is explicitly contemplated in the Constitution. Moreover, he contended that the Eighth Amendment's prohibition of cruel and unusual punishments represented no barrier to capital punishment since its use was rarely if ever "cruel" and could not be considered even remotely "unusual" in light of its use throughout American history.

ATKINS v. VIRGINIA (2002)

Daryl Atkins was arrested for abduction, armed robbery, and capital murder in the Commonwealth of Virginia. Before the trial, a psychologist examined Atkins and found him to be "mildly mentally retarded." A jury, after finding aggravating circumstances, sentenced him to death.

The Supreme Court ruled that executions of mentally retarded criminals are "cruel and unusual punishments" prohibited by the Eighth Amendment to the Constitution. Though the Court had held the opposite thirteen years earlier, the majority in *Atkins* now found that a "national consensus" had developed as evidenced by the "dramatic shift in the state legislative landscape" toward abolishing the death penalty for mentally retarded persons. The Court said it agreed with the states' move and did not believe that "the execution of the mentally retarded criminals will measurably advance the deterrent or the retributive purpose of the death penalty." The Court said the states' shift was part of "a much broader social and professional consensus" and pointed to the opposition of religious leaders and "the world community," including the European Union. In conclusion, the Court said the movement by some states and foreign counties toward abolition of capital punishment for the mentally retarded was a clear indicator that the practice was out of step with "evolving standards of decency."

Justice Scalia's frustration with the decision to limit the states' use of the death penalty comes through quite clearly from the start of his dissenting opinion. Charging the majority with drafting an opinion based on "nothing but the personal views of its members," Scalia said the Court once again ignored the text and history of the Eighth Amendment.

Scalia wrote that the Court "makes no pretense that execution of the mildly mentally retarded would have been considered 'cruel and unusual' in 1791." Thus, Scalia said, the Court needed to show that the practice has become inconsistent with modern standards of decency. Scalia contended the Court failed to support its claim that a "national consensus" had formed against the practice. He argued that the adoption of laws forbidding execution of the mentally retarded in eighteen states, representing less than half of the states that use the death penalty at all, fell far short of establishing a "national consensus" against the practice. He dismissed other arguments advanced by the Court as "feeble," "counter-indicative," and "irrelevant."

All of the majority's arguments are nothing more than "a game," Scalia charged, to distract from the Court's real rationale: the majority believed the Constitution confers on it the right to decide the acceptability of the death penalty based on the justices' personal sense of decency and justice. Scalia scoffed at this interpretation and said the text of the Constitution authorizes no such "arrogant" assumption of authority. He then attempted to refute the majority's specific arguments supporting its view that capital punishment is "excessive" as applied to mentally retarded criminals. Scalia closed by bemoaning the addition of another restriction on states' use of the death penalty.

> *Seldom has an opinion of this Court rested so obviously upon nothing but the personal views of its Members.*

⤜✦⤏

JUSTICE SCALIA, WITH WHOM THE CHIEF JUSTICE AND JUSTICE THOMAS JOIN, DISSENTING.

Today's decision is the pinnacle of our Eighth Amendment death-is-different jurisprudence. Not only does it, like all of that jurisprudence, find no support in the text or history of the Eighth Amendment; it does not even have support in current social attitudes regarding the conditions that render an otherwise just death penalty inappropriate. Seldom has an opinion of this Court rested so obviously upon nothing but the personal views of its members.

I

I begin with a brief restatement of facts that are abridged by the Court but important to understanding this case. After spending the day drinking alcohol and smoking marijuana, petitioner Daryl Renard Atkins and a partner in crime drove to a convenience store, intending to rob a customer. Their victim was Eric Nesbitt, an airman from Langley Air Force Base, whom they abducted, drove to a nearby automated teller machine, and forced to withdraw $200. They then drove him to a deserted area, ignoring his pleas to leave him unharmed. According to the co-conspirator, whose testimony the jury evidently credited, Atkins ordered Nesbitt out of the vehicle and, after he had taken only a few steps, shot him one, two, three, four, five, six, seven, eight times in the thorax, chest, abdomen, arms, and legs.

The jury convicted Atkins of capital murder. At resentencing (the Virginia Supreme Court affirmed his conviction but remanded for resentencing because the trial court had used an improper verdict form), the jury heard extensive evidence of petitioner's alleged mental retardation. A psychologist testified that petitioner was mildly mentally retarded with an IQ of 59, that he was a "slow learne[r]," who showed a "lack of success in pretty much every domain of his life," and that he had an "impaired" capacity to appreciate the criminality of his conduct and to conform his conduct to the law. Petitioner's family members offered additional evidence in support of his mental retardation claim (e.g., that petitioner is a "follower"). The Commonwealth contested the evidence of retardation and presented testimony of a psychologist who found "absolutely no evidence other than the IQ score . . . indicating that [petitioner] was in the least bit mentally retarded" and concluded that petitioner was "of average intelligence, at least."

The jury also heard testimony about petitioner's 16 prior felony convictions for robbery, attempted robbery, abduction, use of a firearm, and maiming. The victims of these offenses provided graphic depictions of petitioner's violent tendencies: He hit one over the head with a beer bottle; he slapped a gun across another victim's face, clubbed her in the head with it, knocked her to the ground, and then helped her up, only to shoot her in the stomach. The jury sentenced petitioner to death. The Supreme Court of Virginia affirmed petitioner's sentence.

II

As the foregoing history demonstrates, petitioner's mental retardation was a *central issue* at sentencing. The jury concluded, however, that his alleged retardation was not a compelling reason to exempt him from the death penalty in light of the brutality of his crime and his long demonstrated propensity for violence. "In upsetting this particularized judgment on the basis of a constitutional absolute," the Court concludes that no one who is even slightly mentally retarded can have sufficient "moral responsibility to be subjected to capital punishment for any crime. As a sociological and moral conclusion that is implausible; and it is doubly implausible as an interpretation of the United States Constitution." *Thompson v. Oklahoma* (1988) (*Scalia, J.,* dissenting).

Under our Eighth Amendment jurisprudence, a punishment is "cruel and unusual" if it falls within one of two categories: "those modes or acts of punishment that had been considered cruel and unusual at the time that the Bill of Rights was adopted," *Ford v. Wainwright* (1986), and modes of punishment that are inconsistent with modern "standards of decency," as evinced by objective indicia, the most important of which is "legislation enacted by the country's legislatures," *Penry v. Lynaugh* (1989).

The Court makes no pretense that execution of the mildly mentally retarded would have been considered "cruel and unusual" in 1791. Only the *severely* or *profoundly* mentally retarded, commonly known as "idiots," enjoyed any special status under the law at that time. They, like lunatics, suffered a "deficiency in will" rendering them unable to tell right from wrong. 4 W. Blackstone, Commentaries on the Laws of England 24 (1769) (hereinafter Blackstone); see also *Penry* ("[T]he term 'idiot' was generally used to describe persons who had a total lack of reason or understanding, or an inability to distinguish between good and evil")...Due to their incompetence, idiots were "excuse[d] from the guilt, and of course from the punishment, of any criminal action committed under such deprivation of the senses." 4 Blackstone 25. Instead, they were often committed to civil confinement or made wards of the State, thereby preventing them from "go[ing] loose, to the terror of the king's subjects." 4 Blackstone 25. Mentally retarded offenders with less severe impairments—those who were not "idiots"—suffered criminal prosecution and punishment, including capital punishment....

The Court is left to argue, therefore, that execution of the mildly retarded is inconsistent with the "evolving standards of decency that mark the progress of a maturing society." *Trop v. Dulles* (1958). Before today, our opinions consistently emphasized that Eighth Amendment judgments regarding the existence of social "standards" "should be informed by objective factors to the maximum possible extent" and "should not be, or appear to be, merely the subjective views of individual Justices." *Coker v. Georgia* (1977). "First" among these objective factors are the "statutes passed by society's elected representatives," *Stanford v. Kentucky* (1989); because it "will rarely if ever be the case that the Members of this Court will have a better sense of the evolution in views of the American people than do their elected representatives," *Thompson* (*Scalia*, J., dissenting).

The Court pays lipservice to these precedents as it miraculously extracts a "national consensus" forbidding execution of the mentally retarded from the fact that 18 States—less than *half* (47%) of the 38 States that permit capital punishment (for whom the issue exists)—have very recently enacted legislation barring execution of the mentally retarded. Even that 47% figure is a distorted one. If one is to say, as the Court does today, that *all* executions of the mentally retarded are so morally repugnant as to violate our national "standards of decency," surely the "consensus" it points to must be one that has set its righteous face against *all* such executions. Not 18 States, but only 7—18% of death penalty jurisdictions—have legislation of that scope. Eleven of those that the Court counts enacted statutes prohibiting execution of mentally retarded defendants *convicted after, or convicted of crimes committed after, the effective date* of the legislation; those already on death row, or consigned there before the statute's effective date, or even (in those States using the date of the crime as the criterion of retroactivity) tried in the future for murders committed many years ago, could be put to death. That is not a statement of absolute moral repugnance, but one of current preference between two tolerable approaches. Two of these States permit execution of the mentally retarded in other situations as well: Kansas apparently permits execution of all except the *severely* mentally retarded; New York permits execution of the mentally retarded who commit murder in a correctional facility.

But let us accept, for the sake of argument, the Court's faulty count. That bare number of States alone—*18*—should be enough to convince any reasonable person that no "national consensus" exists. How is it possible that agreement among 47% of the death penalty jurisdictions amounts to "consensus"? Our prior cases have generally required a much higher degree of agreement before finding a punishment cruel and unusual on "evolving standards" grounds. In *Coker*, we proscribed the death penalty for rape of an adult woman after finding that only one jurisdiction, Georgia, authorized such a punishment. In *Enmund*, we invalidated the death penalty for mere participation in a robbery in which an accomplice took a life, a punishment not permitted in 28 of the death penalty States (78%). In *Ford*, we supported the common-law prohibition of execution of the insane with the observation that "[t]his ancestral legacy has not outlived its time," since not a single State authorizes such punishment. In *Solem v. Helm* (1983), we invalidated a life sentence without parole under a recidivist statute by which the criminal "was treated more severely than he would have been in any other State." What the Court calls evidence of "consensus" in the present case (a fudged 47%) more closely resembles evidence that we found *inadequate* to establish consensus in earlier cases. *Tison v. Arizona* (1987) upheld a state law authorizing capital punishment for major participation in a felony with reckless indifference to life where only 11 of the 37 death penalty States (30%) prohibited such punishment. *Stanford* upheld a state law permitting execution of defendants who committed a capital crime at age 16 where only 15 of the 36 death penalty States (42%) prohibited death for such offenders.

Moreover, a major factor that the Court entirely disregards is that the legislation of all 18 States it relies on is still in its infancy. The oldest of the statutes is only 14 years old; five were enacted last year; over half were enacted within the past eight years. Few, if any, of the States have had sufficient experience with these laws to know whether they are sensible in the long term. It is "myopic to base sweeping constitutional principles upon the narrow experience of [a few] years." *Coker* (Burger, C. J., dissenting).

The Court attempts to bolster its embarrassingly feeble evidence of "consensus" with the following: "It is not so much the number of these States that is significant, but the *consistency* of the direction of change" (emphasis added). But in what *other* direction *could we possibly* see change? Given that 14 years ago *all* the death penalty

statutes included the mentally retarded, *any* change (except precipitate undoing of what had just been done) was *bound to be* in the one
direction the Court finds significant enough to overcome the lack
of real consensus. That is to say, to be accurate the Court's "*consistency*-of-the-direction-of-change" point should be recast into the
following unimpressive observation: "No State has yet undone its
exemption of the mentally retarded, one for as long as 14 whole
years." In any event, reliance upon "trends," even those of much longer duration than a mere 14 years, is a perilous basis for constitutional
adjudication, as Justice O'Connor eloquently explained in *Thompson:*

> In 1846, Michigan became the first State to abolish the death
> penalty. . . . In succeeding decades, other American States con-
> tinued the trend towards abolition. . . . Later, and particularly
> after World War II, there ensued a steady and dramatic decline
> in executions. . . . In the 1950s and 1960s, more States abolished
> or radically restricted capital punishment, and executions ceased
> completely for several years beginning in 1968. . . .
>
> In 1972, when this Court heard arguments on the consti-
> tutionality of the death penalty, such statistics might have sug-
> gested that the practice had become a relic, implicitly rejected
> by a new societal consensus. . . . We now know that any infer-
> ence of a societal consensus rejecting the death penalty would
> have been mistaken. But had this Court then declared the exis-
> tence of such a consensus, and outlawed capital punishment,
> legislatures would very likely not have been able to revive it.
> The mistaken premise of the decision would have been frozen
> into constitutional law, making it difficult to refute and even
> more difficult to reject.

Her words demonstrate, of course, not merely the peril of riding a trend, but also the peril of discerning a consensus where there is none.

The Court's thrashing about for evidence of "consensus" includes reliance upon the *margins* by which state legislatures have enacted bans on execution of the retarded. Presumably, in applying our Eighth Amendment "evolving-standards-of-decency" jurisprudence, we will henceforth weigh not only how many States have agreed, but how many States have agreed *by how much*. Of course if the percentage of legislators voting for the bill is significant, surely the number of people *represented* by the legislators voting for the bill is also significant: the fact that 49% of the legislators in a State with a population of 60 million voted *against* the bill should be more impressive than the fact that 90% of the legislators in a state with a population of 2 million voted *for* it. (By the way, the population of the death penalty States that exclude the mentally retarded is only 44% of the population of all death penalty States.) This is quite absurd. What we have looked for in the past to "evolve" the Eighth Amendment is a consensus of the same sort as the consensus that *adopted* the Eighth Amendment: a consensus of the sovereign States that form the Union, not a nose count of Americans for and against.

What we have looked for in the past to "evolve" the Eighth Amendment is a consensus of the same sort as the consensus that adopted *the Eighth Amendment: a consensus of the sovereign states that form the Union, not a nose count of Americans for and against.*

Even less compelling (if possible) is the Court's argument that evidence of "national consensus" is to be found in the infrequency with which retarded persons are executed in States that do not bar their execution. To begin with, what the Court takes as true is in fact quite doubtful. It is not at all clear that execution of the mentally retarded is "uncommon," as even the sources cited by the Court suggest. *If*, however, execution of the mentally retarded *is* "uncommon"; and if it is not a sufficient explanation of this that the retarded constitute a tiny fraction of society (1% to 3%); then surely the explanation is that mental retardation is a constitutionally mandated mitigating factor at sentencing. For that reason, even if there were uniform national sentiment in *favor* of executing the retarded in appropriate cases, one would still expect execution of the mentally retarded to be "uncommon." To adapt to the present case what the Court itself said in *Stanford*: "[I]t is not only possible, but overwhelmingly probable, that the very considerations which induce [today's majority] to believe that death should *never* be imposed on [mentally retarded] offenders . . . cause prosecutors and juries to believe that it should *rarely* be imposed."

But the prize for the Court's Most Feeble Effort to fabricate "national consensus" must go to its appeal (deservedly relegated to a footnote) to the views of assorted professional and religious organizations, members of the so-called "world community," and respondents to opinion polls.

But the Prize for the Court's Most Feeble Effort to fabricate "national consensus" must go to its appeal (deservedly relegated to a footnote) to the views of assorted professional and religious organizations, members of the so-called "world community," and respondents to opinion polls. I agree with the Chief Justice that the views of professional and religious organizations and the results of opinion polls are irrelevant.

[Footnote] And in some cases positively counterindicative. The Court cites, for example, the views of the United States

Catholic Conference, whose members are the active Catholic Bishops of the United States. The attitudes of that body regarding crime and punishment are so far from being representative, even of the views of Catholics, that they are currently the object of intense national (and entirely ecumenical) criticism.

Equally irrelevant are the practices of the "world community," whose notions of justice are (thankfully) not always those of our people. "We must never forget that it is a Constitution for the United States of America that we are expounding.... [W]here there is not first a settled consensus among our own people, the views of other nations, however enlightened the Justices of this Court may think them to be, cannot be imposed upon Americans through the Constitution." *Thompson* (*Scalia*, J., dissenting).

III

Beyond the empty talk of a "national consensus," the Court gives us a brief glimpse of what really underlies today's decision: pretension to a power confined *neither* by the moral sentiments originally enshrined in the Eighth Amendment (its original meaning) *nor even* by the current moral sentiments of the American people. " '[T]he Constitution,' " the Court says, "contemplates that in the end *our own judgment* will be brought to bear on the question of the acceptability of the death penalty under the Eighth Amendment' " (quoting *Coker*) (emphasis added). (The unexpressed reason for this unexpressed "contemplation" of the Constitution is presumably that really good lawyers have moral sentiments superior to those of the common herd, whether in 1791 or today.) The arrogance of this assumption of power takes one's breath away. And it explains, of course, why the Court can be so cavalier about the evidence of consensus. It is just a game, after all. "[I]n the end," it is the *feelings* and *intuition* of a majority of the Justices that count—"the perceptions of decency, or of penology, or of mercy, entertained . . . by a majority of the small and unrepresentative segment of our society that sits on this Court." *Thompson* (*Scalia*, J., dissenting).

The genuinely operative portion of the opinion, then, is the Court's statement of the reasons why it agrees with the contrived consensus it has found, that the "diminished capacities" of the mentally retarded render the death penalty excessive. The Court's analysis rests on two fundamental assumptions: (1) that the Eighth Amendment prohibits excessive punishments, and (2) that sentencing juries or judges are unable to account properly for the "diminished capacities" of the retarded. The first assumption is wrong, as I explained at length in *Harmelin v. Michigan* (1991). The Eighth Amendment is addressed to always-and-everywhere "cruel" punishments, such as the rack and the thumbscrew. But where the punishment is in itself permissible, "[t]he Eighth Amendment is not a ratchet, whereby a temporary consensus on leniency for a particular crime fixes a permanent constitutional maximum, disabling the States from giving effect to altered beliefs and responding to changed social conditions." The second assumption—inability of judges or juries to take proper account of mental retardation—is not only unsubstantiated, but contradicts the immemorial belief, here and in England, that they play an *indispensable* role in such matters:

[I]t is very difficult to define the indivisible line that divides perfect and partial insanity; but it must rest upon circumstances duly to be weighed and considered both by the judge and jury,

lest on the one side there be a kind of inhu-
manity towards the defects of human nature,
or on the other side too great an indulgence
given to great crimes.

i Hale, Pleas of the Crown

Proceeding from these faulty assumptions,
the Court gives two reasons why the death
penalty is an excessive punishment for all
mentally retarded offenders. First, the "diminished capacities" of the mentally retarded
raise a "serious question" whether their execution contributes to the "social purposes"
of the death penalty, viz., retribution and
deterrence. (The Court conveniently ignores

*Are the mentally
retarded really more dis-
posed (and hence more
likely) to commit willfully
cruel and serious crime
than others? In my exper-
ience, the opposite is true:
being childlike generally
suggests innocence rather
than brutality.*

a third "social purpose" of the death penalty—"incapacitation of
dangerous criminals and the consequent prevention of crimes that
they may otherwise commit in the future," *Gregg v. Georgia* (1976).
But never mind; its discussion of even the other two does not bear
analysis.) Retribution is not advanced, the argument goes, because
the mentally retarded are *no more culpable* than the average murderer,
whom we have already held lacks sufficient culpability to warrant
the death penalty. Who says so? Is there an established correlation
between mental acuity and the ability to conform one's conduct to
the law in such a rudimentary matter as murder? Are the mentally
retarded really more disposed (and hence more likely) to commit
willfully cruel and serious crime than others? In my experience, the
opposite is true: being childlike generally suggests innocence rather
than brutality.

Assuming, however, that there is a direct connection between diminished intelligence and the inability to refrain from murder, what scientific analysis can possibly show that a mildly retarded individual who commits an exquisite torture-killing is "no more culpable" than the "average" murderer in a holdup-gone-wrong or a domestic dispute? Or a moderately retarded individual who commits a series of 20 exquisite torture-killings? Surely culpability, and deservedness of the most severe retribution, depends not merely (if at all) upon the mental capacity of the criminal (above the level where he is able to distinguish right from wrong) but also upon the depravity of the crime—which is precisely why this sort of question has traditionally been thought answerable not by a categorical rule of the sort the Court today imposes upon all trials, but rather by the sentencer's weighing of the circumstances (both degree of retardation and depravity of crime) in the particular case. The fact that juries continue to sentence mentally retarded offenders to death for extreme crimes shows that society's moral outrage sometimes demands execution of retarded offenders. By what principle of law, science, or logic can the Court pronounce that this is wrong? There is none. Once the Court admits (as it does) that mental retardation does not render the offender morally *blameless*, there is no basis for saying that the death penalty is *never* appropriate retribution, no matter *how* heinous the crime. As long as a mentally retarded offender knows "the difference between right and wrong," only the sentencer can assess whether his retardation reduces his culpability enough to exempt him from the death penalty for the particular murder in question.

As for the other social purpose of the death penalty that the Court discusses, deterrence: That is not advanced, the Court tells us, because the mentally retarded are "less likely" than their nonretarded counterparts to "process the information of the possibility of execution as a penalty and...control their conduct based upon that information." Of course this leads to the same conclusion discussed earlier—that the mentally retarded (because they are less deterred) are more likely to kill—which neither I nor the society at large believes. In any event, even the Court does not say that *all* mentally retarded individuals cannot "process the information of the possibility of execution as a penalty and...control their conduct based upon that information"; it merely asserts that they are "less likely" to be able to do so. But surely the deterrent effect of a penalty is adequately vindicated if it successfully deters many, but not all, of the target class. Virginia's death penalty, for example, does not fail of its deterrent effect simply because *some* criminals are unaware that Virginia *has* the death penalty. In other words, the supposed fact that *some* retarded criminals cannot fully appreciate the death penalty has nothing to do with the deterrence rationale, but is simply an echo of the arguments denying a retribution rationale, discussed and rejected above. I am not sure that a murderer is somehow less blameworthy if (though he knew his act was wrong) he did not fully appreciate that he could die for it; but if so, we should treat a mentally retarded murderer the way we treat an offender who may be "less likely" to respond to the death penalty because he was abused as a child. We do not hold him immune from capital punishment, but require his background to be considered by the sentencer as a mitigating factor.

The Court throws one last factor into its grab bag of reasons why execution of the retarded is "excessive" in all cases: Mentally retarded offenders "face a special risk of wrongful execution" because they are less able "to make a persuasive showing of mitigation," "to give meaningful assistance to their counsel," and to be effective witnesses. "Special risk" is pretty flabby language (even flabbier than "less likely")—and I suppose a similar "special risk" could be said to exist for just plain stupid people, inarticulate people, even ugly people. If this unsupported claim has any substance to it (which I doubt), it might support a due process claim in all criminal prosecutions of the mentally retarded; but it is hard to see how it has anything to do with an *Eighth Amendment* claim that execution of the mentally retarded is cruel and unusual. We have never before held it to be cruel and unusual punishment to impose a sentence in violation of some *other* constitutional imperative.

There is something to be said for popular abolition of the death penalty; there is nothing to be said for its incremental abolition by this Court.

Today's opinion adds one more to the long list of substantive and procedural requirements impeding imposition of the death penalty imposed under this Court's assumed power to invent a death-is-different jurisprudence. None of those requirements existed when the Eighth Amendment was adopted, and some of them were not even supported by current moral consensus. They include prohibition of the death penalty for "ordinary" murder, *Godfrey*, for rape of an adult woman, *Coker*, and for felony murder absent a showing that the defendant possessed a sufficiently culpable state of mind, *Enmund*; prohibition of the death penalty for any person under the age of 16 at the time of the crime, *Thompson*; prohibition of the death penalty as the mandatory punishment for any crime, *Woodson v. North Carolina* (1976); a requirement that the sentencer not be given unguided discretion, *Furman v. Georgia* (1972); a requirement that the sentencer be empowered to take into account all mitigating circumstances, *Lockett v. Ohio* (1978); and a requirement that the accused receive a judicial evaluation of his claim of insanity before the sentence can be executed, *Ford*. There is something to be said for popular abolition of the death penalty; there is nothing to be said for its incremental abolition by this Court.

This newest invention promises to be more effective than any of the others in turning the process of capital trial into a game. One need only read the definitions of mental retardation adopted by the American Association of Mental Retardation and the American Psychiatric Association (set forth in the Court's opinion) to realize that the symptoms of this condition can readily be feigned. And whereas the capital defendant who feigns insanity risks commitment to a mental institution until he can be cured (and then tried and executed), the capital defendant who feigns mental retardation risks nothing at all. The mere pendency of the present case has brought us petitions by death row inmates claiming for the first time, after multiple habeas petitions, that they are retarded.

Perhaps these practical difficulties will not be experienced by the minority of capital-punishment States that have very recently changed mental retardation from a mitigating factor (to be accepted or rejected by the sentencer) to an absolute immunity. Time will tell—and the brief time those States have had the new disposition in place (an average of 6.8 years) is surely not enough. But if the practical difficulties do not appear, and if the other States share the Court's perceived moral consensus that *all* mental retardation renders the death penalty inappropriate for *all* crimes, then that majority will presumably follow suit. But there is no justification for this Court's pushing them into the experiment—and turning the experiment into a permanent practice—on constitutional pretext. Nothing has changed the accuracy of Matthew Hale's endorsement of the common law's traditional method for taking account of guilt-reducing factors, written over three centuries ago:

[Determination of a person's incapacity] is a matter of great difficulty, partly from the easiness of counterfeiting this disability...and partly from the variety of the degrees of this infirmity, whereof some are sufficient, and some are insufficient to excuse persons in capital offenses....

Yet the law of England hath afforded the best method of trial, that is possible, of this and all other matters of fact, namely, by a jury of twelve men all concurring in the same judgment, by the testimony of witnesses....and by the inspection and direction of the judge.

I HALE, PLEAS OF THE CROWN

I respectfully dissent.

ROPER v. SIMMONS (2005)

In 1989, the Court in *Stanford v. Kentucky* upheld the possibility of capital punishment for offenders who were sixteen or seventeen years of age when they committed murder. But after the Court decided in *Atkins* that executing mentally retarded offenders was cruel and unusual—because it did not comport with "the evolving standards of decency that mark the progress of a maturing society"—it was unclear whether *Stanford* would survive.

It didn't. Christopher Simmons was seventeen years old when he committed a horrible, premeditated murder. He was tried, convicted, and sentenced to death by a Missouri jury. The Supreme Court of Missouri, however, ruled that capital punishment was cruel and unusual, and thus unconstitutional, when applied to a juvenile offender. The court said that a national consensus had developed against executing juveniles in all cases.

In a 5–4 opinion delivered by Justice Anthony Kennedy, the U.S. Supreme Court upheld the Missouri Supreme Court's decision. In ruling that the Constitution prohibits the death penalty for under-eighteen offenders, Kennedy cited sociological and scientific research that he said demonstrated that juveniles have a lack of maturity and sense of responsibility compared with adults. Awareness of this important difference, Kennedy argued, is what persuaded many states to move away from such executions. When *Stanford* was decided, twenty states allowed for the execution of juveniles. But since that decision, only six states had executed prisoners for crimes committed as juveniles and five states that allowed the juvenile death penalty had since abolished it. Finally, Kennedy pointed to the views of international community, which were overwhelmingly opposed to capital punishment for juvenile offenders. Kennedy noted that only seven countries in addition to the United States had executed juvenile offenders, including such habitual human rights violators as Iran, Pakistan, Saudi Arabia, and China.

Justice Scalia strenuously dissented, writing that no national consensus had formed against imposing capital punishment on juvenile criminals. He said the majority used a different standard from the one it had in the past for calculating a shift in sentiment among the states. In addition, he questioned whether the Court's conclusions relating to psychological and sociological research were sound. Even if juveniles sometimes do fail to consider the consequences of their actions, it does not follow that they always do.

Finally, Scalia railed against the Court's use of foreign law and views to buttress its opinion. He said that foreign views were not relevant to an understanding of our Constitution. The Court could not seriously expect those views to have weight in this case since the Court did not consider foreign views in areas where those views would have conflicted with the majority's sense of justice. Scalia noted that other counties, including England, do not protect criminal defendants' rights as vigorously as we do. He pointed out that the United States is one of only six countries to allow abortion on demand up to the point of viability. The Court certainly had not considered our less popular views in these areas of the law when deciding relevant cases. Scalia charged, "To invoke alien law when it agrees with one's own thinking, and ignore it otherwise, is not reasoned decisionmaking, but sophistry."

~∞∞~

JUSTICE SCALIA, WITH WHOM THE CHIEF JUSTICE AND JUSTICE THOMAS JOIN, DISSENTING.

In urging approval of a constitution that gave life-tenured judges the power to nullify laws enacted by the people's representatives, Alexander Hamilton assured the citizens of New York that there was little risk in this, since "[t]he judiciary ... ha[s] neither FORCE nor WILL but merely judgment." The Federalist No. 78. But Hamilton had in mind a traditional judiciary, "bound down by strict rules and precedents which serve to define and point out their duty in every particular case that comes before them." Bound down, indeed. What a mockery today's opinion makes of Hamilton's expectation, announcing the Court's conclusion that the meaning of our Constitution has changed over the past 15 years—not, mind you, that this Court's decision 15 years ago was wrong, but that the Constitution has changed. The Court reaches this implausible result by purporting to advert, not to the original meaning of the Eighth Amendment, but to "the evolving standards of decency" of our national society. It then finds, on the flimsiest of grounds, that a national consensus which could not be perceived in our people's laws barely 15 years ago now solidly exists. Worse still, the Court says in so many words that what our people's laws say about the issue does not, in the last analysis, matter: "[I]n the end our own judgment will be brought to bear on the question of the acceptability of the death penalty under the Eighth Amendment." The Court thus proclaims itself sole arbiter of our Nation's moral standards—and in the course of discharging that awesome responsibility purports to take guidance from the views of foreign courts and legislatures. Because I do not believe that the meaning of our Eighth Amendment, any more than the meaning of other provisions of our Constitution, should be determined by the subjective views of five Members of this Court and like-minded foreigners, I dissent.

Because I do not believe that the meaning of our Eighth Amendment, any more than the meaning of other provisions of our Constitution, should be determined by the subjective views of five Members of this Court and like-minded foreigners, I dissent.

I

In determining that capital punishment of offenders who committed murder before age 18 is "cruel and unusual" under the Eighth Amendment, the Court first considers, in accordance with our modern (though in my view mistaken) jurisprudence, whether there is a "national consensus," *ibid.* that laws allowing such executions contravene our modern "standards of decency," *Trop v. Dulles* (1958). We have held that this determination should be based on "objective indicia that reflect the public attitude toward a given sanction"— namely, "statutes passed by society's elected representatives." *Stanford v. Kentucky* (1989). As in *Atkins v. Virginia* (2002), the Court dutifully recites this test and claims halfheartedly that a national consensus has emerged since our decision in *Stanford*, because 18 States—or 47% of

States that permit capital punishment—now have legislation prohibiting the execution of offenders under 18, and because all of four States have adopted such legislation since *Stanford*.

Words have no meaning if the views of less than 50% of death penalty States can constitute a national consensus. Our previous cases have required overwhelming opposition to a challenged practice, generally over a long period of time. In *Coker v. Georgia* (1977), a plurality concluded the Eighth Amendment prohibited capital punishment for rape of an adult woman where only one jurisdiction authorized such punishment. The plurality also observed that "[a]t no time in the last 50 years ha[d] a majority of States authorized death as a punishment for rape." In *Ford v. Wainwright* (1986), we held execution of the insane unconstitutional, tracing the roots of this prohibition to the common law and noting that "no State in the union permits the execution of the insane." In *Enmund v. Florida* (1982), we invalidated capital punishment imposed for participation in a robbery in which an accomplice committed murder, because 78% of all death penalty States prohibited this punishment. Even there we expressed some hesitation, because the legislative judgment was "neither 'wholly unanimous among state legislatures,'...nor as compelling as the legislative judgments considered in *Coker*." By contrast, agreement among 42% of death penalty States in *Stanford*, which the Court appears to believe was correctly decided at the time was insufficient to show a national consensus.

In an attempt to keep afloat its implausible assertion of national consensus, the Court throws overboard a proposition well established in our Eighth Amendment jurisprudence. "It should be observed," the Court says, "that the *Stanford* Court should have considered those States that had abandoned the death penalty altogether as part of the

consensus against the juvenile death penalty...;
a State's decision to bar the death penalty altogether of necessity demonstrates a judgment
that the death penalty is inappropriate for all
offenders, including juveniles." The insinua-
tion that the Court's new method of counting contradicts only "the *Stanford* Court" is
misleading. None of our cases dealing with an
alleged constitutional limitation upon the death
penalty has counted, as States supporting a
consensus in favor of that limitation, States that
have eliminated the death penalty entirely. And
with good reason. Consulting States that bar
the death penalty concerning the necessity of
making an exception to the penalty for offenders under 18 is rather like including old-order
Amishmen in a consumer-preference poll on
the electric car. Of course they don't like it,
but that sheds no light whatever on the point at
issue. That 12 States favor no executions says something about consensus against the death penalty, but nothing—absolutely nothing—
about consensus that offenders under 18 deserve special immunity
from such a penalty. In repealing the death penalty, those 12 States
considered none of the factors that the Court puts forth as determinative of the issue before us today—lower culpability of the young,
inherent recklessness, lack of capacity for considered judgment, etc.
What might be relevant, perhaps, is how many of those States permit
16- and 17-year-old offenders to be treated as adults with respect
to noncapital offenses. (They all do; indeed, some even require that

Consulting States that bar the death penalty concerning the necessity of making an exception to the penalty for offenders under 18 is rather like including old-order Amishmen in a consumer-preference poll on the electric car. Of course they don't like it, but that sheds no light whatever on the point at issue.

juveniles as young as 14 be tried as adults if they are charged with murder.) The attempt by the Court to turn its remarkable minority consensus into a faux majority by counting Amishmen is an act of nomological desperation.

Recognizing that its national-consensus argument was weak compared with our earlier cases, the *Atkins* Court found additional support in the fact that 16 States had prohibited execution of mentally retarded individuals since *Penry v. Lynaugh* (1989). Indeed, the *Atkins* Court distinguished *Stanford* on that very ground, explaining that "[a]lthough we decided *Stanford* on the same day as *Penry*, apparently only two state legislatures have raised the threshold age for imposition of the death penalty." Now, the Court says a legislative change in four States is "significant" enough to trigger a constitutional prohibition. It is amazing to think that this subtle shift in numbers can take the issue entirely off the table for legislative debate.

I also doubt whether many of the legislators who voted to change the laws in those four States would have done so if they had known their decision would (by the pronouncement of this Court) be rendered irreversible. After all, legislative support for capital punishment, in any form, has surged and ebbed throughout our Nation's history. As Justice O'Connor has explained:

"The history of the death penalty instructs that there is danger in inferring a settled societal consensus from statistics like those relied on in this case. In 1846, Michigan became the first State to abolish the death penalty ... . In succeeding decades, other American States continued the trend towards abolition.... Later, and particularly after World War II, there ensued a steady and dramatic decline in executions.... In the 1950's and 1960's, more States abolished or radically restricted capital punishment, and executions ceased completely for several years beginning in 1968.

"In 1972, when this Court heard arguments on the constitutionality of the death penalty, such statistics might have suggested that the practice had become a relic, implicitly rejected by a new societal consensus.... . We now know that any inference of a societal consensus rejecting the death penalty would have been mistaken. But had this Court then declared the existence of such a consensus, and outlawed capital punishment, legislatures would very likely not have been able to revive it. The mistaken premise of the decision would have been frozen into constitutional law, making it difficult to refute and even more difficult to reject."

THOMPSON V. OKLAHOMA (1988)

Relying on such narrow margins is especially inappropriate in light of the fact that a number of legislatures and voters have expressly affirmed their support for capital punishment of 16- and 17-year-old offenders since *Stanford*. Though the Court is correct that no State has lowered its death penalty age, both the Missouri and Virginia Legislatures—which, at the time of *Stanford*, had no minimum age requirement—expressly established 16 as the minimum. The people of Arizona and Florida have done the same by ballot initiative. Thus, even States that have not executed an under-18 offender in recent years unquestionably favor the possibility of capital punishment in some circumstances.

The Court's reliance on the infrequency of executions, for under-18 murderers credits an argument that this Court considered and explicitly rejected in *Stanford*. That infrequency is explained, we accurately said, both by "the undisputed fact that a far smaller percentage of capital crimes are committed by persons under 18 than over 18." Thus, "it is not only possible, but overwhelmingly probable, that the very considerations which induce [respondent] and [his] supporters to believe that death should never be imposed on offenders under 18 cause prosecutors and juries to believe that it should rarely be imposed."

It is, furthermore, unclear that executions of the relevant age group have decreased since we decided Stanford. Between 1990 and 2003, 123 of 3,599 death sentences, or 3.4%, were given to individuals who committed crimes before reaching age 18. By contrast, only 2.1% of those sentenced to death between 1982 and 1988 committed the crimes when they were under 18. As for actual executions of under-18 offenders, they constituted 2.4% of the total executions since 1973. In *Stanford*, we noted that only 2% of the executions between 1642 and 1986 were of under-18 offenders and found that that lower number did not demonstrate a national consensus against the penalty. Thus, the numbers of under-18 offenders subjected to the death penalty, though low compared with adults, have either held steady or slightly increased since Stanford. These statistics in no way support the action the Court takes today.

II

Of course, the real force driving today's decision is not the actions of four state legislatures, but the Court's "'own judgment'" that murderers younger than 18 can never be as morally culpable as older counterparts. The Court claims that this usurpation of the role of moral arbiter is simply a "retur[n] to the rul[e] established in decisions predating

Stanford." That supposed rule—which is reflected solely in dicta and never once in a holding that purports to supplant the consensus of the American people with the Justices' views—was repudiated in *Stanford* for the very good reason that it has no foundation in law or logic. If the Eighth Amendment set forth an ordinary rule of law, it would indeed be the role of this Court to say what the law is. But the Court having pronounced that the Eighth Amendment is an ever-changing reflection of "the evolving standards of decency" of our society, it makes no sense for the Justices then to prescribe those standards rather than discern them from the practices of our people. On the evolving-standards hypothesis, the only legitimate function of this Court is to identify a moral consensus of the American people. By what conceivable warrant can nine lawyers presume to be the authoritative conscience of the Nation?

> *By what conceivable warrant can nine lawyers presume to be the authoritative conscience of the Nation?*

The reason for insistence on legislative primacy is obvious and fundamental: " '[I]n a democratic society legislatures, not courts, are constituted to respond to the will and consequently the moral values of the people.' " *Gregg v. Georgia* (1976). For a similar reason we have, in our determination of society's moral standards, consulted the practices of sentencing juries: Juries "'maintain a link between contemporary community values and the penal system'" that this Court cannot claim for itself. *Gregg.*

Today's opinion provides a perfect example of why judges are ill equipped to make the type of legislative judgments the Court insists on making here. To support its opinion that States should be prohibited from imposing the death penalty on anyone who committed murder before age 18, the Court looks to scientific and sociological studies, picking and choosing those that support its position. It never explains why those particular studies are methodologically sound; none was ever entered into evidence or tested in an adversarial proceeding. As The Chief Justice has explained:

> "[M]ethodological and other errors can affect the reliability and validity of estimates about the opinions and attitudes of a population derived from various sampling techniques. Everything from variations in the survey methodology, such as the choice of the target population, the sampling design used, the questions asked, and the statistical analyses used to interpret the data can skew the results."

ATKINS

In other words, all the Court has done today, to borrow from another context, is to look over the heads of the crowd and pick out its friends.

In other words, all the Court has done today, to borrow from another context, is to look over the heads of the crowd and pick out its friends.

We need not look far to find studies contradicting the Court's conclusions. As petitioner points out, the American Psychological Association (APA), which claims in this case that scientific evidence shows persons under 18 lack the ability to take moral responsibility for their decisions, has previously taken precisely the opposite position before this very Court. In its brief in *Hodgson v. Minnesota* (1990), the APA found a "rich body of research" showing that juveniles are mature enough to decide whether to obtain an abortion without parental involvement. The APA brief, citing psychology treatises and studies too numerous to list here, asserted: "[B]y middle adolescence (age 14-15) young people develop abilities similar to adults in reasoning about moral dilemmas, understanding social rules and laws, [and] reasoning about interpersonal relationships and interpersonal problems." Given the nuances of scientific methodology and conflicting views, courts—which can only consider the limited evidence on the record before them—are ill equipped to determine which view of science is the right one. Legislatures "are better qualified to weigh and 'evaluate the results of statistical studies in terms of their own local conditions and with a flexibility of approach that is not available to the courts.' " *McCleskey v. Kemp* (1987).

Even putting aside questions of methodology, the studies cited by the Court offer scant support for a categorical prohibition of the death penalty for murderers under 18. At most, these studies conclude that, on average, or in most cases, persons under 18 are unable to take moral responsibility for their actions. Not one of the cited studies opines that all individuals under 18 are unable to appreciate the nature of their crimes.

Moreover, the cited studies describe only adolescents who engage in risky or antisocial behavior, as many young people do. Murder, however, is more than just risky or antisocial behavior. It is entirely consistent to believe that young people often act impetuously and lack judgment, but, at the same time, to believe that those who commit premeditated murder are—at least sometimes—just as culpable as adults. Christopher Simmons, who was only seven months shy of his 18th birthday when he murdered Shirley Crook, described to his friends beforehand—"[i]n chilling, callous terms," as the Court puts it—the murder he planned to commit. He then broke into the home of an innocent woman, bound her with duct tape and electrical wire, and threw her off a bridge alive and conscious. In their amici brief, the States of Alabama, Delaware, Oklahoma, Texas, Utah, and Virginia offer additional examples of murders committed by individuals under 18 that involve truly monstrous acts. In Alabama, two 17-year-olds, one 16-year-old, and one 19-year-old picked up a female hitchhiker, threw bottles at her, and kicked and stomped her for approximately 30 minutes until she died. They then sexually assaulted her lifeless body and, when they were finished, threw her body off a cliff. They later returned to the crime scene to mutilate her corpse. Other examples in the brief are equally shocking. Though these cases are assuredly the exception rather than the rule, the studies the Court cites in no way justify a constitutional imperative that prevents legislatures and juries from treating exceptional cases in an exceptional way—by determining that some murders are not just the acts of happy-go-lucky teenagers, but heinous crimes deserving of death.

That "almost every State prohibits those under 18 years of age from voting, serving on juries, or marrying without parental consent" is patently irrelevant—and is yet another resurrection of an argument that this Court gave a decent burial in *Stanford*. (What kind of Equal Justice under Law is it that—without so much as a "Sorry about that"—gives as the basis for sparing one person from execution arguments explicitly rejected in refusing to spare another?) As we explained in *Stanford*, it is "absurd to think that one must be mature enough to drive carefully, to drink responsibly, or to vote intelligently, in order to be mature enough to understand that murdering another human being is profoundly wrong, and to conform one's conduct to that most minimal of all civilized standards." Serving on a jury or entering into marriage also involve decisions far more sophisticated than the simple decision not to take another's life.

Moreover, the age statutes the Court lists "set the appropriate ages for the operation of a system that makes its determinations in gross, and that does not conduct individualized maturity tests." *Ibid.* The criminal justice system, by contrast, provides for individualized consideration of each defendant. In capital cases, this Court requires the sentencer to make an individualized determination, which includes weighing aggravating factors and mitigating factors, such as youth. It is hard to see why this context should be any different. Whether to obtain an abortion is surely a much more complex decision for a young person than whether to kill an innocent person in cold blood.

> *Whether to obtain an abortion is surely a much more complex decision for a young person than whether to kill an innocent person in cold blood.*

The Court concludes, however, that juries cannot be trusted with the delicate task of weighing a defendant's youth along with the other mitigating and aggravating factors of his crime. This startling conclusion undermines the very foundations of our capital sentencing system, which entrusts juries with "mak[ing] the difficult and uniquely human judgments that defy codification and that 'buil[d] discretion, equity, and flexibility into a legal system.'" *McCleskey.* The Court says that juries will be unable to appreciate the significance of a defendant's youth when faced with details of a brutal crime. This assertion is based on no evidence; to the contrary, the Court itself acknowledges that the execution of under-18 offenders is "infrequent" even in the States "without a formal prohibition on executing juveniles," suggesting that juries take seriously their responsibility to weigh youth as a mitigating factor.

Nor does the Court suggest a stopping point for its reasoning. If juries cannot make appropriate determinations in cases involving murderers under 18, in what other kinds of cases will the Court find jurors deficient? We have already held that no jury may consider whether a mentally deficient defendant can receive the death penalty, irrespective of his crime. Why not take other mitigating factors, such as considerations of childhood abuse or poverty, away from juries as well? Surely jurors "overpower[ed]" by "the brutality or cold-blooded nature" of a crime could not adequately weigh these mitigating factors either.

The Court's contention that the goals of retribution and deterrence are not served by executing murderers under 18 is also transparently false. The argument that "[r]etribution is not proportional if the law's most severe penalty is imposed on one whose culpability or blameworthiness is diminished" is simply an extension of the earlier, false generalization that youth always defeats culpability. The Court claims that "juveniles will be less susceptible to deterrence" because "'[t]he likelihood that the teenage offender has made the kind of cost-benefit analysis that attaches any weight to the possibility of execution is so remote as to be virtually nonexistent'" *ibid.* (quoting *Thompson*). The Court unsurprisingly finds no support for this astounding proposition, save its own case law. The facts of this very case show the proposition to be false. Before committing the crime, Simmons encouraged his friends to join him by assuring them that they could "get away with it" because they were minors. This fact may have influenced the jury's decision to impose capital punishment despite Simmons' age. Because the Court refuses to entertain the possibility that its own unsubstantiated generalization about juveniles could be wrong, it ignores this evidence entirely.

III

Though the views of our own citizens are essentially irrelevant to the Court's decision today, the views of other countries and the so-called international community take center stage.

The Court begins by noting that "Article 37 of the United Nations Convention on the Rights of the Child, which every country in the world has ratified save for the United States and Somalia, contains an express prohibition on capital punishment for crimes committed by juveniles under 18." The Court also discusses the International Covenant on Civil and Political Rights (ICCPR), which the Senate ratified only subject to a reservation that reads: "The United States reserves the right, subject to its Constitutional restraints, to impose capital punishment on any person (other than a pregnant woman) duly convicted under existing or future laws permitting the imposition of capital punishment, including such punishment for crime

That the Senate and the President—those actors our Constitution empowers to enter into treaties—have declined to join and ratify treaties prohibiting execution of under-18 offenders can only suggest that our country has either not reached a national consensus on the question, or has reached a consensus contrary to what the Court announces.

committed by persons below eighteen years of age." Unless the Court has added to its arsenal the power to join and ratify treaties on behalf of the United States, I cannot see how this evidence favors, rather than refutes, its position. That the Senate and the President—those actors our Constitution empowers to enter into treaties—have declined to join and ratify treaties prohibiting execution of under-18 offenders can only suggest that our country has either not reached a national consensus on the question, or has reached a consensus contrary to what the Court announces. That the reservation to the ICCPR was made in 1992 does not suggest otherwise, since the reservation still remains in place today. It is also worth noting that, in addition to barring the execution of under-18 offenders, the United Nations Convention on the Rights of the Child prohibits punishing them with life in prison without the possibility of release. If we are truly going to get in line with the international community, then the Court's reassurance that the death penalty is really not needed, since "the punishment of life imprisonment without the possibility of parole is itself a severe sanction" gives little comfort.

It is interesting that whereas the Court is not content to accept what the States of our Federal Union say, but insists on inquiring into what they do (specifically, whether they in fact apply the juvenile death penalty that their laws allow), the Court is quite willing to believe that every foreign nation—of whatever tyrannical political makeup and with however subservient or incompetent a court system—in fact adheres to a rule of no death penalty for offenders under 18. Nor does the Court inquire into how many of the countries that have the death penalty, but have forsworn (on paper at least) imposing that penalty on offenders under 18, have what no State of this country can constitutionally have: a mandatory death penalty for certain crimes, with no possibility of mitigation by the sentencing authority, for youth or any other reason. I suspect it is most of them. To forbid the death penalty for juveniles under such a system may be a good idea, but it says nothing about our system, in which the sentencing authority, typically a jury, always can, and almost always does, withhold the death penalty from an under-18 offender except, after considering all the circumstances, in the rare cases where it is warranted. The foreign authorities, in other words, do not even speak to the issue before us here.

More fundamentally, however, the basic premise of the Court's argument—that American law should conform to the laws of the rest of the world—ought to be rejected out of hand. In fact the Court itself does not believe it. In many significant respects the laws of most other countries differ from our law—including not only such explicit provisions of our Constitution as the right to jury trial and grand jury indictment, but even many interpretations of the Constitution prescribed by this Court itself. The Court-pronounced exclusionary rule, for example, is distinctively American. When we adopted that rule in *Mapp v. Ohio* (1961), it was "unique to American Jurisprudence." *Bivens v. Six Unknown Fed. Narcotics Agents* (1971). Since then a categorical exclusionary rule has been "universally rejected" by other countries, including those with rules prohibiting illegal searches and police misconduct, despite the fact that none of these countries "appears to have any alternative form of discipline for police that is effective in preventing search violations." Bradley, *Mapp* Goes Abroad, 52 Case W. Res. L. Rev. 375 (2001). England, for example, rarely excludes evidence found during an illegal search or seizure and has only recently begun excluding evidence from illegally obtained confessions. Canada rarely excludes evidence and will only do so if admission will "bring the administration of justice into disrepute." The European Court of Human Rights has held that introduction of illegally seized evidence does not violate the "fair trial" requirement in Article 6, § 1, of the European Convention on Human Rights.

The Court has been oblivious to the views of other countries when deciding how to interpret our Constitution's requirement that "Congress shall make no law respecting an establishment of religion...." Most other countries—including those committed to religious neutrality—do not insist on the degree of separation between church and state that this Court requires. For example, whereas "we have recognized special Establishment Clause dangers where the government makes direct money payments to sectarian institutions," *Rosenberger v. Rector and Visitors of Univ. of Va.* (1995), countries such as the Netherlands, Germany, and Australia allow direct government funding of religious schools on the ground that "the state can only be truly neutral between secular and religious perspectives if it does not dominate the provision of so key a service as education, and makes it possible for people to exercise their right of religious expression within the context of public funding." S. Monsma & J. Soper, *The Challenge of Pluralism: Church and State in Five Democracies* (1997). England permits the teaching of religion in state schools. *Id.* Even in France, which is considered "America's only rival in strictness of church-state separation," "[t]he practice of contracting for educational services provided by Catholic schools is very widespread." C. Glenn, *The Ambiguous Embrace: Government and Faith-Based Schools and Social Agencies* (2000).

> *And let us not forget the Court's abortion jurisprudence, which makes us one of only six countries that allow abortion on demand until the point of viability.*

And let us not forget the Court's abortion jurisprudence, which makes us one of only six countries that allow abortion on demand until the point of viability. Though the Government and amici in cases following *Roe v. Wade* (1973) urged the Court to follow the international community's lead, these arguments fell on deaf ears.

The Court's special reliance on the laws of the United Kingdom is perhaps the most indefensible part of its opinion. It is of course true that we share a common history with the United Kingdom, and that we often consult English sources when asked to discern the meaning of a constitutional text written against the backdrop of 18th-century English law and legal thought. If we applied that approach today, our task would be an easy one. As we explained in *Harmelin v. Michigan* (1991), the "Cruell and Unusuall Punishments" provision of the English Declaration of Rights was originally meant to describe those punishments " 'out of [the Judges'] Power' "—that is, those punishments that were not authorized by common law or statute, but that were nonetheless administered by the Crown or the Crown's judges. Under that reasoning, the death penalty for under-18 offenders would easily survive this challenge. The Court has, however—I think wrongly—long rejected a purely originalist approach to our Eighth Amendment, and that is certainly not the approach the Court takes today. Instead, the Court undertakes the majestic task of determining (and thereby prescribing) our Nation's current standards of decency. It is beyond comprehension why we should look, for that purpose, to a country that has developed, in the centuries since the Revolutionary War—and with increasing speed since the United Kingdom's recent submission to the jurisprudence of European courts dominated by continental jurists—a legal, political, and social culture quite different from our own. If we took the Court's directive seriously, we would also consider relaxing our double jeopardy prohibition, since the British Law Commission recently published a report that would significantly extend the rights of the prosecution to appeal cases where an acquittal was the result of a judge's ruling that was legally incorrect. We would also curtail our right to jury trial in criminal cases since, despite the jury system's deep roots in our shared common law, England now permits all but the most serious offenders to be tried by magistrates without a jury.

The Court should either profess its willingness to reconsider all these matters in light of the views of foreigners, or else it should cease putting forth foreigners' views as part of the reasoned basis of its decisions. To invoke alien law when it agrees with one's own thinking, and ignore it otherwise, is not reasoned decisionmaking, but sophistry.

The Court responds that "[i]t does not lessen our fidelity to the Constitution or our pride in its origins to acknowledge that the express affirmation of certain fundamental rights by other nations and peoples simply underscores the centrality of those same rights within our own heritage of freedom." To begin with, I do not believe that approval by "other nations and peoples" should buttress our commitment to American principles any more than (what should logically follow) disapproval by "other nations and peoples" should weaken that commitment. More importantly, however, the Court's statement flatly misdescribes what is going on here. Foreign sources are cited today, not to underscore our "fidelity" to the Constitution, our "pride in its origins," and "our own [American] heritage." To the contrary, they are cited to set aside the centuries-old American practice—a practice still engaged in by a large majority of the relevant States—of letting a jury of 12 citizens decide whether, in the particular case, youth should be the basis for withholding the death penalty. What these foreign sources "affirm," rather than repudiate, is the Justices' own notion of how the world ought to be, and their diktat that it shall be so henceforth in America. The Court's parting attempt to downplay the significance of its extensive discussion of foreign law is unconvincing. "Acknowledgment" of foreign approval has no place in the legal opinion of this Court unless it is part of the basis for the Court's judgment—which is surely what it parades as today.

IV

To add insult to injury, the Court affirms the Missouri Supreme Court without even admonishing that court for its flagrant disregard of our precedent in *Stanford*. Until today, we have always held that "it is this Court's prerogative alone to overrule one of its precedents." *State Oil Co. v. Khan* (1997). That has been true even where "'changes in judicial doctrine' ha[ve] significantly undermined" our prior holding, *United States v. Hatter* (2001), and even where our prior holding "appears to rest on reasons rejected in some other line of decisions," *Rodriguez de Quijas v. Shearson/American Express, Inc.* (1989). Today, however, the Court silently approves a state-court decision that blatantly rejected controlling precedent.

One must admit that the Missouri Supreme Court's action, and this Court's indulgent reaction, are, in a way, understandable. In a system based upon constitutional and statutory text democratically adopted, the concept of "law" ordinarily signifies that particular words have a fixed meaning. Such law does not change, and this Court's pronouncement of it therefore remains authoritative until (confessing our prior error) we overrule. The Court has purported to make of the Eighth Amendment, however, a mirror of the passing and changing sentiment of American society regarding penology. The lower courts can look into that mirror as well as we can; and what we saw 15 years ago bears no necessary relationship to what they see today. Since they are not looking at the same text, but at a different scene, why should our earlier decision control their judgment?

> *However sound philosophically, this is no way to run a legal system.*

However sound philosophically, this is no way to run a legal system. We must disregard the new reality that, to the extent our Eighth Amendment decisions constitute something more than a show of hands on the current Justices' current personal views about penology, they purport to be nothing more than a snapshot of American public opinion at a particular point in time (with the timeframes now shortened to a mere 15 years). We must treat these decisions just as though they represented real law, real prescriptions democratically adopted by the American people, as conclusively (rather than sequentially) construed by this Court. Allowing lower courts to reinterpret the Eighth Amendment whenever they decide enough time has passed for a new snapshot leaves this Court's decisions without any force— especially since the "evolution" of our Eighth Amendment is no longer determined by objective criteria. To allow lower courts to behave as we do, "updating" the Eighth Amendment as needed, destroys stability and makes our case law an unreliable basis for the designing of laws by citizens and their representatives, and for action by public officials. The result will be to crown arbitrariness with chaos.

GLOSSIP v. GROSS (2015)

During his tenure on the Supreme Court, Justice Scalia saw a handful of his colleagues embrace the view that the death penalty is always "cruel and unusual," and thus unconstitutional. In 1994, Justice Harry Blackmun had done so. He announced in a dissenting opinion that he would no longer "tinker with machinery of death."[4] He wrote of the defendant facing death, "Intravenous tubes attached to his arms will carry the instrument of death, a toxic fluid designed specifically for the purpose of killing human beings. The witness, standing a few feet away, will behold [him], no longer a defendant, an appellant, or a petitioner, but a man, strapped to a gurney, and seconds away from extinction." It is not clear if Blackmun included such specifics in an attempt to elicit sympathy for the convicted murderer. Whatever Blackmun's motivation, Justice Scalia chose to respond to Blackmun's dissent and argued that lethal injection seems benign compared to the death suffered by most victims of the killers on death row. Scalia wrote:

> The death-by-injection which Justice Blackmun describes looks pretty desirable next to...some of the other cases currently before us which Justice Blackmun did not select as the vehicle for his announcement that the death penalty is always unconstitutional—for example, the case of the 11-year-old girl raped by four men and then killed by stuffing her panties down her throat. How enviable a quiet death by lethal injection compared with that! If the people conclude that such more brutal deaths may be deterred by capital punishment; indeed, if they merely conclude that justice requires such brutal deaths to be avenged by capital punishment; the creation of false, untextual and unhistorical contradictions with "the Court's Eighth Amendment jurisprudence" should not prevent them.

Eleven years later, Justice Stephen Breyer assumed the role of death penalty prohibitionist. In *Glossip v. Gross* (2015), the Court was asked to decide whether the use of the drug midazolam in Oklahoma's execution protocol entailed a substantial risk of severe pain, compared with other alternatives, and was therefore unconstitutionally cruel and unusual. A 5–4 majority answered in the negative, holding that the drug did not create such a risk.

Justice Stephen Breyer wrote a dissent in which he stated that he no longer believed the death penalty was constitutional. He said that capital punishment: (1) is unreliable, resulting in innocent people being executed; (2) is applied arbitrarily, with some criminals facing death after committing less egregious crimes than others who were not sentenced to die; (3) is carried out so slowly, which reduces the death penalty's deterrent value and results in inmates spending long (and "cruel") periods on death row. Breyer argued that these factors have led the country to move away from the death penalty, thus making it an "unusual" punishment.

Justice Scalia concurred with the Court's decision, but wrote a brief separate opinion to address what he described as "Justice Breyer's plea for judicial abolition of the death penalty." Scalia dismissed Breyer's argument as "full of internal contradictions and (it must be said) gobbledy-gook." As he had argued many times before, Scalia wrote that since the Constitution specifically contemplates capital punishment—the Fifth Amendment refers to "a capital...crime"—the Court did not have the authority to declare that punishment unconstitutional.

⚜

Justice Scalia, with whom Justice Thomas joins, concurring.

I join the opinion of the Court, and write to respond to Justice Breyer's plea for judicial abolition of the death penalty.

Welcome to Groundhog Day. The scene is familiar: Petitioners, sentenced to die for the crimes they committed (including, in the case of one petitioner since put to death, raping and murdering an 11-month-old baby), come before this Court asking us to nullify their sentences as "cruel and unusual" under the Eighth Amendment. They rely on this provision because it is the only provision they *can* rely on. They were charged by a sovereign State with murder. They were afforded counsel and tried before a jury of their peers—tried twice, once to determine whether they were guilty and once to determine whether death was the appropriate sentence. They were duly convicted and sentenced. They were granted the right to appeal and to seek postconviction relief, first in state and then in federal court. And now, acknowledging that their convictions are unassailable, they ask us for clemency, as though clemency were ours to give.

The response is also familiar: A vocal minority of the Court, waving over their heads a ream of the most recent abolitionist studies (a superabundant genre) as though they have discovered the lost folios of Shakespeare, insist that *now*, at long last, the death penalty must be abolished for good. Mind you, not once in the history of the American Republic has this Court ever suggested the death penalty is categorically impermissible. The reason is obvious: It is impossible to hold unconstitutional that which the Constitution explicitly *contemplates*. The Fifth Amendment provides that "[n]o person shall be held to answer for a capital...crime, unless on a presentment or indictment

> *A vocal minority of the Court, waving over their heads a ream of the most recent abolitionist studies (a superabundant genre) as though they have discovered the lost folios of Shakespeare, insist that now, at long last, the death penalty must be abolished for good.*

of a Grand Jury," and that no person shall be "deprived of life...without due process of law." Nevertheless, today Justice Breyer takes on the role of the abolitionists in this long-running drama, arguing that the text of the Constitution and two centuries of history must yield to his "20 years of experience on this Court," and inviting full briefing on the continued permissibility of capital punishment.

Historically, the Eighth Amendment was understood to bar only those punishments that added "'terror, pain, or disgrace'" to an otherwise permissible capital sentence. *Baze v. Rees*, (2008). Rather than bother with this troubling detail, Justice Breyer elects to contort the constitutional text. Redefining "cruel" to mean "unreliable," "arbitrary," or causing "excessive delays," and "unusual" to include a "decline in use," he proceeds to offer up a white paper devoid of any meaningful legal argument.

Even accepting Justice Breyer's rewriting of the Eighth Amendment, his argument is full of internal contradictions and (it must be said) gobbledy-gook. He says that the death penalty is cruel because it is unreliable; but it is *convictions*, not *punishments*, that are unreliable. Moreover, the "pressure on police, prosecutors, and jurors to secure a conviction," which he claims increases the risk of wrongful convictions in capital cases, flows from the nature of the crime, not the punishment that follows its commission. Justice Breyer acknowledges as much: "[T]he crimes at issue in capital cases are typically horrendous murders, and thus accompanied by intense community pressure." That same pressure would exist, and the same risk of wrongful convictions, if horrendous death-penalty cases were converted into

Even accepting Justice Breyer's rewriting of the Eighth Amendment, his argument is full of internal contradictions and (it must be said) gobbledy-gook.

equally horrendous life-without-parole cases. The reality is that any innocent defendant is infinitely better off appealing a death sentence than a sentence of life imprisonment. (Which, again, Justice Breyer acknowledges: "[C]ourts (or State Governors) are 130 times more likely to exonerate a defendant where a death sentence is at issue.") The capital convict will obtain endless legal assistance from the abolition lobby (and legal favoritism from abolitionist judges), while the lifer languishes unnoticed behind bars.

Justice Breyer next says that the death penalty is cruel because it is arbitrary. To prove this point, he points to a study of 205 cases that "measured the 'egregiousness' of the murderer's conduct" with "a system of metrics," and then "compared the egregiousness of the conduct of the 9 defendants sentenced to death with the egregiousness of the conduct of defendants in the remaining 196 cases [who were not sentenced to death]." If only Aristotle, Aquinas, and Hume knew that moral philosophy could be so neatly distilled into a pocket-sized, *vade mecum* "system of metrics." Of course it cannot: Egregiousness is a moral judgment susceptible of few hard-and-fast rules. More importantly, egregiousness of the crime is only one of several factors that render a punishment condign—culpability, rehabilitative potential, and the need for deterrence also are relevant. That is why this Court has required an individualized consideration of all mitigating circumstances, rather than formulaic application of some egregiousness test.

It is because these questions are contextual and admit of no easy answers that we rely on juries to make judgments about the people and crimes before them. The fact that these judgments may vary across cases is an inevitable consequence of the jury trial, that cornerstone of Anglo-American judicial procedure. But when a punishment is authorized by law—if you kill you are subject to death—the fact that some defendants receive mercy from their jury no more renders the underlying punishment "cruel" than does the fact that some guilty individuals are never apprehended, are never tried, are acquitted, or are pardoned.

Justice Breyer's third reason that the death penalty is cruel is that it entails delay, thereby (1) subjecting inmates to long periods on death row and (2) undermining the penological justifications of the death penalty. The first point is nonsense. Life without parole is an even lengthier period than the wait on death row; and if the objection is that death row is a more confining environment, the solution should be modifying the environment rather than abolishing the death penalty. As for the argument that delay undermines the penological rationales for the death penalty: In insisting that "the major alternative to capital punishment—namely, life in prison without possibility of parole—also incapacitates," Justice Breyer apparently forgets that one of the plaintiffs *in this very case* was already in prison when he committed the murder that landed him on death row. Justice Breyer further asserts that "whatever interest in retribution might be served by the death penalty as currently administered, that interest can be served almost as well by a sentence of life in prison without parole." My goodness. If he thinks the death penalty not much more harsh (and hence not much more retributive), why is he so keen to get rid of it? With all due respect, whether the death penalty and life imprisonment constitute more-or-less equivalent retribution is a question far above the judiciary's pay grade. Perhaps Justice Breyer is more forgiving—or more enlightened—than those who, like Kant, believe that death is the only just punishment for taking a life. I would not presume to tell parents whose life has been forever altered by the brutal murder of a child that life imprisonment is punishment enough.

And finally, Justice Breyer speculates that it does not "seem likely" that the death penalty has a "significant" deterrent effect. It seems very likely to me, and there are statistical studies that say so. See, *e.g.,* Zimmerman, State Executions, Deterrence, and the Incidence of Murder, J. Applied Econ. (2004) ("[I]t is estimated that each state execution deters approximately fourteen murders per year on average"); Dezhbakhsh, Rubin, & Shepherd, Does Capital Punishment Have a Deterrent Effect? New Evidence from Postmoratorium Panel Data, Am. L. & Econ. Rev. (2003) ("[E]ach execution results, on average, in eighteen fewer murders" per year); Sunstein & Vermeule, Is Capital Punishment Morally Required? Acts, Omissions, and Life-Life Tradeoffs, Stan. L. Rev. (2005) ("All in all, the recent evidence of a deterrent effect from capital punishment seems impressive, especially in light of its 'apparent power and unanimity' "). But we federal judges live in a world apart from the vast majority of Americans. After work, we retire to homes in placid suburbia or to high-rise co-ops with guards at the door. We are not confronted with the threat of violence that is ever present in many Americans' everyday lives. The suggestion that the incremental deterrent effect of capital punishment does not seem "significant" reflects, it seems to me, a let-them-eat-cake obliviousness to the needs of others. Let the People decide how much incremental deterrence is appropriate.

Of course, this delay is a problem of the Court's own making. As Justice Breyer concedes, for more than 160 years, capital sentences were carried out in an average of two years or less. But by 2014, he tells us, it took an average of 18 years to carry out a death sentence. What happened in the intervening years? Nothing other than the proliferation of labyrinthine restrictions on capital punishment, promulgated by this Court under an interpretation of the Eighth

Amendment that empowered it to divine "the evolving standards of decency that mark the progress of a maturing society," *Trop v. Dulles* (1958)—a task for which we are eminently ill suited. Indeed, for the past two decades, Justice Breyer has been the Drum Major in this parade. His invocation of the resultant delay as grounds for abolishing the death penalty calls to mind the man sentenced to death for killing his parents, who pleads for mercy on the ground that he is an orphan. Amplifying the surrealism of his argument, Justice Breyer uses the fact that many States have abandoned capital punishment— have abandoned it *precisely because of* the costs those suspect decisions have imposed—to conclude that it is now "unusual." (A caution to the reader: Do not use the creative arithmetic that Justice Breyer employs in counting the number of States that use the death penalty when you prepare your next tax return; outside the world of our Eighth Amendment abolitionist-inspired jurisprudence, it will be regarded as more misrepresentation than math.)

> *His invocation of the resultant delay as grounds for abolishing the death penalty calls to mind the man sentenced to death for killing his parents, who pleads for mercy on the ground that he is an orphan.*

If we were to travel down the path that Justice Breyer sets out for us and once again consider the constitutionality of the death penalty, I would ask that counsel also brief whether our cases that have abandoned the historical understanding of the Eighth Amendment, beginning with *Trop*, should be overruled. That case has caused more mischief to our jurisprudence, to our federal system, and to our society than any other that comes to mind. Justice Breyer's dissent is the living refutation of *Trop*'s assumption that this Court has the capacity to recognize "evolving standards of decency." Time and again, the People have voted to exact the death penalty as punishment for the most serious of crimes. Time and again, this Court has upheld that decision. And time and again, a vocal minority of this Court has insisted that things have "changed radically," and has sought to replace the judgments of the People with their own standards of decency.

Capital punishment presents moral questions that philosophers, theologians, and statesmen have grappled with for millennia. The Framers of our Constitution disagreed bitterly on the matter. For that reason, they handled it the same way they handled many other controversial issues: they left it to the People to decide. By arrogating to himself the power to overturn that decision, Justice Breyer does not just reject the death penalty, he rejects the Enlightenment.

CHAPTER EIGHT

RIGHTS OF THE ACCUSED

～✕◯✚◯✕～

J USTICE SCALIA'S FORCEFUL opinions in defense of the constitutionality of the death penalty led some people to assume he favored the interests of law enforcement over the rights of criminal defendants. His record, however, revealed a fidelity to fundamental constitutional guarantees, such as the Fourth Amendment's protection against unreasonable searches and seizures, which frequently brought him down on the side of the accused.

Scalia was widely and rightly credited with single-handedly reviving the Sixth Amendment's guarantee that "[i]n all criminal prosecutions, the accused shall enjoy the right... to be confronted with the witnesses against him." Before Scalia joined the Court, it had held that out-of-court statements could be used against a defendant if they were deemed reliable. Scalia convinced his colleagues that the Framers guaranteed the accused more than that, giving them the right to confront witnesses and cross-examine their testimony.

Justice Scalia also sought to ensure that innocent Americans would not be ensnared by vaguely worded criminal laws. In *Sykes v. United States* (2011), he wrote:

We face a Congress that puts forth an ever-increasing volume of laws in general, and of criminal laws in particular. It should be no surprise that as the volume increases, so do the number of imprecise laws. And no surprise that our indulgence of imprecisions that violate the Constitution encourages imprecisions that violate the Constitution. Fuzzy, leave-the-details-to-be-sorted-out-by-the-courts legislation is attractive to the Congressman who wants credit for addressing a national problem but does not have the time (or perhaps the votes) to grapple with the nitty-gritty. In the field of criminal law, at least, it is time to call a halt.[1]

In *Sykes*, Scalia inveighed against a vague provision of the Armed Career Criminal Act, which imposed tough minimum prison sentences on persons who previously had been convicted of three violent felonies. Scalia argued for years that a provision of the law was unconstitutionally vague, and in *Johnson v. United States* (2015) he convinced his colleagues to strike it down. Scalia wrote that the Fifth Amendment's Due Process Clause prohibits the government from "taking away someone's life, liberty, or property under a criminal law so vague that it fails to give ordinary people fair notice of the conduct it punishes, or so standardless that it invites arbitrary enforcement."[2]

Finally, Justice Scalia was a strong defender of the Fourth Amendment's protection against unreasonable searches and seizures. In cases involving law enforcement's use of modern technology, such as thermal imaging to search a house for contraband or a GPS monitor to track a suspected criminal's car, Scalia came down time after time on the side of the defendant and the Constitution.

MARYLAND v. KING (2013)

While Alonzo King was booked on assault charges and processed, the police took a DNA sample with a cheek swab. The swab linked him to an unsolved 2003 rape, and King was charged with that crime. He moved to suppress the DNA match, arguing that the Maryland law permitting the DNA swab was a violation of his Fourth Amendment protection against unreasonable searches and seizures. The circuit court upheld the law, and King was convicted of rape, but the Maryland Court of Appeals agreed with King, struck down the act, and set aside King's conviction.

Writing for a 5–4 majority, Justice Kennedy ruled that taking and analyzing a cheek swab of an arrestee's DNA is, like fingerprinting and photographing, a legitimate law enforcement activity and reasonable under the Fourth Amendment. The majority stressed that DNA testing can improve the criminal justice system by helping law enforcement officers to accurately identify who is being taken into custody. This important benefit, the Court argued, outweighs the minor intrusion of a cheek swab on people who are charged with violent crimes.

Justice Scalia wrote a dissent that was joined by three of his liberal colleagues, Justices Ginsburg, Sotomayor, and Kagan. He argued that the Fourth Amendment prohibits law enforcement from searching a person for evidence of a crime without cause. Suspicionless searches, he argued, have been permitted only where the police have a justifying motive apart from the investigation of a crime. There was no such motive in King's case, Scalia argued.

More broadly, Scalia pointed out, "What DNA adds—what makes it a valuable weapon in the law-enforcement arsenal—is the ability to solve unsolved crimes, by matching old crime-scene evidence against the profiles of people whose identities are already known." That is what clearly was going in King's case, Scalia said, and it was not enough to justify a suspicionless search.

"Solving unsolved crimes is a noble objective," Scalia wrote, "but it occupies a lower place in the American pantheon of noble objectives than the protection of our people from suspicionless law-enforcement searches. The Fourth Amendment must prevail."

After the Court ruled in *Maryland v. King*, the left-leaning constitutional scholar Jeffrey Rosen wrote that Scalia's opinion was "not only one of his own best Fourth Amendment dissents, but one of the best Fourth Amendment dissents ever."

❧

Justice Scalia, with whom Justice Ginsburg, Justice Sotomayor, and Justice Kagan join, dissenting.

The Fourth Amendment forbids searching a person for evidence of a crime when there is no basis for believing the person is guilty of the crime or is in possession of incriminating evidence. That prohibition is categorical and without exception; it lies at the very heart of the Fourth Amendment. Whenever this Court has allowed a suspicionless search, it has insisted upon a justifying motive apart from the investigation of crime.

It is obvious that no such noninvestigative motive exists in this case. The Court's assertion that DNA is being taken, not to solve crimes, but to identify those in the State's custody, taxes the credulity of the credulous. And the Court's comparison of Maryland's DNA searches to other techniques, such as fingerprinting, can seem apt only to those who know no more than today's opinion has chosen to tell them about how those DNA searches actually work.

I

A

At the time of the Founding, Americans despised the British use of so-called "general warrants"—warrants not grounded upon a sworn oath of a specific infraction by a particular individual, and thus not limited in scope and application. The first Virginia Constitution declared that "general warrants, whereby any officer or messenger may be commanded to search suspected places without evidence of a fact committed," or to search a person "whose offence is not particularly described and supported by evidence," "are grievous and oppressive, and ought not be granted." Va. Declaration of Rights § 10 (1776). The Maryland Declaration of Rights similarly provided that general warrants were "illegal."

In the ratification debates, Antifederalists sarcastically predicted that the general, suspicionless warrant would be among the Constitution's "blessings." "Brutus" of New York asked why the Federal Constitution contained no provision like Maryland's, and Patrick Henry warned that the new Federal Constitution would expose the citizenry to searches and seizures "in the most arbitrary manner, without any evidence or reason." 3 Debates on the Federal Constitution 588 (J. Elliot 2d ed. 1854).

Madison's draft of what became the Fourth Amendment answered these charges by providing that the "rights of the people to be secured in their persons...from all unreasonable searches and seizures, shall not be violated by warrants issued without probable cause...or not particularly describing the places to be searched." 1 Annals of Cong. 434–435 (1789). As ratified, the Fourth Amendment's Warrant Clause forbids a warrant to "issue" except "upon probable cause," and requires that it be "particula[r]" (which is to say, individualized) to "the place to be searched, and the persons or things to be seized." And we have held that, even when a warrant is not constitutionally necessary, the Fourth Amendment's general prohibition of "unreasonable" searches imports the same requirement of individualized suspicion. See *Chandler v. Miller* (1997).

Although there is a "closely guarded category of constitutionally permissible suspicionless searches," id., that has never included searches designed to serve "the normal need for law enforcement," *Skinner v. Railway Labor Executives' Assn.* (1989). Even the common name for suspicionless searches—"special needs" searches—itself reflects that they must be justified, always, by concerns "other than crime detection." *Chandler.* We have approved random drug tests of railroad employees, yes—but only because the Government's need to "regulat[e] the conduct of railroad employees to ensure safety" is distinct from "normal law enforcement." *Skinner.* So too we have approved suspicionless searches in public schools—but only because there the government acts in furtherance of its "responsibilities. . . as guardian and tutor of children entrusted to its care." *Vernonia School Dist. 47J v. Acton* (1995).

So while the Court is correct to note that there are instances in which we have permitted searches without individualized suspicion, "[i]n none of these cases. . . did we indicate approval of a [search] whose primary purpose was to detect evidence of ordinary criminal wrongdoing." *Indianapolis v. Edmond* (2000). That limitation is crucial. It is only when a governmental purpose aside from crime-solving is at stake that we engage in the free-form "reasonableness" inquiry that the Court indulges at length today. To put it another way, both the legitimacy of the Court's method and the correctness of its outcome hinge entirely on the truth of a single proposition: that the primary purpose of these DNA searches is something other than simply discovering evidence of criminal wrongdoing. As I detail below, that proposition is wrong.

B

The Court alludes at several points to the fact that King was an arrestee, and arrestees may be validly searched incident to their arrest. But the Court does not really rest on this principle, and for good reason: The objects of a search incident to arrest must be either (1) weapons or evidence that might easily be destroyed, or (2) evidence relevant to the crime of arrest. Neither is the object of the search at issue here.

The Court hastens to clarify that it does not mean to approve invasive surgery on arrestees or warrantless searches of their homes. That the Court feels the need to disclaim these consequences is as damning a criticism of its suspicionless-search regime as any I can muster. And the Court's attempt to distinguish those hypothetical searches from this real one is unconvincing. We are told that the "privacy-related concerns" in the search of a home "are weighty enough that the search may require a warrant, notwithstanding the diminished expectations of privacy of the arrestee." But why are the "privacy-related concerns" not also "weighty" when an intrusion into the body is at stake? (The Fourth Amendment lists "persons" first among the entities protected against unreasonable searches and seizures.) And could the police engage, without any suspicion of wrongdoing, in a "brief and... minimal" intrusion into the home of an arrestee—perhaps just peeking around the curtilage a bit? Obviously not.

At any rate, all this discussion is beside the point. No matter the degree of invasiveness, suspicionless searches are never allowed if their principal end is ordinary crime-solving. A search incident to arrest either serves other ends (such as officer safety, in a search for weapons) or is not suspicionless (as when there is reason to believe the arrestee possesses evidence relevant to the crime of arrest).

Sensing (correctly) that it needs more, the Court elaborates at length the ways that the search here served the special purpose of "identifying" King. But that seems to me quite wrong—unless what one means by "identifying" someone is "searching for evidence that he has committed crimes unrelated to the crime of his arrest." At points the Court does appear to use "identifying" in that peculiar sense—claiming, for example, that knowing "an arrestee's past conduct is essential to an assessment of the danger he poses." If identifying someone means finding out what unsolved crimes he has committed, then identification is indistinguishable from the ordinary law-enforcement aims that have never been thought to justify a suspicionless search. Searching every lawfully stopped car, for example, might turn up information about unsolved crimes the driver had committed, but no one would say that such a search was aimed at "identifying" him, and no court would hold such a search lawful. I will therefore assume that the Court means that the DNA search at issue here was useful to "identify" King in the normal sense of that word—in the sense that

> *I will therefore assume that the Court means that the DNA search at issue here was useful to "identify" King in the normal sense of that word—in the sense that would identify the author of Introduction to the Principles of Morals and Legislation as Jeremy Bentham.*

would identify the author of Introduction to the Principles of Morals and Legislation as Jeremy Bentham.

1

The portion of the Court's opinion that explains the identification rationale is strangely silent on the actual workings of the DNA search at issue here. To know those facts is to be instantly disabused of the notion that what happened had anything to do with identifying King.

King was arrested on April 10, 2009, on charges unrelated to the case before us. That same day, April 10, the police searched him and seized the DNA evidence at issue here. What happened next? Reading the Court's opinion, particularly its insistence that the search was necessary to know "who [had] been arrested," one might guess that King's DNA was swiftly processed and his identity thereby confirmed—perhaps against some master database of known DNA profiles, as is done for fingerprints. After all, was not the suspicionless search here crucial to avoid "inordinate risks for facility staff" or to "existing detainee population"? Surely, then— surely—the State of Maryland got cracking on those grave risks immediately, by rushing to identify King with his DNA as soon as possible.

Nothing could be further from the truth. Maryland officials did not even begin the process of testing King's DNA that day. Or, actually, the next day. Or the day after that. And that was for a simple reason: Maryland law forbids them to do so. A "DNA sample collected from an individual charged with a crime ... may not be tested or placed in the statewide DNA data base system prior to the first scheduled arraignment date." Md. Pub. Saf. Code Ann. § 2-504(d) (1). And King's first appearance in court was not until three days after his arrest. (I suspect, though, that they did not wait three days to ask his name or take his fingerprints.)

This places in a rather different light the Court's solemn declaration that the search here was necessary so that King could be identified at "every stage of the criminal process." I hope that the Maryland officials who read the Court's opinion do not take it seriously. Acting on the Court's misperception of Maryland law could lead to jail time. See Md. Pub. Saf. Code Ann. § 2-512(c)–(e) (punishing by up to five years' imprisonment anyone who obtains or tests DNA information except as provided by statute). Does the Court really believe that Maryland did not know whom it was arraigning? The Court's response is to imagine that release on bail could take so long that the DNA results are returned in time, or perhaps that bail could be revoked if the DNA test turned up incriminating information. That is no answer at all. If the purpose of this Act is to assess "whether [King] should be released on bail," why would it possibly forbid the DNA testing process to begin until King was arraigned? Why would Maryland resign itself to simply hoping that the bail decision will drag out long enough that the "identification" can succeed before the arrestee is released? The truth, known to Maryland and increasingly to the reader: this search had nothing to do with establishing King's identity.

> *The truth, known to Maryland and increasingly to the reader: this search had nothing to do with establishing King's identity.*

It gets worse. King's DNA sample was not received by the Maryland State Police's Forensic Sciences Division until April 23, 2009—two weeks after his arrest. It sat in that office, ripening in a storage area, until the custodians got around to mailing it to a lab for testing on June 25, 2009—two months after it was received, and nearly three since King's arrest. After it was mailed, the data from the lab tests were not available for several more weeks, until July 13, 2009, which is when the test results were entered into Maryland's DNA database, together with information identifying the person from whom the sample was taken. Meanwhile, bail had been set, King had engaged in discovery, and he had requested a speedy trial—presumably not a trial of John Doe. It was not until August 4, 2009—four months after King's arrest—that the forwarded sample transmitted (without identifying information) from the Maryland DNA database to the Federal Bureau of Investigation's national database was matched with a sample taken from the scene of an unrelated crime years earlier.

A more specific description of exactly what happened at this point illustrates why, by definition, King could not have been identified by this match. The FBI's DNA database (known as CODIS) consists of two distinct collections. One of them, the one to which King's DNA was submitted, consists of DNA samples taken from known convicts or arrestees. I will refer to this as the "Convict and Arrestee Collection." The other collection consists of samples taken from crime scenes; I will refer to this as the "Unsolved Crimes Collection." The Convict and Arrestee Collection stores "no names or other personal identifiers of the offenders, arrestees, or detainees." Rather, it contains only the DNA profile itself, the name of the agency that submitted it, the laboratory personnel who analyzed it, and an identification number for the specimen. This is because the submitting state laboratories are expected already to know the identities of the convicts and arrestees from whom samples are taken. (And, of course, they do.)

Moreover, the CODIS system works by checking to see whether any of the samples in the Unsolved Crimes Collection match any of the samples in the Convict and Arrestee Collection. That is sensible, if what one wants to do is solve those cold cases, but note what it requires: that the identity of the people whose DNA has been entered in the Convict and Arrestee Collection already be known. If one wanted to identify someone in custody using his DNA, the logical thing to do would be to compare that DNA against the Convict and Arrestee Collection: to search, in other words, the collection that could be used (by checking back with the submitting state agency) to identify people, rather than the collection of evidence from unsolved crimes, whose perpetrators are by definition unknown. But that is not what was done. And that is because this search had nothing to do with identification.

In fact, if anything was "identified" at the moment that the DNA database returned a match, it was not King—his identity was already known. (The docket for the original criminal charges lists his full name, his race, his sex, his height, his weight, his date of birth, and his address.) Rather, what the August 4 match "identified" was the previously-taken sample from the earlier crime. That sample was genuinely mysterious to Maryland; the State knew that it had probably been left by the victim's attacker, but nothing else. King was not identified by his association with the sample; rather, the sample was identified by its association with King. The Court effectively destroys its own "identification" theory when it acknowledges that the object of this search was "to see what [was] already known about [King]." King was who he was, and volumes of his biography could not make him any more or any less King. No minimally competent speaker of English would say, upon noticing a known arrestee's similarity "to a wanted poster of a previously unidentified suspect," that the arrestee had thereby been identified. It was the previously unidentified suspect who had been identified—just as, here, it was the previously unidentified rapist.

2

That taking DNA samples from arrestees has nothing to do with identifying them is confirmed not just by actual practice (which the Court ignores) but by the enabling statute itself (which the Court also ignores). The Maryland Act at issue has a section helpfully entitled "Purpose of collecting and testing DNA samples." Md. Pub. Saf. Code Ann. § 2-505. (One would expect such a section to play a somewhat larger role in the Court's analysis of the Act's purpose—which is to say, at least some role.) That provision lists five purposes for which DNA samples may be tested. By this point, it will not surprise the reader to learn that the Court's imagined purpose is not among them.

Instead, the law provides that DNA samples are collected and tested, as a matter of Maryland law, "as part of an official investigation into a crime." (Or, as our suspicionless-search cases would put it: for ordinary law-enforcement purposes.) That is certainly how everyone has always understood the Maryland Act until today. The Governor of Maryland, in commenting on our decision to hear this case, said that he was glad, because "[a]llowing law enforcement to collect DNA samples...is absolutely critical to our efforts to continue driving down crime," and "bolsters our efforts to resolve open investigations and bring them to a resolution." The attorney general of Maryland remarked that he "look[ed] forward to the opportunity to defend this important crime-fighting tool," and praised the DNA database for helping to "bring to justice violent perpetrators." Even this Court's order staying the decision below states that the statute "provides a valuable tool for investigating unsolved crimes and thereby helping to remove violent offenders from the general population"—with, unsurprisingly, no mention of identity.

More devastating still for the Court's "identification" theory, the statute does enumerate two instances in which a DNA sample may be tested for the purpose of identification: "to help identify human remains," and "to help identify missing individuals." No mention of identifying arrestees. Inclusio unius est exclusio alterius. And note again that Maryland forbids using DNA records "for any purposes other than those specified"—it is actually a crime to do so.

The Maryland regulations implementing the Act confirm what is now monotonously obvious: These DNA searches have nothing to do with identification. For example, if someone is arrested and law enforcement determines that "a convicted offender State-wide DNA Data Base sample already exists" for that arrestee, "the agency is not required to obtain a new sample." But how could the State know if an arrestee has already had his DNA sample collected, if the point of the sample is to identify who he is? Of course, if the DNA sample is instead taken in order to investigate crimes, this restriction makes perfect sense: Having previously placed an identified someone's DNA on file to check against available crime-scene evidence, there is no sense in going to the expense of taking a new sample. Maryland's regulations further require that the "individual collecting a sample... verify the identity of the individual from whom a sample is taken by name and, if applicable, State identification (SID) number." (But how?) And after the sample is taken, it continues to be identified by the individual's name, fingerprints, etc.—rather than (as the Court believes) being used to identify individuals.

So, to review: DNA testing does not even begin until after arraignment and bail decisions are already made. The samples sit in storage for months, and take weeks to test. When they are tested, they are checked against the Unsolved Crimes Collection—rather than the Convict and Arrestee Collection, which could be used to identify them. The Act forbids the Court's purpose (identification), but prescribes as its purpose what our suspicionless-search cases forbid ("official investigation into a crime"). Against all of that, it is safe to say that if the Court's identification theory is not wrong, there is no such thing as error.

It is safe to say that if the Court's identification theory is not wrong, there is no such thing as error.

II

The Court also attempts to bolster its identification theory with a series of inapposite analogies.

Is not taking DNA samples the same, asks the Court, as taking a person's photograph? No—because that is not a Fourth Amendment search at all. It does not involve a physical intrusion onto the person, and we have never held that merely taking a person's photograph invades any recognized "expectation of privacy," see *Katz v. United States* (1967). Thus, it is unsurprising that the cases the Court cites as authorizing photo-taking do not even mention the Fourth Amendment.

But is not the practice of DNA searches, the Court asks, the same as taking "Bertillon" measurements—noting an arrestee's height, shoe size, and so on, on the back of a photograph? No, because that system was not, in the ordinary case, used to solve unsolved crimes.

It is possible, I suppose, to imagine situations in which such measurements might be useful to generate leads. (If witnesses described a
very tall burglar, all the "tall man" cards could then be pulled.) But
the obvious primary purpose of such measurements, as the Court's
description of them makes clear, was to verify that, for example,
the person arrested today is the same person that was arrested a year
ago. Which is to say, Bertillon measurements were actually used as a
system of identification, and drew their primary usefulness from that
task.

It is on the fingerprinting of arrestees, however, that the
Court relies most heavily. The Court does not actually say
whether it believes that taking a person's fingerprints is a Fourth
Amendment search, and our cases provide no ready answer to
that question. Even assuming so, however, law enforcement's
post-arrest use of fingerprints could not be more different from
its post-arrest use of DNA. Fingerprints of arrestees are taken
primarily to identify them (though that process sometimes solves
crimes); the DNA of arrestees is taken to solve crimes (and nothing else). Contrast CODIS, the FBI's nationwide DNA database,
with IAFIS, the FBI's Integrated Automated Fingerprint Identification System.

FINGERPRINTS	DNA SAMPLES
The "average response time for an electronic criminal fingerprint submission is about 27 minutes." *IAFIS*.	DNA analysis can take months—far too long to be useful for identifying someone.

FINGERPRINTS	DNA SAMPLES
IAFIS includes detailed identification information, including "criminal histories; mug shots; scars and tattoo photos; physical characteristics like height, weight, and hair and eye color."	CODIS contains "[n]o names or other personal identifiers of the offenders, arrestees, or detainees." See CODIS and NDIS Fact Sheet.
"Latent prints" recovered from crime scenes are not systematically compared against the database of known fingerprints, since that requires further forensic work.	The entire *point* of the DNA database is to check crime scene evidence against the profiles of arrestees and convicts as they come in.

The Court asserts that the taking of fingerprints was "constitutional for generations prior to the introduction" of the FBI's rapid computer-matching system. This bold statement is bereft of citation to authority because there is none for it. The "great expansion in fingerprinting came before the modern era of Fourth Amendment jurisprudence," and so we were never asked to decide the legitimacy of the practice. *United States v. Kincade* (CA9 2004). As fingerprint databases expanded from convicted criminals, to arrestees, to civil servants, to immigrants, to everyone with a driver's license, Americans simply "became accustomed to having our fingerprints on file in some government database." But it is wrong to suggest that this was uncontroversial at the time, or that this Court blessed universal fingerprinting for "generations" before it was possible to use it effectively for identification.

The Court also assures us that "the delay in processing DNA from arrestees is being reduced to a substantial degree by rapid technical advances." The idea, presumably, is that the snail's pace in this case is atypical, so that DNA is now readily usable for identification. The Court's proof, however, is nothing but a pair of press releases—each of which turns out to undercut this argument. We learn in them that reductions in backlog have enabled Ohio and Louisiana crime labs to analyze a submitted DNA sample in twenty days. But that is still longer than the eighteen days that Maryland needed to analyze King's sample, once it worked its way through the State's labyrinthine bureaucracy. What this illustrates is that these times do not take into account the many other sources of delay. So if the Court means to suggest that Maryland is unusual, that may be right—it may qualify in this context as a paragon of efficiency. (Indeed, the Governor of Maryland was hailing the elimination of that State's backlog more than five years ago.) Meanwhile, the Court's holding will result in the dumping of a large number of arrestee samples—many from minor offenders—onto an already overburdened system: Nearly one-third of Americans will be arrested for some offense by age 23.

The Court also accepts uncritically the Government's representation at oral argument that it is developing devices that will be able to test DNA in mere minutes. At most, this demonstrates that it may one day be possible to design a program that uses DNA for a purpose other than crime-solving—not that Maryland has in fact designed such a program today. And that is the main point, which the Court's discussion of the brave new world of instant DNA analysis should not obscure. The issue before us is not whether DNA can some day be used for identification; nor even whether it can today be used for identification; but whether it was used for identification here.

Today, it can fairly be said that finger-prints really are used to identify people—so well, in fact, that there would be no need for the expense of a separate, wholly redundant DNA confirmation of the same information. What DNA adds—what makes it a valuable weapon in the law-enforcement arsenal—is the ability to solve unsolved crimes, by matching old crime-scene evidence against the profiles of people whose identities are already known. That is what was going on when King's DNA was taken, and we should

Solving unsolved crimes is a noble objective, but it occupies a lower place in the American pantheon of noble objectives than the protection of our people from suspicionless law-enforcement searches.

not disguise the fact. Solving unsolved crimes is a noble objective, but it occupies a lower place in the American pantheon of noble objectives than the protection of our people from suspicionless law-enforcement searches. The Fourth Amendment must prevail.

The Court disguises the vast (and scary) scope of its holding by promising a limitation it cannot deliver. The Court repeatedly says that DNA testing, and entry into a national DNA registry, will not befall thee and me, dear reader, but only those arrested for "serious offense[s]." I cannot imagine what principle could possibly justify this limitation, and the Court does not attempt to suggest any. If one believes that DNA will "identify" someone arrested for assault, he must believe that it will "identify" someone arrested for a traf-fic offense. This Court does not base its judgments on senseless dis-tinctions. At the end of the day, logic will out. When there comes before us the taking of DNA from an arrestee for a traffic violation, the Court will predictably (and quite rightly) say, "We can find no significant difference between this case and *King*." Make no mistake about it: As an entirely predictable consequence of today's decision, your DNA can be taken and entered into a national DNA database if you are ever arrested, rightly or wrongly, and for whatever reason.

The most regrettable aspect of the suspicionless search that occurred here is that it proved to be quite unnecessary. All parties concede that it would have been entirely permissible, as far as the Fourth Amendment is concerned, for Maryland to take a sample of King's DNA as a consequence of his conviction for second-degree assault. So the ironic result of the Court's error is this: The only arrestees to whom the outcome here will ever make a difference are those who have been acquitted of the crime of arrest (so that their DNA could not have been taken upon conviction). In other words, this Act manages to burden uniquely the sole group for whom the Fourth Amendment's protections ought to be most jealously guarded: people who are innocent of the State's accusations.

Today's judgment will, to be sure, have the beneficial effect of solving more crimes; then again, so would the taking of DNA samples from anyone who flies on an airplane (surely the Transportation Security Administration needs to know the "identity" of the flying public), applies for a driver's license, or attends a public school. Perhaps the construction of such a genetic panopticon is wise. But I doubt that the proud men who wrote the charter of our liberties would have been so eager to open their mouths for royal inspection.

I doubt that the proud men who wrote the charter of our liberties would have been so eager to open their mouths for royal inspection.

I therefore dissent, and hope that today's incursion upon the Fourth Amendment, like an earlier one, will some day be repudiated.

HAMDI v. RUMSFELD (2004)

After the terrorist attacks of September 11, 2001, the U.S. Supreme Court was forced to confront a number of challenges to the executive branch's program to prosecute and detain alleged terrorists. These cases raised questions about the separation of powers questions as well as the right to be free of arbitrary and unlawful detention, known as the right to due process.

The Suspension Clause of the U.S. Constitution, found in article I, section 9, clause 2, helps protect due process by demanding that "The Privilege of the Writ of Habeas Corpus shall not be suspended, unless when in Cases of Rebellion or Invasion the public Safety may require it." Habeas corpus, which is Latin for "you have the body," is a right descended from English common law and was written into federal law by Congress as soon as the Constitution was adopted. Many prisoners today rely on habeas corpus motions to challenge their imprisonment on any number of grounds.

In *Rasul v. Bush* (2004) and *Boumediene v. Bush* (2008), Justice Scalia vigorously dissented from opinions holding that foreign terrorist suspects held at the Guantanamo Naval Base in Cuba had the right to challenge their detention as enemy combatants. He argued that the writ of habeas corpus had never been extended to aliens captured overseas. Moreover, the military clearly did not expect the Court to rule that the terrorism suspects had constitutional protection at Guantanamo; if it did, it would never have brought them there.

The *Boumediene* ruling so clearly infuriated Scalia that he said at the outset of his opinion that he would depart from his "usual practice" of reviewing the legal errors of a decision first and "begin with a description of the disastrous consequences of what the Court has done today." He wrote:

America is at war with radical Islamists. The enemy began by killing Americans and American allies abroad: 241 at the Marine barracks in Lebanon, 19 at the Khobar Towers in Dhahran, 224 at our embassies in Dar es Salaam and Nairobi, and 17 on the USS Cole in Yemen. On September 11, 2001, the enemy brought the battle to American soil, killing 2,749 at the Twin Towers in New York City, 184 at the Pentagon in Washington, D.C., and 40 in Pennsylvania. It has threatened further attacks against our homeland; one need only walk about buttressed and barricaded Washington, or board a plane anywhere in the country, to know that the threat is a serious one. Our Armed Forces are now in the field against the enemy, in Afghanistan and Iraq. Last week, 13 of our countrymen in arms were killed.

The game of bait-and-switch that today's opinion plays upon the Nation's Commander in Chief will make the war harder on us. It will almost certainly cause more Americans to be killed. That consequence would be tolerable if necessary to preserve a time-honored legal principle vital to our constitutional Republic. But it is this Court's blatant *abandonment* of such a principle that produces the decision today.

Scalia, whose opinion was joined by Chief Justice Roberts and Justices Thomas and Alito, concluded by writing, "The Nation will live to regret what the Court has done today."

Four years earlier, Justice Scalia dissented from the Court's 2004 ruling in *Rasul*, in which the Court first held that federal courts had jurisdiction to hear habeas corpus appeals from foreign nationals held at Guantanamo. But on the same day *Rasul* was handed down, the Court decided a case involving the detention of an American citizen who had allegedly taken up arms with the terrorists.

In *Hamdi v. Rumsfeld* (2004), the Supreme Court ruled that U.S. citizens have a right under the Due Process Clause of the Fifth Amendment to challenge their detention by the president, even though their detention has been authorized by an act of Congress. The Bush administration argued that Yaser Esam Hamdi, a U.S. and Saudi citizen, had been caught waging war against the United States in Afghanistan and therefore could be detained and interrogated as an enemy combatant. The administration also argued that Hamdi did not have a right to an attorney or to due process. In June 2002, Hamdi's father filed a habeas corpus petition to challenge his detention.

Justice Sandra Day O'Connor wrote for a plurality of the Supreme Court and ruled that the Authorization for the Use of Military Force, the law passed by Congress after the 9/11 attacks, granted the president the power to hold persons he deemed enemy combatants until the war was over. Despite this authority, O'Connor wrote, Hamdi had a constitutional right to challenge his detention before a neutral decision maker.

In an opinion joined only by liberal Justice John Paul Stevens, Justice Scalia said the plurality had wrongly ignored Hamdi's right as an American citizen to habeas corpus. "The very core of liberty secured by our Anglo-Saxon system of separated powers has been freedom from indefinite imprisonment at the will of the Executive," Scalia wrote. He wrote that the government has two choices when dealing with a citizen who takes up arms against the United States. Either the executive branch can prosecute him in federal court for treason or another crime, or Congress can exercise its constitutional authority to suspend the right to habeas corpus and permit the president to hold the alleged traitor until hostilities end.

Scalia said he shared the plurality's unease at resolving the "conflict between the competing demands of national security and our citizens' constitutional right to personal liberty," but blasted it for adopting a "Mr. Fix-it Mentality" and avoiding the conclusion demanded by the Constitution.

~≈⊙≀⊙≈~

Justice Scalia, with whom Justice Stevens joins, dissenting.

Petitioner, a presumed American citizen, has been imprisoned without charge or hearing in the Norfolk and Charleston Naval Brigs for more than two years, on the allegation that he is an enemy combatant who bore arms against his country for the Taliban. His father claims to the contrary, that he is an inexperienced aid worker caught in the wrong place at the wrong time. This case brings into conflict the competing demands of national security and our citizens' constitutional right to personal liberty. Although I share the Court's evident unease as it seeks to reconcile the two, I do not agree with its resolution.

Where the Government accuses a citizen of waging war against it, our constitutional tradition has been to prosecute him in federal court for treason or some other crime. Where the exigencies of war prevent that, the Constitution's Suspension Clause, Art. I, § 9, cl. 2, allows Congress to relax the usual protections temporarily. Absent suspension, however, the Executive's assertion of military exigency has not been thought sufficient to permit detention without charge. No one contends that the congressional Authorization for Use of Military Force, on which the Government relies to justify its actions here, is an implementation of the Suspension Clause. Accordingly, I would reverse the decision below.

I

The very core of liberty secured by our Anglo-Saxon system of separated powers has been freedom from indefinite imprisonment at the will of the Executive. Blackstone stated this principle clearly:

> "Of great importance to the public is the preservation of this personal liberty: for if once it were left in the power of any, the highest, magistrate to imprison arbitrarily whomever he or his officers thought proper... there would soon be an end of all other rights and immunities.... To bereave a man of life, or by violence to confiscate his estate, without accusation or trial, would be so gross and notorious an act of despotism, as must at once convey the alarm of tyranny throughout the whole kingdom. But confinement of the person, by secretly hurrying him to gaol, where his sufferings are unknown or forgotten; is a less public, a less striking, and therefore a more dangerous engine of arbitrary government....
>
> "To make imprisonment lawful, it must either be, by process from the courts of judicature, or by warrant from some legal officer, having authority to commit to prison; which warrant must be in writing, under the hand and seal of the magistrate, and express the causes of the commitment, in order to be examined into (if necessary) upon a habeas corpus. If there be no cause expressed, the gaoler is not bound to detain the prisoner. For the law judges in this respect,... that it is unreasonable to

send a prisoner, and not to signify withal the crimes alleged against him."

W. BLACKSTONE, COMMENTARIES ON THE LAWS OF ENGLAND (1765)

These words were well known to the Founders. Hamilton quoted from this very passage in The Federalist No. 84. The two ideas central to Blackstone's understanding—due process as the right secured, and habeas corpus as the instrument by which due process could be insisted upon by a citizen illegally imprisoned—found expression in the Constitution's Due Process and Suspension Clauses.

The gist of the Due Process Clause, as understood at the founding and since, was to force the Government to follow those common-law procedures traditionally deemed necessary before depriving a person of life, liberty, or property. When a citizen was deprived of liberty because of alleged criminal conduct, those procedures typically required committal by a magistrate followed by indictment and trial. See, e.g., 2 & 3 Phil. & M., c. 10 (1555); 3 J. Story, Commentaries on the Constitution of the United States § 1783, p. 661 (1833) (hereinafter Story) (equating "due process of law" with "due presentment or indictment, and being brought in to answer thereto by due process of the common law"). The Due Process Clause "in effect affirms the right of trial according to the process and proceedings of the common law." Ibid. See also T. Cooley, General Principles of Constitutional Law 224 (1880) ("When life and liberty are in question, there must in every instance be judicial proceedings; and that requirement implies an accusation, a hearing before an impartial tribunal, with proper jurisdiction, and a conviction and judgment before the punishment can be inflicted" (internal quotation marks omitted)).

To be sure, certain types of permissible noncriminal detention—that is, those not dependent upon the contention that the citizen had committed a criminal act—did not require the protections of criminal procedure. However, these fell into a limited number of well-recognized exceptions—civil commitment of the mentally ill, for example, and temporary detention in quarantine of the infectious. It is unthinkable that the Executive could render otherwise criminal grounds for detention noncriminal merely by disclaiming an intent to prosecute, or by asserting that it was incapacitating dangerous offenders rather than punishing wrongdoing.

These due process rights have historically been vindicated by the writ of habeas corpus. In England before the founding, the writ developed into a tool for challenging executive confinement. It was not always effective. For example, in Darnel's Case, 3 How. St. Tr. 1 (K. B. 1627), King Charles I detained without charge several individuals for failing to assist England's war against France and Spain. The prisoners sought writs of habeas corpus, arguing that without specific charges, "imprisonment shall not continue on for a time, but for ever; and the subjects of this kingdom may be restrained of their liberties perpetually." *Id.* The Attorney General replied that the Crown's interest in protecting the realm justified imprisonment in "a matter of state...not ripe nor timely" for the ordinary process of accusation and trial. *Id.* The court denied relief, producing widespread outrage, and Parliament responded with the Petition of Right, accepted by the King in 1628, which expressly prohibited imprisonment without formal charges.

The struggle between subject and Crown continued, and culminated in the Habeas Corpus Act of 1679, described by Blackstone as a "second magna charta, and stable bulwark of our liberties." The Act

governed all persons "committed or detained...for any crime." In cases
other than felony or treason plainly expressed in the warrant of commitment, the Act required release upon appropriate sureties (unless the
commitment was for a nonbailable offense). Where the commitment
was for felony or high treason, the Act did not require immediate
release, but instead required the Crown to commence criminal proceedings within a specified time. If the prisoner was not "indicted some
Time in the next Term," the judge was "required...to set at Liberty
the Prisoner upon Bail" unless the King was unable to produce his
witnesses. Ibid. Able or no, if the prisoner was not brought to trial by
the next succeeding term, the Act provided that "he shall be discharged
from his Imprisonment." English courts sat four terms per year, so the
practical effect of this provision was that imprisonment without indictment or trial for felony or high treason under § 7 would not exceed
approximately three to six months.

The writ of habeas corpus was preserved in the Constitution—the
only common-law writ to be explicitly mentioned. Hamilton lauded
"the establishment of the writ of habeas corpus" in his Federalist
defense as a means to protect against "the practice of arbitrary impris-
onments...in all ages, [one of] the favourite and most formidable
instruments of tyranny." The Federalist No. 84. Indeed, availability
of the writ under the new Constitution (along with the requirement
of trial by jury in criminal cases) was his basis for arguing that additional, explicit procedural protections were unnecessary.

II

The allegations here, of course, are no ordinary accusations of criminal activity. Yaser Esam Hamdi has been imprisoned because the
Government believes he participated in the waging of war against

the United States. The relevant question, then, is whether there is a different, special procedure for imprisonment of a citizen accused of wrongdoing by aiding the enemy in wartime.

Citizens aiding the enemy have been treated as traitors subject to the criminal process.

A

Justice O'Connor, writing for a plurality of this Court, asserts that captured enemy combatants (other than those suspected of war crimes) have traditionally been detained until the cessation of hostilities and then released. That is probably an accurate description of wartime practice with respect to enemy aliens. The tradition with respect to American citizens, however, has been quite different. Citizens aiding the enemy have been treated as traitors subject to the criminal process.

As early as 1350, England's Statute of Treasons made it a crime to "levy War against our Lord the King in his Realm, or be adherent to the King's Enemies in his Realm, giving to them Aid and Comfort, in the Realm, or elsewhere." In his 1762 Discourse on High Treason, Sir Michael Foster explained:

"With regard to Natural-born Subjects there can be no Doubt. They owe Allegiance to the Crown at all Times and in all Places.

. . . . .

"The joining with Rebels in an Act of Rebellion, or with Enemies in Acts of Hostility, will make a Man a Traitor: in the one Case within the Clause of Levying War, in the other within that of Adhering to the King's enemies.

. . . . .

"States in Actual Hostility with Us, though no War be solemnly Declared, are Enemies within the meaning of the Act. And therefore in an Indictment on the Clause of Adhering to the King's Enemies, it is sufficient to Aver that the Prince or State Adhered to is an Enemy, without shewing any War Proclaimed. . . . And if the Subject of a Foreign Prince in Amity with Us, invadeth the Kingdom without Commission from his Sovereign, He is an Enemy. And a Subject of England adhering to Him is a Traitor within this Clause of the Act."

Subjects accused of levying war against the King were routinely prosecuted for treason. The Founders inherited the understanding that a citizen's levying war against the Government was to be punished criminally. The Constitution provides: "Treason against the United States, shall consist only in levying War against them, or in adhering to their Enemies, giving them Aid and Comfort"; and establishes a heightened proof requirement (two witnesses) in order to "convic[t]" of that offense.

In more recent times, too, citizens have been charged and tried in Article III courts for acts of war against the United States, even when their noncitizen co-conspirators were not. For example, two American citizens alleged to have participated during World War I in a spying conspiracy on behalf of Germany were tried in federal court. A German member of the same conspiracy was subjected to military process. During World War II, the famous German saboteurs of *Ex parte Quirin* (1942) received military process, but the citizens who associated with them (with the exception of one citizen-saboteur, discussed below) were punished under the criminal process.

The modern treason statute is 18 U.S.C. § 2381; it basically tracks the language of the constitutional provision. Other provisions of Title 18 criminalize various acts of warmaking and adherence to the enemy. See, e.g., § 32 (destruction of aircraft or aircraft facilities), § 2332a (use of weapons of mass destruction), § 2332b (acts of terrorism transcending national boundaries), § 2339A (providing material support to terrorists), § 2339B (providing material support to certain terrorist organizations), § 2382 (misprision of treason), § 2383 (rebellion or insurrection), § 2384 (seditious conspiracy), § 2390 (enlistment to serve in armed hostility against the United States). The only citizen other than Hamdi known to be imprisoned in connection with military hostilities in Afghanistan against the United States was subjected to criminal process and convicted upon a guilty plea.

B

There are times when military exigency renders resort to the traditional criminal process impracticable. English law accommodated such exigencies by allowing legislative suspension of the writ of habeas corpus for brief periods. Blackstone explained:

"And yet sometimes, when the state is in real danger, even this [i.e., executive detention] may be a necessary measure. But the happiness of our constitution is, that it is not left to the executive power to determine when the danger of the state is so great, as to render this measure expedient. For the parliament only, or legislative power, whenever it sees proper, can authorize the crown, by suspending the habeas corpus act for a short and limited time, to imprison suspected persons without giving any reason for so doing.... In like manner this experiment ought only to be tried in case of extreme emergency; and in these the nation parts with it[s] liberty for a while, in order to preserve it for ever."

1 BLACKSTONE 132

Where the Executive has not pursued the usual course of charge, committal, and conviction, it has historically secured the Legislature's explicit approval of a suspension. In England, Parliament on numerous occasions passed temporary suspensions in times of threatened invasion or rebellion. Not long after Massachusetts had adopted a clause in its constitution explicitly providing for habeas corpus, it suspended the writ in order to deal with Shay's Rebellion.

Our Federal Constitution contains a provision explicitly permitting suspension, but limiting the situations in which it may be invoked: "The privilege of the Writ of Habeas Corpus shall not be suspended, unless when in Cases of Rebellion or Invasion the public Safety may require it." Although this provision does not state that suspension must be effected by, or authorized by, a legislative act, it has been so understood, consistent with English practice and the Clause's placement in Article I.

The Suspension Clause was by design a safety valve, the Constitution's only "express provision for exercise of extraordinary authority because of a crisis," *Youngstown Sheet & Tube Co. v. Sawyer* (1952). Very early in the Nation's history, President Jefferson unsuccessfully sought a suspension of habeas corpus to deal with Aaron Burr's conspiracy to overthrow the Government. During the Civil War, Congress passed its first Act authorizing Executive suspension of the writ of habeas corpus to the relief of those many who thought President Lincoln's unauthorized proclamations of suspension unconstitutional. Later Presidential proclamations of suspension relied upon the congressional authorization. During Reconstruction, Congress passed the Ku Klux Klan Act, which included a provision authorizing suspension of the writ, invoked by President Grant in quelling a rebellion in nine South Carolina counties.

Two later Acts of Congress provided broad suspension authority to governors of U. S. possessions. The Philippine Civil Government Act of 1902 provided that the Governor of the Philippines could suspend the writ in case of rebellion, insurrection, or invasion. In 1905 the writ was suspended for nine months by proclamation of the Governor. The Hawaiian Organic Act of 1900 likewise provided that the Governor of Hawaii could suspend the writ in case of rebellion or invasion (or threat thereof).

III

Of course the extensive historical evidence of criminal convictions and habeas suspensions does not necessarily refute the Government's position in this case. When the writ is suspended, the Government is entirely free from judicial oversight. It does not claim such total liberation here, but argues that it need only produce what it calls "some evidence" to satisfy a habeas court that a detained individual is an enemy combatant. Even if suspension of the writ on the one hand, and committal for criminal charges on the other hand, have been the only traditional means of dealing with citizens who levied war against their own country, it is theoretically possible that the Constitution does not require a choice between these alternatives.

I believe, however, that substantial evidence does refute that possibility. First, the text of the 1679 Habeas Corpus Act makes clear that indefinite imprisonment on reasonable suspicion is not an available option of treatment for those accused of aiding the enemy, absent a suspension of the writ. In the United States, this Act was read as "enforc[ing] the common law," *Ex parte Watkins* (1830), and shaped the early understanding of the scope of the writ. As noted above, § 7 of the Act specifically addressed those committed for high treason, and provided a remedy if they were not indicted and tried by the second succeeding court term. That remedy was not a bobtailed judicial inquiry into whether there were reasonable grounds to believe the prisoner had taken up arms against the King. Rather, if the prisoner was not indicted and tried within the prescribed time, "he shall be discharged from his Imprisonment." The Act does not contain any exception for wartime. That omission is conspicuous, since § 7 explicitly addresses the offense of "High Treason," which often involved offenses of a military nature.

Writings from the founding generation also suggest that, without exception, the only constitutional alternatives are to charge the crime or suspend the writ. In 1788, Thomas Jefferson wrote to James Madison questioning the need for a Suspension Clause in cases of rebellion in the proposed Constitution. His letter illustrates the constraints under which the Founders understood themselves to operate:

> "Why suspend the Hab. corp. in insurrections and rebellions? The parties who may be arrested may be charged instantly with a well defined crime. Of course the judge will remand them. If the publick safety requires that the government should have a man imprisoned on less probable testimony in those than in other emergencies; let him be taken and tried, retaken and

retried, while the necessity continues, only giving him redress against the government for damages."

PAPERS OF THOMAS JEFFERSON (JULY 31, 1788) (J. BOYD ED. 1956)

A similar view was reflected in the 1807 House debates over suspension during the armed uprising that came to be known as Burr's conspiracy:

"With regard to those persons who may be implicated in the conspiracy, if the writ of habeas corpus be not suspended, what will be the consequence? When apprehended, they will be brought before a court of justice, who will decide whether there is any evidence that will justify their commitment for farther prosecution. From the communication of the Executive, it appeared there was sufficient evidence to authorize their commitment. Several months would elapse before their final trial, which would give time to collect evidence, and if this shall be sufficient, they will not fail to receive the punishment merited by their crimes, and inflicted by the laws of their country."

16 ANNALS OF CONGRESS (REMARKS OF REP. BURWELL)

The absence of military authority to imprison citizens indefinitely in wartime—whether or not a probability of treason had been established by means less than jury trial—was confirmed by three cases decided during and immediately after the War of 1812. In the first, *In re Stacy* (N. Y. 1813), a citizen was taken into military custody on suspicion that he was "carrying provisions and giving information to the enemy." Stacy petitioned for a writ of habeas corpus, and, after the defendant custodian attempted to avoid complying, Chief Justice Kent ordered attachment against him. Kent noted that the military was "without any color of authority in any military tribunal to try a citizen for that crime" and that it was "holding him in the closest confinement, and contemning the civil authority of the state."

Two other cases, later cited with approval by this Court in *Ex parte Milligan* (1866), upheld verdicts for false imprisonment against military officers. In *Smith v. Shaw* (N.Y. 1815), the court affirmed an award of damages for detention of a citizen on suspicion that he was, among other things, "an enemy's spy in time of war." The court held that "[n]one of the offences charged against Shaw were cognizable by a court-martial, except that which related to his being a spy; and if he was an American citizen, he could not be charged with such an offence. He might be amenable to the civil authority for treason; but could not be punished, under martial law, as a spy." *Ibid.* "If the defendant was justifiable in doing what he did, every citizen of the United States would, in time of war, be equally exposed to a like exercise of military power and authority." *Id.* Finally, in *M'Connell v. Hampton* (N.Y. 1815), a jury awarded $9,000 for false imprisonment after a military officer confined a citizen on charges of treason; the judges on appeal did not question the verdict but found the damages excessive, in part because "it does not appear that [the defendant]... knew [the plaintiff] was a citizen." *Id.*

President Lincoln, when he purported to suspend habeas corpus without congressional authorization during the Civil War, apparently did not doubt that suspension was required if the prisoner was to be held without criminal trial. In his famous message to Congress on July 4, 1861, he argued only that he could suspend the writ, not that even without suspension, his imprisonment of citizens without criminal trial was permitted.

Further evidence comes from this Court's decision in *Ex parte Milligan*. There, the Court issued the writ to an American citizen who had been tried by military commission for offenses that included conspiring to overthrow the Government, seize munitions, and liberate prisoners of war. The Court rejected in no uncertain terms the Government's assertion that military jurisdiction was proper "under the 'laws and usages of war,'" *id*.:

> "It can serve no useful purpose to inquire what those laws and usages are, whence they originated, where found, and on whom they operate; they can never be applied to citizens in states which have upheld the authority of the government, and where the courts are open and their process unobstructed." *Ibid.*

Milligan is not exactly this case, of course, since the petitioner was threatened with death, not merely imprisonment. But the reasoning and conclusion of *Milligan* logically cover the present case. The Government justifies imprisonment of Hamdi on principles of the law of war and admits that, absent the war, it would have no such authority. But if the law of war cannot be applied to citizens where courts are open, then Hamdi's imprisonment without criminal trial is no less unlawful than Milligan's trial by military tribunal.

Milligan responded to the argument, repeated by the Government in this case, that it is dangerous to leave suspected traitors at large in time of war:

"If it was dangerous, in the distracted condition of affairs, to leave Milligan unrestrained of his liberty, because he 'conspired against the government, afforded aid and comfort to rebels, and incited the people to insurrection,' the law said arrest him, confine him closely, render him powerless to do further mischief; and then present his case to the grand jury of the district, with proofs of his guilt, and, if indicted, try him according to the course of the common law. If this had been done, the Constitution would have been vindicated, the law of 1863 enforced, and the securities for personal liberty preserved and defended." *Id.*

Thus, criminal process was viewed as the primary means—and the only means absent congressional action suspending the writ—not only to punish traitors, but to incapacitate them.

The proposition that the Executive lacks indefinite wartime detention authority over citizens is consistent with the Founders' general mistrust of military power permanently at the Executive's disposal. In the Founders' view, the "blessings of liberty" were threatened by "those military establishments which must gradually poison its very fountain." The Federalist No. 45 (J. Madison). No fewer than 10 issues of the Federalist were devoted in whole or part to allaying fears of oppression from the proposed Constitution's authorization of standing armies in peacetime. Many safeguards in the Constitution reflect these concerns. Congress's authority "[t]o raise and support Armies" was hedged with the proviso that "no Appropriation of Money to that Use shall be for a longer Term than two Years." U.S. Const., Art. 1, § 8, cl. 12. Except for the actual command of military forces, all authorization for their maintenance and all explicit authorization for their use is placed in the control of Congress under Article

I, rather than the President under Article II. As Hamilton explained, the President's military authority would be "much inferior" to that of the British King:

> "It would amount to nothing more than the supreme command and direction of the military and naval forces, as first general and admiral of the confederacy: while that of the British king extends to the declaring of war, and to the raising and regulating of fleets and armies; all which, by the constitution under consideration, would appertain to the legislature."
>
> THE FEDERALIST No. 69

A view of the Constitution that gives the Executive authority to use military force rather than the force of law against citizens on American soil flies in the face of the mistrust that engendered these provisions.

IV

The Government argues that our more recent jurisprudence ratifies its indefinite imprisonment of a citizen within the territorial jurisdiction of federal courts. It places primary reliance upon *Ex parte Quirin* (1942), a World War II case upholding the trial by military commission of eight German saboteurs, one of whom, Hans Haupt, was a U.S. citizen. The case was not this Court's finest hour. The Court upheld the commission and denied relief in a brief per curiam issued the day after oral argument concluded; a week later the Government carried out the commission's death sentence upon six saboteurs, including Haupt. The Court eventually explained its reasoning in a written opinion issued several months later.

Only three paragraphs of the Court's lengthy opinion dealt with the particular circumstances of Haupt's case. The Government argued that Haupt, like the other petitioners, could be tried by military commission under the laws of war. In agreeing with that contention, *Quirin* purported to interpret the language of *Milligan* quoted above (the law of war "can never be applied to citizens in states which have upheld the authority of the government, and where the courts are open and their process unobstructed") in the following manner:

> "Elsewhere in its opinion...the Court was at pains to point out that Milligan, a citizen twenty years resident in Indiana, who had never been a resident of any of the states in rebellion, was not an enemy belligerent either entitled to the status of a prisoner of war or subject to the penalties imposed upon unlawful belligerents. We construe the Court's statement as to the inapplicability of the law of war to Milligan's case as having particular reference to the facts before it. From them the Court concluded that Milligan, not being a part of or associated with the armed forces of the enemy, was a non-belligerent, not subject to the law of war...."

In my view this seeks to revise *Milligan* rather than describe it. *Milligan* had involved (among other issues) two separate questions: (1) whether the military trial of Milligan was justified by the laws of war, and if not (2) whether the President's suspension of the writ, pursuant to congressional authorization, prevented the issuance of habeas corpus. The Court's categorical language about the law of war's inapplicability to citizens where the courts are open (with no exception mentioned for citizens who were prisoners of war) was contained in its discussion of the first point. The factors pertaining to whether Milligan could reasonably be considered a belligerent and prisoner of war, while mentioned earlier in the opinion were made relevant and brought to bear in the Court's later discussion of whether Milligan came within the statutory provision that effectively made an exception to Congress's authorized suspension of the writ for (as the Court described it) "all parties, not prisoners of war, resident in their respective jurisdictions,... who were citizens of states in which the administration of the laws in the Federal tribunals was unimpaired," *id.* Milligan thus understood was in accord with the traditional law of habeas corpus I have described: Though treason often occurred in wartime, there was, absent provision for special treatment in a congressional suspension of the writ, no exception to the right to trial by jury for citizens who could be called "belligerents" or "prisoners of war."

Absent suspension of the writ, a citizen held where the courts are open is entitled either to criminal trial or to a judicial decree requiring his release.

But even if *Quirin* gave a correct description of *Milligan*, or made an irrevocable revision of it, *Quirin* would still not justify denial of the writ here. In *Quirin* it was uncontested that the petitioners were members of enemy forces. They were "admitted enemy invaders" and it was "undisputed" that they had landed in the United States in service of German forces. The specific holding of the Court was only that, "upon the conceded facts," the petitioners were "plainly within [the] boundaries" of military jurisdiction. But where those jurisdictional facts are not conceded—where the petitioner insists that he is not a belligerent—*Quirin* left the pre-existing law in place: Absent suspension of the writ, a citizen held where the courts are open is entitled either to criminal trial or to a judicial decree requiring his release.

V

It follows from what I have said that Hamdi is entitled to a habeas decree requiring his release unless (1) criminal proceedings are promptly brought, or (2) Congress has suspended the writ of habeas corpus. A suspension of the writ could, of course, lay down conditions for continued detention, similar to those that today's opinion prescribes under the Due Process Clause. But there is a world of difference between the people's representatives' determining the need for that suspension (and prescribing the conditions for it), and this Court's doing so.

The plurality finds justification for Hamdi's imprisonment in the Authorization for Use of Military Force, which provides:

> "That the President is authorized to use all necessary and appropriate force against those nations, organizations, or persons he determines planned, authorized, committed, or aided the terrorist attacks that occurred on September 11, 2001, or harbored such organizations or persons, in order to prevent any future acts of international terrorism against the United States by such nations, organizations or persons." § 2(a).

This is not remotely a congressional suspension of the writ, and no one claims that it is. Contrary to the plurality's view, I do not think this statute even authorizes detention of a citizen with the clarity necessary to satisfy the interpretive canon that statutes should be construed so as to avoid grave constitutional concerns...or with the clarity necessary to overcome the statutory prescription that "[n]o citizen shall be imprisoned or otherwise detained by the United States except pursuant to an Act of Congress." But even if it did, I would not permit it to overcome Hamdi's entitlement to habeas corpus relief. The Suspension Clause of the Constitution, which carefully circumscribes the conditions under which the writ can be withheld, would be a sham if it could be evaded by congressional prescription of requirements other than the common-law requirement of committal for criminal prosecution that render the writ, though available, unavailing. If the Suspension Clause does not guarantee the citizen that he will either be tried or released, unless the conditions for suspending the writ exist and the grave action of suspending the writ has been taken; if it merely guarantees the citizen that he will not be detained unless Congress by ordinary legislation says he can be detained; it guarantees him very little indeed.

It should not be thought, however, that the plurality's evisceration of the Suspension Clause augments, principally, the power of Congress. As usual, the major effect of its constitutional improvisation is to increase the power of the Court. Having found a congressional authorization for detention of citizens where none clearly exists; and having discarded the categorical procedural protection of the Suspension Clause; the plurality then proceeds, under the guise of the Due Process Clause, to prescribe what procedural protections it thinks appropriate. It "weigh[s] the private interest... against the Government's asserted interest," and—just as though writing a new Constitution—comes up with an unheard-of system in which the citizen rather than the Government bears the burden of proof, testimony is by hearsay rather than live witnesses, and the presiding officer may well be a "neutral" military officer rather than judge and jury. It claims authority to engage in this sort of "judicious balancing" from *Mathews v. Eldridge* (1976), a case involving... the withdrawal of disability benefits! Whatever the merits of this technique when newly recognized property rights are at issue (and even there they are questionable), it has no place where the Constitution and the common law already supply an answer.

Having distorted the Suspension Clause, the plurality finishes up by transmogrifying the Great Writ—disposing of the present habeas petition by remanding for the District Court to "engag[e] in a factfinding process that is both prudent and incremental." "In the absence of [the Executive's prior provision of procedures that satisfy due process],... a court that receives a petition for a writ of habeas corpus from an alleged enemy combatant must itself ensure that the minimum requirements of due process are achieved." This judicial remediation of executive default is unheard of. The role of habeas corpus is to determine the legality of executive detention, not to supply the omitted process necessary to make it legal. It is not the habeas court's function to make illegal detention legal by supplying a process that the Government could have provided, but chose not to. If Hamdi is being imprisoned in violation of the Constitution (because without due process of law), then his habeas petition should be granted; the Executive may then hand him over to the criminal authorities, whose detention for the purpose of prosecution will be lawful, or else must release him.

The plurality seems to view it as its mission to Make Everything Come Out Right.

There is a certain harmony of approach in the plurality's making up for Congress's failure to invoke the Suspension Clause and its making up for the Executive's failure to apply what it says are needed procedures—an approach that reflects what might be called a Mr. Fix-it Mentality. The plurality seems to view it as its mission to Make Everything Come Out Right, rather than merely to decree the consequences, as far as individual rights are concerned, of the other two branches' actions and omissions. Has the Legislature failed to suspend the writ in the current dire emergency? Well, we will remedy that failure by prescribing the reasonable conditions that a suspension should have included. And has the Executive failed to live up to those reasonable conditions? Well, we will ourselves make that failure good, so that this dangerous fellow (if he is dangerous) need not be set free. The problem with this approach is not only that it steps out of the courts' modest and limited role in a democratic society; but that by repeatedly doing what it thinks the political branches ought to do it encourages their lassitude and saps the vitality of government by the people.

VI

Several limitations give my views in this matter a relatively narrow compass. They apply only to citizens, accused of being enemy combatants, who are detained within the territorial jurisdiction of a federal court. This is not likely to be a numerous group; currently we know of only two, Hamdi and Jose Padilla. Where the citizen is captured outside and held outside the United States, the constitutional requirements may be different. Moreover, even within the United States, the accused citizen-enemy combatant may lawfully

If civil rights are to be curtailed during wartime, it must be done openly and democratically, as the Constitution requires, rather than by silent erosion through an opinion of this Court.

be detained once prosecution is in progress or in contemplation. The Government has been notably successful in securing conviction, and hence long-term custody or execution, of those who have waged war against the state.

I frankly do not know whether these tools are sufficient to meet the Government's security needs, including the need to obtain intelligence through interrogation. It is far beyond my competence, or the Court's competence, to determine that. But it is not beyond Congress's. If the situation demands it, the Executive can ask Congress to authorize suspension of the writ—which can be made subject to whatever conditions Congress deems appropriate, including even the procedural novelties invented by the plurality today. To be sure, suspension is limited by the Constitution to cases of rebellion or invasion. But whether the attacks of September 11, 2001, constitute an "invasion," and whether those attacks still justify suspension several years later, are questions for Congress rather than this Court. If civil rights are to be curtailed during wartime, it must be done openly and democratically, as the Constitution requires, rather than by silent erosion through an opinion of this Court.

The Founders well understood the difficult tradeoff between safety and freedom. "Safety from external danger," Hamilton declared,

> "is the most powerful director of national conduct. Even the ardent love

Whatever the general merits of the view that war silences law or modulates its voice, that view has no place in the interpretation and application of a Constitution designed precisely to confront war and, in a manner that accords with democratic principles, to accommodate it.

of liberty will, after a time, give way to its dictates. The violent destruction of life and property incident to war; the continual effort and alarm attendant on a state of continual danger, will compel nations the most attached to liberty, to resort for repose and security to institutions which have a tendency to destroy their civil and political rights. To be more safe, they, at length, become willing to run the risk of being less free."

THE FEDERALIST NO. 8

The Founders warned us about the risk, and equipped us with a Constitution designed to deal with it.

Many think it not only inevitable but entirely proper that liberty give way to security in times of national crisis—that, at the extremes of military exigency, *inter arma silent leges*. Whatever the general merits of the view that war silences law or modulates its voice, that view has no place in the interpretation and application of a Constitution designed precisely to confront war and, in a manner that accords with democratic principles, to accommodate it. Because the Court has proceeded to meet the current emergency in a manner the Constitution does not envision, I respectfully dissent.

CHAPTER NINE

RELIGIOUS FREEDOM

THE VERY FIRST WORDS in the Bill of Rights protect the freedom of Americans to practice their religion and guard them against the potential tyranny of government-sponsored religion: "Congress shall make no law respecting an establishment of religion, or prohibiting the free exercise thereof." The amendment's two clauses—known as the Establishment Clause and the Free Exercise Clause—have generated two separate issues for analysis by the courts.

The Establishment Clause of the First Amendment is the textual basis for what many consider the Constitution's requirement of a "wall of separation between church and state." Though the "wall of separation" is not to be found in the Constitution—the phrase comes from a private letter written by Thomas Jefferson—the metaphor stuck and has been adopted by those who feel religion has no place in the public square. The Framers of the Constitution, of course, did not subscribe to such a separationist view. They were primarily concerned with preventing the establishment of a national church; indeed, the Establishment Clause was not even applied to state governments until 1947.[1] In that year, the Supreme Court, citing Jefferson's "wall," extended the clause to the states and expanded the range of prohibited government actions. Laws that aid only one religion or that reveal a preference for one religion over another are unconstitutional, the Court said, but so too are laws that "aid all religions."[2]

As the Court constructed a higher wall between church and state, it was forced to consider the constitutionality of many government policies that arguably aided "all religions." For example, was it permissible for a state to provide any assistance to religious schools for textbooks or supplies? How would state laws fare that required students to observe a moment of silence that might be used for prayer? More fundamentally, what standards or guides should courts use to answer such questions?

Before Justice Scalia joined the Supreme Court, it had adopted in the case of *Lemon v. Kurtzman* (1971) a three-prong test for deciding legal challenges to government practices that purportedly "established" religion. Under the *Lemon* test, as it became known, the Court will strike down laws appearing to promote or aid religion unless it determines that (1) the law has a secular purpose, (2) the law's primary effect is not to advance religion, and (3) the law does not foster an "excessive entanglement" with religion. The *Lemon* test has been fiercely criticized by many legal scholars and even current Supreme Court justices for tipping the scales against religion.[3] These critics argue, among other things, that the Constitution does not forbid government from "advancing" religion generally, so long as it does not "play favorites" between various religions. Lately, the *Lemon* test is fallen into such disrepute that the Court sometimes ignores it altogether. This practice of ignoring but not overruling produced one of Scalia's most vivid and humorous opinions in *Lamb's Chapel*, which is included in this chapter.

Overall, Justice Scalia was unsympathetic to claims that government action had unlawfully aided religion. Indeed, during his three decades on the Court, Scalia never wrote or joined an opinion that found a government authority had violated the Establishment Clause.[4]

The other religion clause of the First Amendment, the Free Exercise Clause, prohibits Congress and the states from interfering with a person's ability to practice his religion. What constitutes interference is not always easy to determine. For example, the Court has held that the military's ban on wearing any hat (other than an official one) while on duty does not violate the Free Exercise right of an Orthodox Jewish soldier who wished to wear a yarmulke.[5] On the other hand, the Court has held that the Free Exercise rights of Seventh-Day Adventists were unconstitutionally abridged by a state law denying unemployment benefits to persons who do not work on Saturdays, the sabbath day for Adventists.[6]

The two religion clauses are often raised in the same case. The Court examines whether a government action violates the Establishment Clause and, if it does not, whether it overly burdens a person's right to adhere to his religious customs.

Justice Scalia was an active participant in the religion clause cases. His most important opinion in the area was not one of his trademark colorful dissents. Rather, Scalia's opinion for the majority in *Employment Division of Oregon v. Smith* (1990) was noteworthy because it established a new rule for judging Free Exercise claims and because it disappointed many political conservatives. In *Smith*, Scalia and the Court ruled that Oregon could deny benefits to Native Americans who, in violation of the state's drug laws, used peyote in their traditional religious ceremonies. Though recognizing the religious use of peyote, Scalia wrote that the Free Exercise Clause does not protect activities that are made criminal by generally applicable and religion-neutral laws. To hold otherwise, Scalia argued, the Court would have to create special exemptions to all sorts of laws that various religious groups within the United States object to, for example, laws requiring payment of taxes and registration for military service, animal cruelty laws, and child labor laws.

Scalia appreciated the potential hardship that might arise from the Court's restraint. He wrote, "It may fairly be said that leaving accommodation to the political process will place at a disadvantage those religious practices that are not widely engaged in; but that unavoidable consequence of democratic government must be preferred to a system in which each conscience is a law unto itself or in which judges weigh the social importance of all laws against the centrality of all religious beliefs."[7] In Scalia's view, the Court was ill-suited to make determinations as to what religious practices are "central" to the exercise of a person's faith. To avoid such questions, he left the decision in the hands of the people acting through their elected officials.

In *Smith*, Scalia noted that Oregon could change its law to allow religious use of peyote, as other states had done. This acknowledgment was consistent with Scalia's strong belief that the Court should be deferential to legislative efforts to accommodate religious practices. "When a legislature acts to accommodate religion, particularly a minority sect, 'it follows the best of our traditions,'" Scalia wrote in one opinion.[8]

Besides *Smith*, Justice Scalia's most notable opinions were dissents filed in cases where the majority used the Establishment Clause to invalidate legislative accommodations of religion and public expressions of faith. Scalia argued that public religious observances that were practiced at the time the First Amendment was drafted cannot reasonably be considered unconstitutional when practiced today. His dissenting opinion in *Lee v. Weisman* (below) best represents his originalist argument.

LEE v. WEISMAN (1992)

This case arose from a challenge to a Rhode Island public school system's practice of inviting members of the clergy to offer prayers at the graduation ceremonies of its middle schools and high schools. In 1989, a middle school principal invited a rabbi to offer invocation and benediction prayers at the school's graduation. The principal provided the rabbi with a pamphlet titled "Guide for Civic Occasions," which was prepared by the National Conference of Christians and Jews. The principal instructed the rabbi to make the prayers nonsectarian. The rabbi's prayers included thanksgiving to God for the blessings found in America. A student and her father sued the school district, charging that the prayers amounted to government-required participation in religion.

A closely divided majority of the Supreme Court agreed that the school's practice violated the Establishment Clause of the First Amendment. The Court's decision did not rely on the *Lemon* test. Instead, it focused on the issue of coercion and the pressure that school sponsorship of the prayer would put on the non-believing student. The government has a duty, wrote Justice Anthony Kennedy for the Court, "to guard and respect that sphere of inviolable conscience and belief which is the mark of a free people."

Writing for the four dissenting justices, Scalia blasted the Court's decision for being completely out of touch with the history and traditions of religious freedom in the United States—specifically, the use of voluntary prayer at high school graduations and other public ceremonies. Scalia traced the long history of prayer in governmental ceremonies and proclamations. He argued that the potential harm of "coercion" that may be felt by the nonbeliever is outweighed by the benefit of having people of many different faiths be able to come together in the "unifying mechanism" of public prayer. Moreover, he belittled the Court for dabbling in psychology to support its finding of coercion.

Scalia began his dissent by pointing out the inconsistency in Justice Kennedy's religion clause interpretations. Scalia said he could not agree with Kennedy's majority opinion here because he already professed support for an analysis based on history and culture that the Court had employed "three terms ago." That opinion was written by Justice Kennedy as well.

Scalia also referred to the *Durham* rule for insanity defense.[9] That rule, since abandoned, was widely criticized for allowing criminal defendants to escape punishment so long as a single psychiatrist testified that the crime was the product of "mental disease or defect." Scalia seemed to suggest that the Court's reliance on coercion in *Lee v. Weisman* might lead to a similarly absurd result whereby psychiatrists will have enormous influence in deciding which public displays of religion are permissible under the Constitution.

Last, Scalia's ability to see the logical consequences of the Court's reasoning was showcased here, as he foresaw the potential for a fight over the Pledge of Allegiance, in particular the words "under God." Scalia said the Court's argument—that young adults need to be protected from even the slightest coercion—would likely lead it to find recitation of the Pledge at public ceremonies to violate the Establishment Clause. That issue reached the Supreme Court in 2003.

⚜

JUSTICE SCALIA, WITH WHOM THE CHIEF JUSTICE, JUSTICE WHITE, AND JUSTICE THOMAS JOIN, DISSENTING.

Three Terms ago, I joined an opinion recognizing that the Establishment Clause must be construed in light of the "[g]overnment policies of accommodation, acknowledgment, and support for religion [that] are an accepted part of our political and cultural heritage." That opinion affirmed that "the meaning of the Clause is to be determined by reference to historical practices and understandings." It said that "[a] test for implementing the protections of the Establishment Clause that, if applied with consistency, would invalidate longstanding traditions cannot be a proper reading of the Clause." *County of Allegheny v. American Civil Liberties Union, Greater Pittsburgh Chapter* (1989) (Kennedy, J., concurring in judgment in part and dissenting in part).

These views, of course, prevent me from joining today's opinion, which is conspicuously bereft of any reference to history. In holding that the Establishment Clause prohibits invocations and benedictions at public school graduation ceremonies, the Court—with nary a mention that it is doing so—lays waste a tradition that is as old as public school graduation ceremonies themselves, and that is a component of an even more longstanding American tradition of nonsectarian prayer to God at public celebrations generally. As its instrument of destruction, the bulldozer of its social engineering, the Court invents a boundless, and boundlessly manipulable, test of psychological coercion, which promises to do for the Establishment Clause what the *Durham* rule did for the insanity defense. Today's opinion shows more forcefully than volumes of argumentation why our Nation's protection, that fortress which is our Constitution, cannot possibly rest upon the changeable philosophical predilections of the Justices of this Court, but must have deep foundations in the historic practices of our people.

I

Justice Holmes' aphorism that "a page of history is worth a volume of logic" applies with particular force to our Establishment Clause jurisprudence. As we have recognized, our interpretation of the Establishment Clause should "compor[t] with what history reveals was the contemporaneous understanding of its guarantees." *Lynch v. Donnelly* (1984). "[T]he line we must draw between the permissible and the impermissible is one which accords with history and faithfully reflects the understanding of the Founding Fathers." *School Dist. of Abington v. Schempp* (1963). "[H]istorical evidence sheds light not only on what the draftsmen intended the Establishment Clause to mean, but also on how they thought that Clause applied" to contemporaneous practices. *Marsh v. Chambers* (1983). Thus, "[t]he existence from the beginning of the Nation's life of a practice, [while] not conclusive of its constitutionality . . . is a fact of considerable import in the interpretation" of the Establishment Clause. *Walz v. Tax Comm'n of New York City* (1970) (Brennan, J., concurring).

The history and tradition of our Nation are replete with public ceremonies featuring prayers of thanksgiving and petition. Illustrations of this point have been amply provided in our prior opinions, but since the Court is so oblivious to our history as to suggest that the Constitution restricts "preservation and transmission of religious beliefs . . . to the private sphere," it appears necessary to provide another brief account.

From our Nation's origin, prayer has been a prominent part of governmental ceremonies and proclamations. The Declaration of Independence, the document marking our birth as a separate people, "appeal[ed] to the Supreme Judge of the world for the rectitude of our intentions" and avowed "a firm reliance on the protection of divine Providence." In his first inaugural address, after swearing his oath of office on a Bible, George Washington deliberately made a prayer a part of his first official act as President:

[I]t would be peculiarly improper to omit in this first official act my fervent supplications to that Almighty Being who rules over the universe, who presides in the councils of nations, and whose providential aids can supply every human defect, that His benediction may consecrate to the liberties and happiness of the people of the United States a Government instituted by themselves for these essential purposes.

Such supplications have been a characteristic feature of inaugural addresses ever since. Thomas Jefferson, for example, prayed in his first inaugural address: "[M]ay that Infinite Power which rules the destinies of the universe lead our councils to what is best, and give them a favorable issue for your peace and prosperity." In his second inaugural address, Jefferson acknowledged his need for divine guidance and invited his audience to join his prayer:

I shall need, too, the favor of that Being in whose hands we are, who led our fathers, as Israel of old, from their native land and planted them in a country flowing with all the necessaries and comforts of life; who has covered our infancy with His providence and our riper years with His wisdom and power, and to whose goodness I ask you to join in supplications with me that He will so enlighten the minds of your servants, guide their councils, and prosper their measures that whatsoever they do shall result in your good, and shall secure to you the peace, friendship, and approbation of all nations.

Similarly, James Madison, in his first inaugural address, placed his confidence:

[I]n the guardianship and guidance of that Almighty Being whose power regulates the destiny of nations, whose blessings have been so conspicuously dispensed to this rising Republic, and to whom we are bound to address our devout gratitude for the past, as well as our fervent supplications and best hopes for the future.

Most recently, President Bush, continuing the tradition established by President Washington, asked those attending his inauguration to bow their heads, and made a prayer his first official act as President.

Our national celebration of Thanksgiving likewise dates back to President Washington. As we recounted in *Lynch*:

The day after the First Amendment was proposed, Congress urged President Washington to proclaim "a day of public thanksgiving and prayer, to be observed by acknowledging with grateful hearts the many and signal favours of Almighty God." President Washington proclaimed November 26, 1789, a day of thanksgiving to "offe[r] our prayers and supplications to the Great Lord and Ruler of Nations, and beseech Him to pardon our national and other transgressions. . . .

This tradition of Thanksgiving Proclamations—with their religious theme of prayerful gratitude to God—has been adhered to by almost every President.

The other two branches of the Federal Government also have a long-established practice of prayer at public events. As we detailed in *Marsh*, congressional sessions have opened with a chaplain's prayer ever since the First Congress. And this Court's own sessions have opened with the invocation "God save the United States and this Honorable Court" since the days of Chief Justice Marshall.

In addition to this general tradition of prayer at public ceremonies, there exists a more specific tradition of invocations and benedictions at public school graduation exercises. By one account, the first public high school graduation ceremony took place in Connecticut in July 1868—the very month, as it happens, that the Fourteenth Amendment (the vehicle by which the Establishment Clause has been applied against the States) was ratified—when "15 seniors from the Norwich Free Academy marched in their best Sunday suits and dresses into a church hall and waited through majestic music and long prayers." Brodinsky, Commencement Rites Obsolete? Not At All, A 10 Week Study Shows, 10 Updating School Board Policies, No. 4 (Apr. 1979). As the Court obliquely acknowledges in describing the "customary features" of high school graduations, and as respondents do not contest, the invocation and benediction have long been recognized to be "as traditional as any other parts of the [school] graduation program and are widely established." H. McKown, Commencement Activities (1931).

II

I find it a sufficient embarrassment that our Establishment Clause jurisprudence regarding holiday displays has come to "require scrutiny more commonly associated with interior decorators than with the judiciary." But interior decorating is a rock-hard science compared to psychology practiced by amateurs.

The Court presumably would separate graduation invocations and benedictions from other instances of public "preservation and transmission of religious beliefs" on the ground that they involve "psychological coercion." I find it a sufficient embarrassment that our Establishment Clause jurisprudence regarding holiday displays has come to "requir[e] scrutiny more commonly associated with interior decorators than with the judiciary." *American Jewish Congress v. Chicago* (CA 7 1987) (Easterbrook, J., dissenting). But interior decorating is a rock-hard science compared to psychology practiced by amateurs. A few citations of "[r]esearch in psychology" that have no particular bearing upon the precise issue here cannot disguise the fact that the Court has gone beyond the realm where judges know what they are doing. The Court's argument that state officials have "coerced" students to take part in the invocation and benediction at graduation ceremonies is, not to put too fine a point on it, incoherent.

The Court identifies two "dominant facts" that it says dictate its ruling that invocations and benedictions at public school graduation ceremonies violate the Establishment Clause. Neither of them is, in any relevant sense, true.

A

The Court declares that students' "attendance and participation in the [invocation and benediction] are, in a fair and real sense, obligatory." But what exactly is this "fair and real sense"? According to the Court, students at graduation who want "to avoid the fact or appearance of participation," in the invocation and benediction are *psychologically* obligated by "public pressure, as well as peer pressure, . . . to stand as a group or, at least, maintain respectful silence" during those prayers. This assertion—*the very linchpin of the Court's opinion*—is almost as intriguing for what it does not say as for what it says. It does not say, for example, that students are psychologically coerced to bow their heads, place their hands in a Durer-like prayer position, pay attention to the prayers, utter "Amen," or in fact pray. (Perhaps further intensive psychological research remains to be done on these matters.) It claims only that students are psychologically coerced "to stand . . . or, at least, maintain respectful silence." (emphasis added). Both halves of this disjunctive (both of which must amount to the fact or appearance of participation in prayer if the Court's analysis is to survive on its own terms) merit particular attention.

To begin with the latter: the Court's notion that a student who simply sits in "respectful silence" during the invocation and benediction (when all others are standing) has somehow joined—or would somehow be perceived as having joined—in the prayers is nothing short of ludicrous. We indeed live in a vulgar age. But surely "our social conventions" have not coarsened to the point that anyone who does not stand on his chair and shout obscenities can reasonably be deemed to have assented to everything said in his presence. Since the Court does not dispute that students exposed to prayer at graduation ceremonies retain (despite "subtle coercive pressures") the free will to sit, there is absolutely no basis for the Court's decision. It is fanciful enough to say that "a reasonable dissenter," standing head erect in a class of bowed heads, "could believe that the group exercise signified her own participation or approval of it." It is beyond the absurd to say that she could entertain such a belief while pointedly declining to rise.

But let us assume the very worst, that the nonparticipating graduate is "subtly coerced"...to stand! Even that half of the disjunctive does not remotely establish a "participation" (or an "appearance of participation") in a religious exercise. The Court acknowledges that, "in our culture, standing...can signify adherence to a view or simple respect for the views of others." (Much more often the latter than the former, I think, except perhaps in the proverbial town meeting, where one votes by standing.) But if it is a permissible inference that one who is standing is doing so simply out of respect for the prayers of others that are in progress, then how can it possibly be said that a "reasonable dissenter...could believe that the group exercise signified her own participation or approval"? Quite obviously, it cannot. I may add, moreover, that maintaining respect for the religious observances of others is a fundamental civic virtue that government (including the public schools) can and should cultivate—so that, even if it were the case that the displaying of such respect might be mistaken for taking part in the prayer, I would deny that the dissenter's interest in avoiding *even the false appearance of participation* constitutionally trumps the government's interest in fostering respect for religion generally.

> *In* Barnette, *we held that a public school student could not be compelled to recite the Pledge; we did not even hint that she could not be compelled to observe respectful silence.... Logically, that ought to be the next project for the Court's bulldozer.*

The opinion manifests that the Court itself has not given careful consideration to its test of psychological coercion. For if it had, how could it observe, with no hint of concern or disapproval, that students stood for the Pledge of Allegiance, which immediately preceded Rabbi Gutterman's invocation? The government can, of course, no more coerce political orthodoxy than religious orthodoxy. Moreover, since the Pledge of Allegiance has been revised since *Barnette* to include the phrase "under God," recital of the Pledge would appear to raise the same Establishment Clause issue as the invocation and benediction. If students were psychologically coerced to remain standing during the invocation, they must also have been psychologically coerced, moments before, to stand for (and thereby, in the Court's view, take part in or appear to take part in) the Pledge. Must the Pledge therefore be barred from the public schools (both from graduation ceremonies and from the classroom)? In *Barnette*, we held that a public school student could not be compelled to recite the Pledge; we did not even hint that she could not be compelled to observe respectful silence—indeed, even to stand in respectful silence—when those who wished to recite it did so. Logically, that ought to be the next project for the Court's bulldozer.

I also find it odd that the Court concludes that high school graduates may not be subjected to this supposed psychological coercion, yet refrains from addressing whether "mature adults" may. I had thought that the reason graduation from high school is regarded as so significant an event is that it is generally associated with transition from adolescence to young adulthood. Many graduating seniors, of course, are old enough to vote. Why, then, does the Court treat them as though they were first-graders? Will we soon have a jurisprudence that distinguishes between mature and immature adults?

B

The other "dominant fac[t]" identified by the Court is that "[s]tate officials direct the performance of a formal religious exercise" at school graduation ceremonies. "Direct[ing] the performance of a formal religious exercise" has a sound of liturgy to it, summoning up images of the principal directing acolytes where to carry the cross, or showing the rabbi where to unroll the Torah. A Court professing to be engaged in a "delicate and fact-sensitive" line-drawing would better describe what it means as "prescribing the content of an invocation and benediction." But even that would be false. All the record shows is that principals of the Providence public schools, acting within their delegated authority, have invited clergy to deliver invocations and benedictions at graduations; and that Principal Lee invited Rabbi Gutterman, provided him a two-page pamphlet, prepared by the National Conference of Christians and Jews, giving general advice on inclusive prayer for civic occasions, and advised him that his prayers at graduation should be nonsectarian. How these facts can fairly be transformed into the charges that Principal Lee "directed and controlled the content of [Rabbi Gutterman's] prayer," that school officials "monitor prayer," and attempted to "'compose official prayers,'" and that the "government involvement with religious activity in this case is pervasive" is difficult to fathom. The Court identifies nothing in the record remotely suggesting that school officials have ever drafted, edited, screened, or censored graduation prayers, or that Rabbi Gutterman was a mouthpiece of the school officials.

These distortions of the record are, of course, not harmless error: without them, the Court's solemn assertion that the school officials could reasonably be perceived to be "enforc[ing] a religious orthodoxy," would ring as hollow, as it ought.

III

The deeper flaw in the Court's opinion does not lie in its wrong answer to the question whether there was state-induced "peer-pressure" coercion; it lies, rather, in the Court's making violation of the Establishment Clause hinge on such a precious question. The coercion that was a hallmark of historical establishments of religion was coercion of religious orthodoxy and of financial support by force of law and threat of penalty. Typically, attendance at the state church was required; only clergy of the official church could lawfully perform sacraments; and dissenters, if tolerated, faced an array of civil disabilities. Thus, for example, in the colony of Virginia, where the Church of England had been established, ministers were required by law to conform to the doctrine and rites of the Church of England; and all persons were required to attend church and observe the Sabbath, were tithed for the public support of Anglican ministers, and were taxed for the costs of building and repairing churches.

The Establishment Clause was adopted to prohibit such an establishment of religion at the federal level (and to protect state establishments of religion from federal interference). I will further acknowledge for the sake of argument that, as some scholars have argued, by 1790, the term "establishment" had acquired an additional meaning—"financial support of religion generally, by public taxation"—that reflected the development of "general or multiple" establishments, not limited to a single church. But that would still be an establishment coerced by *force of law*. And I will further concede that our constitutional tradition, from the Declaration of Independence and the first inaugural address of Washington, quoted earlier, down to the present day, has, with a few aberrations ruled out of order government-sponsored endorsement of religion—even when no legal coercion is present, and indeed

even when no ersatz, "peer-pressure" psycho-coercion is present—
where the endorsement is sectarian, in the sense of specifying details
upon which men and women who believe in a benevolent, omnipotent Creator and Ruler of the world are known to differ (for example, the divinity of Christ). But there is simply no support for the proposition that the officially sponsored nondenominational invocation and benediction read by Rabbi Gutterman—with no one legally coerced to recite them—violated the Constitution of the United States. To the contrary, they are so characteristically American they could have come from the pen of George Washington or Abraham Lincoln himself.

> *I see no warrant for expanding the concept of coercion beyond acts backed by threat of penalty—a brand of coercion that, happily, is readily discernible to those of us who have made a career of reading the disciples of Blackstone, rather than of Freud.*

Thus, while I have no quarrel with the Court's general proposition that the Establishment Clause "guarantees that government may not coerce anyone to support or participate in religion or its exercise," I see no warrant for expanding the concept of coercion beyond acts backed by threat of penalty—a brand of coercion that, happily, is readily discernible to those of us who have made a career of reading the disciples of Blackstone, rather than of Freud. The Framers were indeed opposed to coercion of religious worship by the National Government; but, as their own sponsorship of nonsectarian prayer in public events demonstrates, they understood that "[s]peech is not coercive; the listener may do as he likes." *American Jewish Congress v. Chicago*, 827 F.2d, at 132 (Easterbrook, J., dissenting).

This historical discussion places in revealing perspective the Court's extravagant claim that the State has, "for all practical purposes," and "in every practical sense," compelled students to participate in prayers at graduation. Beyond the fact, stipulated to by the parties, that attendance at graduation is voluntary, there is nothing in the record to indicate that failure of attending students to take part in the invocation or benediction was subject to any penalty or discipline. Contrast this with, for example, the facts of *Barnette*: Schoolchildren were required by law to recite the Pledge of Allegiance; failure to do so resulted in expulsion, threatened the expelled child with the prospect of being sent to a reformatory for criminally inclined juveniles, and subjected his parents to prosecution (and incarceration) for causing delinquency. To characterize the "subtle coercive pressures" allegedly present here as the "practical" equivalent of the legal sanctions in *Barnette* is . . . well, let me just say it is not a "delicate and fact-sensitive" analysis.

The Court relies on our "school prayer" cases, *Engel v. Vitale* (1962) and *School Dist. of Abington v. Schempp* (1963). But whatever the merit of those cases, they do not support, much less compel, the Court's psychojourney. In the first place, *Engel* and *Schempp* do not constitute an exception to the rule, distilled from historical practice, that public ceremonies may include prayer; rather, they simply do not fall within the scope of the rule (for the obvious reason that school instruction is not a public ceremony). Second, we have made clear our understanding that school prayer occurs within a framework in which legal coercion to attend school (i.e., coercion under threat of penalty) provides the ultimate backdrop. In *Schempp*, for example, we emphasized that the prayers

> *The Court relies on our "school prayer" cases,* Engel v. Vitale *and* School District of Abington v. Schempp. *But whatever the merit of those cases, they do not support, much less compel, the Court's psychojourney.*

were "prescribed as part of the curricular activities of students who are *required by law* to attend school." (emphasis added). *Engel*'s suggestion that the school prayer program at issue there—which permitted students "to remain silent or be excused from the room"—involved "indirect coercive pressure" should be understood against this backdrop of legal coercion. The question whether the opt-out procedure in *Engel* sufficed to dispel the coercion resulting from the mandatory attendance requirement is quite different from the question whether forbidden coercion exists in an environment utterly devoid of legal compulsion. And finally, our school prayer cases turn in part on the fact that the classroom is inherently an instructional setting, and daily prayer there—where parents are not present to counter "the students' emulation of teachers as role models and the children's susceptibility to peer pressure," *Edwards v. Aguillard* (1987)—might be thought to raise special concerns regarding state interference with the liberty of parents to direct the religious upbringing of their children: "Families entrust public schools with the education of their children, but condition their trust on the understanding that the classroom will not purposely be used to advance religious views that may conflict with the private beliefs of the student and his or her family." Voluntary prayer at graduation—a one-time ceremony at which parents, friends, and relatives are present—can hardly be thought to raise the same concerns.

IV

Our Religion Clause jurisprudence has become bedeviled (so to speak) by reliance on formulaic abstractions that are not derived from, but positively conflict with, our long-accepted constitutional traditions. Foremost among these has been the so-called *Lemon* test, which has received well-earned criticism from many Members of this Court. The Court today demonstrates the irrelevance of *Lemon* by essentially ignoring it, and the interment of that case may be the one happy byproduct of the Court's otherwise lamentable decision. Unfortunately, however, the Court has replaced *Lemon* with its psycho-coercion test, which suffers the double disability of having no roots whatever in our people's historic practice and being as infinitely expandable as the reasons for psychotherapy itself.

Another happy aspect of the case is that it is only a jurisprudential disaster, and not a practical one. Given the odd basis for the Court's decision, invocations and benedictions will be able to be given at public school graduations next June, as they have for the past century and a half, so long as school authorities make clear that anyone who abstains from screaming in protest does not necessarily participate in the prayers. All that is seemingly needed is an announcement, or perhaps a written insertion at the beginning of the graduation program, to the effect that, while all are asked to rise for the invocation and benediction, none is compelled to join in them, nor will be assumed, by rising, to have done so. That obvious fact recited, the graduates and their parents may proceed to thank God, as Americans have always done, for the blessings He has generously bestowed on them and on their country.

The reader has been told much in this case about the personal interest of Mr. Weisman and his daughter, and very little about the personal interests on the other side. They are not inconsequential. Church and state would not be such a difficult subject if religion were, as the Court apparently thinks it to be, some purely personal avocation that can be indulged entirely in secret, like pornography, in the privacy of one's room. For most believers, it is not that, and has never been. Religious men and women of almost all denominations have felt it necessary to acknowledge and beseech the blessing of God as a people, and not just as individuals, because they believe in the "protection of divine Providence," as the Declaration of Independence put it, not just for individuals but for societies; because they believe God to be, as Washington's first Thanksgiving Proclamation put it, the "Great Lord and Ruler of Nations." One can believe in the effectiveness of such public worship, or one can deprecate and deride it. But the longstanding American tradition of prayer at official ceremonies displays with unmistakable clarity that the Establishment Clause does not forbid the government to accommodate it.

The narrow context of the present case involves a community's celebration of one of the milestones in its young citizens' lives, and it is a bold step for this Court to seek to banish from that occasion, and from thousands of similar celebrations throughout this land, the expression of gratitude to God that a majority of the community wishes to make. The issue before us today is not the abstract philosophical question whether the alternative of frustrating this desire of a religious majority is to be preferred over the alternative of imposing "psychological coercion," or a feeling of exclusion, upon nonbelievers. Rather, the question is *whether a mandatory choice in favor of the former has been imposed by the United States Constitution.* As the age-old practices of our people show, the answer to that question is not at all in doubt.

I must add one final observation: the Founders of our Republic knew the fearsome potential of sectarian religious belief to generate civil dissension and civil strife. And they also knew that nothing, absolutely nothing, is so inclined to foster among religious believers of various faiths a toleration—no, an affection—for one another than voluntarily joining in prayer together, to the God whom they all worship and seek. Needless to say, no one should be compelled to do that, but it is a shame to deprive our public culture of the opportunity, and indeed the encouragement, for people to do it voluntarily. The Baptist or Catholic who heard and joined in the simple and inspiring prayers of Rabbi Gutterman on this official and patriotic occasion was inoculated from religious bigotry and prejudice in a manner that cannot be replicated. To deprive our society of that important unifying mechanism in order to spare the nonbeliever what seems to me the minimal inconvenience of standing, or even sitting in respectful nonparticipation, is as senseless in policy as it is unsupported in law.

For the foregoing reasons, I dissent.

LAMB'S CHAPEL v. CENTER MORICHES UNION FREE SCHOOL DISTRICT (1993)

The Center Moriches Union Free School District in New York enacted a policy of allowing civic and social uses of its schools but prohibited use by any group for religious purposes. This policy was enforced to exclude the pastor of Lamb's Chapel, who sought to use the school facilities to show a film series by Dr. James Dobson on issues related to family values and child rearing. The pastor sued alleging violation of free speech under the First Amendment.

In ruling that the policy indeed violated the free speech rights of the pastor and his church, the Court majority also stated that use of the school by the church for its film presentation would not violate the Establishment

Clause. The Court, after ignoring the *Lemon* test a year earlier in *Lee v. Weisman*, applied the test here and found the church's use of the school harmless.

Justice Scalia agreed with the Court's free speech conclusion, but wrote a separate opinion to point out the absurdity of the Court's use of *Lemon*. The image Scalia evokes to make his point qualifies this short opinion as one of his most memorable.

~~∽⬥∼~~

Justice Scalia,
with whom Justice Thomas
joins, concurring in the judgment.

I join the Court's conclusion that the District's refusal to allow use of school facilities for petitioners' film viewing, while generally opening the schools for community activities, violates petitioners' First Amendment free speech rights...I also agree with the Court that allowing Lamb's Chapel to use school facilities poses "no realistic danger" of a violation of the Establishment Clause, but I cannot accept most of its reasoning in this regard. The Court explains that the showing of petitioners' film on school property after school hours would not cause the community to "think that the District was endorsing religion or any particular creed," and further notes that access to school property would not violate the three–part test articulated in *Lemon v. Kurtzman* (1971).

As to the Court's invocation of the *Lemon* test: Like some ghoul in a late-night horror movie that repeatedly sits up in its grave and shuffles abroad after being repeatedly killed and buried, *Lemon* stalks our Establishment Clause jurisprudence once again, frightening the little children and school attorneys of Center Moriches Union Free

School District. Its most recent burial, only last Term, was, to be sure, not fully six feet under: Our decision in *Lee v. Weisman* conspicuously avoided using the supposed "test," but also declined the invitation to repudiate it. Over the years, however, no fewer than five of the currently sitting Justices have, in their own opinions, personally driven pencils through the creature's heart (the author of today's opinion repeatedly), and a sixth has joined an opinion doing so.

The secret of the *Lemon* test's survival, I think, is that it is so easy to kill. It is there to scare us (and our audience) when we wish it to do so, but we can command it to return to the tomb at will. When we wish to strike down a practice it forbids, we invoke it, see, e.g., *Aguilar v. Fenton* (1985) (striking down state remedial education program administered in part in

Like some ghoul in a late-night horror movie that repeatedly sits up in its grave and shuffles abroad after being repeatedly killed and buried, Lemon *stalks our Establishment Clause jurisprudence once again, frightening the little children and school attorneys of Center Moriches Union Free School District.*

parochial schools); when we wish to uphold a practice it forbids, we ignore it entirely, see *Marsh v. Chambers* (1983) (upholding state legislative chaplains). Sometimes, we take a middle course, calling its three prongs "no more than helpful signposts," *Hunt v. McNair* (1973). Such a docile and useful monster is worth keeping around, at least in a somnolent state; one never knows when one might need him.

For my part, I agree with the long list of constitutional scholars who have criticized *Lemon* and bemoaned the strange Establishment Clause geometry of crooked lines and wavering shapes its intermittent use has produced. I will decline to apply *Lemon*—whether it validates or invalidates the government action in question—and therefore cannot join the opinion of the Court today.

I cannot join for yet another reason: the Court's statement that the proposed use of the school's facilities is constitutional because (among other things) it would not signal endorsement of religion in general. What a strange notion, that a Constitution which itself gives "religion in general" preferential treatment (I refer to the Free Exercise Clause) forbids endorsement of religion in general. The attorney general of New York not only agrees with that strange notion, he has an explanation for it: "Religious advocacy," he writes, "serves the community only in the eyes of its adherents, and yields a benefit only to those who already believe." Brief for Respondent Attorney General 24. That was *not* the view of those who adopted our Constitution, who believed that the public virtues inculcated by religion are a public good. It suffices to point out that, during the summer of 1789, when it was in the process of drafting the First Amendment, Congress enacted the Northwest Territory Ordinance that the Confederation Congress had adopted, in 1787—Article III of which provides, "Religion, morality, and knowledge, *being necessary to good government and the happiness of mankind*, schools and the means of education shall forever be encouraged." Unsurprisingly, then, indifference to "religion in general" is not what our cases, both old and recent, demand.

For the reasons given by the Court, I agree that the Free Speech Clause of the First Amendment forbids what respondents have done here. As for the asserted Establishment Clause justification, I would hold, simply and clearly, that giving Lamb's Chapel nondiscriminatory access to school facilities cannot violate that provision because it does not signify state or local embrace of a particular religious sect.

McCREARY COUNTY v. ACLU (2005)

Two counties in Kentucky posted large, readily visible copies of the Ten Commandments in their courthouses. After the American Civil Liberties Union sued to remove the displays on the grounds that they violated the First Amendment's Establishment Clause, the counties adopted resolutions (nearly identical to each other) calling for a more extensive exhibit showing that the Commandments are Kentucky's "precedent legal code." The resolutions noted several grounds for taking that position, including the state legislature's acknowledgment of Christ as the "Prince of Ethics." The new displays included eight smaller, historical documents, including the Declaration of Independence.

After changing lawyers, the counties revised their displays once again. They did not, however, pass a new resolution authorizing the new exhibits, nor did the counties repeal their earlier resolutions. The new display, called "The Foundations of American Law and Government," consisted of nine framed documents of equal size, one of which was the text of the Ten Commandments with an explanation of their influence on Western legal thought. Other items displayed included the Declaration of Independence and the lyrics of the "Star-Spangled Banner," each accompanied by a statement about its historical and legal significance.

The district court blocked the exhibitions, ruling that they lacked any secular purpose, as required by the Supreme Court's *Lemon* decision. The lower court ruled that the Ten Commandments are a distinctly religious document. Even the revised display was problematic because the counties selected documents that specifically referred to Christianity.

In a five-to-four decision, the Supreme Court agreed that the displays violated the Establishment Clause because their purpose had been to advance religion. Writing for the majority, Justice David Souter said that an objective observer would have viewed all three iterations of the displays as a governmental endorsement of religion, especially because the counties' original resolutions showed their intent to promote religion. Courts, Souter wrote, should look at the real motives underlying government actions with respect to religion. The Establishment Clause requires the government "to stay neutral on religious belief, which is reserved for the conscience of the individual."

Justice Scalia dissented. As he did in his opinion in *Lee v. Weisman*, Scalia argued that public expressions of faith had a long history in the United States and clearly would not have violated the Constitution in the eyes of the Framers. A public display of the Ten Commandments, like a public prayer at a school graduation, should not elicit any legal controversy. But Scalia used his dissent to promote bolder conclusions about the limits of the Establishment Clause. First, he argued that the Constitution does not require government to be neutral between religion and irreligion. The insistence on neutrality, he objected, is rooted not in the history of our country's practices but in mistaken Court precedents. "Nothing stands behind the Court's assertion that governmental affirmation of the society's belief in God is unconstitutional except the Court's own say-so, citing as support only the unsubstantiated say-so of earlier Courts going back no farther than the mid-20th century," Scalia wrote.

Scalia also argued that the Constitution does not prevent the government from favoring some religious beliefs over others in the context of public acknowledgments. He wrote that "97.7% of all believers," including Christians, Jews, and Muslims, are monotheistic. Public expressions of faith that favor this great majority of believers over others do not offend the Constitution. "With respect to public acknowledgment of religious faith, it is entirely clear from our Nation's historical practices that the Establishment Clause permits this disregard of polytheists and believers in unconcerned deities, just as it permits the disregard of devout atheists."

Justice Scalia, with whom the Chief Justice and Justice Thomas join, and with whom Justice Kennedy joins as to Parts II and III, dissenting.

I would uphold McCreary County and Pulaski County, Kentucky's (hereinafter Counties) displays of the Ten Commandments. I shall discuss first, why the Court's oft repeated assertion that the government cannot favor religious practice is false; second, why today's opinion extends the scope of that falsehood even beyond prior cases; and third, why even on the basis of the Court's false assumptions the judgment here is wrong.

I

A

On September 11, 2001, I was attending in Rome, Italy an international conference of judges and lawyers, principally from Europe and the United States. That night and the next morning virtually all of the participants watched, in their hotel rooms, the address to the Nation by the President of the United States concerning the murderous attacks upon the Twin Towers and the Pentagon, in which thousands of Americans had been killed. The address ended, as Presidential addresses often do, with the prayer "God bless America." The next afternoon I was approached by one of the judges from a European country, who, after extending his profound condolences for my country's loss, sadly observed "How I wish that the Head of State of my country, at a similar time of national tragedy and distress, could conclude his address 'God bless _____.' It is of course absolutely forbidden."

That is one model of the relationship between church and state—a model spread across Europe by the armies of Napoleon, and reflected in the Constitution of France, which begins "France is [a]...secular...Republic." Religion is to be strictly excluded from the public forum. This is not, and never was, the model adopted by America. George Washington added to the form of Presidential oath prescribed by Art. II, § 1, cl. 8, of the Constitution, the concluding words "so help me God." The Supreme Court under John Marshall opened its sessions with the prayer, "God save the United States and this Honorable Court." The First Congress instituted the practice of beginning its legislative sessions with a prayer. *Marsh v. Chambers* (1983). The same week that Congress submitted the Establishment Clause as part of the Bill of Rights for ratification by the States, it enacted legislation providing for paid chaplains in the House and Senate. The day after the First Amendment was proposed, the same Congress that had proposed it requested the President to proclaim "a day of public thanksgiving and prayer, to be observed, by acknowledging, with grateful hearts, the many and signal favours of Almighty God." President Washington offered the first Thanksgiving Proclamation shortly thereafter, devoting November 26, 1789 on behalf of the American people " 'to the service of that great and glorious Being who is the beneficent author of all the good that is, that was, or that will be,' " *Van Orden v. Perry*, thus beginning a tradition of offering gratitude to God that continues today. The same Congress also reenacted the Northwest Territory Ordinance of 1787, Article III of which provided: "Religion, morality, and knowledge, being necessary to good government and the happiness of mankind, schools and the means of education shall forever be encouraged." And of course the First Amendment itself accords religion (and no other manner of belief) special constitutional protection.

These actions of our First President and Congress and the Marshall Court were not idiosyncratic; they reflected the beliefs of the period. Those who wrote the Constitution believed that morality was essential to the well-being of society and that encouragement of religion was the best way to foster morality. The "fact that the Founding Fathers believed devotedly that there was a God and that the unalienable rights of man were rooted in Him is clearly evidenced in their writings, from the Mayflower Compact to the Constitution itself." *School Dist. of Abington Township v. Schempp* (1963). President Washington opened his Presidency with a prayer, and reminded his fellow citizens at the conclusion of it that "reason and experience both forbid us to expect that National morality can prevail in exclusion of religious principle." President John Adams wrote to the Massachusetts Militia, "we have no government armed with power capable of contending with human passions unbridled by morality and religion.... Our Constitution was made only for a moral and religious people. It is wholly inadequate to the government of any other." Thomas Jefferson concluded his second inaugural address by inviting his audience to pray:

> "I shall need, too, the favor of that Being in whose hands we are, who led our fathers, as Israel of old, from their native land and planted them in a country flowing with all the necessaries and comforts of life; who has covered our infancy with His providence and our riper years with His wisdom and power and to whose goodness I ask you to join in supplications with me that He will so enlighten the minds of your servants, guide their councils, and prosper their measures that whatsoever they do shall result in your good, and shall secure to you the peace, friendship, and approbation of all nations."

James Madison, in his first inaugural address, likewise placed his confidence "in the guardianship and guidance of that Almighty Being whose power regulates the destiny of nations, whose blessings have been so conspicuously dispensed to this rising Republic, and to whom we are bound to address our devout gratitude for the past, as well as our fervent supplications and best hopes for the future."

Nor have the views of our people on this matter significantly changed. Presidents continue to conclude the Presidential oath with the words "so help me God." Our legislatures, state and national, continue to open their sessions with prayer led by official chaplains. The sessions of this Court continue to open with the prayer "God save the United States and this Honorable Court." Invocation of the Almighty by our public figures, at all levels of government, remains commonplace. Our coinage bears the motto "IN GOD WE TRUST." And our Pledge of Allegiance contains the acknowledgment that we are a Nation "under God." As one of our Supreme Court opinions rightly observed, "We are a religious people whose institutions presuppose a Supreme Being." *Zorach v. Clauson* (1952)...

> *Nothing stands behind the Court's assertion that governmental affirmation of the society's belief in God is unconstitutional except the Court's own say-so, citing as support only the unsubstantiated say-so of earlier Courts going back no farther than the mid-20th century.*

With all of this reality (and much more) staring it in the face, how can the Court possibly assert that " 'the First Amendment mandates governmental neutrality between... religion and nonreligion,' " and that "[m]anifesting a purpose to favor... adherence to religion generally" is unconstitutional? Who says so? Surely not the words of the Constitution. Surely not

the history and traditions that reflect our society's constant understanding of those words. Surely not even the current sense of our
society, recently reflected in an Act of Congress adopted unanimously
by the Senate and with only 5 nays in the House of Representatives
criticizing a Court of Appeals opinion that had held "under God" in
the Pledge of Allegiance unconstitutional. Nothing stands behind the
Court's assertion that governmental affirmation of the society's belief
in God is unconstitutional except the Court's own say-so, citing as
support only the unsubstantiated say-so of earlier Courts going back
no farther than the mid-20th century. And it is, moreover, a thoroughly discredited say-so. It is discredited, to begin with, because a
majority of the Justices on the current Court (including at least one
Member of today's majority) have, in separate opinions, repudiated
the brain-spun "*Lemon* test" that embodies the supposed principle
of neutrality between religion and irreligion. And it is discredited
because the Court has not had the courage (or the foolhardiness) to
apply the neutrality principle consistently.

What distinguishes the rule of law from the dictatorship of a shifting Supreme Court majority is the absolutely indispensable requirement that judicial opinions be grounded in consistently applied
principle. That is what prevents judges from ruling now this way,
now that—thumbs up or thumbs down—as their personal preferences dictate. Today's opinion forthrightly (or actually, somewhat
less than forthrightly) admits that it does not rest upon consistently
applied principle. In a revealing footnote, the Court acknowledges
that the "Establishment Clause doctrine" it purports to be applying
"lacks the comfort of categorical absolutes." What the Court means
by this lovely euphemism is that sometimes the Court chooses to
decide cases on the principle that government cannot favor religion,

and sometimes it does not. The footnote goes on to say that "[i]n special instances we have found good reason" to dispense with the principle, but "[n]o such reasons present themselves here." It does not identify all of those "special instances," much less identify the "good reason" for their existence.

I have cataloged elsewhere the variety of circumstances in which this Court—even after its embrace of *Lemon*'s stated prohibition of such behavior—has approved government action "undertaken with the specific intention of improving the position of religion," *Edwards v. Aguillard* (1987) (Scalia, J., dissenting). Suffice it to say here that when the government relieves churches from the obligation to pay property taxes, when it allows students to absent themselves from public school to take religious classes, and when it exempts religious organizations from generally applicable prohibitions of religious discrimination, it surely means to bestow a benefit on religious practice—but we have approved it. Indeed, we have even approved (post-*Lemon*) government-led prayer to God. In *Marsh v. Chambers*, the Court upheld the Nebraska State Legislature's practice of paying a chaplain to lead it in prayer at the opening of legislative sessions. The Court explained that "[t]o invoke Divine guidance on a public body entrusted with making the laws is not...an 'establishment' of religion or a step toward establishment; it is simply a tolerable acknowledgment of beliefs widely held among the people of this country." (Why, one wonders, is not respect for the Ten Commandments a tolerable acknowledgment of beliefs widely held among the people of this country?)

The only "good reason" for ignoring the neutrality principle set forth in any of these cases was the antiquity of the practice at issue. That would be a good reason for finding the neutrality principle a mistaken interpretation of the Constitution, but it is hardly a good reason for letting an unconstitutional practice continue. We did not hide behind that reason in *Reynolds v. Sims* (1964), which found unconstitutional bicameral state legislatures of a sort that had existed since the beginning of the Republic. And almost monthly, it seems, the Court has not shrunk from invalidating aspects of criminal procedure and penology of similar vintage. See, e.g., *Deck v. Missouri* (2005) (invalidating practice of shackling defendants absent "special circumstances"); *Roper v. Simmons* (2005) (invalidating practice of executing under-18-year-old offenders). What, then, could be the genuine "good reason" for occasionally ignoring the neutrality principle? I suggest it is the instinct for self-preservation, and the recognition that the Court, which "has no influence over either the sword or the purse," The Federalist No. 78, cannot go too far down the road of an enforced neutrality that contradicts both historical fact and current practice without losing all that sustains it: the willingness of the people to accept its interpretation of the Constitution as definitive, in preference to the contrary interpretation of the democratically elected branches.

If religion in the public forum had to be entirely nondenominational, there could be no religion in the public forum at all.

Besides appealing to the demonstrably false principle that the government cannot favor religion over irreligion, today's opinion suggests that the posting of the Ten Commandments violates the principle that the government cannot favor one religion over another. That is indeed a valid principle where public aid or assistance to religion is concerned or where the free exercise of religion is at issue, but it necessarily applies in a more limited sense to public acknowledgment of the Creator. If religion in the public forum had to be entirely nondenominational, there could be no religion in the public forum at all. One cannot say the word "God," or "the Almighty," one cannot offer public supplication or thanksgiving, without contradicting the beliefs of some people that there are many gods, or that God or the gods pay no attention to human affairs. With respect to public acknowledgment of religious belief, it is entirely clear from our Nation's historical practices that the Establishment Clause permits this disregard of polytheists and believers in unconcerned deities, just as it permits the disregard of devout atheists. The Thanksgiving Proclamation issued by George Washington at the instance of the First Congress was scrupulously nondenominational—but it was monotheistic. In *Marsh v. Chambers*, we said that the fact the particular prayers offered in the Nebraska Legislature were "in the Judeo-Christian tradition" posed no additional problem, because "there is no indication that the prayer opportunity has been exploited to proselytize or advance any one, or to disparage any other, faith or belief."

Historical practices thus demonstrate that there is a distance between the acknowledgment of a single Creator and the establishment of a religion. The former is, as *Marsh v. Chambers* put it, "a tolerable acknowledgment of beliefs widely held among the people of this country." The three most popular religions in the United States, Christianity, Judaism, and Islam—which combined account for 97.7% of all believers—are monotheistic. All of them, moreover (Islam included), believe that the Ten Commandments were given by God to Moses, and are divine prescriptions for a virtuous life. Publicly honoring the Ten Commandments is thus indistinguishable, insofar as discriminating against other religions is concerned, from publicly honoring God. Both practices are recognized across such a broad and diverse range of the population—from Christians to Muslims—that they cannot be reasonably understood as a government endorsement of a particular religious viewpoint.

B

A few remarks are necessary in response to the criticism of this dissent by the Court, as well as Justice Stevens' criticism in the related case of *Van Orden v. Perry*. Justice Stevens' writing is largely devoted to an attack upon a straw man. "[R]eliance on early religious proclamations and statements made by the Founders is...problematic," he says, "because those views were not espoused at the Constitutional Convention in 1787 nor enshrined in the Constitution's text." *Van Orden*. But I have not relied upon (as he and the Court in this case do) mere "proclamations and statements" of the Founders. I have relied primarily upon official acts and official proclamations of the United States or of the component branches of its Government, including the First Congress's beginning of the tradition of legislative prayer to God, its appointment of congressional chaplains, its legislative proposal of a Thanksgiving Proclamation, and its reenactment of the Northwest Territory Ordinance; our first President's issuance of a Thanksgiving Proclamation; and invocation of God at the opening of sessions of the Supreme Court. The only mere "proclamations and statements" of the Founders I have relied upon were statements of Founders who occupied federal office, and spoke in at least a quasi-official capacity—Washington's prayer at the opening of his Presidency and his Farewell Address, President John Adams' letter to the Massachusetts Militia, and Jefferson's and Madison's inaugural addresses. The Court and Justice Stevens, by contrast, appeal to no official or even quasi-official action in support of their view of the Establishment Clause—only James Madison's Memorial and Remonstrance Against Religious Assessments, written before the federal Constitution had even been proposed, two letters written by Madison long after he was President, and the quasi-official inaction of Thomas Jefferson in refusing to issue a Thanksgiving Proclamation. The Madison Memorial and Remonstrance, dealing as it does with enforced contribution to religion rather than public acknowledgment of God, is irrelevant; one of the letters is utterly ambiguous as to the point at issue here, and should not be read to contradict Madison's statements in his first inaugural address, quoted earlier; even the other letter does not disapprove public acknowledgment of God, unless one posits (what Madison's own actions as President would contradict) that reference to God contradicts "the equality of all religious sects." And as to Jefferson: the notoriously self-contradicting Jefferson did not choose to have his nonauthorship of a Thanksgiving Proclamation inscribed on his tombstone. What he did have inscribed was his authorship of the Virginia Statute for Religious Freedom, a governmental act which begins "Whereas Almighty God hath created the mind free...."

It is no answer for Justice Stevens to say that the understanding that these official and quasi-official actions reflect was not "enshrined in the Constitution's text." The Establishment Clause, upon which Justice Stevens would rely, was enshrined in the Constitution's text, and these official actions show what it meant. There were doubtless some who thought it should have a broader meaning, but those views were plainly rejected. Justice Stevens says that reliance on these actions is "bound to paint a misleading picture," but it is hard to see why. What is more probative of the meaning of the Establishment Clause than the actions of the very Congress that proposed it, and of the first President charged with observing it?

Justice Stevens also appeals to the undoubted fact that some in the founding generation thought that the Religion Clauses of the First Amendment should have a narrower meaning, protecting only the Christian religion or perhaps only Protestantism. I am at a loss to see how this helps his case, except by providing a cloud of obfuscating smoke. (Since most thought the Clause permitted government invocation of monotheism, and some others thought it permitted government invocation of Christianity, he proposes that it be construed not to permit any government invocation of religion at all.) At any rate, those narrower views of the Establishment Clause were as clearly rejected as the more expansive ones. Washington's First Thanksgiving Proclamation is merely an example. All of the actions of Washington and the First Congress upon which I have relied, virtually all Thanksgiving Proclamations throughout our history, and all the other examples of our Government's favoring religion that I have cited, have invoked God, but not Jesus Christ.

[Footnote] Justice Stevens finds that Presidential inaugural and farewell speeches (which are the only speeches upon which I have relied) do not violate the Establishment Clause only because everyone knows that they express the personal religious views of the speaker, and not government policy. This is a peculiar stance for one who has voted that a student-led invocation at a high school football game and a rabbi-led invocation at a high school graduation did constitute the sort of governmental endorsement of religion that the Establishment Clause forbids.

Rather than relying upon Justice Stevens' assurance that "[t]he original understanding of the type of 'religion' that qualified for constitutional protection under the First amendment certainly did not include...followers of Judaism and Islam," I would prefer to take the word of George Washington, who, in his famous Letter to the Hebrew Congregation of Newport, Rhode Island, wrote that,

Even assuming that the meaning of the Constitution ought to change according to "democratic aspirations," why are those aspirations to be found in Justices' notions of what the Establishment Clause ought to mean, rather than in the democratically adopted dispositions of our current society?

"All possess alike liberty of conscience and immunities of citizenship. It is now no more that toleration is spoken of, as if it was by the indulgence of one class of people, that another enjoyed the exercise of their inherent natural rights."

The letter concluded, by the way, with an invocation of the one God:

"May the father of all mercies scatter light and not darkness in our paths, and make us all in our several vocations useful here, and in his own due time and way everlastingly happy."

Justice Stevens says that if one is serious about following the original understanding of the Establishment Clause, he must repudiate its incorporation into the Fourteenth Amendment, and hold that it does not apply against the States. This is more smoke. Justice Stevens did not feel that way last Term, when he joined an opinion insisting upon the original meaning of the Confrontation Clause, but nonetheless applying it against the State of Washington. The notion that incorporation empties the incorporated provisions of their original meaning has no support in either reason or precedent.

Justice Stevens argues that original meaning should not be the touchstone anyway, but that we should rather "expoun[d] the meaning of constitutional provisions with one eye towards our Nation's history and the other fixed on its democratic aspirations." *Van Orden.* This is not the place to debate the merits of the "living Constitution," though I must observe that Justice Stevens' quotation from *McCulloch v. Maryland* (1819) refutes rather than supports that approach. Even assuming, however, that the meaning of the Constitution ought to change according to "democratic aspirations," why are those aspirations to be found in Justices' notions of what the Establishment Clause ought to mean, rather than in the democratically adopted dispositions of our current society? As I have observed above, numerous provisions of our laws and numerous continuing practices of our people demonstrate that the government's invocation of God (and hence the government's invocation of the Ten Commandments) is unobjectionable—including a statute enacted by Congress almost unanimously less than three years ago, stating that "under God" in the Pledge of Allegiance is constitutional. To ignore all this is not to give effect to "democratic aspirations" but to frustrate them.

Finally, I must respond to Justice Stevens' assertion that I would "marginaliz[e] the belief systems of more than 7 million Americans" who adhere to religions that are not monotheistic. Surely that is a gross exaggeration. The beliefs of those citizens are entirely protected by the Free Exercise Clause, and by those aspects of the Establishment Clause that do not relate to government acknowledgment of the Creator. Invocation of God despite their beliefs is permitted not because nonmonotheistic religions cease to be religions recognized by the religion clauses of the First Amendment, but because governmental invocation of God is not an establishment. Justice Stevens fails to recognize that in the context of public acknowledgments of God there are legitimate competing interests: On the one hand, the interest of that minority in not feeling "excluded"; but on the other, the interest of the overwhelming majority of religious believers in being able to give God thanks and supplication as a people, and with respect to our national endeavors. Our national tradition has resolved that conflict in favor of the majority. It is not for this Court to change a disposition that accounts, many Americans think, for the phenomenon remarked upon in a quotation attributed to various authors, including Bismarck, but which I prefer to associate with Charles de Gaulle: "God watches over little children, drunkards, and the United States of America."

II

As bad as the *Lemon* test is, it is worse for the fact that, since its inception, its seemingly simple mandates have been manipulated to fit whatever result the Court aimed to achieve. Today's opinion is no different. In two respects it modifies *Lemon* to ratchet up the Court's hostility to religion. First, the Court justifies inquiry into legislative purpose, not as an end itself, but as a means to ascertain the appearance of the government action to an " 'objective observer.' " Because in the Court's view the true danger to be guarded against is that the objective observer would feel like an "outside[r]" or "not [a] full membe[r] of the political community," its inquiry focuses not on the actual purpose of government action, but the "purpose apparent from government action." Under this approach, even if a government could show that its actual purpose was not to advance religion, it would presumably violate the Constitution as long as the Court's objective observer would think otherwise.

I have remarked before that it is an odd jurisprudence that bases the unconstitutionality of a government practice that does not actually advance religion on the hopes of the government that it would do so. But that oddity pales in comparison to the one invited by today's analysis: the legitimacy of a government action with a wholly secular effect would turn on the misperception of an imaginary observer that the government officials behind the action had the intent to advance religion.

Second, the Court replaces *Lemon's* requirement that the government have "a secular...purpose," In *Edwards*, the Court did say that the state action was invalid because its "primary" or "preeminent" purpose was to advance a particular religious belief, but that statement was unnecessary to the result, since the Court rejected the State's only proffered secular purpose as a sham.

I have urged that Lemon's purpose prong be abandoned, because (as I have discussed in Part I) even an exclusive purpose to foster or assist religious practice is not necessarily invalidating. But today's extension makes things even worse. By shifting the focus of *Lemon's* purpose prong from the search for a genuine, secular motivation to the hunt for a predominantly religious purpose, the Court converts what has in the past been a fairly limited inquiry into a rigorous review of the full record. Those responsible for the adoption of the

Religion Clauses would surely regard it as a bitter irony that the religious values they designed those Clauses to protect have now become so distasteful to this Court that if they constitute anything more than a subordinate motive for government action they will invalidate it.

III

Even accepting the Court's Lemon-based premises, the displays at issue here were constitutional.

A

To any person who happened to walk down the hallway of the McCreary or Pulaski County Courthouse during the roughly nine months when the Foundations Displays were exhibited, the displays must have seemed unremarkable—if indeed they were noticed at all. The walls of both courthouses were already lined with historical documents and other assorted portraits; each Foundations Display was exhibited in the same format as these other displays and nothing in the record suggests that either County took steps to give it greater prominence.

Entitled "The Foundations of American Law and Government Display," each display consisted of nine equally sized documents: the original version of the Magna Carta, the Declaration of Independence, the Bill of Rights, the Star Spangled Banner, the Mayflower Compact of 1620, a picture of Lady Justice, the National Motto of the United States ("In God We Trust"), the Preamble to the Kentucky Constitution, and the Ten Commandments. The displays did not emphasize any of the nine documents in any way: The frame holding the Ten Commandments was of the same size and had the same appearance as that which held each of the other documents.

Posted with the documents was a plaque, identifying the display, and explaining that it "contains documents that played a significant role in the foundation of our system of law and government." The explanation related to the Ten Commandments was third in the list of nine and did not serve to distinguish it from the other documents. It stated:

> "The Ten Commandments have profoundly influenced the formation of Western legal thought and the formation of our country. That influence is clearly seen in the Declaration of Independence, which declared that, 'We hold these truths to be self-evident, that all men are created equal, that they are endowed by their Creator with certain unalienable Rights, that among these are Life, Liberty, and the pursuit of Happiness.' The Ten Commandments provide the moral background of the Declaration of Independence and the foundation of our legal tradition."

B

On its face, the Foundations Displays manifested the purely secular purpose that the Counties asserted before the District Court: "to display documents that played a significant role in the foundation of our system of law and government." That the Displays included the Ten Commandments did not transform their apparent secular purpose into one of impermissible advocacy for Judeo-Christian beliefs. Even an isolated display of the Decalogue conveys, at worst, "an equivocal message, perhaps of respect for Judaism, for religion in general, or for law." *Allegheny County*. But when the Ten Commandments appear alongside other documents of secular significance in a display devoted to the foundations of American law and government, the context communicates that the Ten Commandments are included, not to teach their binding nature as a religious text, but to show their unique contribution to the development of the legal system. This is doubly true when the display is introduced by a document that informs passersby that it "contains documents that played a significant role in the foundation of our system of law and government."

The same result follows if the Ten Commandments display is viewed in light of the government practices that this Court has countenanced in the past. The acknowledgment of the contribution that religion in general, and the Ten Commandments in particular, have made to our Nation's legal and governmental heritage is surely no more of a step towards establishment of religion than was the practice of legislative prayer we approved in *Marsh v. Chambers* (1983), and it seems to be on par with the inclusion of a crèche or a menorah in a "Holiday" display that incorporates other secular symbols. . . .

Acknowledgment of the contribution that religion has made to our Nation's legal and governmental heritage partakes of a centuries-old tradition. Members of this Court have themselves often detailed the degree to which religious belief pervaded the National Government during the founding era. Display of the Ten Commandments is well within the mainstream of this practice of acknowledgment. Federal, State, and local governments across the Nation have engaged in such display. The Supreme Court Building itself includes depictions of Moses with the Ten Commandments in the Courtroom and on the east pediment of the building, and symbols of the Ten Commandments "adorn the metal gates lining the north and south sides of the Courtroom as well as the doors leading into the Courtroom." *Van Orden*. Similar depictions of the Decalogue appear on public buildings and monuments throughout our Nation's Capital. The frequency of these displays testifies to the popular understanding that the Ten Commandments are a foundation of the rule of law, and a symbol of the role that religion played, and continues to play, in our system of government.

Displays erected in silence (and under the direction of good legal advice) are permissible, while those hung after discussion and debate are deemed unconstitutional.

Perhaps in recognition of the centrality of the Ten Commandments as a widely recognized symbol of religion in public life, the Court is at pains to dispel the impression that its decision will require governments across the country to sandblast the Ten Commandments from the public square. The constitutional problem, the Court says, is with the Counties' purpose in erecting the Foundations Displays, not the displays themselves. The Court adds in a footnote: "One consequence of taking account of the purpose underlying past actions is that the same government action may be constitutional if taken in the first instance and unconstitutional if it has a sectarian heritage."

This inconsistency may be explicable in theory, but I suspect that the "objective observer" with whom the Court is so concerned will recognize its absurdity in practice. By virtue of details familiar only to the parties to litigation and their lawyers, McCreary and Pulaski Counties, Kentucky, and Rutherford County, Tennessee, have been ordered to remove the same display that appears in courthouses from Mercer County, Kentucky to Elkhart County, Indiana. Displays erected in silence (and under the direction of good legal advice) are permissible, while those hung after discussion and debate are deemed unconstitutional. Reduction of the Establishment Clause to such minutiae trivializes the Clause's protection against religious establishment; indeed, it may inflame religious passions by making the passing comments of every government official the subject of endless litigation.

C

In any event, the Court's conclusion that the Counties exhibited the Foundations Displays with the purpose of promoting religion is doubtful. In the Court's view, the impermissible motive was apparent from the initial displays of the Ten Commandments all by themselves: When that occurs, the Court says, "a religious object is unmistakable." Surely that cannot be. If, as discussed above, the Commandments have a proper place in our civic history, even placing them by themselves can be civically motivated—especially when they are placed, not in a school (as they were in the Stone case upon which the Court places such reliance), but in a courthouse. And the fact that at the posting of the exhibit a clergyman was present is unremarkable (clergymen taking particular pride in the role of the Ten Commandments in our civic history); and even more unremarkable the fact that the clergyman "testified to the certainty of the existence of God."

The Court has in the past prohibited government actions that "proselytize or advance any one, or…disparage any other, faith or belief," see *Marsh*, or that apply some level of coercion (though I and others have disagreed about the form that coercion must take), see, e.g., *Lee v. Weisman* (Scalia, J., dissenting). The passive display of the Ten Commandments, even standing alone, does not begin to do either. What Justice Kennedy said of the crèche in Allegheny County is equally true of the Counties' original Ten Commandments displays:

"No one was compelled to observe or participate in any religious ceremony or activity. [T]he count[ies] [did not] contribut[e] significant amounts of tax money to serve the cause of one religious faith. [The Ten Commandments] are purely passive symbols of [the religious foundation for many of our laws and governmental institutions]. Passersby who disagree with the message conveyed by th[e] displays are free to ignore them, or even to turn their backs, just as they are free to do when they disagree with any other form of government speech."

Nor is it the case that a solo display of the Ten Commandments advances any one faith. They are assuredly a religious symbol, but they are not so closely associated with a single religious belief that their display can reasonably be understood as preferring one religious sect over another. The Ten Commandments are recognized by Judaism, Christianity, and Islam alike as divinely given.

The Court also points to the Counties' second displays, which featured a number of statements in historical documents reflecting a religious influence, and the resolutions that accompanied their erection, as evidence of an impermissible religious purpose. In the Court's view, "[t]he [second] display's unstinting focus...on religious passages, show[s] that the Counties were posting the Commandments precisely because of their sectarian content." No, all it necessarily shows is that the exhibit was meant to focus upon the historic role of religious belief in our national life—which is entirely permissible. And the same can be said of the resolution. To forbid any government focus upon this aspect of our history is to display what Justice Goldberg called "untutored devotion to the concept of neutrality," *Abington Township*, that would commit the Court (and the Nation) to a revisionist agenda of secularization.

Turning at last to the displays actually at issue in this case, the Court faults the Counties for not repealing the resolution expressing what the Court believes to be an impermissible intent. Under these circumstances, the Court says, "no reasonable observer could swallow the claim that the Counties had cast off the objective so unmistakable in the earlier displays." Even were I to accept all that the Court has said before, I would not agree with that assessment. To begin with, of course, it is unlikely that a reasonable observer would even have been aware of the resolutions, so there would be nothing to "cast off." The Court implies that the Counties may have been able to remedy the "taint" from the old resolutions by enacting a new one. But that action would have been wholly unnecessary in light of the explanation that the Counties included with the displays themselves: A plaque next to the documents informed all who passed by that each display "contains documents that played a significant role in the foundation of our system of law and government." Additionally, there was no reason for the Counties to repeal or repudiate the resolutions adopted with the hanging of the second displays, since they related only to the second displays. After complying with the District Court's order to remove the second displays "immediately," and erecting new displays that in content and by express assertion reflected a different purpose from that identified in the resolutions, the Counties had no reason to believe that their previous resolutions would be deemed to be the basis for their actions. After the Counties discovered that the sentiments expressed in the resolutions could be attributed to their most recent displays (in oral argument before this Court), they repudiated them immediately.

In sum: The first displays did not necessarily evidence an intent to further religious practice; nor did the second displays, or the resolutions authorizing them; and there is in any event no basis for attributing whatever intent motivated the first and second displays to the third. Given the presumption of regularity that always accompanies our review of official action, the Court has identified no evidence of a purpose to advance religion in a way that is inconsistent with our cases. The Court may well be correct in identifying the third displays as the fruit of a desire to display the Ten Commandments, but neither our cases nor our history support its assertion that such a desire renders the fruit poisonous.

For the foregoing reasons, I would reverse the judgment of the Court of Appeals.

CHAPTER TEN

ILLEGAL IMMIGRATION

✦

A RTICLE I, SECTION 8, of the U.S. Constitution grants to Congress the power "[t]o establish an uniform Rule of Naturalization." Congress has exercised its authority by passing laws, such as the Immigration and Nationality Act, which govern many aspects of immigration law. Federal law specifies which categories of aliens are ineligible to be admitted to the United States, requires aliens to register with the federal government and to carry proof of status, imposes sanctions on employers who hire unauthorized workers, and specifies which aliens may be removed and the procedures for doing so.

Another constitutional provision relevant to immigration is the Supremacy Clause, found in Article VI, which gives Congress the power to preempt (or to prevent enforcement of) state law. Sometimes Congress will say directly that it is preempting state law. In other cases, courts will infer federal preemption if Congress has occupied the field with laws and regulations so extensive that federal interests can be said to dominate. Lastly, federal power will be determined to preempt state action when state laws conflict with federal law. This last category was at issue when a challenge to a tough Arizona immigration law made its way to thé Supreme Court in 2010.

ARIZONA v. UNITED STATES (2012)

Arizona had an estimated 460,000 undocumented aliens in 2010, five times as many as it had in 1990. State leaders had frequently expressed their frustration with the lack of support from the federal government in securing the state's border with Mexico and dealing with the economic, safety, and social effects of rising numbers of illegal immigrants.

In 2010, the state passed S.B. 1070, the Support Our Law Enforcement and Safe Neighborhoods Act, a bill designed to address illegal immigration. This law, extremely controversial, received a great deal of media attention. The law's supporters saw it as a modest effort to help federal officials stop the tide of illegal immigration. Opponents said the new law would increase racial discrimination. Some immigrants' rights groups called for a boycott of the state of Arizona.

As soon as the law was enacted, the Obama administration's Justice Department sued Arizona in federal court, arguing that federal immigration law preempted the new state law. The district court issued an injunction preventing four provisions of the new law from going into effect, and Arizona appealed.

In a five-to-three decision (with Justice Elena Kagan not taking part), the Court agreed that federal law preempted three sections of Arizona's immigration law. These sections (1) made failure to comply with federal alien registration requirements a state misdemeanor (Section 3); (2) made an illegal immigrant's attempt to solicit or perform work a misdemeanor (Section 5(c)); and (3) authorized state and local officers to arrest without a warrant a person "the officer has probable cause to believe... has committed any public offense that makes the person removable from the United States" (Section 6). Writing for the majority, Justice Anthony Kennedy said these provisions conflicted with federal immigration policies as well as with the administration's enforcement priorities. The Court said the fourth section of the Arizona statute—which required officers conducting a stop, detention, or arrest to make efforts to verify the person's immigration status with the federal government (Section 2(b))—should be allowed to take effect unless evidence were offered to show that it would conflict with federal immigration law.

Justice Scalia wrote a solo opinion blasting the court's decision and reasoning. He examined the history of immigration enforcement and acknowledged that the federal government had taken the leading role in setting immigration policy over time. But he argued that the states continue to possess the authority as sovereigns to exclude "people who have no right to be there." Scalia wrote, "Arizona is entitled to have 'its own immigration policy'—including a more rigorous enforcement policy—so long as that does not conflict with federal law." Scalia then examined each of the four sections of the Arizona law at issue and concluded that none contradicted federal law; instead, he wrote, they enforce federal immigration restrictions more effectively. Finally, countering the Justice Department's argument that S.B. 1070 conflicts with the administration's freedom to set enforcement priorities, Scalia argued that Arizona does not have to sit idle when Congress chooses not to fund border security and the president chooses not to enforce immigration laws vigorously.

～⊂⊛⊃～

JUSTICE SCALIA, CONCURRING IN PART AND DISSENTING IN PART.

Today's opinion deprives States of what most would consider the defining characteristic of sovereignty: the power to exclude from the sovereign's territory people who have no right to be there.

The United States is an indivisible "Union of sovereign States." *Hinderlider v. La Plata River & Cherry Creek Ditch Co.* (1938). Today's opinion, approving virtually all of the Ninth Circuit's injunction against enforcement of the four challenged provisions of Arizona's law, deprives States of what most would consider the defining characteristic of sovereignty: the power to exclude from the sovereign's territory people who have no right to be there. Neither the Constitution itself nor even any law passed by Congress supports this result. I dissent.

I

As a sovereign, Arizona has the inherent power to exclude persons from its territory, subject only to those limitations expressed in the Constitution or constitutionally imposed by Congress. That power to exclude has long been recognized as inherent in sovereignty. Emer de Vattel's seminal 1758 treatise on the Law of Nations stated:

> "The sovereign may forbid the entrance of his territory either to foreigners in general, or in particular cases, or to certain persons, or for certain particular purposes, according as he may think it advantageous to the state. There is nothing in all this, that does not flow from the rights of domain and sovereignty: every one is obliged to pay respect to the prohibition; and whoever dares violate it, incurs the penalty decreed to render it effectual."

There is no doubt that "before the adoption of the constitution of the United States" each State had the authority to "prevent [itself] from being burdened by an influx of persons." *Mayor of New York v. Miln* (1837). And the Constitution did not strip the States of that authority. To the contrary, two of the Constitution's provisions were designed to enable the States to prevent "the intrusion of obnoxious aliens through other States." Letter from James Madison to Edmund Randolph (Aug. 27, 1782), in The Writings of James Madison (1900). The Articles of Confederation had provided that "the free inhabitants of each of these States, paupers, vagabonds and fugitives from justice excepted, shall be entitled to all privileges and immunities of free citizens in the several States." This meant that an unwelcome alien could obtain all the rights of a citizen of one State simply by first becoming an inhabitant of another. To remedy this, the Constitution's Privileges and Immunities Clause provided that "[t]he Citizens of each State shall be entitled to all Privileges and Immunities of Citizens in the several States." But if one State had particularly lax citizenship standards, it might still serve as a gateway for the entry of "obnoxious aliens" into other States. This problem was solved "by authorizing the general government to establish a uniform rule of naturalization throughout the United States." The Federalist No. 42. In other words, the naturalization power was given to Congress not to abrogate States' power to exclude those they did not want, but to vindicate it.

Two other provisions of the Constitution are an acknowledgment of the States' sovereign interest in protecting their borders. Article I provides that "[n]o State shall, without the Consent of the Congress, lay any Imposts or Duties on Imports or Exports, except what may be absolutely necessary for executing it's inspection Laws." This assumed what everyone assumed: that the States could exclude from their territory dangerous or unwholesome goods. A later portion of the same section provides that "[n]o State shall, without the Consent of Congress,... engage in War, unless actually invaded, or in such imminent Danger as will not admit of delay." This limits the States' sovereignty (in a way not relevant here) but leaves intact their inherent power to protect their territory.

Notwithstanding "[t]he myth of an era of unrestricted immigration" in the first 100 years of the Republic, the States enacted numerous laws restricting the immigration of certain classes of aliens, including convicted criminals, indigents, persons with contagious diseases, and (in Southern States) freed blacks. Neuman, *The Lost Century of American Immigration (1776–1875)*, 93 Colum. (1993). State laws not only provided for the removal of unwanted immigrants but also imposed penalties on unlawfully present aliens and those who aided their immigration.

In fact, the controversy surrounding the Alien and Sedition Acts involved a debate over whether, under the Constitution, the States had exclusive authority to enact such immigration laws. Criticism of the Sedition Act has become a prominent feature of our First Amendment jurisprudence, but one of the Alien Acts also aroused controversy at the time:

"Be it enacted by the Senate and House of Representatives of the United States of America in Congress assembled, That it shall be lawful for the President of the United States at any time during the continuance of this act, to order all such aliens as he shall judge dangerous to the peace and safety of the United States, or shall have reasonable grounds to suspect are

concerned in any treasonable or secret machinations against
the government thereof, to depart out of the territory of the
United States. . . ."

The Kentucky and Virginia Resolutions, written in denunci-
ation of these Acts, insisted that the power to exclude unwanted
aliens rested solely in the States. Jefferson's Kentucky Resolutions
insisted "that alien friends are under the jurisdiction and protection of the laws of the state wherein they are [and] that no power
over them has been delegated to the United States, nor prohibited
to the individual states, distinct from their power over citizens."
Madison's Virginia Resolutions likewise contended that the Alien
Act purported to give the President "a power nowhere delegated
to the federal government." Notably, moreover, the Federalist
proponents of the Act defended it primarily on the ground that
"[t]he removal of aliens is the usual preliminary of hostility" and
could therefore be justified in exercise of the Federal Government's war powers.

In *Mayor of New York v. Miln*, this Court considered a New York
statute that required the commander of any ship arriving in New
York from abroad to disclose "the name, place of birth, and last legal
settlement, age and occupation . . . of all passengers . . . with the
intention of proceeding to the said city." After discussing the sovereign authority to regulate the entrance of foreigners described by De
Vattel, the Court said:

"The power . . . of New York to pass this law having undeniably existed at the formation of the constitution, the simply
inquiry is, whether by that instrument it was taken from the

states, and granted to congress; for if it were not, it yet remains
with them."

And the Court held that it remains.

II

One would conclude from the foregoing that after the adoption
of the Constitution there was some doubt about the power of the
Federal Government to control immigration, but no doubt about
the power of the States to do so. Since the founding era (though
not immediately), doubt about the Federal Government's power
has disappeared. Indeed, primary responsibility for immigration policy has shifted from the States to the Federal Government. Congress
exercised its power "[t]o establish an uniform Rule of Naturalization," Art. I, § 8, cl. 4, very early on, see An Act to establish an
uniform Rule of Naturalization. But with the fleeting exception
of the Alien Act, Congress did not enact any legislation regulating
immigration for the better part of a century. In 1862, Congress
passed "An Act to prohibit the 'Coolie Trade' by American Citizens in American Vessels," which prohibited "procuring [Chinese
nationals]. . . to be disposed of, or sold, or transferred, for any term
of years or for any time whatever, as servants or apprentices, or to
be held to service or labor." Then, in 1875, Congress amended that
act to bar admission to Chinese, Japanese, and other Asian immigrants who had "entered into a contract or agreement for a term of
service within the United States, for lewd and immoral purposes."
And in 1882, Congress enacted the first general immigration statute. Of course, it hardly bears mention that Federal immigration
law is now extensive.

I accept that as a valid exercise of federal power—not because of the Naturalization Clause (it has no necessary connection to citizenship) but because it is an inherent attribute of sovereignty no less for the United States than for the States. As this Court has said, it is an "'accepted maxim of international law, that every sovereign nation has the power, as inherent in sovereignty, and essential to self-preservation, to forbid the entrance of foreigners within its dominions.'" *Fong Yue Ting v. United States* (1893). That is why there was no need to set forth control of immigration as one of the enumerated powers of Congress, although an acknowledgment of that power (as well as of the States' similar power, subject to federal abridgment) was contained in Art. I, § 9, which provided that "[t]he Migration or Importation of such Persons as any of the States now existing shall think proper to admit, shall not be prohibited by the Congress prior to the Year one thousand eight hundred and eight...."

In light of the predominance of federal immigration restrictions in modern times, it is easy to lose sight of the States' traditional role in regulating immigration—and to overlook their sovereign prerogative to do so. I accept as a given that State regulation is excluded by the Constitution when (1) it has been prohibited by a valid federal law, or (2) it conflicts with federal regulation—when, for example, it admits those whom federal regulation would exclude, or excludes those whom federal regulation would admit.

Possibility (1) need not be considered here: there is no federal law prohibiting the States' sovereign power to exclude (assuming federal authority to enact such a law). The mere existence of federal action in the immigration area—and the so-called field preemption arising from that action, upon which the Court's opinion so heavily relies—cannot be regarded as such a prohibition. We are not talking here

We are not talking here about a federal law prohibiting the States from regulating bubble-gum advertising, or even the construction of nuclear plants. We are talking about a federal law going to the core of state sovereignty: the power to exclude.

about a federal law prohibiting the States from regulating bubble-gum advertising, or even the construction of nuclear plants. We are talking about a federal law going to the core of state sovereignty: the power to exclude. Like elimination of the States' other inherent sovereign power, immunity from suit, elimination of the States' sovereign power to exclude requires that "Congress... unequivocally expres[s] its intent to abrogate," *Seminole Tribe of Fla. v. Florida* (1996). Implicit "field preemption" will not do.

Nor can federal power over illegal immigration be deemed exclusive because of what the Court's opinion solicitously calls "foreign countries['] concern[s] about the status, safety, and security of their nationals in the United States." The Constitution gives all those on our shores the protections of the Bill of Rights—but just as those rights are not expanded for foreign nationals because of their countries' views (some countries, for example, have recently discovered the death penalty to be barbaric), neither are the fundamental sovereign powers of the States abridged to accommodate foreign countries' views. Even in its international relations, the Federal Government must live with the inconvenient fact that it is a Union of independent States, who have their own sovereign powers. This is not the first time it has found that a nuisance and a bother in the conduct of foreign policy. Four years ago, for example, the Government importuned us to interfere with thoroughly constitutional state judicial procedures in the criminal trial of foreign nationals because the international community, and even an opinion of the International Court of Justice, disapproved them. We rejected that request, as we should reject the Executive's invocation of foreign-affairs considerations here. Though it may upset foreign powers—and even when the Federal Government desperately wants to avoid upsetting foreign powers—the States have the right to protect their borders against foreign nationals, just as they have the right to execute foreign nationals for murder.

What this case comes down to, then, is whether the Arizona law conflicts with federal immigration law—whether it excludes those whom federal law would admit, or admits those whom federal law would exclude. It does not purport to do so. It applies only to aliens who neither possess a privilege to be present under federal law nor have been removed pursuant to the Federal Government's inherent authority. I proceed to consider the challenged provisions in detail.

§ 2(B)

"For any lawful stop, detention or arrest made by a law enforcement official... in the enforcement of any other law or ordinance of a county, city or town or this state where reasonable suspicion exists that the person is an alien and is unlawfully present in the United States, a reasonable attempt shall be made, when practicable, to determine the immigration status of the person, except if the determination may hinder or obstruct an investigation. Any person who is arrested shall have the person's immigration status determined before the person is released...."

S.B. 1070, § 2(B)

The Government has conceded that "even before Section 2 was enacted, state and local officers had state-law authority to inquire of DHS [the Department of Homeland Security] about a suspect's unlawful status and otherwise cooperate with federal immigration officers." That concession, in my view, obviates the need for further inquiry. The Government's conflict-pre-emption claim calls on us "to determine whether, under the circumstances of this particular case, [the State's] law stands as an obstacle to the accomplishment and execution of the full purposes and objectives of Congress." *Hines v. Davidowitz* (1941). It is impossible to make such a finding without a factual record concerning the manner in which Arizona is implementing these provisions—something the Government's pre-enforcement challenge has pretermitted. "The fact that [a law] might operate unconstitutionally under some conceivable set of circumstances is insufficient to render it wholly invalid, since we have not recognized an 'overbreadth' doctrine outside the limited context of the First Amendment." *United States v. Salerno* (1987). And on its face, § 2(B) merely tells state officials that they are authorized to do something that they were, by the Government's concession, already authorized to do.

The Court therefore properly rejects the Government's challenge, recognizing that, "[a]t this stage, without the benefit of a definitive interpretation from the state courts, it would be inappropriate to assume § 2B will be construed in a way that creates a conflict with federal law." Before reaching that conclusion, however, the Court goes to great length to assuage fears that "state officers will be required to delay the release of some detainees for no reason other than to verify their immigration status." Of course, any investigatory detention, including one under § 2(B), may become an "unreasonable ... seizur[e]" if it lasts too long. But that has nothing to do with this case, in which the Government claims that § 2(B) is pre-empted by federal immigration law, not that anyone's Fourth Amendment rights have been violated. And I know of no reason why a protracted detention that does not violate the Fourth Amendment would contradict or conflict with any federal immigration law.

§ 6

"A peace officer, without a warrant, may arrest a person if the officer has probable cause to believe...[t]he person to be arrested has committed any public offense that makes the person removable from the United States."

S.B. 1070, § 6(A)(5)

This provision of S.B. 1070 expands the statutory list of offenses for which an Arizona police officer may make an arrest without a warrant. If an officer has probable cause to believe that an individual is "removable" by reason of a public offense, then a warrant is not required to make an arrest. The Government's primary contention is that § 6 is pre-empted by federal immigration law because it allows state officials to make arrests "without regard to federal priorities." The Court's opinion focuses on limits that Congress has placed on federal officials' authority to arrest removable aliens and the possibility that state officials will make arrests "to achieve [Arizona's] own immigration policy" and "without any input from the Federal Government."

Of course on this pre-enforcement record there is no reason to assume that Arizona officials will ignore federal immigration policy (unless it be the questionable policy of not wanting to identify illegal aliens who have committed offenses that make them removable). As Arizona points out, federal law expressly provides that state officers may "cooperate with the Attorney General in the identification, apprehension, detention, or removal of aliens not lawfully present in the United States," and "cooperation" requires neither identical efforts nor prior federal approval.

> *The most important point is that, as we have discussed, Arizona is entitled to have "its own immigration policy"—including a more rigorous enforcement policy—so long as that does not conflict with federal law.*

It is consistent with the Arizona statute, and with the "cooperat[ive]" system that Congress has created, for state officials to arrest a removable alien, contact federal immigration authorities, and follow their lead on what to do next. And it is an assault on logic to say that identifying a removable alien and holding him for federal determination of whether he should be removed "violates the principle that the removal process is entrusted to the discretion of the Federal Government." The State's detention does not represent commencement of the removal process unless the Federal Government makes it so.

But that is not the most important point. The most important point is that, as we have discussed, Arizona is entitled to have "its own immigration policy"—including a more rigorous enforcement policy—so long as that does not conflict with federal law. The Court says, as though the point is utterly dispositive, that "it is not a crime for a removable alien to remain present in the United States." It is not a federal crime, to be sure. But there is no reason Arizona cannot make it a state crime for a removable alien (or any illegal alien, for that matter) to remain present in Arizona.

The Court quotes 8 U.S.C. § 1226(a), which provides that, "[o]n a warrant issued by the Attorney General, an alien may be arrested and detained pending a decision on whether the alien is to be removed from the United States." Section 1357(a)(2) also provides that a federal immigration official "shall have power without warrant... to arrest any alien in the United States, if he has reason to believe that the alien so arrested is in the United States in violation of any [federal immigration] law or regulation and is likely to escape before a warrant can be obtained for his arrest." But statutory limitations upon the actions of federal officers in enforcing the United States' power to protect its borders do not on their face apply to the actions of state officers in enforcing the State's power to protect its borders. There is no more reason to read these provisions as implying that state officials are subject to similar limitations than there is to read them as implying that only federal officials may arrest removable aliens. And in any event neither implication would constitute the sort of clear elimination of the States' sovereign power that our cases demand.

> *But we have no license to assume, without any support in the record, that Arizona officials would use their arrest authority under § 6 to harass anyone.*

The Court raises concerns about "unnecessary harassment of some aliens... whom federal officials determine should not be removed." But we have no license to assume, without any support in the record, that Arizona officials would use their arrest authority under § 6 to harass anyone. And it makes no difference that federal officials might "determine [that some unlawfully present aliens] should not be removed." They may well determine not to remove from the United States aliens who have no right to be here; but unless and until these aliens have been given the right to remain, Arizona is entitled to arrest them and at least bring them to federal officials' attention, which is all that § 6 necessarily entails. (In my view, the State can go further than this, and punish them for their unlawful entry and presence in Arizona.)

The Government complains that state officials might not heed "federal priorities." Indeed they might not, particularly if those priorities include willful blindness or deliberate inattention to the presence of removable aliens in Arizona. The State's whole complaint—the reason this law was passed and this case has arisen—is that the citizens of Arizona believe federal priorities are too lax. The State has the sovereign power to protect its borders more rigorously if it wishes, absent any valid federal prohibition. The Executive's policy choice of lax federal enforcement does not constitute such a prohibition.

§ 3

"In addition to any violation of federal law, a person is guilty of willful failure to complete or carry an alien registration document if the person is in violation of 8 [U.S.C.] § 1304(e) or § 1306(a)."

S.B. 1070, § 3(A)

It is beyond question that a State may make violation of federal law a violation of state law as well. We have held that to be so even when the interest protected is a distinctively federal interest, such as protection of the dignity of the national flag, or protection of the Federal Government's ability to recruit soldiers. *Gilbert v. Minnesota* (1920). "[T]he State is not inhibited from making the national purposes its own purposes to the extent of exerting its police power to prevent its own citizens from obstructing the accomplishment of such purposes." *Id.* Much more is that so when, as here, the State is protecting its own interest, the integrity of its borders. And we have said that explicitly with regard to illegal immigration: "Despite the exclusive federal control of this Nation's borders, we cannot conclude that the States are without any power to deter the influx of persons entering the United States against federal law, and whose numbers might have a discernible impact on traditional state concerns." *Plyler v. Doe* (1982).

The Court's opinion relies upon *Hines v. Davidowitz.* But that case did not, as the Court believes, establish a "field preemption" that implicitly eliminates the States' sovereign power to exclude those whom federal law excludes. It held that the States are not permitted to establish "additional or auxiliary" registration requirements for aliens. But § 3 does not establish additional or auxiliary registration requirements. It merely makes a violation of state law the very same failure to register and failure to carry evidence of registration that are violations of federal law. *Hines* does not prevent the State from relying on the federal registration system as "an available aid in the enforcement of a number of statutes of the state applicable to aliens whose constitutional validity has not been questioned." One such statute is Arizona's law forbidding illegal aliens to collect unemployment benefits. To enforce that and other laws that validly turn on alien status, Arizona has, in Justice Stone's words, an interest in knowing "the number and whereabouts of aliens within the state" and in having "a means of their identification." And it can punish the aliens' failure to comply with the provisions of federal law that make that knowledge and identification possible.

In some areas of uniquely federal concern—e.g., fraud in a federal administrative process or perjury in violation of a federally required oath—this Court has held that a State has no legitimate interest in enforcing a federal scheme. But the federal alien registration system is certainly not of uniquely federal interest. States, private entities, and individuals rely on the federal registration system (including the E-Verify program) on a regular basis. Arizona's legitimate interest in protecting (among other things) its unemployment-benefits system is an entirely adequate basis for making the violation of federal registration and carry requirements a violation of state law as well.

The Court points out, however, that in some respects the state law exceeds the punishments prescribed by federal law: It rules out probation and pardon, which are available under federal law. The answer is that it makes no difference. Illegal immigrants who violate § 3 violate Arizona law. It is one thing to say that the Supremacy Clause prevents Arizona law from excluding those whom federal law admits. It is quite something else to say that a violation of Arizona law cannot be punished more severely than a violation of federal law. Especially where (as here) the State is defending its own sovereign interests, there is no precedent for such a limitation. The sale of illegal drugs, for example, ordinarily violates state law as well as federal law, and no one thinks that the state penalties cannot exceed the federal. As I have discussed, moreover, "field preemption" cannot establish a prohibition of additional state penalties in the area of immigration.

> *What I do fear—and what Arizona and the States that support it fear—is that "federal policies" of nonenforcement will leave the States helpless before those evil effects of illegal immigration.*

Finally, the Government also suggests that § 3 poses an obstacle to the administration of federal immigration law, but "there is no conflict in terms, and no possibility of such conflict, [if] the state statute makes federal law its own," *California v. Zook* (1949).

It holds no fear for me, as it does for the Court, that "[w]ere § 3 to come into force, the State would have the power to bring criminal charges against individuals for violating a federal law even in circumstances where federal officials in charge of the comprehensive scheme determine that prosecution would frustrate federal policies." That seems to me entirely appropriate when the State uses the federal law (as it must) as the criterion for the exercise of its own power, and the implementation of its own policies of excluding those who do not belong there. What I do fear—and what Arizona and the States that support it fear—is that "federal policies" of nonenforcement will leave the States helpless before those evil effects of illegal immigration that the Court's opinion dutifully recites in its prologue (ante, at 6) but leaves unremedied in its disposition.

§ 5(C)

"It is unlawful for a person who is unlawfully present in the United States and who is an unauthorized alien to knowingly apply for work, solicit work in a public place or perform work as an employee or independent contractor in this state."

S.B. 1070, § 5(C), AS AMENDED, ARIZ. REV. STAT. ANN. § 13-2928(C)

Here, the Court rightly starts with *De Canas v. Bica* (1976), which involved a California law providing that "'[n]o employer shall knowingly employ an alien who is not entitled to lawful residence in the United States if such employment would have an adverse effect on lawful resident workers.'" This Court concluded that the California law was not pre-empted, as Congress had neither occupied the field of "regulation of employment of illegal aliens" nor expressed "the clear and manifest purpose" of displacing such state regulation. Thus, at the time *De Canas* was decided, § 5(C) would have been indubitably lawful.

The only relevant change is that Congress has since enacted its own restrictions on employers who hire illegal aliens in legislation that also includes some civil (but no criminal) penalties on illegal aliens who accept unlawful employment. The Court concludes from this (reasonably enough) "that Congress made a deliberate choice not to impose criminal penalties on aliens who seek, or engage in, unauthorized employment." But that is not the same as a deliberate choice to prohibit the States from imposing criminal penalties. Congress's intent with regard to exclusion of state law need not be guessed at, but is found in the law's express pre-emption provision, which excludes "any State or local law imposing civil or criminal sanctions (other than through licensing and similar laws) upon those who employ, or recruit or refer for a fee for employment, unauthorized aliens." Common sense, reflected in the canon expressio unius est exclusio alterius, suggests that the specification of pre-emption for laws punishing "those who employ" implies the lack of pre-emption for other laws, including laws punishing "those who seek or accept employment."

The Court has no credible response to this. It quotes our jurisprudence to the effect that an "express pre-emption provisio[n] does not bar the ordinary working of conflict pre-emption principles." True enough—conflict preemption principles. It then goes on say that since "Congress decided it would be inappropriate to impose criminal penalties on aliens who seek or engage in unauthorized employment," "[i]t follows that a state law to the contrary is an obstacle to the regulatory system Congress chose." For "'[w]here a comprehensive federal scheme intentionally leaves a portion of the regulated field without controls, then the pre-emptive inference can be drawn.'" All that is a classic description not of conflict pre-emption but of field pre-emption, which (concededly) does not occur beyond the terms of an express pre-emption provision.

The Court concludes that § 5(C) "would interfere with the careful balance struck by Congress," (another field pre-emption notion, by the way) but that is easy to say and impossible to demonstrate. The Court relies primarily on the fact that "[p]roposals to make unauthorized work a criminal offense were debated and discussed during the long process of drafting [the Immigration Reform and Control Act of 1986 (IRCA)]," "[b]ut Congress rejected them." There is no more reason to believe that this rejection was expressive of a desire that there be no sanctions on employees, than expressive of a desire that such sanctions be left to the States. To tell the truth, it was most likely expressive of what inaction ordinarily expresses: nothing at all. It is a "naïve assumption that the failure of a bill to make it out of committee, or to be adopted when reported to the floor, is the same as a congressional rejection of what the bill contained." *Crosby v. National Foreign Trade Council* (2000).

The brief for the Government in this case asserted that "the Executive Branch's ability to exercise discretion and set priorities is particularly important because of the need to allocate scarce enforcement resources wisely." Of course there is no reason why the Federal Executive's need to allocate its scarce enforcement resources should

disable Arizona from devoting its resources to illegal immigration in
Arizona that in its view the Federal Executive has given short shrift.
Despite Congress's prescription that "the immigration laws of the
United States should be enforced vigorously and uniformly," Arizona
asserts without contradiction and with supporting citations:

> "[I]n the last decade federal enforcement efforts have focused
> primarily on areas in California and Texas, leaving Arizona's
> border to suffer from comparative neglect. The result has been
> the funneling of an increasing tide of illegal border crossings
> into Arizona. Indeed, over the past decade, over a third of the
> Nation's illegal border crossings occurred in Arizona."

Must Arizona's ability to protect its borders yield to the reality
that Congress has provided inadequate funding for federal enforcement—or, even worse, to the Executive's unwise targeting of that
funding?

But leave that aside. It has become clear that federal enforcement
priorities—in the sense of priorities based on the need to allocate
"scarce enforcement resources"—is not the problem here. After this
case was argued and while it was under consideration, the Secretary of Homeland Security announced a program exempting from
immigration enforcement some 1.4 million illegal immigrants under
the age of 30. If an individual unlawfully present in the United
States

> "• came to the United States under the age of sixteen;
> "• has continuously resided in the United States for at least five
> years...,

"• is currently in school, has graduated from high school, has
    obtained a general education development certificate, or is an
    honorably discharged veteran...,

"• has not been convicted of a [serious crime]; and

"• is not above the age of thirty,"

then U.S. immigration officials have been directed to "defe[r] action"
against such individual "for a period of two years, subject to renewal."
The husbanding of scarce enforcement resources can hardly be the
justification for this, since the considerable administrative cost of
conducting as many as 1.4 million background checks, and ruling
on the biennial requests for dispensation that
the nonenforcement program envisions, will
necessarily be deducted from immigration
enforcement. The President said at a news
conference that the new program is "the right
thing to do" in light of Congress's failure to
pass the Administration's proposed revision of
the Immigration Act. Perhaps it is, though Arizona may not think so. But to say, as the Court
does, that Arizona contradicts federal law by
enforcing applications of the Immigration Act
that the President declines to enforce boggles the mind.

> *To say, as the Court does, that Arizona contradicts federal law by enforcing applications of the Immigration Act that the President declines to enforce boggles the mind.*

The Court opinion's looming specter of inutterable horror—"[i]f §
3 of the Arizona statute were valid, every State could give itself independent authority to prosecute federal registration violations"—seems
to me not so horrible and even less looming. But there has come to
pass, and is with us today, the specter that Arizona and the States that
support it predicted: A Federal Government that does not want to

enforce the immigration laws as written, and leaves the States' borders unprotected against immigrants whom those laws would exclude. So the issue is a stark one. Are the sovereign States at the mercy of the Federal Executive's refusal to enforce the Nation's immigration laws?

A good way of answering that question is to ask: Would the States conceivably have entered into the Union if the Constitution itself contained the Court's holding? Today's judgment surely fails that test. At the Constitutional Convention of 1787, the delegates con-tended with "the jealousy of the states with regard to their sovereignty." 1 Records of the Federal Convention 19 (M. Farrand ed. 1911). Through ratification of the fundamen-tal charter that the Convention produced, the States ceded much of their sovereignty to the Federal Government. But much of it remained jealously guarded—as reflected in

> *Would the States conceivably have entered into the Union if the Constitution itself contained the Court's holding?*

the innumerable proposals that never left Independence Hall. Now, imagine a provision—perhaps inserted right after Art. I, § 8, cl. 4, the Naturalization Clause—which included among the enumerated powers of Congress "To establish Limitations upon Immigration that will be exclusive and that will be enforced only to the extent the President deems appropriate." The delegates to the Grand Conven-tion would have rushed to the exits.

As is often the case, discussion of the dry legalities that are the proper object of our attention suppresses the very human realities that gave rise to the suit. Arizona bears the brunt of the country's illegal immigration problem. Its citizens feel themselves under siege by large numbers of illegal immigrants who invade their property, strain their social services, and even place their lives in jeopardy.

Federal officials have been unable to remedy the problem, and indeed have recently shown that they are unwilling to do so. Thousands of Arizona's estimated 400,000 illegal immigrants—including not just children but men and women under 30—are now assured immunity from enforcement, and will be able to compete openly with Arizona citizens for employment.

Arizona has moved to protect its sovereignty—not in contradiction of federal law, but in complete compliance with it. The laws under challenge here do not extend or revise federal immigration restrictions, but merely enforce those restrictions more effectively. If securing its territory in this fashion is not within the power of Arizona, we should cease referring to it as a sovereign State. I dissent.

CHAPTER ELEVEN

HOMOSEXUALITY

❦

JUST AS THE GOVERNMENT sometimes classifies people by race and sex, it also enacts policies providing for different treatment based on sexuality. Prohibitions of adoption by homosexual couples is one example. All classifications other than those based on race, national origin, sex, or illegitimacy have traditionally been given the broadest deference by the courts. Courts will uphold distinctions based on sexuality if they find that there was a rational basis for the classification. This is a very low threshold to meet, since state legislatures usually have some reason for passing the laws they do.

In its 1986 decision in *Bowers v. Hardwick*, the Supreme Court upheld a Georgia law that criminalized sodomy. Though the law did not single out homosexual sodomy, the challenge to the law was brought by a homosexual man who was caught in the act and arrested. The Court specifically refused to extend to sodomy the privacy right it had created and invoked previously to protect the use of contraceptives by married persons in *Griswold v. Connecticut* (1965) and abortion in *Roe v. Wade* (1973). Writing for the majority, Justice White ruled that not all "private sexual conduct between consenting adults" deserves constitutional protection.[1] Because sodomy had been outlawed by all fifty states as late as 1961 and remained illegal in half the states when *Bowers* was decided, the Court found it could not properly be considered a "fundamental right" that was "deeply rooted in this Nation's history or tradition." Finding no support for a right to sodomy in the text of the Constitution or in the country's history, the Court ruled that consensual sodomy could be regulated by the state.

Justice Scalia's opinions make clear that he believes a state's desire to protect traditional sexual mores constituted a rational basis for regulating private sexual conduct. Indeed, Scalia argued, if *Bowers* exempted consensual sodomy from criminal prosecution and punishment, certainly a state could take more modest steps to disfavor homosexual conduct or, at least, to avoid giving preferential treatment to homosexuals.

This latter issue came to the Supreme Court in 1996 in a challenge to an amendment to the constitution of Colorado. The amendment, adopted by the voters of the state in a referendum, prohibited the state government and any counties or cities within the state from giving homosexuals, as a class, special protection. In *Romer v. Evans* (1996), the Supreme Court struck down the Colorado amendment, ruling that the law did not have a rational justification and therefore violated the Equal Protection Clause of the Fourteenth Amendment.[2]

Justice Scalia vigorously disagreed. In his view, the Court's holding in *Bowers* protected the right of states to pass laws that disfavor homosexuality. The amendment at issue in *Romer* did not even go that far, but merely denied them from receiving special treatment under Colorado law. Scalia wrote that the Court's opinion contradicted *Bowers* and "places the prestige of this institution behind the proposition that opposition to homosexuality is as reprehensible as racial or religious bias."[3]

Particularly galling to Scalia, it seems, was the Court's assertion that the constitutional amendment was fueled by simple bigotry. Scalia wrote, "The Court has mistaken a Kulturkampf for a fit of spite." In that Kulturkampf (or culture war), Scalia says, many Americans view homosexuality as morally repugnant not out of hatred but rather in the same way they view other harmful conduct—"murder, for example, polygamy, or cruelty to animals"—as immoral. Far from being "un-American," Scalia argued, this moral disapproval is what "produced the centuries-old criminal laws that we held constitutional in *Bowers*."

In *Romer*, the Court, without addressing *Bowers* head-on, specifically took the reason and hence the life out of it. It would be seven years until *Bowers*' death was officially pronounced in *Lawrence v. Texas*.

LAWRENCE v. TEXAS (2003)

In 2003, a challenge against a Texas law prohibiting certain intimate sexual conduct between persons of the same sex was brought by two homosexual men who were arrested and convicted for engaging in sodomy in their home. A majority of the Supreme Court, while not declaring homosexual sodomy a "fundamental right," struck down the law saying it was protected by the same "right to privacy" created by the Court in *Griswold* and extended thereafter. In striking down the law, the Court expressly overruled *Bowers v. Hardwick*. The majority did not explicitly apply "strict-scrutiny" review (appropriate when "fundamental rights" are abridged) or "rational basis" review (which the Court applied in *Bowers* to homosexual conduct). Instead, it said simply that moral opposition by a majority of voters is not a sufficient reason for outlawing consensual sex between persons of the same sex. The Texas law furthered "no legitimate state interest which can justify its intrusion into the personal and private life of the individual," the majority held.

In a concurring opinion, Justice Sandra Day O'Connor agreed the law should be invalidated but disagreed with the Court's analysis and overturning of *Bowers*. Instead of relying on "substantive due process" and the right to privacy in the Fourteenth Amendment, O'Connor, said the Court should have used Equal Protection analysis as it did in *Romer* to strike down the law. Because the law discriminated against homosexuals—only sex acts between persons of the same sex were punishable—it could be upheld only if there was a rational basis for the law. O'Connor found the state's justification—the promotion of morality—insufficient. She wrote, "Moral disapproval of a group, like a bare desire to harm the group, is an interest that is insufficient to satisfy rational basis review under the Equal Protection Clause."

The biting opening of Justice Scalia's dissenting opinion can be appreciated only if one is familiar with the *Casey* joint opinion's refusal a decade earlier to overturn *Roe* out of concern for *stare decisis* (see chapter five). Scalia ridiculed the joint opinion authors' chest-beating adherence to the nineteen-year-old *Roe* with the *Lawrence* majority's breezy reversal of the seventeen-year-old *Bowers*. Further, he noted that the majority's argument for overturning *Bowers*—it had been undermined by a torrent of heavy criticism—also applied with equal force to *Roe*. In *Casey*, however, the joint opinion said that the criticism of *Roe* was a reason to uphold it—"to overrule under fire . . . would subvert the Court's legitimacy," the joint opinion read.

In addition to pointing out the Court's hypocrisy, Scalia chastised the majority for criticizing *Bowers'* conclusion that sodomy is not a fundamental right but not having the temerity to expressly reverse that determination. Scalia said the country's long tradition of criminalizing homosexual sodomy makes clear that it is not a fundamental right. He argued that the state's interest in protecting morality—the same reason it outlaws bigamy, adult incest, and obscenity—provided a rational basis for maintaining the law against sodomy. Conversely, he argued, if the majority of the Court does not believe promoting morality is even a legitimate state interest, none of these prohibitions could be defended from challenge.

Scalia then turned his attention to Justice O'Connor's concurring opinion. He refuted her equal protection argument by noting that Texas's sodomy law on its face applies equally to men and women, homosexuals and heterosexuals. Further, he wrote that even if there were unequal treatment, the state's interest in protecting morality provides a rational basis to uphold the distinction.

Finally, Scalia took aim at both the Court and O'Connor for undercutting the rationale for prohibiting same-sex marriages. "If moral disapprobation of homosexual conduct is 'no legitimate state interest' for purposes of proscribing that conduct . . . what justification could there possibly be for denying the benefits of marriage to homosexuals exercising '[t]he liberty protected by the Constitution'?" Scalia asked rhetorically. Eight months after *Lawrence* was decided, the Massachusetts Supreme Judicial Court ruled that the commonwealth could not deny the civil institution of marriage to same-sex couples, and the United States Supreme Court would follow suit a dozen years later.

⌖

Justice Scalia, with whom the Chief Justice and Justice Thomas join, dissenting.

"Liberty finds no refuge in a jurisprudence of doubt." *Planned Parenthood of Southeastern Pa. v. Casey* (1992). That was the Court's sententious response, barely more than a decade ago, to those seeking to overrule *Roe v. Wade*. The Court's response today, to those who have engaged in a 17-year crusade to overrule *Bowers v. Hardwick*

(1986) is very different. The need for stability and certainty presents no barrier.

Most of the rest of today's opinion has no relevance to its actual holding—that the Texas statute "furthers no legitimate state interest which can justify" its application to petitioners under rational-basis review. Though there is discussion of "fundamental proposition[s]" and "fundamental decisions" nowhere does the Court's opinion declare that homosexual sodomy is a "fundamental right" under the Due Process Clause; nor does it subject the Texas law to the standard of review that would be appropriate (strict scrutiny) if homosexual sodomy *were* a "fundamental right." Thus, while overruling the *outcome* of *Bowers*, the Court leaves strangely untouched its central legal conclusion: "[R]espondent would have us announce . . . a fundamental right to engage in homosexual sodomy. This we are quite unwilling to do." Instead the Court simply describes petitioners' conduct as "an exercise of their liberty"—which it undoubtedly is—and proceeds to apply an unheard-of form of rational-basis review that will have far-reaching implications beyond this case.

I

I begin with the Court's surprising readiness to reconsider a decision rendered a mere 17 years ago in *Bowers v. Hardwick.* I do not myself believe in rigid adherence to *stare decisis* in constitutional cases; but I do believe that we should be consistent rather than manipulative in invoking the doctrine. Today's opinions in support of reversal do not bother to distinguish—or indeed, even bother to mention—the paean to *stare decisis* coauthored by three Members of today's majority in *Planned Parenthood v. Casey.* There, when *stare decisis* meant preservation of judicially invented abortion rights, the widespread criticism of *Roe* was strong reason to *reaffirm* it:

> Where, in the performance of its judicial duties, the Court decides a case in such a way as to resolve the sort of intensely divisive controversy reflected in *Roe*[,] ... its decision has a dimension that the resolution of the normal case does not carry.... [T]o overrule under fire in the absence of the most compelling reason ... would subvert the Court's legitimacy beyond any serious question.

Today, however, the widespread opposition to *Bowers*, a decision resolving an issue as "intensely divisive" as the issue in *Roe*, is offered as a reason in favor of *overruling* it. Gone, too, is any "enquiry" (of the sort conducted in *Casey*) into whether the decision sought to be overruled has "proven 'unworkable,'" *Casey*.

Today's approach to *stare decisis* invites us to overrule an erroneously decided precedent (including an "intensely divisive" decision) *if*: (1) its foundations have been "eroded" by subsequent decisions; (2) it has been subject to "substantial and continuing" criticism; and (3) it has not induced "individual or societal reliance" that counsels against overturning. The problem is that *Roe* itself—which today's majority surely has no disposition to overrule—satisfies these conditions to at least the same degree as *Bowers*.

(1) A preliminary digressive observation with regard to the first factor: The Court's claim that *Planned Parenthood v. Casey* "casts some doubt" upon the holding in *Bowers* (or any other case, for that matter) does not withstand analysis. As far as its holding is concerned, *Casey* provided a *less* expansive right to abortion than did *Roe, which was already*

on the books when Bowers was decided. And if the Court is referring not to the holding of *Casey*, but to the dictum of its famed sweet-mystery-of-life passage ("'At the heart of liberty is the right to define one's own concept of existence, of meaning, of the universe, and of the mystery of human life'"): That "casts some doubt" upon either the totality of our jurisprudence or else (presumably the right answer) nothing at all. I have never heard of a law that attempted to restrict one's "right to define" certain concepts; and if the passage calls into question the government's power to regulate *actions based on* one's self-defined "concept of existence, etc.," it is the passage that ate the rule of law.

> *I have never heard of a law that attempted to restrict one's "right to define" certain concepts; and if the passage calls into question the government's power to regulate actions based on one's self-defined "concept of existence, etc.," it is the passage that ate the rule of law.*

I do not quarrel with the Court's claim that *Romer v. Evans* "eroded" the "foundations" of *Bowers'* rational-basis holding. But *Roe* and *Casey* have been equally "eroded" by *Washington v. Glucksberg* (1997) which held that *only* fundamental rights which are " 'deeply rooted in this Nation's history and tradition'" qualify for anything other than rational basis scrutiny under the doctrine of "substantive due process." *Roe* and *Casey*, of course, subjected the restriction of abortion to heightened scrutiny without even attempting to establish that the freedom to abort *was* rooted in this Nation's tradition.

(2) *Bowers*, the Court says, has been subject to "substantial and continuing [criticism], disapproving of its reasoning in all respects, not just as to its historical assumptions." Exactly what those nonhistorical criticisms are, and whether the Court even agrees with them,

are left unsaid, although the Court does cite two books. Of course, *Roe* too (and by extension *Casey*) had been (and still is) subject to unrelenting criticism, including criticism from the two commentators cited by the Court today.

(3) That leaves, to distinguish the rock-solid, unamendable disposition of *Roe* from the readily overrulable *Bowers*, only the third factor. "[T]here has been," the Court says, "no individual or societal reliance on *Bowers* of the sort that could counsel against overturning its holding..." It seems to me that the "societal reliance" on the principles confirmed in *Bowers* and discarded today has been overwhelming. Countless judicial decisions and legislative enactments have relied on the ancient proposition that a governing majority's belief that certain sexual behavior is "immoral and unacceptable" constitutes a rational basis for regulation. We ourselves relied extensively on *Bowers* when we concluded, in *Barnes v. Glen Theatre, Inc.* (1991), that Indiana's public indecency statute furthered "a substantial government interest in protecting order and morality." State laws against bigamy, same-sex marriage, adult incest, prostitution, masturbation, adultery, fornication, bestiality, and obscenity are likewise sustainable only in light of *Bowers'* validation of laws based on moral choices. Every single one of these laws is called into question by today's decision; the Court makes no effort to cabin the scope of its decision to exclude them from its holding. The impossibility of distinguishing homosexuality from other traditional "morals" offenses is precisely why *Bowers* rejected the rational-basis challenge. "The law," it said, "is constantly based on notions of morality, and if all laws representing essentially moral choices are to be invalidated under the Due Process Clause, the courts will be very busy indeed."

What a massive disruption of the current social order, therefore, the overruling of *Bowers* entails. Not so the overruling of *Roe*, which would simply have restored the regime that existed for centuries before 1973, in which the permissibility of and restrictions upon abortion were determined legislatively State-by-State. *Casey*, however, chose to base its *stare decisis* determination on a different "sort" of reliance. "[P]eople," it said, "have organized intimate relationships and made choices that define their views of themselves and their places in society, in reliance on the availability of abortion in the event that contraception should fail." This falsely assumes that the consequence of overruling *Roe* would have been to make abortion unlawful. It would not; it would merely have *permitted* the States to do so. Many States would unquestionably have declined to prohibit abortion, and others would not have prohibited it within six months (after which the most significant reliance interests would have expired). Even for persons in States other than these, the choice would not have been between abortion and childbirth, but between abortion nearby and abortion in a neighboring State.

To tell the truth, it does not surprise me, and should surprise no one, that the Court has chosen today to revise the standards of *stare decisis* set forth in *Casey*. It has thereby exposed *Casey*'s extraordinary deference to precedent for the result-oriented expedient that it is.

II

Having decided that it need not adhere to *stare decisis*, the Court still must establish that *Bowers* was wrongly decided and that the Texas statute, as applied to petitioners, is unconstitutional.

[The Texas anti-sodomy statute] undoubtedly imposes constraints on liberty. So do laws prohibiting prostitution, recreational use of heroin, and, for that matter, working more than 60 hours per week in a bakery. But there is no right to "liberty" under the Due Process Clause, though today's opinion repeatedly makes that claim. ("The liberty protected by the Constitution allows homosexual persons the right to make this choice"); ("'These matters...are central to the liberty protected by the Fourteenth Amendment'"); ("Their right to liberty under the Due Process Clause gives them the full right to engage in their conduct without intervention of the government"). The Fourteenth Amendment *expressly allows* States to deprive their citizens of "liberty," so long as "due process of law" is provided:

> No state shall...deprive any person of life, liberty, or property, *without due process of law*.
>
> AMDT. 14 (EMPHASIS ADDED)

Our opinions applying the doctrine known as "substantive due process" hold that the Due Process Clause prohibits States from infringing *fundamental* liberty interests, unless the infringement is narrowly tailored to serve a compelling state interest. *Washington v. Glucksberg*. We have held repeatedly, in cases the Court today does not overrule, that *only* fundamental rights qualify for this so-called "heightened scrutiny" protection—that is, rights which are "'deeply rooted in this Nation's history and tradition,'" *ibid*. All other liberty interests may be abridged or abrogated pursuant to a validly enacted state law if that law is rationally related to a legitimate state interest.

Bowers held, first, that criminal prohibitions of homosexual sodomy are not subject to heightened scrutiny because they do not implicate a "fundamental right" under the Due Process Clause. Noting that "[p]roscriptions against that conduct have ancient roots," that "[s]odomy was a criminal offense at common law and was forbidden by the laws of the original 13 States when they ratified the Bill of Rights," and that many States had retained their bans on sodomy, *Bowers* concluded that a right to engage in homosexual sodomy was not "'deeply rooted in this Nation's history and tradition.'"

The Court today does not overrule this holding. Not once does it describe homosexual sodomy as a "fundamental right" or a "fundamental liberty interest," nor does it subject the Texas statute to strict scrutiny. Instead, having failed to establish that the right to homosexual sodomy is "'deeply rooted in this Nation's history and tradition,'" the Court concludes that the application of Texas's statute to petitioners' conduct fails the rational-basis test, and overrules *Bowers'* holding to the contrary. "The Texas statute furthers no legitimate state interest which can justify its intrusion into the personal and private life of the individual."

I shall address that rational-basis holding presently. First, however, I address some aspersions that the Court casts upon *Bowers'* conclusion that homosexual sodomy is not a "fundamental right"—even though, as I have said, the Court does not have the boldness to reverse that conclusion.

III

The Court's description of "the state of the law" at the time of *Bowers* only confirms that *Bowers* was right. The Court points to *Griswold v. Connecticut* (1965). But that case *expressly disclaimed* any reliance on the doctrine of "substantive due process," and grounded the so-called "right to privacy" in penumbras of constitutional provisions *other than* the Due Process Clause. *Eisenstadt v. Baird* (1972), likewise had nothing to do with "substantive due process"; it invalidated a Massachusetts law prohibiting the distribution of contraceptives to unmarried persons solely on the basis of the Equal Protection Clause. Of course *Eisenstadt* contains well known dictum relating to the "right to privacy," but this referred to the right recognized in *Griswold*—a right penumbral to the *specific* guarantees in the Bill of Rights, and not a "substantive due process" right.

Roe v. Wade recognized that the right to abort an unborn child was a "fundamental right" protected by the Due Process Clause. The *Roe* Court, however, made no attempt to establish that this right was "'deeply rooted in this Nation's history and tradition'"; instead, it based its conclusion that "the Fourteenth Amendment's concept of personal liberty . . . is broad enough to encompass a woman's decision whether or not to terminate her pregnancy" on its own normative judgment that anti-abortion laws were undesirable. We have since rejected *Roe*'s holding that regulations of abortion must be narrowly tailored to serve a compelling state interest, see *Planned Parenthood v. Casey*. . . and thus, by logical implication, *Roe*'s holding that the right to abort an unborn child is a "fundamental right."

After discussing the history of antisodomy laws, the Court proclaims that, "it should be noted that there is no longstanding history in this country of laws directed at homosexual conduct as a distinct matter." This observation in no way casts into doubt the "definitive [historical] conclusion" on which *Bowers* relied: that our Nation has a longstanding history of laws prohibiting *sodomy in general*—regardless of whether it was performed by same-sex or opposite-sex couples:

It is obvious to us that neither of these formulations would extend a fundamental right to homosexuals to engage in acts of consensual sodomy. Proscriptions against that conduct have ancient roots. *Sodomy* was a criminal offense at common law and was forbidden by the laws of the original 13 States when they ratified the Bill of Rights. In 1868, when the Fourteenth Amendment was ratified, all but 5 of the 37 States in the Union had *criminal sodomy laws*. In fact, until 1961, all 50 States outlawed *sodomy*, and today, 24 States and the District of Columbia continue to provide criminal penalties for *sodomy* performed in private and between consenting adults. Against this background, to claim that a right to engage in such conduct is "deeply rooted in this Nation's history and tradition" or "implicit in the concept of ordered liberty" is, at best, facetious.

I do not know what "acting in private" means; surely consensual sodomy, like heterosexual intercourse, is rarely performed on stage.

It is (as *Bowers* recognized) entirely irrelevant whether the laws in our long national tradition criminalizing homosexual sodomy were "directed at homosexual conduct as a distinct matter." Whether homosexual sodomy was prohibited by a law targeted at same-sex sexual relations or by a more general law prohibiting both homosexual and heterosexual sodomy, the only relevant point is that it *was* criminalized—which suffices to establish that homosexual sodomy is not a right "deeply rooted in our Nation's history and tradition." The Court today agrees that homosexual sodomy was criminalized and thus does not dispute the facts on which *Bowers actually* relied.

Next the Court makes the claim, again unsupported by any citations, that "[l]aws prohibiting sodomy do not seem to have been enforced against consenting adults acting in private." The key qualifier here is "acting in private"—since the Court admits that sodomy laws *were* enforced against consenting adults (although the Court contends that prosecutions were "infrequent"). I do not know what "acting in private" means; surely consensual sodomy, like heterosexual intercourse, is rarely performed on stage. If all the Court means by "acting in private" is "on private premises, with the doors closed and windows covered," it is entirely unsurprising that evidence of enforcement would be hard to come by. (Imagine the circumstances that would enable a search warrant to be obtained for a residence on the ground that there was probable cause to believe that consensual sodomy was then and there occurring.) Surely that lack of evidence would not sustain the proposition that consensual sodomy on private premises with the doors closed and windows covered was regarded as a "fundamental right," even though all other consensual sodomy was criminalized. There are 203 prosecutions for consensual, adult homosexual sodomy reported in the West Reporting system and official state reporters from the years 1880–1995. See W. Eskridge, Gaylaw: Challenging the Apartheid of the Closet (1999) (hereinafter Gaylaw). There are also records of 20 sodomy prosecutions and 4 executions during the colonial period. J. Katz, Gay/Lesbian Almanac (1983). Bowers' conclusion that homosexual sodomy is not a fundamental right "deeply rooted in this Nation's history and tradition" is utterly unassailable.

Realizing that fact, the Court instead says: "[W]e think that our laws and traditions in the past half century are of most relevance here. These references show *an emerging awareness* that liberty gives substantial protection to adult persons in deciding how to conduct their private lives *in matters pertaining to sex*." (emphasis added). Apart from the fact that such an "emerging awareness" does not establish a "fundamental right," the statement is factually false. States continue to prosecute all sorts of crimes by adults "in matters pertaining to sex": prostitution, adult incest, adultery, obscenity, and child pornography. Sodomy laws, too, have been enforced "in the past half century," in which there have been 134 reported cases involving prosecutions for consensual, adult, homosexual sodomy. In relying, for evidence of an "emerging recognition," upon the American Law Institute's 1955 recommendation not to criminalize "'consensual sexual relations conducted in private,'" the Court ignores the fact that this recommendation was "a point of resistance in most of the states that considered adopting the Model Penal Code" Gaylaw 159.

In any event, an "emerging awareness" is by definition not "deeply rooted in this Nation's history and tradition[s]," as we have said "fundamental right" status requires. Constitutional entitlements do not spring into existence because some States choose to lessen or eliminate criminal sanctions on certain behavior. Much less do they spring into existence, as the Court seems to believe, because *foreign nations* decriminalize conduct. The *Bowers* majority opinion *never* relied on "values we share with a wider civilization," but rather rejected the claimed right to sodomy on the ground that such a right was not "'deeply rooted in *this Nation's* history and tradition,'" (emphasis added). *Bowers'* rational-basis holding is likewise devoid of any reliance on the views of a "wider civilization." The Court's discussion of these foreign views (ignoring, of course, the many countries that have retained criminal prohibitions on sodomy) is therefore meaningless dicta. Dangerous dicta, however, since "this Court...should not impose foreign moods, fads, or fashions on Americans." *Foster v. Florida* (2002) (Thomas, J., concurring in denial of certiorari).

IV

I turn now to the ground on which the Court squarely rests its holding: the contention that there is no rational basis for the law here under attack. This proposition is so out of accord with our jurisprudence—indeed, with the jurisprudence of *any* society we know—that it requires little discussion.

The Texas statute undeniably seeks to further the belief of its citizens that certain forms of sexual behavior are "immoral and unacceptable"—the same interest furthered by criminal laws against fornication, bigamy, adultery, adult incest, bestiality, and obscenity. *Bowers* held that this *was* a legitimate state interest. The Court today reaches the opposite conclusion. The Texas statute, it says, "furthers *no legitimate state interest* which can justify its intrusion into the personal and private life of the individual" (emphasis addded). The Court embraces instead Justice Stevens' declaration in his *Bowers* dissent, that "the fact that the governing majority in a State has traditionally viewed a particular practice as immoral is not a sufficient reason for upholding a law prohibiting the practice." This effectively decrees the end of all morals legislation. If, as the Court asserts, the promotion of majoritarian sexual morality is not even a *legitimate* state interest, none of the above-mentioned laws can survive rational-basis review.

V

Finally, I turn to petitioners' equal-protection challenge, which no Member of the Court save Justice O'Connor embraces: On its face [the Texas law] applies equally to all persons. Men and women, heterosexuals and homosexuals, are all subject to its prohibition of deviate sexual intercourse with someone of the same sex. To be sure, § 21.06 does distinguish between the sexes insofar as concerns the partner with whom the sexual acts are performed: men can violate the law only with other men, and women only with other women. But this cannot itself be a denial of equal protection, since it is precisely the same distinction regarding partner that is drawn in state laws prohibiting marriage with someone of the same sex while permitting marriage with someone of the opposite sex.

The objection is made, however, that the antimiscegenation laws invalidated in *Loving v. Virginia* (1967), similarly were applicable to whites and blacks alike, and only distinguished between the races insofar as the *partner* was concerned. In *Loving*, however, we correctly applied heightened scrutiny, rather than the usual rational-basis review, because the Virginia statute was "designed to maintain White Supremacy." A racially discriminatory purpose is always sufficient to subject a law to strict scrutiny, even a facially neutral law that makes no mention of race. No purpose to discriminate against men or women as a class can be gleaned from the Texas law, so rational-basis review applies. That review is readily satisfied here by the same rational basis that satisfied it in *Bowers*—society's belief that certain forms of sexual behavior are "immoral and unacceptable." This is the same justification that supports many other laws regulating sexual behavior that make a distinction based upon the identity of the partner—for example, laws against adultery, fornication, and adult incest, and laws refusing to recognize homosexual marriage.

Justice O'Connor argues that the discrimination in this law which must be justified is not its discrimination with regard to the sex of the partner but its discrimination with regard to the sexual proclivity of the principal actor.

While it is true that the law applies only to conduct, the conduct targeted by this law is conduct that is closely correlated

with being homosexual. Under such circumstances, Texas' sodomy law is targeted at more than conduct. It is instead directed
toward gay persons as a class.

Of course the same could be said of any law. A law against public
nudity targets "the conduct that is closely correlated with being a
nudist," and hence "is targeted at more than conduct"; it is "directed
toward nudists as a class." But be that as it may. Even if the Texas law
does deny equal protection to "homosexuals as a class," that denial *still*
does not need to be justified by anything more than a rational basis,
which our cases show is satisfied by the enforcement of traditional
notions of sexual morality.

Justice O'Connor simply decrees application of "a more searching
form of rational basis review" to the Texas statute. The cases she cites
do not recognize such a standard, and reach their conclusions only
after finding, as required by conventional rational-basis analysis, that
no conceivable legitimate state interest supports the classification at
issue. Nor does Justice O'Connor explain precisely what her "more
searching form" of rational-basis review consists of. It must at least
mean, however, that laws exhibiting "'a . . . desire to harm a politically
unpopular group,'" are invalid *even though* there may be a conceivable
rational basis to support them.

This reasoning leaves on pretty shaky grounds state laws limiting
marriage to opposite-sex couples. Justice O'Connor seeks to preserve
them by the conclusory statement that "preserving the traditional institution of marriage" is a legitimate state interest. But "preserving the
traditional institution of marriage" is just a kinder way of describing
the State's *moral disapproval* of same-sex couples. Texas's interest in §
21.06 could be recast in similarly euphemistic terms: "preserving the

traditional sexual mores of our society." In the jurisprudence Justice O'Connor has seemingly created, judges can validate laws by characterizing them as "preserving the traditions of society" (good); or invalidate them by characterizing them as "expressing moral disapproval" (bad).

Today's opinion is the product of a Court, which is the product of a law-profession culture, that has largely signed on to the so-called homosexual agenda, by which I mean the agenda promoted by some homosexual activists directed at eliminating the moral opprobrium that has traditionally attached to homosexual conduct. I noted in an earlier opinion the fact that the American Association of Law Schools (to which any reputable law school *must* seek to belong) excludes from membership any school that refuses to ban from its job-interview facilities a law firm (no matter how small) that does not wish to hire as a prospective partner a person who openly engages in homosexual conduct.

So imbued is the Court with the law profession's anti-anti-homosexual culture, that it is seemingly unaware that the attitudes of that culture are not obviously "mainstream."

One of the most revealing statements in today's opinion is the Court's grim warning that the criminalization of homosexual conduct is "an invitation to subject homosexual persons to discrimination both in the public and in the private spheres." It is clear from this that the Court has taken sides in the culture war, departing from its role of assuring, as neutral observer, that the democratic rules of engagement are observed. Many Americans do not want persons who openly engage in homosexual conduct as partners in their business, as scoutmasters for their children, as teachers in their children's schools, or as boarders in their home.

They view this as protecting themselves and their families from a lifestyle that they believe to be immoral and destructive. The Court views it as "discrimination" which it is the function of our judgments to deter. So imbued is the Court with the law profession's anti-anti-homosexual culture, that it is seemingly unaware that the attitudes of that culture are not obviously "mainstream"; that in most States what the Court calls "discrimination" against those who engage in homosexual acts is perfectly legal; that proposals to ban such "discrimination" under Title VII have repeatedly been rejected by Congress; that in some cases such "discrimination" is *mandated* by federal statute, see 10 U.S.C. § 654(b)(1) (mandating discharge from the armed forces of any service member who engages in or intends to engage in homosexual acts); and that in some cases such "discrimination" is a constitutional right, see *Boy Scouts of America v. Dale* (2000).

Let me be clear that I have nothing against homosexuals, or any other group, promoting their agenda through normal democratic means. Social perceptions of sexual and other morality change over time, and every group has the right to persuade its fellow citizens that its view of such matters is the best. That homosexuals have achieved some success in that enterprise is attested to by the fact that Texas is one of the few remaining States that criminalize private, consensual homosexual acts. But persuading one's fellow citizens is one thing, and imposing one's views in absence of democratic majority will is something else. I would no more *require* a State to criminalize homosexual acts—or, for that matter, display *any* moral disapprobation of them— than I would *forbid* it to do so. What Texas has chosen to do is well within the range of traditional democratic action, and its hand should not be stayed through the invention of a brand-new "constitutional right" by a Court that is impatient of democratic change. It is indeed true that "later generations can see that laws once thought necessary and proper in fact serve only to oppress"; and when that happens, later generations can repeal those laws. But it is the premise of our system that those judgments are to be made by the people, and not imposed by a governing caste that knows best.

> *One of the benefits of leaving regulation of this matter to the people rather than to the courts is that the people, unlike judges, need not carry things to their logical conclusion.*

One of the benefits of leaving regulation of this matter to the people rather than to the courts is that the people, unlike judges, need not carry things to their logical conclusion. The people may feel that their disapprobation of homosexual conduct is strong enough to disallow homosexual marriage, but not strong enough to criminalize private homosexual acts—and may legislate accordingly. The Court today pretends that it possesses a similar freedom of action, so that that we need not fear judicial imposition of homosexual marriage, as has recently occurred in Canada (in a decision that the Canadian Government has chosen not to appeal). At the end of its opinion—after having laid waste the foundations of our rational-basis jurisprudence—the Court says that the present case "does not involve whether the government must give formal recognition to any relationship that homosexual persons seek to enter." Do not believe it. More illuminating than this bald, unreasoned disclaimer is the progression of thought displayed by an earlier passage in the Court's opinion, which notes the constitutional protections afforded to "personal decisions relating to *marriage*, procreation, contraception, family relationships, child rearing, and education," and then declares that "[p]ersons in a homosexual relationship may seek autonomy for these purposes, just as heterosexual persons do." (emphasis added). Today's opinion dismantles the structure of constitutional law that has permitted a distinction to be made between heterosexual and homosexual unions, insofar as formal recognition in marriage is concerned. If moral disapprobation of homosexual conduct is "no legitimate state interest" for purposes of proscribing that conduct; and if, as the Court coos (casting aside all pretense of neutrality), "[w]hen sexuality finds overt expression in intimate conduct with another person, the conduct can be but one element in a personal bond that is more enduring," what justification could there possibly be for denying the benefits of marriage to homosexual couples exercising "[t]he liberty protected by the Constitution." Surely not the encouragement of procreation, since the sterile and the elderly are allowed to marry. This case "does not involve" the issue of homosexual marriage only if one entertains the belief that principle and logic have nothing to do with the decisions of this Court. Many will hope that, as the Court comfortingly assures us, this is so.

The matters appropriate for this Court's resolution are only three: Texas's prohibition of sodomy neither infringes a "fundamental right" (which the Court does not dispute), nor is unsupported by a rational relation to what the Constitution considers a legitimate state interest, nor denies the equal protection of the laws. I dissent.

UNITED STATES v. WINDSOR (2013)

In 2003, the majority of the American public opposed same-sex marriage, a fact that likely prompted the Court in *Lawrence* to deny that its decision striking down sodomy laws would affect the Court's thinking about whether

it might recognize a constitutional right to same-sex marriage. Scalia told
readers in his *Lawrence* dissent not to believe it. He said the majority's reasoning would necessarily lead to that result. A decade later, the Court began
the journey.

Edith Windsor married another woman in Ontario, Canada, in 2007.
The couple lived in New York State, which recognized their marriage.
Windsor's spouse died in 2009 leaving her estate to Windsor, who sought
to claim the federal estate tax exemption for surviving spouses. Her claim
was barred, however, by a provision of the federal Defense of Marriage
Act (DOMA), which Congress passed and President Bill Clinton signed in
1996. That law amended federal law to define "marriage" and "spouse" as
excluding same-sex partners.

Windsor sued, arguing that DOMA was unconstitutional. While the suit
was pending, the Obama administration's Justice Department announced
that it would no longer defend the law. In response, a legal advisory group
of the House of Representatives voted to intervene in order to defend the
law.

Writing for a five-to-four majority, Justice Anthony Kennedy ruled that
DOMA unconstitutionally deprived homosexual Americans of equal liberty. He argued that DOMA's clear purpose and practical effect were to
impose a disadvantage, a separate status, and a stigma upon all who enter
into same-sex marriages, even where those marriages were made lawful by
states, which historically have had primary jurisdiction over marriage.

Justice Scalia sharply dissented. He began by challenging the Court's
rationale for deciding the case at all. Because Windsor prevailed in the lower
courts and the Justice Department decided not to defend the law, there was
no dispute for the Supreme Court to resolve. "In the more than two centuries that this Court has existed as an institution," Scalia wrote, "we have
never suggested that we have the power to decide a question when every

party agrees with both its nominal opponent and the court below on that question's answer."

Scalia then moved to the substance of the Court's holding. He dismissed the majority's accusation that the only motivation for DOMA was "animus" or bias against homosexuals. Consistent with his originalist philosophy, Scalia argued that because the Constitution is silent on the question of same-sex marriage, the issue should be left to the people and their representatives. He wrote, "We might have covered ourselves with honor today, by promising all sides of this debate that it was theirs to settle and that we would respect their resolution. We might have let the People decide."

~✧~

Justice Scalia, with whom Justice Thomas joins, and with whom the Chief Justice joins as to Part I, dissenting.

This case is about power in several respects. It is about the power of our people to govern themselves, and the power of this Court to pronounce the law. Today's opinion aggrandizes the latter, with the predictable consequence of diminishing the former. We have no power to decide this case. And even if we did, we have no power under the Constitution to invalidate this democratically adopted legislation. The Court's errors on both points spring forth from the same diseased root: an exalted conception of the role of this institution in America.

I

A

The Court is eager—hungry—to tell everyone its view of the legal question at the heart of this case. Standing in the way is an obstacle, a technicality of little interest to anyone but the people of We the People, who created it as a barrier against judges' intrusion into their lives. They gave judges, in Article III, only the "judicial Power," a power to decide not abstract questions but real, concrete "Cases" and "Controversies." Yet the plaintiff and the Government agree entirely on what should happen in this lawsuit. They agree that the court below got it right; and they agreed in the court below that the court below that one got it right as well. What, then, are we doing here?

The answer lies at the heart of the jurisdictional portion of today's opinion, where a single sentence lays bare the majority's vision of our role. The Court says that we have the power to decide this case because if we did not, then our "primary role in determining the constitutionality of a law" (at least one that "has inflicted real injury on a plaintiff") would "become only secondary to the President's." But wait, the reader wonders—Windsor won below, and so cured her injury, and the President was glad to see it. True, says the majority, but judicial review must march on regardless, lest we "undermine the clear dictate of the separation-of-powers principle that when an Act of Congress is alleged to conflict with the Constitution, it is emphatically the province and duty of the judicial department to say what the law is."

> *It envisions a Supreme Court standing (or rather enthroned) at the apex of government, empowered to decide all constitutional questions, always and everywhere "primary" in its role.*

That is jaw-dropping. It is an assertion of judicial supremacy over the people's Representatives in Congress and the Executive. It envisions a Supreme Court standing (or rather enthroned) at the apex of government, empowered to decide all constitutional questions, always and everywhere "primary" in its role.

This image of the Court would have been unrecognizable to those who wrote and ratified our national charter. They knew well the dangers of "primary" power, and so created branches of government that would be "perfectly co-ordinate by the terms of their common commission," none of which branches could "pretend to an exclusive or superior right of settling the boundaries between their respective powers." The Federalist, No. 49. The people did this to protect themselves. They did it to guard their right to self-rule against the black-robed supremacy that today's majority finds so attractive. So it was that Madison could confidently state, with no fear of contradiction, that there was nothing of "greater intrinsic value" or "stamped with the authority of more enlightened patrons of liberty" than a government of separate and coordinate powers.

For this reason we are quite forbidden to say what the law is whenever (as today's opinion asserts) "'an Act of Congress is alleged to conflict with the Constitution.'" We can do so only when that allegation will determine the outcome of a lawsuit, and is contradicted by the other party. The "judicial Power" is not, as the majority believes, the power "'to say what the law is,'" giving the Supreme Court the "primary role in determining the constitutionality of laws." The majority must have in mind one of the foreign constitutions that pronounces such primacy for its constitutional court and allows that primacy to be exercised in contexts other than a lawsuit. The judicial power as Americans have understood it (and their English ancestors before them) is the power to adjudicate, with conclusive effect, disputed government claims (civil or criminal) against private

persons, and disputed claims by private persons against the government or other private persons. Sometimes (though not always) the
parties before the court disagree not with regard to the facts of their
case (or not only with regard to the facts) but with regard to the
applicable law—in which event (and only in which event) it becomes
the "'province and duty of the judicial department to say what the
law is.'"

In other words, declaring the compatibility of state or federal
laws with the Constitution is not only not the "primary role" of this
Court, it is not a separate, free-standing role at all. We perform that
role incidentally—by accident, as it were—when that is necessary to
resolve the dispute before us. Then, and only then, does it become
"'the province and duty of the judicial department to say what the
law is.'" That is why, in 1793, we politely declined the Washington Administration's request to "say what the law is" on a particular
treaty matter that was not the subject of a concrete legal controversy.
And that is why, as our opinions have said, some questions of law
will never be presented to this Court, because there will never be
anyone with standing to bring a lawsuit. As Justice Brandeis put it,
we cannot "pass upon the constitutionality of legislation in a friendly,
non-adversary, proceeding"; absent a "'real, earnest and vital controversy between individuals,'" we have neither any work to do nor
any power to do it. *Ashwander v. TVA* (1936). Our authority begins
and ends with the need to adjudge the rights of an injured party who
stands before us seeking redress.

That is completely absent here. Windsor's injury was cured by
the judgment in her favor. And while, in ordinary circumstances,
the United States is injured by a directive to pay a tax refund, this
suit is far from ordinary. Whatever injury the United States has

suffered will surely not be redressed by the action that it, as a litigant, asks us to take. The final sentence of the Solicitor General's brief on the merits reads: "For the foregoing reasons, the judgment of the court of appeals should be affirmed." That will not cure the Government's injury, but carve it into stone. One could spend many fruitless afternoons ransacking our library for any other petitioner's brief seeking an affirmance of the judgment against it. What the petitioner United States asks us to do in the case before us is exactly what the respondent Windsor asks us to do: not to provide relief from the judgment below but to say that that judgment was correct. And the same was true in the Court of Appeals: Neither party sought to undo the judgment for Windsor, and so that court should have dismissed the appeal (just as we should dismiss) for lack of jurisdiction. Since both parties agreed with the judgment of the District Court for the Southern District of New York, the suit should have ended there. The further proceedings have been a contrivance, having no object in mind except to elevate a District Court judgment that has no precedential effect in other courts, to one that has precedential effect throughout the Second Circuit, and then (in this Court) precedential effect throughout the United States.

We have never before agreed to speak—to "say what the law is"—where there is no controversy before us. In the more than two centuries that this Court has existed as an institution, we have never suggested that we have the power to decide a question when every party agrees with both its nominal opponent and the court below on that question's answer. The United States reluctantly conceded that at oral argument.

. . . . .

II

For the reasons above, I think that this Court has, and the Court of Appeals had, no power to decide this suit. We should vacate the decision below and remand to the Court of Appeals for the Second Circuit, with instructions to dismiss the appeal. Given that the majority has volunteered its view of the merits, however, I proceed to discuss that as well.

A

There are many remarkable things about the majority's merits holding. The first is how rootless and shifting its justifications are. For example, the opinion starts with seven full pages about the traditional power of States to define domestic relations—initially fooling many readers, I am sure, into thinking that this is a federalism opinion. But we are eventually told that "it is unnecessary to decide whether this federal intrusion on state power is a violation of the Constitution," and that "[t]he State's power in defining the marital relation is of central relevance in this case quite apart from principles of federalism" because "the State's decision to give this class of persons the right to marry conferred upon them a dignity and status of immense import." But no one questions the power of the States to define marriage (with the concomitant conferral of dignity and status), so what is the point of devoting seven pages to describing how long and well established that power is? Even after the opinion has formally disclaimed reliance upon principles of federalism, mentions of "the usual tradition of recognizing and accepting state definitions of marriage" continue. What to make of this? The opinion never explains. My guess is that the majority, while reluctant to suggest that defining the meaning of "marriage" in federal statutes is unsupported by any of the Federal Government's enumerated powers, nonetheless needs some rhetorical basis to support its pretense that today's prohibition of laws excluding same-sex marriage is confined to the Federal Government (leaving the second, state-law shoe to be dropped later, maybe next Term). But I am only guessing.

Equally perplexing are the opinion's references to "the Constitution's guarantee of equality." Near the end of the opinion, we are told that although the "equal protection guarantee of the Fourteenth Amendment makes [the] Fifth Amendment [due process] right all the more specific and all the better understood and preserved"—what can that mean?—"the Fifth Amendment itself withdraws from Government the power to degrade or demean in the way this law does." The only possible interpretation of this statement is that the Equal Protection Clause, even the Equal Protection Clause as incorporated in the Due Process Clause, is not the basis for today's holding. But the portion of the majority opinion that explains why DOMA is unconstitutional (Part IV) begins by citing *Bolling v. Sharpe* (1954), *Department of Agriculture v. Moreno* (1973), and *Romer v. Evans* (1996)—all of which are equal-protection cases. And those three cases are the only authorities that the Court cites in Part IV about the Constitution's meaning, except for its citation of *Lawrence v. Texas* (2003) (not an equal-protection case) to support its passing assertion that the Constitution protects the "moral and sexual choices" of same-sex couples.

Moreover, if this is meant to be an equal-protection opinion, it is a confusing one. The opinion does not resolve and indeed does not even mention what had been the central question in this litigation: whether, under the Equal Protection Clause, laws restricting marriage to a man and a woman are reviewed for more than mere rationality. That is the issue that divided the parties and the court below.

In accord with my previously expressed skepticism about the Court's "tiers of scrutiny" approach, I would review this classification only for its rationality. As nearly as I can tell, the Court agrees with that; its opinion does not apply strict scrutiny, and its central propositions are taken from rational-basis cases like *Moreno*. But the Court certainly does not apply anything that resembles that deferential framework.

The majority opinion need not get into the strict-vs.-rational-basis scrutiny question, and need not justify its holding under either, because it says that DOMA is unconstitutional as "a deprivation of the liberty of the person protected by the Fifth Amendment of the Constitution": that it violates "basic due process" principles and that it inflicts an "injury and indignity" of a kind that denies "an essential part of the liberty protected by the Fifth Amendment." The majority never utters the dread words "substantive due process," perhaps sensing the disrepute into which that doctrine has fallen, but that is what those statements mean. Yet the opinion does not argue that same-sex marriage is "deeply rooted in this Nation's history and tradition," *Washington v. Glucksberg* (1997), a claim that would of course be quite absurd. So would the further suggestion (also necessary, under our substantive-due-process precedents) that a world in which DOMA exists is one bereft of "'ordered liberty.'" *Id.*

Some might conclude that this loaf could have used a while longer in the oven. But that would be wrong; it is already overcooked. The most expert care in preparation cannot redeem a bad recipe. The sum of all the Court's nonspecific hand-waving is that this law is invalid (maybe on equal-protection grounds, maybe on substantive-due-process grounds, and perhaps with some amorphous federalism component playing a role) because it is motivated by a "'bare...desire to harm'" couples in same-sex marriages. It is this proposition with which I will therefore engage.

B

As I have observed before, the Constitution does not forbid the government to enforce traditional moral and sexual norms. I will not swell the U.S. Reports with restatements of that point. It is enough to say that the Constitution neither requires nor forbids our society to approve of same-sex marriage, much as it neither requires nor forbids us to approve of no-fault divorce, polygamy, or the consumption of alcohol.

> *The Constitution neither requires nor forbids our society to approve of same-sex marriage, much as it neither requires nor forbids us to approve of no-fault divorce, polygamy, or the consumption of alcohol.*

However, even setting aside traditional moral disapproval of same-sex marriage (or indeed same-sex sex), there are many perfectly valid—indeed, downright boring—justifying rationales for this legislation. Their existence ought to be the end of this case. For they give the lie to the Court's conclusion that only those with hateful hearts could have voted "aye" on this Act. And more importantly, they serve to make the contents of the legislators' hearts quite irrelevant: "It is a familiar principle of constitutional law that this Court will not strike down an otherwise constitutional statute on the basis of an alleged illicit legislative motive." *United States v. O'Brien* (1968). Or at least it was a familiar principle. By holding to the contrary, the majority has declared open season on any law that (in the opinion of the law's opponents and any panel of like-minded federal judges) can be characterized as mean-spirited.

The majority concludes that the only motive for this Act was the "bare...desire to harm a politically unpopular group." Bear in mind that the object of this condemnation is not the legislature of some once-Confederate Southern state (familiar objects of the Court's scorn), but our respected coordinate branches, the Congress and Presidency of the United States. Laying such a charge against them should require the most extraordinary evidence, and I would have thought that every attempt would be made to indulge a more anodyne explanation for the statute. The majority does the opposite—affirmatively concealing from the reader the arguments that exist in justification. It makes only a passing mention of the "arguments put forward" by the Act's defenders, and does not even trouble to paraphrase or describe them. I imagine that this is because it is harder to maintain the illusion of the Act's supporters as unhinged members of a wild-eyed lynch mob when one first describes their views as they see them.

To choose just one of these defenders' arguments, DOMA avoids difficult choice-of-law issues that will now arise absent a uniform federal definition of marriage. Imagine a pair of women who marry in Albany and then move to Alabama, which does not "recognize as valid any marriage of parties of the same sex." When the couple files their next federal tax return, may it be a joint one? Which State's law controls, for federal-law purposes: their State of celebration (which recognizes the marriage) or their State of domicile (which does not)? (Does the answer depend on whether they were just visiting in Albany?) Are these questions to be answered as a matter of federal common law, or perhaps by borrowing a State's choice-of-law rules? If so, which State's? And what about States where the status of an out-of-state same-sex marriage is an unsettled question under local law? DOMA avoided all of this uncertainty by specifying which marriages would be recognized for federal purposes. That is a classic purpose for a definitional provision.

Further, DOMA preserves the intended effects of prior legislation against then-unforeseen changes in circumstance. When Congress provided (for example) that a special estate-tax exemption would exist for spouses, this exemption reached only opposite-sex spouses— those being the only sort that were recognized in any State at the time of DOMA's passage. When it became clear that changes in state law might one day alter that balance, DOMA's definitional section was enacted to ensure that state-level experimentation did not automatically alter the basic operation of federal law, unless and until Congress made the further judgment to do so on its own. That is not animus—just stabilizing prudence. Congress has hardly demonstrated itself unwilling to make such further, revising judgments upon due deliberation. See, e.g., Don't Ask, Don't Tell Repeal Act of 2010.

The Court mentions none of this. Instead, it accuses the Congress that enacted this law and the President who signed it of something much worse than, for example, having acted in excess of enumerated federal powers—or even having drawn distinctions that prove to be irrational. Those legal errors may be made in good faith, errors though they are. But the majority says that the supporters of this Act acted with malice—with the "purpose" "to disparage and to injure" same-sex couples. It says that the motivation for DOMA was to "demean," to "impose inequality," to "impose...a stigma," to deny people "equal dignity," to brand gay people as "unworthy," and to "humiliat[e]" their children.

I am sure these accusations are quite untrue. To be sure (as the majority points out), the legislation is called the Defense of Marriage

Act. But to defend traditional marriage is not to condemn, demean, or humiliate those who would prefer other arrangements, any more than to defend the Constitution of the United States is to condemn, demean, or humiliate other constitutions. To hurl such accusations so casually demeans this institution. In the majority's judgment, any resistance to its holding is beyond the pale of reasoned disagreement. To question its high-handed invalidation of a presumptively valid statute is to act (the majority is sure) with the purpose to "disparage," "injure," "degrade," "demean," and "humiliate" our fellow human beings, our fellow citizens, who are homosexual. All that, simply for supporting an Act that did no more than codify an aspect of marriage that had been unquestioned in our society for most of its existence—indeed, had been unquestioned in virtually all societies for virtually all of human history. It is one thing for a society to elect change; it is another for a court of law to impose change by adjudging those who oppose it hostes humani generis, enemies of the human race.

> *It is one thing for a society to elect change; it is another for a court of law to impose change by adjudging those who oppose it hostes humani generis, enemies of the human race.*

The penultimate sentence of the majority's opinion is a naked declaration that "[t]his opinion and its holding are confined" to those couples "joined in same-sex marriages made lawful by the State." I have heard such "bald, unreasoned disclaimer[s]" before. When the Court declared a constitutional right to homosexual sodomy, we were assured that the case had nothing, nothing at all to do with "whether the government must give formal recognition to any relationship that homosexual persons seek to enter." Now we are told that DOMA is invalid because it "demeans the couple, whose moral and sexual choices the Constitution protects"—with an accompanying citation of *Lawrence*. It takes real cheek for today's majority to assure us, as it is going out the door, that a constitutional requirement to give formal recognition to same-sex marriage is not at issue here—when what has preceded that assurance is a lecture on how superior the majority's moral judgment in favor of same-sex marriage is to the Congress's hateful moral judgment against it. I promise you this: The only thing that will "confine" the Court's holding is its sense of what it can get away with.

I do not mean to suggest disagreement with The Chief Justice's view (dissenting opinion) that lower federal courts and state courts can distinguish today's case when the issue before them is state denial of marital status to same-sex couples—or even that this Court could theoretically do so. Lord, an opinion with such scatter-shot rationales as this one (federalism noises among them) can be distinguished in many ways. And deserves to be. State and lower federal courts should take the Court at its word and distinguish away.

In my opinion, however, the view that this Court will take of state prohibition of same-sex marriage is indicated beyond mistaking by today's opinion. As I have said, the real rationale of today's opinion, whatever disappearing trail of its legalistic argle-bargle one chooses to follow, is that DOMA is motivated by "'bare...desire to harm'" couples in same-sex marriages. How easy it is, indeed how inevitable, to

> *The real rationale of today's opinion, whatever disappearing trail of its legalistic argle-bargle one chooses to follow, is that DOMA is motivated by "'bare... desire to harm'" couples in same-sex marriages.*

reach the same conclusion with regard to state laws denying same-sex couples marital status. Consider how easy (inevitable) it is to make the following substitutions in a passage from today's opinion:

> "~~DOMA's~~ *This state law's* principal effect is to identify a subset of ~~state-sanctioned marriages~~ *constitutionally protected sexual relationships*, see *Lawrence*, and make them unequal. The principal purpose is to impose inequality, not for other reasons like governmental efficiency. Responsibilities, as well as rights, enhance the dignity and integrity of the person. And ~~DOMA~~ *this state law* contrives to deprive some couples ~~married under the laws of their State~~ *enjoying constitutionally protected sexual relationships*, but not other couples, of both rights and responsibilities."

Or try this passage, from ante:

> "[~~DOMA~~] *This state law* tells those couples, and all the world, that their otherwise valid ~~marriages~~ *relationships* are unworthy of ~~federal~~ *state* recognition. This places same-sex couples in an unstable position of being in a second-tier ~~marriage~~ *relationship*. The differentiation demeans the couple, whose moral and sexual choices the Constitution protects, see *Lawrence*,...."

Or this—which does not even require alteration, except as to the invented number:

> "And it humiliates tens of thousands of children now being raised by same-sex couples. The law in question makes it even

more difficult for the children to understand the integrity and closeness of their own family and its concord with other families in their community and in their daily lives."

Similarly transposable passages—deliberately transposable, I think—abound. In sum, that Court which finds it so horrific that Congress irrationally and hatefully robbed same-sex couples of the "personhood and dignity" which state legislatures conferred upon them, will of a certitude be similarly appalled by state legislatures' irrational and hateful failure to acknowledge that "personhood and dignity" in the first place. As far as this Court is concerned, no one should be fooled; it is just a matter of listening and waiting for the other shoe.

By formally declaring anyone opposed to same-sex marriage an enemy of human decency, the majority arms well every challenger to a state law restricting marriage to its traditional definition. Henceforth those challengers will lead with this Court's declaration that there is "no legitimate purpose" served by such a law, and will claim that the traditional definition has "the purpose and effect to disparage and to injure" the "personhood and dignity" of same-sex couples. The majority's limiting assurance will be meaningless in the face of language like that, as the majority well knows. That is why the language is there. The result will be a judicial distortion of our society's debate over marriage—a debate that can seem in need of our clumsy "help" only to a member of this institution.

As to that debate: Few public controversies touch an institution so central to the lives of so many, and few inspire such attendant passion by good people on all sides. Few public controversies will ever demonstrate so vividly the beauty of what our Framers gave us, a gift the Court pawns today to buy its stolen moment in the spotlight: a system of government that permits us to rule ourselves.

It is hard to admit that one's political opponents are not monsters, especially in a struggle like this one, and the challenge in the end proves more than today's Court can handle.

Since DOMA's passage, citizens on all sides of the question have seen victories and they have seen defeats. There have been plebiscites, legislation, persuasion, and loud voices—in other words, democracy. Victories in one place for some, see North Carolina Const., Amdt. 1 (providing that "[m]arriage between one man and one woman is the only domestic legal union that shall be valid or recognized in this State") (approved by a popular vote, 61% to 39% on May 8, 2012), are offset by victories in other places for others, see Maryland Question 6 (establishing "that Maryland's civil marriage laws allow gay and lesbian couples to obtain a civil marriage license") (approved by a popular vote, 52% to 48%, on November 6, 2012). Even in a single State, the question has come out differently on different occasions. Compare Maine Question 1 (permitting "the State of Maine to issue marriage licenses to same-sex couples") (approved by a popular vote, 53% to 47%, on November 6, 2012) with Maine Question 1 (rejecting "the new law that lets same-sex couples marry") (approved by a popular vote, 53% to 47%, on November 3, 2009).

In the majority's telling, this story is black-and-white: Hate your neighbor or come along with us. The truth is more complicated. It is hard to admit that one's political opponents are not monsters, especially in a struggle like this one, and the challenge in the end proves more than today's Court can handle. Too bad. A reminder that disagreement over something so fundamental as marriage can still be politically legitimate would have been a fit task for what in earlier times was called the judicial temperament. We might have covered ourselves with honor today, by promising all sides of this debate that it was theirs to settle and that we would respect their resolution. We might have let the People decide.

But that the majority will not do. Some will rejoice in today's decision, and some will despair at it; that is the nature of a controversy that matters so much to so many. But the Court has cheated both sides, robbing the winners of an honest victory, and the losers of the peace that comes from a fair defeat. We owed both of them better. I dissent.

OBERGEFELL v. HODGES (2015)

In his dissenting opinion in *United States v. Windsor* (above), Justice Scalia wrote that the Court's opinion undercut the basis not only of the Defense of Marriage Act but of any state law prohibiting same-sex marriage: "By formally declaring anyone opposed to same-sex marriage an enemy of human decency, the majority arms well every challenger to a state law restricting marriage to its traditional definition." He predicted that the Court was "leaving the second, state-law shoe to be dropped later, maybe next Term." He was off by one term.

In *Obergefell v. Hodges*, a divided Supreme Court ruled that states' bans on same-sex marriage (and the refusal to recognize legal same-sex marriages that occurred in states that permitted such marriages) violated the Due Process Clause of the Fourteenth Amendment. Writing for the majority, Justice Anthony Kennedy opened his opinion by stating, "The Constitution promises liberty to all within its reach, a liberty that includes certain specific rights that allow persons, within a lawful realm, to define and express their identity." He argued that the right to marry is one of the fundamental liberties protected by the Due Process Clause, and that the liberty extends equally to same-sex and opposite-sex couples.

Chief Justice John Roberts and Justices Scalia, Thomas, and Alito filed dissenting opinions in which they argued that the Court had overstepped its bounds in taking the debate over same-sex marriage away from the democratic process. In his dissent, Scalia wrote, "Until the courts put a stop to it, public debate over same-sex marriage displayed American democracy at its best. Individuals on both sides of the issue passionately, but respectfully, attempted to persuade their fellow citizens to accept their views."

Scalia attacked the flowery language Justice Kennedy used to describe the liberty established by his majority opinion. Scalia wrote, "If, even as the price to be paid for a fifth vote, I ever joined an opinion for the Court that began: 'The Constitution promises liberty to all within its reach, a liberty that includes certain specific rights that allow persons, within a lawful realm, to define and express their identity,' I would hide my head in a bag."

～◈◈◈◈～

Justice Scalia, with whom Justice Thomas joins, dissenting.

I join The Chief Justice's opinion in full. I write separately to call attention to this Court's threat to American democracy.

The substance of today's decree is not of immense personal importance to me. The law can recognize as marriage whatever sexual attachments and living arrangements it wishes, and can accord them favorable civil consequences, from tax treatment to rights of inheritance. Those civil consequences—and the public approval that conferring the name of marriage evidences—can perhaps have adverse social effects, but no more adverse than the effects of many other controversial laws. So it is not of special importance to me what the law says about marriage. It is of overwhelming importance, however, who it is that rules me. Today's decree says that my Ruler, and the Ruler of 320 million Americans coast-to-coast,

Today's decree says that my Ruler, and the Ruler of 320 million Americans coast-to-coast, is a majority of the nine lawyers on the Supreme Court.

is a majority of the nine lawyers on the Supreme Court. The opinion in these cases is the furthest extension in fact—and the furthest extension one can even imagine—of the Court's claimed power to create "liberties" that the Constitution and its Amendments neglect to mention. This practice of constitutional revision by an unelected committee of nine, always accompanied (as it is today) by extravagant praise of liberty, robs the People of the most important liberty they asserted in the Declaration of Independence and won in the Revolution of 1776: the freedom to govern themselves.

I

Until the courts put a stop to it, public debate over same-sex marriage displayed American democracy at its best. Individuals on both sides of the issue passionately, but respectfully, attempted to persuade their fellow citizens to accept their views. Americans considered the arguments and put the question to a vote. The electorates of 11 States, either directly or through their representatives, chose to expand the traditional definition of marriage. Many more decided not to. Win or lose, advocates for both sides continued pressing their cases, secure in the knowledge that an electoral loss can be negated by a later electoral win. That is exactly how our system of government is supposed to work.

The Constitution places some constraints on self-rule—constraints adopted *by the People themselves* when they ratified the Constitution and its Amendments. Forbidden are laws "impairing the Obligation of Contracts," denying "Full Faith and Credit" to the "public Acts" of other States, prohibiting the free exercise of religion, abridging the freedom of speech, infringing the right to keep and bear arms, authorizing unreasonable searches and seizures, and so forth. Aside from these limitations, those powers "reserved to the States respectively, or to the people" can be exercised as the States or the People desire. These cases ask us to decide whether the Fourteenth Amendment contains a limitation that requires the States to license and recognize marriages between two people of the same sex. Does it remove *that* issue from the political process?

Of course not. It would be surprising to find a prescription regarding marriage in the Federal Constitution since, as the author of today's opinion reminded us only two years ago (in an opinion joined by the same Justices who join him today):

> "[R]egulation of domestic relations is an area that has long been regarded as a virtually exclusive province of the States."

> "[T]he Federal Government, through our history, has deferred to state-law policy decisions with respect to domestic relations."

But we need not speculate. When the Fourteenth Amendment was ratified in 1868, every State limited marriage to one man and one woman, and no one doubted the constitutionality of doing so. That resolves these cases. When it comes to determining the meaning of a vague constitutional provision—such as "due process of law" or "equal protection of the laws"—it is unquestionable that the People who ratified that provision did not understand it to prohibit a practice that remained both universal and uncontroversial in the years after ratification. We have no basis for striking down a practice that is not expressly prohibited by the Fourteenth Amendment's text, and that bears the endorsement of a long tradition of open, widespread, and unchallenged use dating back to the Amendment's ratification. Since there is no doubt whatever that the People never decided to prohibit the limitation of marriage to opposite-sex couples, the public debate over same-sex marriage must be allowed to continue.

But the Court ends this debate, in an opinion lacking even a thin veneer of law. Buried beneath the mummeries and straining-to-be-memorable passages of the opinion is a candid and startling assertion: No matter *what* it was the People ratified, the Fourteenth Amendment protects those rights that the Judiciary, in its "reasoned judgment," thinks the Fourteenth Amendment ought to protect. That is so because "[t]he generations that wrote and ratified the Bill of Rights and the Fourteenth Amendment did not presume to know the extent of freedom in all of its dimensions...." One would think that sentence would continue: "...and therefore they provided for a means by which the People could amend the Constitution," or perhaps "...and therefore they left the creation of additional liberties, such as the freedom to marry someone of the same sex, to the People, through the never-ending process of legislation." But no. What logically follows, in the majority's judge-empowering estimation, is: "and so they entrusted to future generations a charter protecting the right of all persons to enjoy liberty as we learn its meaning." The "we," needless to say, is the nine of us. "History and tradition guide and discipline [our] inquiry but do not set its outer boundaries." Thus, rather than focusing on *the People's* understanding of "liberty"—at the time of ratification or even today—the majority focuses on four "principles and traditions" that, *in the majority's view*, prohibit States from defining marriage as an institution consisting of one man and one woman.

> *A system of government that makes the People subordinate to a committee of nine unelected lawyers does not deserve to be called a democracy.*

This is a naked judicial claim to legislative—indeed, *super*-legislative—power; a claim fundamentally at odds with our system of government. Except as limited by a constitutional prohibition agreed to by the People, the States are free to adopt whatever laws they like, even those that offend the esteemed Justices' "reasoned judgment." A system of government that makes the People subordinate to a committee of nine unelected lawyers does not deserve to be called a democracy.

Judges are selected precisely for their skill as lawyers; whether they reflect the policy views of a particular constituency is not (or should not be) relevant. Not surprisingly then, the Federal Judiciary is hardly a cross-section of America. Take, for example, this Court, which consists of only nine men and women, all of them successful lawyers who studied at Harvard or Yale Law School. Four of the nine are natives of New York City. Eight of them grew up in east- and west-coast States. Only one hails from the vast expanse in-between. Not a single Southwesterner or even, to tell the truth, a genuine Westerner (California does not count). Not a single evangelical Christian (a group that comprises about one quarter of Americans), or even a Protestant of any denomination. The strikingly unrepresentative character of the body voting on today's social upheaval would be irrelevant if they were functioning as *judges*, answering the legal question whether the American people had ever ratified a constitutional provision that was understood to proscribe the traditional definition of marriage. But of course the Justices in today's majority are not voting on that basis; *they say they are not.* And to allow the policy question of same-sex marriage to be considered and resolved by a select, patrician, highly unrepresentative panel of nine is to violate a principle even more fundamental than no taxation without representation: no social transformation without representation.

II

But what really astounds is the hubris reflected in today's judicial Putsch. The five Justices who compose today's majority are entirely comfortable concluding that every State violated the Constitution for all of the 135 years between the Fourteenth Amendment's ratification and Massachusetts' permitting of same-sex marriages in 2003. They have discovered in the Fourteenth Amendment a "fundamental right" overlooked by every person alive at the time of ratification, and almost everyone else in the time since. They see what lesser legal minds—minds like Thomas Cooley, John Marshall Harlan, Oliver Wendell Holmes, Jr., Learned Hand, Louis Brandeis, William Howard Taft, Benjamin Cardozo, Hugo Black, Felix Frankfurter, Robert Jackson, and Henry Friendly—could not. They are certain that the People ratified the Fourteenth Amendment to bestow on them the power to remove questions from the democratic process when that is called for by their "reasoned judgment." These Justices *know* that limiting marriage to one man and one woman is contrary to reason; they *know* that an institution as old as government itself, and accepted by every nation in history until 15 years ago, cannot possibly be supported by anything other than ignorance or bigotry. And they are willing to say that any citizen who does not agree with that, who adheres to what was, until 15 years ago, the unanimous judgment of all generations and all societies, stands against the Constitution.

> *The opinion is couched in a style that is as pretentious as its content is egotistic.*

The opinion is couched in a style that is as pretentious as its content is egotistic. It is one thing for separate concurring or dissenting opinions to contain extravagances, even silly extravagances, of thought and expression; it is something else for the official opinion of the Court to do so.

[Footnote] If, even as the price to be paid for a fifth vote, I ever joined an opinion for the Court that began: "The Constitution promises liberty to all within its reach, a liberty that includes certain specific rights that allow persons, within a lawful realm, to define and express their identity," I would hide my head in a bag. The Supreme Court of the United States has descended from the disciplined legal reasoning of John Marshall and Joseph Story to the mystical aphorisms of the fortune cookie.

Of course the opinion's showy profundities are often profoundly incoherent. "The nature of marriage is that, through its enduring bond, two persons together can find other freedoms, such as expression, intimacy, and spirituality."(Really? Who ever thought that intimacy and spirituality [whatever that means] were freedoms? And if intimacy is, one would think Freedom of Intimacy is abridged rather than expanded by marriage. Ask the nearest hippie. Expression, sure enough, *is* a freedom, but anyone in a long-lasting marriage will attest that that happy state constricts, rather than expands, what one can prudently say.) Rights, we are told, can "rise... from a better informed understanding of how constitutional imperatives define a liberty that remains urgent in our own era." (Huh? How can a better informed understanding of how constitutional imperatives [whatever that means] define [whatever that means] an urgent liberty [never mind], give birth to a right?) And we are told that, "[i]n any particular case," either the Equal Protection or Due Process Clause "may be thought to capture the essence of [a] right in a more accurate and comprehensive way," than the other, "even as the two Clauses may converge in the identification and definition of the right."(What say? What possible "essence" does substantive due process "capture" in an "accurate and comprehensive way"? It stands for nothing whatever, except those freedoms and entitlements that this Court *really* likes. And the Equal Protection Clause, as employed today, identifies nothing except a difference in treatment that this Court *really* dislikes. Hardly a distillation of essence. If the opinion is correct that the two clauses "converge in the identification and definition of [a] right," that is only because the majority's likes and dislikes are predictably compatible.) I could go on. The world does not expect logic and precision in poetry or inspirational pop-philosophy; it demands them in the law. The stuff contained in today's opinion has to diminish this Court's reputation for clear thinking and sober analysis.

Hubris is sometimes defined as o'erweening pride; and pride, we know, goeth before a fall. The Judiciary is the "least dangerous" of the federal branches because it has "neither Force nor Will, but merely judgment; and must ultimately depend upon the aid of the executive arm" and the States, "even for the efficacy of its judgments." With each decision of ours that takes from the People a question properly left to them—with each decision that is unabashedly based not on law, but on the "reasoned judgment" of a bare majority of this Court—we move one step closer to being reminded of our impotence.

CHAPTER TWELVE

SEXUAL EQUALITY

~≈◈⊹◉≈~

A s with race, the Equal Protection Clause of the Fourteenth Amendment protects persons from being unreasonably classified by sex. Before the 1970s, however, the Supreme Court gave wide latitude to the government to draw lines by sex. So long as the classification was considered "rationally related" to some "legitimate" government objective, it would be allowed.

From the 1970s, as attitudes about women's role in society changed, the Court began to take a harder look at classifications based on sex. From 1976 until its decision in *United States v. Virginia* in 1996, the Court upheld such classifications only if they served "important" (as opposed to merely "legitimate") government objectives and were "substantially related" (not merely "rationally related") to achievement of those objectives.[1] This level of review, commonly referred to as "intermediate scrutiny," is easier to satisfy than the strict-scrutiny standard applied in race cases, but it often results in classifications' being struck down as unconstitutional. There have been exceptions. For example, the Supreme Court upheld the law requiring only men to register for the military draft[2] and also found constitutional a California law holding adult men, but not women, criminally liable for statutory rape.[3]

Justice Scalia followed the Court's precedents and applied intermediate scrutiny to laws that distinguished between men and women. As the reader will observe in Scalia's dissent in *United States v. Virginia* below, he contended that this level of review was more than sufficient given that women had a greater voice in our democratic system than racial and ethnic minorities. Women's greater political power, he believed, was simply a matter of numbers. Women, making up the majority of eligible voters in the United States, were less likely to be the victims of discriminatory laws that violated the Equal Protection Clause.

UNITED STATES v. VIRGINIA (1996)

The Supreme Court was asked to decide the constitutionality of the admissions policy of the Virginia Military Institute (VMI). The Commonwealth of Virginia, which had operated VMI as an all-male college since 1839, argued that this policy was justified by the institute's rigorous physical training requirements, deprivation of students' privacy, and boot camp–style training, including hazing. The state also argued that the VMI's men-only military education furthered Virginia's efforts to provide diversity in educational approaches. Finally, the state proposed a separate military program at a preexisting all-women private liberal arts college in Virginia.

In a 7–1 decision (Justice Thomas did not participate in the case because his son attended VMI at the time), the Supreme Court ruled that VMI's admissions policy violated the Equal Protection Clause of the Fourteenth Amendment. The majority said the admissions policy was based on overly broad generalizations about how women would fare in VMI's physically challenging program. Even if most women would be unable to keep up, some would be able, the Court ruled, and therefore should not be denied the opportunity to attend. The Court also dismissed the state's argument about its policy of diversity in higher education, pointing out that Virginia did not have any all-women public universities. Lastly, the Court ruled that the proposed all-women military program would not correct the state's Equal Protection problems because the women's alternative did not include the same level of military training or have the same standard of academic excellence as VMI.

In holding the VMI admissions policy unconstitutional, the Court ruled that sex-based distinctions will be invalidated unless a state demonstrates an "exceedingly persuasive justification." In addition, the Court's majority warned that it would be skeptical of government distinctions based on sex, which can be justified only by actual state purposes, not rationalizations that hide discriminatory motivations.

Justice Scalia, the lone dissenter, wrote a long opinion that challenged the Court on nearly every facet of its decision. First, Scalia wrote that the Court completely ignored the long-standing tradition of government support for men's military colleges. Using a line of reasoning he employed often in religious freedom cases, Scalia argued that the Constitution cannot be read to outlaw a policy that has been in place for more than 150 years.

Next, Scalia charged that the new burden on the state to show an "exceedingly persuasive justification" for excluding women from VMI amounted to a "redefinition of intermediate scrutiny that makes it indistinguishable from strict scrutiny." He said this more searching scrutiny was unwarranted given that women are not a minority group that lacks recourse to change policy through the democratic process. Rejecting the new standard, Scalia went on to apply that traditional intermediate-scrutiny analysis, concluding that Virginia had a legitimate, if not compelling, interest in providing "effective" education. He criticized the Court for ignoring the case's factual record, which made it clear that single-sex education at the college level was beneficial for both male and female students.

Scalia's opinion also responded to a concurring opinion written by Chief Justice Rehnquist, who agreed that VMI's admissions policy was unconstitutional but argued that the Court should not have used the new "exceedingly persuasive justification" test. Even under the standard "intermediate-scrutiny" review, the chief justice wrote, the policy would fail because the state did not offer sufficient evidence to support its mission of providing educational diversity or of the benefits of VMI's "adversative" method. Scalia responded that the evidence sought by the chief justice was either amply provided by the state or was considered a given in the litigation.

Scalia predicted the Court's rationale for invalidating VMI's admissions policy would someday be extended to close all single-sex schools in the United States, public and private. Finally, his opinion closed with a poignant reflection on the code of conduct all first-year students at VMI were required to keep with them. The code sets forth basic rules of gentlemanly behavior. Scalia said he did not know whether the men of VMI followed the rules but nevertheless found it "powerfully impressive that a public institution of higher education still in existence sought to have them do so."

≼⊹⊙⊹≽

Justice Scalia, dissenting.

Today the Court shuts down an institution that has served the people of the Commonwealth of Virginia with pride and distinction for over a century and a half. To achieve that desired result, it rejects (contrary to our established practice) the factual findings of two courts below, sweeps aside the precedents of this Court, and ignores the history of our people. As to facts: it explicitly rejects the finding that there exist "gender-based developmental differences" supporting Virginia's restriction of the "adversative" method to only a men's institution, and the finding that the all-male composition of the Virginia Military Institute (VMI) is essential to that institution's character. As to precedent: it drastically revises our established standards for reviewing sex-based classifications. And as to history: it counts for nothing the long tradition, enduring down to the present, of men's military colleges supported by both States and the Federal Government.

Today the Court shuts down an institution that has served the people of the Commonwealth of Virginia with pride and distinction for over a century and a half.

Much of the Court's opinion is devoted to deprecating the closed-mindedness of our forebears with regard to women's education, and even with regard to the treatment of women in areas that have nothing to do with education. Closed-minded they were—as every age is, including our own, with regard to matters it cannot guess, because it simply does not consider them debatable. The virtue of a democratic system with a First Amendment is that it readily enables the people, over time, to be persuaded that what they took for granted is not so, and to change their laws accordingly. That system is destroyed if the smug assurances of each age are removed from the democratic process and written into the Constitution. So to counterbalance the Court's criticism of our ancestors, let me say a word in their praise: they left us free to change. The same cannot be said of this most illiberal Court, which has embarked on a course of inscribing one after another of the current preferences of the society (and in some cases only the counter-majoritarian preferences of the society's law-trained elite) into our Basic Law. Today it enshrines the notion that no substantial educational value is to be served by an all-men's military academy—so that the decision by the people of Virginia to maintain such an institution denies equal protection to women who cannot attend that institution but can attend others. Since it is entirely clear that the Constitution of the United States—the old one—takes no sides in this educational debate, I dissent.

I

I shall devote most of my analysis to evaluating the Court's opinion on the basis of our current equal protection jurisprudence, which regards this Court as free to evaluate everything under the sun by applying one of three tests: "rational basis" scrutiny, intermediate scrutiny, or strict scrutiny. These tests are no more scientific than their names suggest, and a further element of randomness is added by the fact that it is largely up to us which test will be applied in each case. Strict scrutiny, we have said, is reserved for state "classifications based on race or national origin and classifications affecting fundamental rights," *Clark v. Jeter* (1988). It is my position that the term "fundamental rights" should be limited to "interest[s] traditionally protected by our society," *Michael H. v. Gerald D.* (1989); but the Court has not accepted that view, so that strict scrutiny will be applied to the deprivation of whatever sort of right we consider "fundamental." We have no established criterion for "intermediate scrutiny" either, but essentially apply it when it seems like a good idea to load the dice. So far it has been applied to content-neutral restrictions that place an incidental burden on speech, to disabilities attendant to illegitimacy, and to discrimination on the basis of sex.

I have no problem with a system of abstract tests such as rational-basis, intermediate, and strict scrutiny (though I think we can do better than applying strict-scrutiny and intermediate scrutiny whenever we feel like it). Such formulas are essential to evaluating whether the new restrictions that a changing society constantly imposes upon private conduct comport with that "equal protection" our society has always accorded in the past. But in my view the function of this Court is to *preserve* our society's values regarding (among other things) equal protection, not to *revise* them; to prevent backsliding from the degree of restriction the Constitution imposed upon democratic government, not to prescribe, on our own authority, progressively higher degrees. For that reason it is my view that, whatever abstract tests we may choose to devise, they cannot supersede—and indeed ought to be crafted *so as to reflect*—those constant and unbroken national traditions that embody the people's understanding of ambiguous constitutional texts. More specifically, it is my view that "when a practice not expressly prohibited by the text of the Bill of Rights bears the endorsement of a long tradition of open, widespread, and unchallenged use that dates back to the beginning of the Republic, we have no proper basis for striking it down." *Rutan v. Republican Party of Ill.* (1990) (Scalia, J., dissenting). The same applies, mutatis mutandis, to a practice asserted to be in violation of the post–Civil War Fourteenth Amendment.

The all-male constitution of VMI comes squarely within such a governing tradition. Founded by the Commonwealth of Virginia in 1839 and continuously maintained by it since, VMI has always admitted only men. And in that regard it has not been unusual. For almost all of VMI's more than a century and a half of existence, its single-sex status reflected the uniform practice for government-supported military colleges. Another famous Southern institution, The Citadel, has existed as a state-funded school of South Carolina since 1842. And all the federal military colleges—West Point, the Naval Academy at Annapolis, and even the Air Force Academy, which was not established until 1954—admitted only males for most of their history. Their admission of women in 1976 (upon which the Court today relies) came not by court decree, but because the people, through their elected representatives, decreed a change. In other words, the tradition of having government-funded military schools for men is as well rooted in the traditions of this country as the tradition of sending only men into military combat. The people may decide to change the one tradition, like the other, through democratic processes; but the assertion that either tradition has been unconstitutional through the centuries is not law, but politics-smuggled-into-law.

> *The tradition of having government-funded military schools for men is as well rooted in the traditions of this country as the tradition of sending only men into military combat. The people may decide to change the one tradition, like the other, through democratic processes; but the assertion that either tradition has been unconstitutional through the centuries is not law, but politics-smuggled-into-law.*

And the same applies, more broadly, to single-sex education in general, which, as I shall discuss, is threatened by today's decision with the cut-off of all state and federal support. Government-run nonmilitary educational institutions for the two sexes have until very recently also been part of our national tradition. "[It is] [c]oeducation, historically, [that] is a novel educational theory. From grade school through high school, college, and graduate and professional training, much of the Nation's population during much of our history has been educated in sexually segregated classrooms." *Missis-sippi Univ. for Women v. Hogan* (1982) (Powell, J., dissenting). These traditions may of course be changed by the democratic decisions of the people, as they largely have been.

Today, however, change is forced upon Virginia, and reversion to sin-gle-sex education is prohibited nationwide, not by democratic processes but by order of this Court. Even while bemoaning the sorry, bygone days of "fixed notions" concerning women's education, the Court favors current notions so fixedly that it is willing to write them into the Consti-tution of the United States by application of custom-built "tests." This is not the interpretation of a Constitution, but the creation of one.

II

To reject the Court's disposition today, however, it is not necessary to accept my view that the Court's made-up tests cannot displace longstanding national traditions as the primary determinant of what the Constitution means. It is only necessary to apply honestly the test the Court has been applying to sex-based classifications for the past two decades. It is well settled, as Justice O'Connor stated some time ago for a unanimous Court, that we evaluate a statutory classification based on sex under a standard that lies "[b]etween th[e] extremes of rational basis review and strict scrutiny." *Clark v. Jeter.* We have denominated this standard "intermediate scrutiny" and under it have inquired whether the statutory classification is "substantially related to an important governmental objective." *Ibid.*

Before I proceed to apply this standard to VMI, I must comment upon the manner in which the Court avoids doing so. Notwithstand-ing our above-described precedents and their " 'firmly established principles,' " *Heckler v. Mathews* (1984) (quoting *Hogan*), the United

States urged us to hold in this case "that strict scrutiny is the correct constitutional standard for evaluating classifications that deny opportunities to individuals based on their sex." (This was in flat contradiction of the Government's position below, which was, in its own words, to "stat[e] *unequivocally* that the appropriate standard in this case is 'intermediate scrutiny.'" The Court, while making no reference to the Government's argument, effectively accepts it.

Although the Court in two places recites the test as stated in *Hogan*, which asks whether the State has demonstrated "that the classification serves important governmental objectives and that the discriminatory means employed are substantially related to the achievement of those objectives," the Court never answers the question presented in anything resembling that form. When it engages in analysis, the Court instead prefers the phrase "exceedingly persuasive justification" from *Hogan*. The Court's nine invocations of that phrase and even its fanciful description of that imponderable as "the core instruction" of the Court's decisions in *J.E.B. v. Alabama ex rel. T. B.* and *Hogan* would be unobjectionable if the Court acknowledged that whether a "justification" is "exceedingly persuasive" must be assessed by asking "[whether] the classification serves important governmental objectives and [whether] the discriminatory means employed are substantially related to the achievement of those objectives." Instead, however, the Court proceeds to interpret "exceedingly persuasive justification" in a fashion that contradicts the reasoning of *Hogan* and our other precedents.

That is essential to the Court's result, which can only be achieved by establishing that intermediate scrutiny is not survived if there are *some* women interested in attending VMI, capable of undertaking its activities, and able to meet its physical demands. Thus, the Court summarizes its holding as follows:

In contrast to the generalizations about women on which Virginia rests, we note again these *dispositive* realities: VMI's implementing methodology is not *inherently* unsuitable to women; *some* women do well under the adversative model; *some* women, at least, would want to attend VMI if they had the opportunity; *some* women are capable of all of the individual activities required of VMI cadets and can meet the physical standards VMI now imposes on men.

Similarly, the Court states that "[t]he Commonwealth's justification for excluding all women from 'citizen-soldier' training for which some are qualified...cannot rank as 'exceedingly persuasive'...."

Only the amorphous "exceedingly persuasive justification" phrase, and not the standard elaboration of intermediate scrutiny, can be made to yield this conclusion that VMI's single-sex composition is unconstitutional because there exist several women (or, one would have to conclude under the Court's reasoning, a single woman) willing and able to undertake VMI's program. Intermediate scrutiny has never required a least-restrictive-means analysis, but only a "substantial relation" between the classification and the state interests that it serves. Thus, in *Califano v. Webster* (1977), we upheld a congressional statute that provided higher Social Security benefits for women than for men. We reasoned that "women...as such have been unfairly hindered from earning as much as men," but we did not require proof that each woman so benefited had suffered discrimination or that each disadvantaged man had not; it was sufficient that even under the former congressional scheme "women *on the average* received lower retirement benefits than men." The reasoning in our other intermediate-scrutiny cases has similarly required only a substantial relation between end and means, not a perfect fit. In *Rostker v. Goldberg* (1981), we held that selective-service registration could constitutionally exclude women, because even "assuming that a small number of women could be drafted for noncombat roles, Congress simply did not consider it worth the added burdens of including women in draft and registration plans." In *Metro Broadcasting, Inc. v. FCC* (1990), we held that a classification need not be accurate "in every case" to survive intermediate scrutiny so long as, "in the aggregate," it advances the underlying objective. There is simply no support in our cases for the notion that a sex-based classification is invalid unless it relates to characteristics that hold true in every instance.

Not content to execute a *de facto* abandonment of the intermediate scrutiny that has been our standard for sex-based classifications for some two decades, the Court purports to reserve the question whether, even in principle, a higher standard (*i.e.,* strict scrutiny) should apply. "The Court has," it says, "*thus far* reserved most stringent judicial scrutiny for classifications based on race or national origin ... "; and it describes our earlier cases as having done no more than decline to "equat[e] gender classifications, *for all purposes,* to classifications based on race or national origin." The wonderful thing about these statements is that they are not actually false—just as it would not be actually false to say that "our cases have thus far reserved the 'beyond a reasonable doubt' standard of proof for criminal cases," or that "we have not equated tort actions, for all purposes, to criminal prosecutions." But the statements are misleading, insofar as they suggest that we have not already categorically *held* strict scrutiny to be inapplicable to sex-based classifications. And the statements are irresponsible, insofar as they are calculated to destabilize current law. Our task is to clarify the law—not to muddy the waters, and not to exact overcompliance by intimidation. The States and the Federal Government are entitled to know *before they act* the standard to which they will be held, rather than be compelled to guess about the outcome of Supreme Court peek-a-boo.

The Court's intimations are particularly out of place because it is perfectly clear that, if the question of the applicable standard of review for sex-based classifications were to be regarded as an appropriate subject for reconsideration, the stronger argument would be not for elevating the standard to strict scrutiny, but for reducing it to rational-basis review. The latter certainly has a firmer foundation in our past jurisprudence: Whereas no majority of the Court has ever applied strict scrutiny in a case involving sex-based classifications, we routinely applied rational-basis review until the 1970s. And of course normal, rational-basis review of sex-based classifications would be much more in accord with the genesis of heightened standards of judicial review, the famous footnote in *United States v. Carolene Products Co.* (1938), which said (intimatingly) that we did not have to inquire in the case at hand:

> [W]hether prejudice against discrete and insular minorities may be a special condition, which tends seriously to curtail the operation of those political processes ordinarily to be relied upon to protect minorities, and which may call for a correspondingly more searching judicial inquiry.

The States and the Federal Government are entitled to know before they act the standard to which they will be held, rather than be compelled to guess about the outcome of Supreme Court peek-a-boo.

It is hard to consider women a "discrete and insular minority" unable to employ the "political processes ordinarily to be relied upon," when they constitute a majority of the electorate.

It is hard to consider women a "discrete and insular minorit[y]" unable to employ the "political processes ordinarily to be relied upon," when they constitute a majority of the electorate. And the suggestion that they are incapable of exerting that political power smacks of the same paternalism that the Court so roundly condemns. Moreover, a long list of legislation proves the proposition false. See, *e.g.,* Equal Pay Act of 1963; Title VII of the Civil Rights Act of 1964; Title IX of the Education Amendments of 1972; Women's Business Ownership Act of 1988; Violence Against Women Act of 1994.

III

With this explanation of how the Court has succeeded in making its analysis seem orthodox—and indeed, if intimations are to be believed, even overly generous to VMI—I now proceed to describe how the analysis should have been conducted. The question to be answered, I repeat, is whether the exclusion of women from VMI is "substantially related to an important governmental objective."

A

It is beyond question that Virginia has an important state interest in providing effective college education for its citizens. That single-sex instruction is an approach substantially related to that interest should be evident enough from the long and continuing history in this country of men's and women's colleges. But beyond that, as the Court of Appeals here stated: "That single-gender education at the college level is beneficial to both sexes is a *fact established in this case*" (emphasis added).

The evidence establishing that fact was overwhelming—indeed, "virtually uncontradicted" in the words of the court that received the evidence. As an initial matter, Virginia demonstrated at trial that "[a] substantial body of contemporary scholarship and research supports the proposition that, although males and females have significant areas of developmental overlap, they also have differing developmental needs that are deep-seated." While no one questioned that for many students a coeducational environment was nonetheless not inappropriate, that could not obscure the demonstrated benefits of single-sex colleges. For example, the District Court stated as follows:

> One empirical study in evidence, not questioned by any expert, demonstrates that single-sex colleges provide better educational experiences than coeducational institutions. Students of both sexes become more academically involved, interact with faculty frequently, show larger increases in intellectual self-esteem and are more satisfied with practically all aspects of college experience (the sole exception is social life) compared with their counterparts in coeducational institutions. Attendance at an all-male college substantially increases the likelihood that a student will carry out career plans in law, business and college teaching, and also has a substantial positive effect on starting salaries in business. Women's colleges increase the chances that those who attend will obtain positions of leadership, complete the baccalaureate degree, and aspire to higher degrees.

"[I]n the light of this very substantial authority favoring single-sex education," the District Court concluded that "the VMI Board's decision to maintain an all-male institution is fully justified even without taking into consideration the other unique features of VMI's teaching and training." This finding alone, which even this Court cannot dispute, should be sufficient to demonstrate the constitutionality of VMI's all-male composition.

But besides its single-sex constitution, VMI is different from other colleges in another way. It employs a "distinctive educational method," sometimes referred to as the "adversative, or doubting, model of education." "Physical rigor, mental stress, absolute equality of treatment, absence of privacy, minute regulation of behavior, and indoctrination in desirable values are the salient attributes of the VMI educational experience." No one contends that this method is appropriate for all individuals; education is not a "one size fits all" business. Just as a State may wish to support junior colleges, vocational institutes, or a law school that emphasizes case practice instead of classroom study, so too a State's decision to maintain within its system one school that provides the adversative method is "substantially related" to its goal of good education. Moreover, it was uncontested that "if the state were to establish a women's VMI-type [*i.e.,* adversative] program, the program would attract an insufficient number of participants to make the program work" and it was found by the District Court that if Virginia were to include women in VMI, the school "would eventually find it necessary to drop the adversative system altogether." Thus, Virginia's options were an adversative method that excludes women or no adversative method at all.

There can be no serious dispute that, as the District Court found, single-sex education and a distinctive educational method "represent legitimate contributions to diversity in the Virginia higher education system." As a theoretical matter, Virginia's educational interest would have been *best* served (insofar as the two factors we have mentioned are concerned) by six different types of public colleges—an all-men's, an all-women's, and a coeducational college run in the "adversative method," and an all-men's, an all-women's, and a coeducational college run in the "traditional method." But as a practical matter, of course, Virginia's financial resources, like any State's, are not limitless, and the Commonwealth must select among the available options. Virginia thus has decided to fund, in addition to some 14 coeducational 4-year colleges, one college that is run as an all-male school on the adversative model: the Virginia Military Institute.

Virginia did not make this determination regarding the make-up of its public college system on the unrealistic assumption that no other colleges exist. Substantial evidence in the District Court demonstrated that the Commonwealth has long proceeded on the principle that "'[h]igher education resources should be viewed as a whole—public and private'"—because such an approach enhances diversity and because "'it is academic and economic waste to permit unwarranted duplication.'" (quoting 1974 Report of the General Assembly Commission on Higher Education to the General Assembly of Virginia). It is thus significant that, whereas there are "four all-female private [colleges] in Virginia," there is only "one private all-male college," which "indicates that the private sector is providing for th[e] [former] form of education to a much greater extent that it provides for all-male education." In these circumstances, Virginia's election to fund one public all-male institution and one on the adversative model—and to concentrate its resources in a single entity that serves both these interests in diversity—is substantially related to the Commonwealth's important educational interests.

B

The Court today has no adequate response to this clear demonstration of the conclusion produced by application of intermediate scrutiny. Rather, it relies on a series of contentions that are irrelevant or erroneous as a matter of law, foreclosed by the record in this litigation, or both.

1. I have already pointed out the Court's most fundamental error, which is its reasoning that VMI's all-male composition is unconstitutional because "some women are capable of all of the individual activities required of VMI cadets" and would prefer military training on the adversative model. This unacknowledged adoption of what amounts to (at least) strict scrutiny is without antecedent in our sex-discrimination cases and by itself discredits the Court's decision.

2. The Court suggests that Virginia's claimed purpose in maintaining VMI as an all-male institution—its asserted interest in promoting diversity of educational options—is not "genuin[e]," but is a pretext for discriminating against women. To support this charge, the Court would have to impute that base motive to VMI's Mission Study Committee, which conducted a 3-year study from 1983 to 1986 and recommended to VMI's Board of Visitors that the school remain all male. The committee, a majority of whose members consisted of non-VMI graduates, "read materials on education and on women in the military," "made site visits to single-sex and newly coeducational institutions" including West Point and the Naval Academy, and "considered the reasons that other institutions had changed from single-sex to coeducational status"; its work was praised as "thorough"

in the accreditation review of VMI conducted by the Southern Association of Colleges and Schools. The Court states that "[w]hatever internal purpose the Mission Study Committee served—and however well meaning the framers of the report—we can hardly extract from that effort any Commonwealth policy evenhandedly to advance diverse educational options." But whether it is part of the evidence to prove that diversity *was* the Commonwealth's objective (its short report said nothing on that particular subject) is quite separate from whether it is part of the evidence to prove that anti-feminism *was not*. The relevance of the Mission Study Committee is that its very creation, its sober 3-year study, and the analysis it produced utterly refute the claim that VMI has elected to maintain its all-male student-body composition for some misogynistic reason.

The Court also supports its analysis of Virginia's "actual state purposes" in maintaining VMI's student body as all male by stating that there is no explicit statement in the record " 'in which the Commonwealth has expressed itself' " concerning those purposes. That is wrong on numerous grounds. First and foremost, in its implication that such an explicit statement of "actual purposes" is needed. The Court adopts, in effect, the argument of the United States that since the exclusion of women from VMI in 1839 was based on the "assumptions" of the time "that men alone were fit for military and leadership roles," and since "[b]efore this litigation was initiated, Virginia never sought to supply a valid, contemporary rationale for VMI's exclusionary policy," "[t]hat failure itself renders the VMI policy invalid." This is an unheard-of doctrine. Each state decision to adopt or maintain a governmental policy need not be accompanied—in anticipation of litigation and on pain of being found to lack a relevant state interest—by a lawyer's contemporaneous recitation of the

State's purposes. The Constitution is not some giant Administrative Procedure Act, which imposes upon the States the obligation to set forth a "statement of basis and purpose" for their sovereign Acts. The situation would be different if what the Court assumes to have been the 1839 policy *had* been enshrined *and remained enshrined* in legislation—a VMI charter, perhaps, pronouncing that the institution's purpose is to keep women in their place. But since the 1839 policy was no more explicitly recorded than the Court contends the present one is, the mere fact that *today's* Commonwealth continues to fund VMI "is enough to answer [the United States'] contention that the [classification] was the 'accidental by-product of a traditional way of thinking about females.'" *Michael M.* (quoting *Califano*).

It is, moreover, not true that Virginia's contemporary reasons for maintaining VMI are not explicitly recorded. It is hard to imagine a more authoritative source on this subject than the 1990 Report of the Virginia Commission on the University of the 21st Century. As the parties stipulated, that report "notes that the hallmarks of Virginia's educational policy are 'diversity and autonomy.'" It said: "The formal system of higher education in Virginia includes a great array of institutions: state-supported and independent, two-year and senior, research and highly specialized, traditionally black *and single-sex*." (emphasis added). The Court's only response to this is repeated reliance on the Court of Appeals' assertion that "'the only explicit [statement] that we have found in the record in which the Commonwealth has expressed itself with respect to gender distinctions'" (namely, the statement in the 1990 Report that the Commonwealth's institutions must "deal with faculty, staff, and students without regard to sex") had nothing to do with the purpose of diversity. This proves, I suppose, that the Court of Appeals did not find a statement dealing with sex and diversity in the record; but the pertinent question (accepting the need for such a statement) is *whether it was there*. And the plain fact, which the Court does not deny, is that it *was*.

The Court contends that "[a] purpose genuinely to advance an array of educational options ... is not served" by VMI. It relies on the fact that all of Virginia's *other* public colleges have become coeducational. The apparent theory of this argument is that unless Virginia pursues a great deal of diversity, its pursuit of some diversity must be a sham. This fails to take account of the fact that Virginia's resources cannot support all possible permutations of schools, and of the fact that Virginia coordinates its public educational offerings with the offerings of in-state private educational institutions that the Commonwealth provides money for its residents to attend and otherwise assists—which include four women's colleges.

Finally, the Court unreasonably suggests that there is some pretext in Virginia's reliance upon decentralized decisionmaking to achieve diversity—its granting of substantial autonomy to each institution with regard to student-body composition and other matters. The Court adopts the suggestion of the Court of Appeals that it is not possible for "one institution with autonomy, but with no authority over any other state institution, [to] give effect to a state policy of diversity among institutions." If it were impossible for individual human beings (or groups of human beings) to act autonomously in effective pursuit of a common goal, the game of soccer would not exist. And where the goal is diversity in a free market for services, that tends to be achieved even by autonomous actors who

> *The apparent theory of this argument is that unless Virginia pursues a great deal of diversity, its pursuit of some diversity must be a sham.*

If it were impossible for individual human beings (or groups of human beings) to act autonomously in effective pursuit of a common goal, the game of soccer would not exist.

act out of entirely selfish interests and make no effort to cooperate. Each Virginia institution, that is to say, has a natural incentive to make itself distinctive in order to attract a particular segment of student applicants. And of course none of the institutions is *entirely* autonomous; if and when the legislature decides that a particular school is not well serving the interest of diversity—if it decides, for example, that a men's school is not much needed—funding will cease.

[Footnote] The Court, unfamiliar with the Commonwealth's policy of diverse and independent institutions, and in any event careless of state and local traditions, must be forgiven by Virginians for quoting a reference to "'the Charlottesville campus'" of the University of Virginia. The University of Virginia, an institution even older than VMI, though not as old as another of the Commonwealth's universities, the College of William and Mary, occupies the portion of Charlottesville known, not as the "campus," but as "the grounds." More importantly, even if it were a "campus," there would be no need to specify "the Charlottesville campus," as one might refer to the Bloomington or Indianapolis campus of Indiana University. Unlike university systems with which the Court is perhaps more familiar, such as those in New York (*e.g.,* the State University of New York at Binghamton or Buffalo), Illinois (University of Illinois at Urbana-Champaign or at Chicago), and California (University of California, Los Angeles, or University of California,

Berkeley), there is only *one* University of Virginia. It happens (because Thomas Jefferson lived near there) to be located at Charlottesville. To many Virginians it is known, simply, as "the University," which suffices to distinguish it from the Commonwealth's other institutions offering 4-year college instruction....

3. In addition to disparaging Virginia's claim that VMI's single-sex status serves a state interest in diversity, the Court finds fault with Virginia's failure to offer education based on the adversative training method to women. It dismisses the District Court's "'findings' on 'gender-based developmental differences'" on the ground that "[t]hese 'findings' restate the opinions of Virginia's expert witnesses, opinions about typically male or typically female 'tendencies.'" How remarkable to criticize the District Court on the ground that its findings rest on the evidence (*i.e.,* the testimony of Virginia's witnesses)! That is what findings are supposed to do. It is indefensible to tell the Commonwealth that "[t]he burden of justification is demanding and it rests entirely on [you]," and then to ignore the District Court's findings *because* they rest on the evidence put forward by the Commonwealth—particularly when, as the District Court said, "[t]he evidence in the case . . . is *virtually uncontradicted.*"

Ultimately, in fact, the Court does not deny the evidence supporting these findings. It instead makes evident that the parties to this litigation could have saved themselves a great deal of time, trouble, and expense by omitting a trial. The Court simply dispenses with the evidence submitted at trial—it never says that a single finding of the District Court is clearly erroneous—in favor of the Justices' own view of the world, which the Court proceeds to support with (1) references to observations of someone who is not a witness, nor even an educational expert, nor even a judge who reviewed the record or participated in the judgment below, but rather a judge who merely dissented from the Court of Appeals' decision not to rehear this litigation en banc, (2) citations of nonevidentiary materials such as *amicus curiae* briefs filed in this Court, and (3) various historical anecdotes designed to demonstrate that Virginia's support for VMI as currently constituted reminds the Justices of the "bad old days."

It is not too much to say that this approach to the litigation has rendered the trial a sham. But treating the evidence as irrelevant is absolutely necessary for the Court to reach its conclusion. Not a single witness contested, for example, Virginia's "substantial body of 'exceedingly persuasive' evidence ... that some students, both male and female, benefit from attending a single-sex college" and "[that] [f]or those students, the opportunity to attend a single-sex college is a valuable one, likely to lead to better academic and professional achievement." Even the United States' expert witness "called himself a 'believer in single-sex education,'" although it was his "personal, philosophical preference," not one "born of educational-benefit considerations," "that single-sex education should be provided only by the private sector."

4. The Court contends that Virginia, and the District Court, erred, and "misperceived our precedent," by "train[ing] their argument on 'means' rather than 'end.'" The Court focuses on "VMI's mission," which is to produce individuals "imbued with love of learning, confident in the functions and attitudes of leadership, possessing a high sense of public service, advocates of the American democracy and free enterprise system, and ready ... to defend their country in time of national peril." (quoting Mission Study Committee of the VMI Board of Visitors, Report, May 16, 1986). "Surely," the Court says, "that goal is great enough to accommodate women."

This is lawmaking by indirection. What the Court describes as "VMI's mission" is no less the mission of *all* Virginia colleges. Which of them would the Old Dominion continue to fund if they did *not* aim to create individuals "imbued with love of learning, etc.," right down to being ready "to defend their country in time of national peril"? It can be summed up as "learning, leadership, and patriotism." To be sure, those general educational values are described in a particularly martial fashion in VMI's mission statement, in accordance with the military, adversative, and all-male character of the institution. But imparting those values *in that fashion*—*i.e.,* in a military, adversative, all-male environment—is the *distinctive* mission of VMI. And as I have discussed (and both courts below found), *that* mission is *not* "great enough to accommodate women."

The Court's analysis at least has the benefit of producing foreseeable results. Applied generally, it means that whenever a State's ultimate objective is "great enough to accommodate women" (as it always will be), then the State will be held to have violated the Equal Protection Clause if it restricts to men even one means by which it pursues that objective—no matter how few women are interested in pursuing the objective by that means, no matter how much the single-sex program will have to be changed if both sexes are admitted, and no matter how beneficial that program has theretofore been to its participants.

5. The Court argues that VMI would not have to change very much if it were to admit women. The principal response to that argument is that it is irrelevant: If VMI's single-sex status is substantially related to the government's important educational objectives, as I have demonstrated above and as the Court refuses to discuss, that concludes the inquiry. There should be no debate in the federal judiciary over "how much" VMI would be required to change if

it admitted women and whether that would constitute "too much" change.

But if such a debate were relevant, the Court would certainly be on the losing side. The District Court found as follows: "[T]he evidence establishes that key elements of the adversative VMI educational system, with its focus on barracks life, would be fundamentally altered, and the distinctive ends of the system would be thwarted, if VMI were forced to admit females and to make changes necessary to accommodate their needs and interests." Changes that the District Court's detailed analysis found would be required include new allowances for personal privacy in the barracks, such as locked doors and coverings on windows, which would detract from VMI's approach of regulating minute details of student behavior, "contradict the principle that everyone is constantly subject to scrutiny by everyone else," and impair VMI's "total egalitarian approach" under which every student must be "treated alike"; changes in the physical training program, which would reduce "[t]he intensity and aggressiveness of the current program"; and various modifications in other respects of the adversative training program that permeates student life. As the Court of Appeals summarized it, "the record supports the district court's findings that at least these three aspects of VMI's program—physical training, the absence of privacy, and the adversative approach—would be materially affected by coeducation, leading to a substantial change in the egalitarian ethos that is a critical aspect of VMI's training."

> *The Court argues that VMI would not have to change very much if it were to admit women. The principal response to that argument is that it is irrelevant.*

In the face of these findings by two courts below, amply supported by the evidence, and resulting in the conclusion that VMI would be fundamentally altered if it admitted women, this Court simply pronounces that "[t]he notion that admission of women would downgrade VMI's stature, destroy the adversative system and, with it, even the school, is a judgment hardly proved." The point about "downgrad[ing] VMI's stature" is a straw man; no one has made any such claim. The point about "destroy[ing] the adversative system" is simply false; the District Court not only stated that "[e]vidence supports this theory," but specifically concluded that while "[w]ithout a doubt" VMI could assimilate women, "it is equally without a doubt that VMI's present methods of training and education would have to be changed" by a "move away from its adversative new cadet system." And the point about "destroy[ing] the school," depending upon what that ambiguous phrase is intended to mean, is either false or else sets a standard much higher than VMI had to meet. It sufficed to establish, as the District Court stated, that VMI would be "significantly different" upon the admission of women and "would eventually find it necessary to drop the adversative system altogether."

6. Finally, the absence of a precise "all-women's analogue" to VMI is irrelevant. In *Mississippi Univ. for Women v. Hogan*, we attached no constitutional significance to the absence of an all-male nursing school. As Virginia notes, if a program restricted to one sex is necessarily unconstitutional unless there is a parallel program restricted to the other sex, "the opinion in *Hogan* could have ended with its first footnote, which observed that 'Mississippi maintains no other single-sex public university or college.'"

Although there is no precise female-only analogue to VMI, Virginia has created during this litigation the Virginia Women's Institute for Leadership (VWIL), a state-funded all-women's program run by Mary Baldwin College. I have thus far said nothing about VWIL because it is, under our established test, irrelevant, so long as *VMI's* all-male character is "substantially related" to an important state goal. But VWIL now exists, and the Court's treatment of it shows how far reaching today's decision is.

VWIL was carefully designed by professional educators who have long experience in educating young women. The program *rejects* the proposition that there is a "difference in the respective spheres and destinies of man and woman," *Bradwell v. State* (1873), and is designed to "provide an all-female program that will achieve substantially similar outcomes [to VMI's] in an all-female environment." After holding a trial where voluminous evidence was submitted and making detailed findings of fact, the District Court concluded that "there is a legitimate pedagogical basis for the different means employed [by VMI and VWIL] to achieve the substantially similar ends." The Court of Appeals undertook a detailed review of the record and affirmed. But it is Mary Baldwin College, which runs VWIL, that has made the point most succinctly:

> It would have been possible to develop the VWIL program to more closely resemble VMI, with adversative techniques associated with the rat line and barracks-like living quarters. Simply replicating an existing program would have required far less thought, research, and educational expertise. But such a facile approach would have produced a paper program with no real prospect of successful implementation.
>
> BRIEF FOR MARY BALDWIN COLLEGE

It is worth noting that none of the United States' ǒwn experts in the remedial phase of this litigation was willing to testify that VMI's adversative method was an appropriate methodology for educating women. This Court, however, does not care. Even though VWIL was carefully designed by professional educators who have tremendous experience in the area, and survived the test of adversarial litigation, the Court simply declares, with no basis in the evidence, that these professionals acted on "'overbroad' generalizations."

C

A few words are appropriate in response to the concurrence, which finds VMI unconstitutional on a basis that is more moderate than the Court's but only at the expense of being even more implausible. The concurrence offers three reasons: First, that there is "scant evidence in the record" that diversity of educational offering was the real reason for Virginia's maintaining VMI. "Scant" has the advantage of being an imprecise term. I have cited the clearest statements of diversity as a goal for higher education in the 1990 Report, the 1989 Virginia Plan for Higher Education, the Budget Initiatives prepared in 1989 by the State Council of Higher Education for Virginia, the 1974 Report of the General Assembly Commission on Higher Education to the General Assembly of Virginia, and the 1969 Report of the Virginia Commission on Constitutional Revision. There is *no* evidence to the contrary, once one rejects (as the concurrence rightly does) the relevance of VMI's founding in days when attitude towards the education of women were different. Is this conceivably not enough to foreclose rejecting as clearly erroneous the District Court's determination regarding "the Commonwealth's objective of educational diversity"? Especially since it is absurd on its face even to *demand* "evidence" to prove that the Commonwealth's reason for maintaining a men's military academy is that a men's military academy provides a distinctive type of educational experience (*i.e.*, fosters diversity). What other purpose *would* the Commonwealth have? One may argue, as the Court does, that this *type* of diversity is designed only to indulge hostility toward women—but that is a separate point, explicitly rejected by the concurrence, and amply refuted by the evidence I have mentioned in discussing the Court's opinion. What is now under discussion—the concurrence's making central to the disposition of this litigation the supposedly "scant" evidence that Virginia maintained VMI in order to offer a diverse educational experience—is rather like making crucial to the lawfulness of the United States Army record "evidence" that its purpose is to do battle. A legal culture that has forgotten the concept of *res ipsa loquitur* ["the thing speaks for itself"] deserves the fate that it today decrees for VMI.

> *A legal culture that has forgotten the concept of* res ipsa loquitur *[the thing speaks for itself] deserves the fate that it today decrees for VMI.*

Second, the concurrence dismisses out of hand what it calls Virginia's "second justification for the single-sex admissions policy: maintenance of the adversative method." The concurrence reasons that "this justification does not serve an important governmental objective" because, whatever the record may show about the pedagogical benefits of *single-sex* education, "there is no similar evidence in the record that an adversative method is pedagogically beneficial or is any more likely to produce character traits than other methodologies." That is simply wrong. In reality, the pedagogical benefits of VMI's adversative approach were not only proved, but were a *given* in this litigation. The reason the woman applicant who prompted this suit wanted to enter VMI was assuredly not that she wanted to go to an all-male school; it would cease being all-male as soon as she entered. She wanted the distinctive adversative education that VMI provided, and the battle was joined (in the main) over whether VMI had a basis for excluding women from that approach. The Court's opinion recognizes this, and devotes much of its opinion to demonstrating that "'some women . . . do well under [the] adversative model'" and that "[i]t is on behalf of these women that the United States has instituted this suit." Of course, in the last analysis it does not matter whether there are any benefits to the adversative method. The concurrence does not contest that there are benefits to *single-sex* education, and that alone suffices to make Virginia's case, since admission of a woman will even more surely put an end to VMI's single-sex education than it will to VMI's adversative methodology.

A third reason the concurrence offers in support of the judgment is that the Commonwealth and VMI were not quick enough to react to the "further developments" in this Court's evolving jurisprudence. Specifically, the concurrence believes it should have been clear after *Hogan* that "[t]he difficulty with [Virginia's] position is that the diversity benefited only one sex; there was single-sex public education available for men at VMI, but no corresponding single-sex public education available for women." If only, the concurrence asserts, Virginia had "made a genuine effort to devote comparable public resources to a facility for women, and followed through on such a plan, it might well have avoided an equal protection violation." That is to say, the concurrence believes that after our decision in *Hogan* (which held a program

of the Mississippi University for Women to be unconstitutional—
without any reliance on the fact that there was no corresponding
Mississippi all-men's program), the Commonwealth should have
known that what this Court expected of it was . . . yes!, the creation
of a state all-women's program. Any lawyer who gave that advice
to the Commonwealth ought to have been either disbarred or
committed. (The proof of that pudding is today's 6-Justice majority opinion.) And any Virginia politician who proposed such a step
when there were already four 4-year women's colleges in Virginia
(assisted by state support that may well exceed, in the aggregate,
what VMI costs) ought to have been recalled.

In any event, "diversity in the form of single-sex, as well as coeducational, institutions of higher learning" *is* "available to women as
well as to men" in Virginia. The concurrence is able to assert the
contrary only by disregarding the four all-women's private colleges
in Virginia (generously assisted by public funds) and the Commonwealth's longstanding policy of coordinating public with private educational offerings. According to the concurrence, the *reason* Virginia's
assistance to its four all-women's private colleges does not count is
that "[t]he private women's colleges are treated by the State *exactly*
as all other private schools are treated." But if Virginia cannot get
credit for assisting women's education if it only treats women's private
schools as it does all other private schools, then why should it get
blame for assisting men's education if it only treats VMI as it does all
other public schools? This is a great puzzlement.

IV

As is frequently true, the Court's decision today will have consequences that extend far beyond the parties to the litigation. What I

take to be the Court's unease with these consequences, and its result-ing unwillingness to acknowledge them, cannot alter the reality.

A

Under the constitutional principles announced and applied today, single-sex public education is unconstitutional. By going through the motions of applying a balancing test—asking whether the State has adduced an "exceedingly persuasive justification" for its sex-based classification—the Court creates the illusion that government officials in some future case will have a clear shot at justifying some sort of single-sex public education. Indeed, the Court seeks to cre-ate even a greater illusion than that: It purports to have said nothing of relevance to *other* public schools at all. "We address specifically and only an educational opportunity recognized . . . as 'unique'."

The Supreme Court of the United States does not sit to announce "unique" dispositions. Its principal function is to establish *precedent*—that is, to set forth principles of law that every court in America must follow. As we said only this Term, we expect both ourselves and lower courts to adhere to the "*rationale* upon which the Court based the results of its earlier decisions." *Seminole Tribe of Fla v. Florida* (1996). That is the principal reason we publish our opinions.

And the rationale of today's decision is sweeping: for sex-based classifications, a redefinition of intermediate scrutiny that makes it indistinguishable from strict scrutiny. Indeed, the Court indicates that if any program restricted to one sex is "uniqu[e]," it must be opened to members of the opposite sex "who have the will and capacity" to participate in it. I suggest that the single-sex program that will not be capable of being characterized as "unique" is not only unique but nonexistent.

[Footnote] In this regard, I note that the Court—which I concede is under no obligation to do so—provides no example of a program that *would* pass muster under its reasoning today: not even, for example, a football or wrestling program. On the Court's theory, any woman ready, willing, and physically able to participate in such a program would, *as a constitutional matter,* be entitled to do so.

> *The enemies of single-sex education have won; by persuading only seven Justices (five would have been enough) that their view of the world is enshrined in the Constitution, they have effectively imposed that view on all 50 States.*

In any event, regardless of whether the Court's rationale leaves some small amount of room for lawyers to argue, it ensures that single-sex public education is functionally dead. The costs of litigating the constitutionality of a single-sex education program, and the risks of ultimately losing that litigation, are simply too high to be embraced by public officials. Any person with standing to challenge any sex-based classification can haul the State into federal court and compel it to establish by evidence (presumably in the form of expert testimony) that there is an "exceedingly persuasive justification" for the classification. Should the courts happen to interpret that vacuous phrase as establishing a standard that is not utterly impossible of achievement, there is considerable risk that whether the standard has been met will not be determined on the basis of the record evidence—indeed, that will necessarily be the approach of any court that seeks to walk the path the Court has trod today. No state official in his right mind will buy such a high-cost, high-risk lawsuit by commencing a single-sex program. The enemies of single-sex education have won; by persuading only seven Justices (five would have been enough) that their view of the world is enshrined in the Constitution, they have effectively imposed that view on all 50 States.

This is especially regrettable because, as the District Court here determined, educational experts in recent years have increasingly come to "suppor[t] [the] view that substantial educational benefits flow from a single-gender environment, be it male or female, *that cannot be replicated in a coeducational setting.*" (emphasis added). "The evidence in th[is] case," for example, "is virtually uncontradicted" to that effect. Until quite recently, some public officials have attempted to institute new single-sex programs, at least as experiments. In 1991, for example, the Detroit Board of Education announced a program to establish three boys-only schools for inner-city youth; it was met with a lawsuit, a preliminary injunction was swiftly entered by a District Court that purported to rely on *Hogan* and the Detroit Board of Education voted to abandon the litigation and thus abandon the plan. Today's opinion assures that no such experiment will be tried again.

B

There are few extant single-sex public educational programs. The potential of today's decision for widespread disruption of existing institutions lies in its application to *private* single-sex education. Government support is immensely important to private educational institutions. Mary Baldwin College—which designed and runs VWIL—notes that private institutions of higher education in the 1990–1991 school year derived approximately 19 percent of their budgets from federal, state, and local government funds, *not including financial aid to students.* Charitable status under the tax laws is also highly significant for private educational institutions, and it is certainly not beyond the Court that rendered today's decision to hold that a donation to a single-sex college should be deemed contrary to public policy and therefore not deductible if the college discriminates on the basis of sex.

The Court adverts to private single-sex education only briefly, and only to make the assertion (mentioned above) that "[w]e address specifically and only an educational opportunity recognized by the District Court and the Court of Appeals as 'unique.'" As I have already remarked, that assurance assures nothing, unless it is to be taken as a promise that in the future the Court will disclaim the reasoning it has used today to destroy VMI. The Government, in its briefs to this Court, at least purports to address the consequences of its attack on VMI for public support of private single-sex education. It contends that private colleges that are the direct or indirect beneficiaries of government funding are not thereby necessarily converted into state actors to which the Equal Protection Clause is then applicable. That is true. It is also virtually meaningless.

The issue will be not whether government assistance turns private colleges into state actors, but whether the government *itself* would be violating the Constitution by providing state support to single-sex colleges. For example, in *Norwood v. Harrison* (1973), we saw no room to distinguish between state operation of racially segregated schools and state support of privately run segregated schools. "Racial discrimination in state-operated schools is barred by the Constitution and '[i]t is also axiomatic that a state may not induce, encourage or promote private persons to accomplish what it is constitutionally forbidden to accomplish.'" *Id.* When the Government was pressed at oral argument concerning the implications of these cases for private single-sex education if government-provided single-sex education is unconstitutional, it stated that the implications will not be so disastrous, since States *can* provide funding to *racially* segregated private schools, "depend[ing] on the circumstances." I cannot imagine what those "circumstances" might be, and it would be as foolish for private-school administrators to think that that assurance from the Justice Department will outlive the day it was made, as it was for VMI to think that the Justice Department's "unequivoca[l]" support for an intermediate-scrutiny standard in this litigation would survive the Government's loss in the courts below.

The only hope for state-assisted single-sex private schools is that the Court will not apply in the future the principles of law it has applied today. That is a substantial hope, I am happy and ashamed to say. After all, did not the Court today abandon the principles of law it has applied in our earlier sex-classification cases? And does not the Court positively invite private colleges to rely upon our ad-hocery by assuring them this litigation is "unique"? I would not advise the foundation of any new single-sex college (especially an all-male one) with the expectation of being allowed to receive any government support; but it is too soon to abandon in despair those single-sex colleges already in existence. It will certainly be possible for this Court to write a future opinion that ignores the broad principles of law set forth today, and that characterizes as utterly dispositive the opinion's perceptions that VMI was a uniquely prestigious all-male institution, conceived in chauvinism, etc., etc. I will not join that opinion.

Justice Brandeis said it is "one of the happy incidents of the federal system that a single courageous State may, if its citizens choose, serve as a laboratory; and try novel social and economic experiments without risk to the rest of the country." *New State Ice Co. v. Lieb-mann* (1932) (dissenting opinion). But it is one of the unhappy inci-dents of the federal system that a self-righteous Supreme Court, acting on its Members' per-sonal view of what would make a "'more perfect Union,'" (a criterion only slightly more restric-tive than a "more perfect world"), can impose its own favored social and economic dispositions nationwide. As today's disposition, and others this single Term, show, this places it beyond the power of a "single courageous State," not only to introduce novel dispositions that the Court frowns upon, but to reintroduce, or indeed even adhere to, disfavored dispositions that are centu-ries old. The sphere of self-government reserved to the people of the Republic is progressively narrowed.

> *It is one of the unhappy incidents of the federal system that a self-righteous Supreme Court, acting on its Members' personal view of what would make a "more perfect Union," (a criterion only slightly more restrictive than a "more perfect world"), can impose its own favored social and economic dispositions nationwide.*

In the course of this dissent, I have referred approvingly to the opinion of my former col-league, Justice Powell, in *Mississippi Univ. for Women v. Hogan.* Many of the points made in his dissent apply with equal force here—in par-ticular, the criticism of judicial opinions that purport to be "narro[w]" but whose "logic" is "sweepin[g]." But there is one statement with which I cannot agree. Justice Powell observed that the Court's decision in *Hogan,* which struck down a single-sex program offered by the Mississippi Univer-sity for Women, had thereby "[l]eft without honor . . . an element of diversity that has characterized much of American education and enriched much of American life." Today's decision does not leave VMI without honor; no court opinion can do that.

In an odd sort of way, it is precisely VMI's attachment to such old-fashioned concepts as manly "honor" that has made it, and the system it represents, the target of those who today succeed in abolishing public single-sex education. The record contains a booklet that all first-year VMI students (the so-called "rats") were required to keep in their possession at all times. Near the end there appears the following period piece, entitled "The Code of a Gentleman": "Without a strict observance of the fundamental Code of Honor, no man, no matter how 'polished,' can be considered a gentleman. The honor of a gentleman demands the inviolability of his word, and the incorruptibility of his principles. He is the descendant of the knight, the crusader; he is the defender of the defenseless and the champion of justice...or he is not a Gentleman. "A Gentleman...Does not discuss his family affairs in public or with acquaintances...Does not speak more than casually about his girl friend."

"Does not go to a lady's house if he is affected by alcohol. He is temperate in the use of alcohol. Does not lose his temper; nor exhibit anger, fear, hate, embarrassment, ardor or hilarity in public. Does not hail a lady from a club window. A gentleman never discusses the merits or demerits of a lady. Does not mention names exactly as he avoids the mention of what things cost. Does not borrow money from a friend, except in dire need. Money borrowed is a debt of honor, and must be repaid as promptly as possible. Debts incurred by a deceased parent, brother, sister or grown child are assumed by honorable men as a debt of honor. Does not display his wealth, money or possessions. Does not put his manners on and off, whether in the club or in a ballroom. He treats people with courtesy, no matter what their social position may be. Does not slap strangers on the back nor so much as lay a finger on a lady. Does not 'lick the boots of those above' nor 'kick the face of those below him on the social ladder.' Does not take advantage of another's helplessness or ignorance and assumes that no gentleman will take advantage of him."

"A Gentleman respects the reserves of others, but demands that others respect those which are his. A Gentleman can become what he wills to be...." I do not know whether the men of VMI lived by this code; perhaps not. But it is powerfully impressive that a public institution of higher education still in existence sought to have them do so. I do not think any of us, women included, will be better off for its destruction.

CHAPTER THIRTEEN

FREE SPEECH

❦

"Congress shall make no law abridging the freedom of speech." Many Americans cherish the First Amendment's protection of freedom of speech more than any other liberty in the Bill of Rights. It was written into the Constitution by a generation of Americans that did not always permit or enjoy the full exercise of that freedom. Yet the Framers believed that truth—so necessary for enlightened self-government—would best be served by competition in a "marketplace of ideas."[1]

That marketplace has grown over the years. The First Amendment has been extended by federal courts to cover nude dancing, shouting obscenities, flag burning, pornography, and even refusing to wear a necktie.[2] Although some doubt whether the First Amendment was meant to cover such "speech," no one doubts that a fundamental purpose of the First Amendment was the protection of political speech. Indeed, political speech is said to lie at the heart of the First Amendment.

Justice Scalia supported efforts to protect traditional speech. He supported protection of expressive activity when government laws sought to limit that activity solely because of its communicative aspect. The clearest example of this was his vote to strike down a federal law criminalizing the destruction of the American flag. Scalia joined the Court's opinion in *United States v. Eichman* (1990), which held the law was aimed directly and unconstitutionally at suppressing a manner of communicating opposition to the U.S. government and its policies.

Although Scalia had not been as willing as his colleagues to protect some categories of speech—pornography, to name one—he forcefully defended two clear (but unpopular) exercises of First Amendment rights: election-related speech and anti-abortion protest. Scalia accused the Court of using an "ad hoc nullification machine" to eliminate its normal constitutional analyses whenever the issue before it involved abortion.

In *Hill v. Colorado* (2000), the Court upheld a Colorado law that prohibited any person from approaching within eight feet of another person near a health care facility without that person's consent.[3] Although the Court is normally hostile to prior restraints on speech, it upheld the restriction because it was narrowly tailored, as required by its precedents, to advance the state's interest in protecting its citizens' rights to avoid unwanted speech.

Though the Court said the statute did not regulate content of speech, Scalia noted that statute specifically targeted "oral protest," "counseling," and "education" outside medical clinics, making clear that silencing anti-abortion protest was the objective of the law. "I have no doubt this regulation would be deemed content based in an instant if the case before us involved antiwar protesters, or union members seeking to 'educate' the public about the reasons for their strike," he wrote.[4] In addition to challenging the law's purpose, Scalia attacked the Court's finding that the law was narrowly tailored to serve the state's interest. He wrote, "[I]f protecting people from unwelcome communications . . . is a compelling state interest, the First Amendment is a dead letter. And if . . . forbidding peaceful, nonthreatening, but uninvited speech from a distance closer than eight feet is a 'narrowly tailored' means of preventing the obstruction of entrance to medical facilities, . . . the narrow tailoring must refer not to the standards of Versace, but to those of Omar the tentmaker."[5]

The Court decided *Hill* on the same day it issued its opinion in *Stenberg v. Carhart* invalidating Nebraska's law banning partial-birth abortions (see chapter five). Scalia observed that since abortion—"even abortion of a live-and-kicking child"—was removed from the democratic process by the Court, the only way anti-abortion advocates could have a voice was to persuade individuals of the rightness of their views. The *Hill* decision, he said, made even that effort more difficult. Scalia concluded:

Does the deck seem stacked? You bet. . . . [T]oday's decision is not an isolated distortion of our traditional constitutional principles, but is one of many aggressively proabortion novelties announced by the Court in recent years. Today's distortions, however, are particularly blatant. Restrictive views of the First Amendment that have been in dissent since the 1930s suddenly find themselves in the majority. "Uninhibited, robust, and wide open" debate is replaced by the power of the State to protect an unheard-of "right to be left alone" on the public streets.[6]

Scalia also fought to protect the freedom of individuals, groups, and corporations to participate in political campaigns. Specifically, he argued that campaign contributions and expenditures are too closely associated with protected political speech to be regulated by the government without a showing of compelling interest in limiting them. And trying to ensure a "level playing field," Scalia argued, is not compelling. In *Austin v. Michigan Chamber of Commerce* (1990), a case involving Michigan's ban on corporate contributions, Scalia wrote:

> Perhaps the Michigan law before us here has an unqualifiedly noble objective—to equalize the political debate by preventing disproportionate expression of corporations' point of view. But governmental abridgement of liberty is always undertaken with the very best of announced objectives (dictators promise to bring order, not tyranny), and often with the very best of genuinely intended objectives (zealous policemen conduct unlawful searches in order to put dangerous felons behind bars). The premise of our Bill of Rights, however, is that there are some things—even some seemingly desirable things—that government cannot be trusted to do. The very first of these is establishing restrictions upon speech that will assure "fair" political debate.

Because Scalia believed political speech was at the core of the First Amendment, he was highly skeptical of any legislative effort to limit election-related speech. Of course, there are some who do not think limiting the amount of money an individual or corporate entity can contribute to a campaign, or prohibiting some sources from contributing at all, is a substantial limitation on speech protected by the First Amendment. In addition, some think that the large amounts of money spent on campaigns alone create at least an "appearance of corruption" that must be remedied to preserve the integrity of our democratic government. These forces were behind the law that was challenged in *McConnell v. Federal Election Commission* (2003).

MCCONNELL v. FEDERAL ELECTION COMMISSION (2003)

In response to the widely condemned abuses of the 1972 presidential election, Congress in 1974 passed an amendment to strengthen the Federal Election Campaign Act of 1971. The original law and the amendment, designed to provide greater regulation of the system of financing federal campaigns, established the Federal Election Commission, set new limits on the amounts that could be contributed to and spent by candidates, and provided a voluntary system of public financing for presidential campaigns.

After a challenge to the laws' constitutionality, the Supreme Court in its landmark *Buckley v. Valeo* (1976) decision upheld parts of the regulatory regime, including limits on contributions to candidates, and invalidated others. The Court found that campaign fundraising and spending involved First Amendment freedoms and therefore could be limited only if the government had a compelling purpose and the regulation was narrowly tailored to serve that purpose. The Court ruled that limiting the amount of money that could be given directly to a candidate was justified as a way of reducing corruption or the appearance of corruption that might arise from making a large donation of money.

Congress and the Court left donations from individuals and corporations to national political parties unregulated because the fear of corruption was not as great; the parties were barred from using unregulated money to directly benefit candidates. The contributions were used for party-building activities, get-out-the-vote efforts, and issue advocacy. With limits on direct giving upheld, the unregulated contributions to the parties— known commonly as "soft money"—began to grow in size and number.

Some members of Congress and so-called good government groups began to complain that these large contributions were corrupting the legislative process. They pointed out that soft money was sometimes solicited by the parties with lures of access to members of Congress. If the system was not actually corrupt, they said, it certainly looked like it.

In 2002, Congress passed the Bipartisan Campaign Finance Reform Act (BCRA).[7] This complex law had two major features: a ban on soft money and the regulation of "issue advocacy." Issue advocacy, as its name suggests, refers to advertising designed to call attention to one or more public policy issues. Sponsors of issue advertisements were not required by law to disclose the names of their donors or the amount they spent on such ads. Only advertisements that urged listeners or viewers to support or oppose a particular candidate were regulated.

Issue ads began to closely resemble candidate ads. "Pollution is killing children," the issue ad might say. "Senator Jones supports pollution. Call Senator Jones and tell him to save our children by opposing pollution." Deciding that such ads should be more tightly regulated, especially those most likely to influence an election, Congress banned issue ads that mention a candidate's name during the sixty days before a general election. The ban was controversial because it muffled groups that truly wished to educate voters about politicians' records at the most effective time, the days preceding the election. A diverse group of politically active associations ranging from the AFL–CIO to the National Rifle Association argued that BCRA abridged their First Amendment rights.

In 2003 the Supreme Court narrowly voted to uphold both main provisions of BCRA. The Court said new evidence helped to establish that enormous soft-money contributions, especially from corporations, had a corrosive effect on the legislative process and citizens' confidence in the integrity of their government. Combating that corrosion represented a compelling government interest, and prohibiting these donations was deemed a legitimate means, the Court said.

Scalia joined three dissenting opinions that largely argued that the Court's opinion was not faithful to the text and spirit of the First Amendment or to the Court's own precedents. In his separate dissent, Scalia did not go far into the weeds about the Court's constitutional analyses of each provision of BCRA. Instead, he expressed confusion that the Court, which in recent years had wrapped a constitutional blanket around "virtual child pornography" and other "inconsequential forms of expression," did not in *McConnell* protect speech "the First Amendment is meant to protect: the right to criticize the government."

He then attacked three "fallacious propositions" upon which BCRA was premised and which, he said, were accepted by the Court. Scalia's opinion—especially his argument concerning the amount of money spent on elections—is a good example of his willingness to challenge the Court's majority when it advanced a policy argument to limit a freedom that is explicitly protected by the Constitution. Disputing the claim that there is too much money spent on politics, Scalia wrote, "If our democracy is drowning from this much spending, it cannot swim."

Scalia said the motivation behind BCRA and the resulting litigation was suppressing speech that criticizes the government. He argued that some members of Congress might be motivated by a noble purpose, but since others might merely wish to avoid criticism, the course most faithful to the First Amendment is "to assume the worst, and to rule the regulation of political speech 'for fairness' sake' simply out of bounds." Scalia concluded by predicting that Congress would enact additional measures to limit spending and speech and that the Court's decision in *McConnell* would make it difficult, if not impossible, to rescue the First Amendment by striking down those future measures.

❧❀☙

Justice Scalia, concurring with respect to BCRA Titles III and IV, dissenting with respect to BCRA Titles I and V, and concurring in the judgment in part and dissenting in part with respect to BCRA Title II.

... This is a sad day for the freedom of speech. Who could have imagined that the same Court which, within the past four years, has sternly disapproved of restrictions upon such inconsequential forms of expression as virtual child pornography, tobacco advertising, dissemination of illegally intercepted communications, and sexually explicit cable programming, would smile with favor upon a law that cuts to the heart of what the First Amendment is meant to protect: the right to criticize the government. For that is what the most offensive provisions of this legislation are all about. We are governed by Congress, and this legislation prohibits the criticism of Members of Congress by those entities most capable of giving such criticism loud voice: national political parties and corporations, both of the commercial and the not-for-profit sort. It forbids pre-election criticism of incumbents by corporations, even not-for-profit corporations, by use of their general funds; and forbids national-party use of "soft" money to fund "issue ads" that incumbents find so offensive.

To be sure, the legislation is evenhanded: It similarly prohibits criticism of the candidates who oppose Members of Congress in their reelection bids. But as everyone knows, this is an area in which evenhandedness is not fairness. If *all* electioneering were evenhandedly prohibited, incumbents would have an enormous advantage. Likewise, if incumbents and challengers are limited to the same quantity of electioneering, incumbents are favored. In other words, *any* restriction upon a type of campaign speech that is equally available to challengers and incumbents tends to favor incumbents.

Beyond that, however, the present legislation *targets* for prohibition certain categories of campaign speech that are particularly harmful to incumbents. Is it accidental, do you think, that incumbents raise about three times as much "hard money"—the sort of funding generally *not* restricted by this legislation—as do their challengers? Or that lobbyists (who seek the favor of incumbents) give 92 percent of their money in "hard" contributions? Is it an oversight, do you suppose, that the so-called "millionaire provisions" raise the contribution limit for a candidate running against an individual who devotes to the campaign (as challengers often do) great personal wealth, but do not raise the limit for a candidate running against an individual who devotes to the campaign (as incumbents often do) a massive election "war chest"? And is it mere happenstance, do you estimate, that national-party funding, which is severely limited by the Act, is more likely to assist cash-strapped challengers than flush-with-hard-money incumbents? Was it unintended, by any chance, that incumbents are free personally to receive some soft money and even to solicit it for other organizations, while national parties are not?

I wish to address three fallacious propositions that might be thought to justify some or all of the provisions of this legislation—only the

> *Is it mere happenstance, do you estimate, that national-party funding, which is severely limited by the Act, is more likely to assist cash-strapped challengers than flush-with-hard-money incumbents?*

last of which is explicitly embraced by the principal opinion for the Court, but all of which underlie, I think, its approach to these cases.

(A) MONEY IS NOT SPEECH

It was said by congressional proponents of this legislation, with support from the law reviews, that since this legislation regulates nothing but the expenditure of money for speech, as opposed to speech itself, the burden it imposes is not subject to full First Amendment scrutiny; the government may regulate the raising and spending of campaign funds just as it regulates other forms of conduct, such as burning draft cards or camping out on the National Mall. That proposition has been endorsed by one of the two authors of today's principal opinion: "The right to use one's own money to hire gladiators, [and] to fund 'speech by proxy,'... [are] property rights... not entitled to the same protection as the right to say what one pleases." *Nixon v. Shrink Missouri Government PAC* (2000) (Stevens, J., concurring). Until today, however, that view has been categorically rejected by our jurisprudence. As we said in *Buckley v. Valeo* (1976), "this Court has never suggested that the dependence of a communication on the expenditure of money operates itself to introduce a nonspeech element or to reduce the exacting scrutiny required by the First Amendment."

Our traditional view was correct, and today's cavalier attitude toward regulating the financing of speech (the "exacting scrutiny" test of *Buckley* is not uttered in any majority opinion, and is not observed in the ones from which I dissent) frustrates the fundamental purpose of the First Amendment. In any economy operated on even the most rudimentary principles of division of labor, effective public communication requires the speaker to make use of the services of others. An author may write a novel, but he will seldom publish and distribute it himself. A freelance reporter may write a story, but he will rarely edit, print, and deliver it to subscribers. To a government bent on suppressing speech, this mode of organization presents opportunities: Control any cog in the machine, and you can halt the whole apparatus. License printers, and it matters little whether authors are still free to write. Restrict the sale of books, and it matters little who prints them. Predictably, repressive regimes have exploited these principles by attacking all levels of the production and dissemination of ideas. See, *e.g.*, Printing Act of 1662 (punishing printers, importers, and booksellers); Printing Act of 1649 (punishing authors, printers, booksellers, importers, and buyers). In response to this threat, we have interpreted the First Amendment broadly. See, *e.g.*, *Bantam Books, Inc. v. Sullivan* (1963) ("The constitutional guarantee of freedom of the press embraces the circulation of books as well as their publication...").

Division of labor requires a means of mediating exchange, and in a commercial society, that means is supplied by money. The publisher pays the author for the right to sell his book; it pays its staff who print and assemble the book; it demands payments from booksellers who bring the book to market. This, too, presents opportunities for repression: Instead of regulating the various parties to the enterprise individually, the government can suppress their ability to coordinate by regulating their use of money. What good is the right to print books without a right to buy works from authors? Or the right to publish newspapers without the right to pay deliverymen? The right to speak would be largely ineffective if it did not include the right to engage in financial transactions that are the incidents of its exercise.

This is not to say that *any* regulation of money is a regulation of speech. The government may apply general commercial regulations to those who use money for speech if it applies them evenhandedly to those who use money for other purposes. But where the government singles out money used to fund speech as its legislative object, it is acting against speech as such, no less than if it had targeted the paper on which a book was printed or the trucks that deliver it to the bookstore.

History and jurisprudence bear this out. The best early examples derive from the British efforts to tax the press after the lapse of licensing statutes by which the press was first regulated. The Stamp Act of 1712 imposed levies on all newspapers, including an additional tax for each advertisement. It was a response to unfavorable war coverage, "obvious[ly] ... designed to check the publication of those newspapers and pamphlets which depended for their sale on their cheapness and sensationalism." F. Siebert, Freedom of the Press in England, 1476–1776 (1952). It succeeded in killing off approximately half the newspapers in England in its first year. *Id.* In 1765, Parliament applied a similar Act to the Colonies. The colonial Act likewise placed exactions on sales and advertising revenue, the latter at 2s. per advertisement, which was "by any standard ... excessive, since the publisher himself received only from 3 to 5s. and still less for repeated insertions." A. Schlesinger, Prelude to Independence: The Newspaper War on Britain, 1764–1776 (1958). The founding generation saw these taxes as grievous incursions on the freedom of the press.

We have kept faith with the Founders' tradition by prohibiting the selective taxation of the press. And we have done so whether the tax was the product of illicit motive or not. These press-taxation cases belie the claim that regulation of money used to fund speech is not regulation of speech itself. A tax on a newspaper's advertising revenue does not prohibit anyone from saying anything; it merely appropriates part of the revenue that a speaker would otherwise obtain. That is even a step short of totally prohibiting advertising rev-enue—which would be analogous to the total prohibition of certain campaign-speech contributions in the present cases. Yet it is unques-tionably a violation of the First Amendment.

Many other cases exemplify the same principle that an attack upon the funding of speech is an attack upon speech itself. In *Schaumburg v. Citizens for a Better Environment* (1980), we struck down an ordinance limiting the amount charities could pay their solicitors. In *Simon & Schuster, Inc. v. Members of N. Y. State Crime Victims Bd.* (1991), we held unconstitutional a state statute that appropriated the proceeds of criminals' biographies for payment to the victims. And in *Rosenberger v. Rector and Visitors of Univ. of Va.* (1995), we held unconstitutional a university's discrimination in the disbursement of funds to speakers on the basis of viewpoint. Most notable, perhaps, is our famous opinion in *New York Times Co. v. Sullivan* (1964), holding that paid advertisements in a newspaper were entitled to full First Amendment protection:

> Any other conclusion would discourage newspapers from carrying "editorial advertisements" of this type, and so might shut off an important outlet for the promulgation of informa-tion and ideas by persons who do not themselves have access to publishing facilities—who wish to exercise their freedom of speech even though they are not members of the press. The effect would be to shackle the First Amendment in its attempt to secure "the widest possible dissemination of information from diverse and antagonistic sources." *Id.* (citations omitted).

This passage was relied on in *Buckley* for the point that restrictions on the expenditure of money for speech are equivalent to restrictions on speech itself. That reliance was appropriate. If denying protection to paid-for speech would "shackle the First Amendment," so also does forbidding or limiting the right to pay for speech.

It should be obvious, then, that a law limiting the amount a person can spend to broadcast his political views is a direct restriction on speech. That is no different from a law limiting the amount a newspaper can pay its editorial staff or the amount a charity can pay its leafletters. It is equally clear that a limit on the amount a candidate can *raise* from any one individual for the purpose of speaking is also a direct limitation on speech. That is no different from a law limiting the amount a publisher can accept from any one shareholder or lender, or the amount a newspaper can charge any one advertiser or customer.

(B) POOLING MONEY IS NOT SPEECH

Another proposition which could explain at least some of the results of today's opinion is that the First Amendment right to spend money for speech does not include the right to combine with others in spending money for speech. Such a proposition fits uncomfortably with the concluding words of our Declaration of Independence: "And for the support of this Declaration, . . . we mutually pledge to each other our Lives, *our Fortunes* and our sacred Honor." (Emphasis added.) The freedom to associate with others for the dissemination of ideas—not just by singing or speaking in unison, but by pooling financial resources for expressive purposes—is part of the freedom of speech.

Our form of government is built on the premise that every citizen shall have the right to engage in political expression and association. This right was enshrined in the First Amendment of the Bill of Rights. Exercise of these basic freedoms in America has traditionally been through the media of political associations. Any interference with the freedom of a party is simultaneously an interference with the freedom of its adherents.

NAACP v. BUTTON (1963) (INTERNAL QUOTATION MARKS OMITTED)

The First Amendment protects political association as well as political expression. The constitutional right of association explicated in *NAACP v. Alabama* (1958) stemmed from the Court's recognition that "[e]ffective advocacy of both public and private points of view, particularly controversial ones, is undeniably enhanced by group association." Subsequent decisions have made clear that the First and Fourteenth Amendments guarantee "freedom to associate with others for the common advancement of political beliefs and ideas, ...

BUCKLEY

We have said that "implicit in the right to engage in activities protected by the First Amendment" is "a corresponding right to associate with others in pursuit of a wide variety of political, social, economic, educational, religious, and cultural ends." *Roberts v. United States Jaycees* (1984). That "right to associate . . . in pursuit" includes the right to pool financial resources.

If it were otherwise, Congress would be empowered to enact legislation requiring newspapers to be sole proprietorships, banning their use of partnership or corporate form. That sort of restriction would be an obvious violation of the First Amendment, and it is incomprehensible why the conclusion should change when what is at issue is the pooling of funds for the most important (and most perennially threatened) category of speech: electoral speech. The principle that such financial association does not enjoy full First Amendment protection threatens the existence of all political parties.

(c) Speech by Corporations Can Be Abridged

The last proposition that might explain at least some of today's casual abridgment of free-speech rights is this: that the particular form of association known as a corporation does not enjoy full First Amendment protection. Of course the text of the First Amendment does not limit its application in this fashion, even though "[b]y the end of the eighteenth century the corporation was a familiar figure in American economic life." C. Cooke, Corporation, Trust and Company 92 (1951). Nor is there any basis in reason why First Amendment rights should not attach to corporate associations—and we have said so. In *First Nat. Bank of Boston v. Bellotti* (1978), we held unconstitutional a state prohibition of corporate speech designed to influence the vote on referendum proposals. We said:

> [T]here is practically universal agreement that a major purpose of [the First] Amendment was to protect the free discussion of governmental affairs. If the speakers here were not corporations, no one would suggest that the State could silence their proposed speech. It is the type of speech indispensable to decisionmaking in a democracy, and this is no less true because the speech comes from a corporation rather than an individual. The inherent worth of the speech in terms of its capacity for informing the public does not depend upon the identity of its source, whether

corporation, association, union, or individual. *Id*. (internal quotation marks, footnotes, and citations omitted).

In *NAACP v. Button,* we held that the NAACP could assert First Amendment rights "on its own behalf, ... though a corporation," and that the activities of the corporation were "modes of expression and association protected by the First and Fourteenth Amendments." In *Pacific Gas & Elec. Co. v. Public Util. Comm'n of Cal.* (1986), we held unconstitutional a state effort to compel corporate speech. "The identity of the speaker," we said, "is not decisive in determining whether speech is protected. Corporations and other associations, like individuals, contribute to the 'discussion, debate, and the dissemination of information and ideas' that the First Amendment seeks to foster." And in *Buckley*, we held unconstitutional FECA's limitation upon independent corporate expenditures.

The Court changed course in *Austin v. Michigan Chamber of Commerce* (1990), upholding a state prohibition of an independent corporate expenditure in support of a candidate for state office. I dissented in that case and remain of the view that it was error. In the modern world, giving the government power to exclude corporations from the political debate enables it effectively to muffle the voices that best represent the most significant segments of the economy and the most passionately held social and political views. People who associate—who pool their financial resources—for purposes of economic enterprise overwhelmingly do so in the corporate form; and with increasing frequency, incorporation is chosen by those who associate to defend and promote particular ideas—such as the American Civil Liberties Union and the National Rifle Association, parties to these cases. Imagine, then, a government that wished to suppress nuclear power—or oil and gas exploration, or automobile manufacturing, or gun ownership, or civil liberties—and that had the power to prohibit corporate advertising against its proposals. To be sure, the individuals involved in, or benefited by, those industries, or interested in those causes, could (given enough time) form political action committees or other associations to make their case. But the organizational form in which those enterprises already *exist*, and in which they can most quickly and most effectively get their message across, is the corporate form. The First Amendment does not in my view permit the restriction of that political speech. And the same holds true for corporate electoral speech: A candidate should not be insulated from the most effective speech that the major participants in the economy and major incorporated interest groups can generate.

The premise of the First Amendment is that the American people are neither sheep nor fools.

But what about the danger to the political system posed by "amassed wealth"? The most direct threat from that source comes in the form of undisclosed favors and payoffs to elected officials—which have already been criminalized, and will be rendered no more discoverable by the legislation at issue here. The use of corporate wealth (like individual wealth) to speak to the electorate is unlikely to "distort" elections—*especially* if disclosure requirements *tell* the people where the speech is coming from. The premise of the First Amendment is that the American people are neither sheep nor fools, and hence fully capable of considering both the substance of the speech presented to them and its proximate and ultimate source. If that premise is wrong, our democracy has a much greater problem to overcome than merely the influence of amassed wealth. Given the premises of democracy, there is no such thing as *too much* speech.

But, it is argued, quite apart from its effect upon the electorate, corporate speech in the form of contributions to the candidate's campaign, or even in the form of independent expenditures supporting the candidate, engenders an obligation which is later paid in the form of greater access to the officeholder, or indeed in the form of votes on particular bills. Any *quid-pro-quo* agreement for votes would of course violate criminal law, and actual payoff *votes* have not even been claimed by those favoring the restrictions on corporate speech. It cannot be denied, however, that corporate (like noncorporate) allies will have greater access to the officeholder, and that he will tend to favor the same causes as those who support him (which is usually *why* they supported him). That is the nature of politics—if not indeed human nature—and how this can properly be considered "corruption" (or "the appearance of corruption") with regard to corporate allies and not with regard to other allies is beyond me. If the Bill of Rights had intended an exception to the freedom of speech in order to combat this malign proclivity of the officeholder to agree with those who agree with him, and to speak more with his supporters than

> *But let us not be deceived. While the Government's briefs and arguments before this Court focused on the horrible "appearance of corruption," the most passionate floor statements during the debates on this legislation pertained to so-called attack ads, which the Constitution surely protects, but which Members of Congress analogized to "crack cocaine," "drive-by shootings," and "air pollution."*

his opponents, it would surely have said so. It did not do so, I think, because the juice is not worth the squeeze. Evil corporate (and private affluent) influences are well enough checked (so long as adequate campaign-expenditure disclosure rules exist) by the politician's fear of being portrayed as "in the pocket" of so-called moneyed interests. The incremental benefit obtained by muzzling corporate speech is more than offset by loss of the information and persuasion that corporate speech can contain. That, at least, is the assumption of a constitutional guarantee which prescribes that Congress shall make no law abridging the freedom of speech.

But let us not be deceived. While the Government's briefs and arguments before this Court focused on the horrible "appearance of corruption," the most passionate floor statements during the debates on this legislation pertained to so-called attack ads, which the Constitution surely protects, but which Members of Congress analogized to "crack cocaine," "drive-by shooting[s]," and "air pollution." There is good reason to believe that the ending of negative campaign ads was the principal attraction of the legislation. A Senate sponsor said, "I hope that we will not allow our attention to be distracted from the real issues at hand—how to raise the tenor of the debate in our elections and give people real choices. No one benefits from negative ads. They don't aid our Nation's political dialog." Cong. Rec. (remarks of Sen. McCain). He assured the body that "[y]ou cut off the soft money, you are going to see a lot less of that [attack ads]. Prohibit unions and corporations, and you will see a lot less of that. If you demand full disclosure for those who pay for those ads, you are going to see a lot less of that...." Cong. Rec. (remarks of Sen. McCain).

Another theme prominent in the legislative debates was the notion that there is too much money spent on elections. The first principle of "reform" was that "there should be less money in politics." (remarks of Sen. Murray). "The enormous amounts of special interest money that flood our political system have become a cancer in our democracy" (remarks of Sen. Kennedy). "[L]arge sums of money drown out the voice of the average voter" (remarks of Rep. Langevin). The system of campaign finance is "drowning in money." (remarks of Rep. Menendez). And most expansively:

> Despite the ever-increasing sums spent on campaigns, we have not seen an improvement in campaign discourse, issue discussion or voter education. More money does not mean more ideas, more substance or more depth. Instead, it means more of what voters complain about most. More 30-second spots, more negativity and an increasingly longer campaign period.
>
> REMARKS OF SENATOR KERRY

Perhaps voters do detest these 30-second spots—though I suspect they detest even more hour-long campaign-debate interruptions of their favorite entertainment programming. Evidently, however, these ads *do persuade* voters, or else they would not be so routinely used by sophisticated politicians of all parties. The point, in any event, is that it is not the proper role of those who govern us to judge which campaign speech has "substance" and "depth" (do you think it might be that which is least damaging to incumbents?) and to abridge the rest.

Americans spent about half as much electing all their Nation's officials, state and federal, as they spent on movie tickets ($7.8 billion); about a fifth as much as they spent on cosmetics and perfume ($18.8 billion); and about a sixth as much as they spent on pork (the nongovernmental sort) ($22.8 billion). If our democracy is drowning from this much spending, it cannot swim.

And what exactly are these outrageous sums frittered away in determining who will govern us? A report prepared for Congress concluded that the total amount, in hard and soft money, spent on the 2000 federal elections was between $2.4 and $2.5 billion. *All* campaign spending in the United States, including state elections, ballot initiatives, and judicial elections, has been estimated at $3.9 billion for 2000, which was a year that "shattered spending and contribution records." Even taking this last, larger figure as the benchmark, it means that Americans spent about half as much electing all their Nation's officials, state and federal, as they spent on movie tickets ($7.8 billion); about a fifth as much as they spent on cosmetics and perfume ($18.8 billion); and about a sixth as much as they spent on pork (the nongovernmental sort) ($22.8 billion). If our democracy is drowning from this much spending, it cannot swim.

> *Those in power, even giving them the benefit of the greatest good will, are inclined to believe that what is good for them is good for the country.*

Which brings me back to where I began: This litigation is about preventing criticism of the government. I cannot say for certain that many, or some, or even any, of the Members of Congress who voted for this legislation did so not to produce "fairer" campaigns, but to mute criticism of their records and facilitate reelection. Indeed, I will stipulate that all those who voted for the Act believed they were acting for the good of the country. There remains the problem of the Charlie Wilson Phenomenon, named after Charles Wilson, former president of General Motors, who is supposed to have said during the Senate hearing on his nomination as Secretary of Defense that "what's good for General Motors is good for the country." Those in power, even giving them the benefit of the greatest good will, are inclined to believe that what is good for them is good for the country. Whether in prescient recognition of the Charlie Wilson Phenomenon, or out of fear of good old-fashioned, malicious, self-interested manipulation, "[t]he fundamental approach of the First Amendment . . . was to assume the worst, and to rule the regulation of political speech 'for fairness' sake' simply out of bounds." *Austin* (Scalia, J., dissenting). Having abandoned that approach to a limited extent in *Buckley*, we abandon it much further today.

We will unquestionably be called upon to abandon it further still in the future. The most frightening passage in the lengthy floor debates on this legislation is the following assurance given by one of the cosponsoring Senators to his colleagues:

> This is a modest step, it is a first step, it is an essential step, but it does not even begin to address, in some ways, the fundamental problems that exist with the hard money aspect of the system.
>
> CONGRESSIONAL RECORD (STATEMENT OF SENATOR FEINGOLD)

The system indeed. The first instinct of power is the retention of power, and, under a Constitution that requires periodic elections, that is best achieved by the suppression of election-time speech. We have witnessed merely the second scene of Act I of what promises to be a lengthy tragedy. In scene 3 the Court, having abandoned most of the First Amendment weaponry that *Buckley* left intact, will be even less equipped to resist the incumbents' writing of the rules of political debate. The federal election campaign laws, which are already (as today's opinions show) so voluminous, so detailed, so complex, that no ordinary citizen dare run for office, or even contribute a significant sum, without hiring an expert advisor in the field, can be expected to grow more voluminous, more detailed, and more complex in the years to come—and always, always, with the objective of reducing the excessive amount of speech.

CITIZENS UNITED v. FEDERAL ELECTION COMMISSION (2010)

After *McConnell*, Scalia continued to believe that the Supreme Court had failed to protect core political speech, especially speech made through associations, including corporations. As new disputes over how the Bipartisan Campaign Reform Act (BCRA) should be applied reached the Court, Scalia used the opportunities to show that bans on corporate and union spending were unconstitutional and unwise.

In *Federal Election Commission v. Wisconsin Right to Life* (2007), the Supreme Court was asked to decide whether a pro-life group could run ads urging Wisconsin residents to call their U.S. Senators to urge them to oppose a filibuster against federal judicial nominees. The Court ruled that, even though the Wisconsin corporation was paying for the ads from its general treasury and the ads mentioned elected officials within thirty days of an election, the ads were permissible because they were true issue ads, not campaign ads endorsing political candidates.

Scalia argued that the Court should have directly overruled *Austin v. Michigan Chamber of Commerce* and, to the extent that it approved restrictions on corporate political speech, *McConnell* as well. These decisions and BCRA, in his view, had failed in their mission to keep large, corporate contributions out of politics, as evidenced by the growth of super PACS and section 527 organizations. He wrote:

There is wondrous irony to be found in both the genesis and the consequences of BCRA. In the fact that the institutions it was designed to muzzle—unions and nearly all manner of corporations—for all the "corrosive and distorting effects" of their "immense aggregations of wealth," were utterly impotent to prevent the passage of this legislation that forbids them to criticize candidates (including incumbents). In the fact that the effect of BCRA has been to concentrate more political power in the hands of the country's wealthiest individuals and their so-called 527 organizations, unregulated by [BCRA]. (In the 2004 election cycle, a mere 24 individuals contributed an astounding total of $142 million to 527s.) And in the fact that while these wealthy individuals dominate political discourse, it is this small, grass-roots organization of Wisconsin Right to Life that is muzzled.[8]

Scalia's views soon prevailed. In 2008, a nonprofit corporation named Citizens United released a documentary film about then-Senator Hillary Clinton, who was running for the Democratic nomination for president. The group planned to make the movie available on cable television up through the election. Because the documentary referred directly to Senator Clinton, it seemed to violate BCRA.

In *Citizens United v. Federal Election Commission* (2010), the Supreme Court overruled *Austin* and struck down the provisions of BCRA that prevented corporations and unions from making independent expenditures on behalf of political candidates. Writing for the majority, Justice Anthony Kennedy found that the ban on corporate spending amounted to an outright ban on speech, violating the First Amendment's clear statement that "Congress shall make no law...abridging the freedom of speech." He wrote that government lacks the power to restrict political speech based on the speaker's corporate identity.

In a separate opinion concurring in part and dissenting in part from the majority's opinion, Justice John Paul Stevens borrowed Justice Scalia's originalist approach to interpretation, arguing that the Framers would not have protected political speech by funded by corporations. Justice Scalia, whose long-held views were vindicated by the *Citizens United* decision, wrote a separate concurring opinion specifically to take issue with Justice Stevens's venture into originalism.

⚜

JUSTICE SCALIA, WITH WHOM JUSTICE ALITO JOINS, AND WITH WHOM JUSTICE THOMAS JOINS IN PART, CONCURRING.

I join the opinion of the Court.

I write separately to address Justice Stevens' discussion of "Original Understandings." This section of the dissent purports to show that today's decision is not supported by the original understanding of the First Amendment. The dissent attempts this demonstration, however, in splendid isolation from the text of the First Amendment. It never shows why "the freedom of speech" that was the right of Englishmen did not include the freedom to speak in association with other individuals, including association in the corporate form. To be sure, in 1791 (as now) corporations could pursue only the objectives set forth in their charters; but the dissent provides no evidence that their speech in the pursuit of those objectives could be censored.

Instead of taking this straightforward approach to determining the Amendment's meaning, the dissent embarks on a detailed exploration of the Framers' views about the "role of corporations in society." The Framers didn't like corporations, the dissent concludes, and therefore it follows (as night the day) that corporations had no rights of free speech. Of course the Framers' personal affection or disaffection for corporations is relevant only insofar as it can be thought to be reflected in the understood meaning of the text they enacted—not, as the dissent suggests, as a freestanding substitute for that text. But the dissent's distortion of proper analysis is even worse than that. Though faced with a constitutional text that makes no distinction between types of speakers, the dissent feels no necessity to provide even an isolated statement from the founding era to the effect that corporations are not covered, but places the burden on petitioners to bring forward statements showing that they are ("there is not a scintilla of evidence to support the notion that anyone believed [the First Amendment] would preclude regulatory distinctions based on the corporate form").

Despite the corporation-hating quotations the dissent has dredged up, it is far from clear that by the end of the 18th century corporations were despised. If so, how came there to be so many of them? The dissent's statement that there were few business corporations during the eighteenth century—"only a few hundred during all of the 18th century"—is misleading. There were approximately 335 charters issued to business corporations in the United States by the end of the 18th century. See J. Davis, *Essays in the Earlier History of American Corporations* (1917). This was a "considerable extension of corporate enterprise in the field of business," Davis, and represented "unprecedented growth," *id*. Moreover, what seems like a small number by today's standards surely does not indicate the relative importance of corporations when the Nation was considerably smaller. As I have previously noted, "[b]y the end of the eighteenth century the corporation was a familiar figure in American economic life." *McConnell v. Federal Election Comm'n*, 540 U. S. 93, 256 (2003).

Even if we thought it proper to apply the dissent's approach of excluding from First Amendment coverage what the Founders disliked, and even if we agreed that the Founders disliked founding-era corporations; modern corporations might not qualify for exclusion. Most of the Founders' resentment towards corporations was directed at the state-granted monopoly privileges that individually chartered corporations enjoyed. Modern corporations do not have such privileges, and would probably have been favored by most of our enterprising Founders—excluding, perhaps, Thomas Jefferson and others favoring perpetuation of an agrarian society. Moreover, if the Founders' specific intent with respect to corporations is what matters, why does the dissent ignore the Founders' views about other legal entities that have more in common with modern business corporations than the founding-era corporations? At the time of the founding, religious, educational, and literary corporations were incorporated under general incorporation statutes, much as business corporations are today. There were also small unincorporated business associations, which some have argued were the " 'true progenitors' " of today's business corporations. Friedman (quoting S. Livermore, *Early American Land Companies: Their Influence on Corporate Development* (1939)). Were all of these silently excluded from the protections of the First Amendment?

The lack of a textual exception for speech by corporations cannot be explained on the ground that such organizations did not exist or did not speak. To the contrary, colleges, towns and cities, religious institutions, and guilds had long been organized as corporations at common law and under the King's charter, and as I have discussed, the practice of incorporation only expanded in the United States. Both corporations and voluntary associations actively petitioned the Government and expressed their views in newspapers and pamphlets. For example: An antislavery Quaker corporation petitioned the First Congress, distributed pamphlets, and communicated through the press in 1790. The New York Sons of Liberty sent a circular to colonies farther south in 1766. And the Society for the Relief and Instruction of Poor Germans circulated a biweekly paper from 1755 to 1757. The dissent offers no evidence—none whatever—that the First Amendment's unqualified text was originally understood to exclude such associational speech from its protection.

The notion which follows from the dissent's view, that modern newspapers, since they are incorporated, have free-speech rights only at the sufferance of Congress, boggles the mind.

Historical evidence relating to the textually similar clause "the freedom of...the press" also provides no support for the proposition that the First Amendment excludes conduct of artificial legal entities from the scope of its protection. The freedom of "the press" was widely understood to protect the publishing activities of individual editors and printers. But these individuals often acted through newspapers, which (much like corporations) had their own names, outlived the individuals who had founded them, could be bought and sold, were sometimes owned by more than one person, and were operated for profit. Their activities were not stripped of First Amendment protection simply because they were carried out under the banner of an artificial legal entity. And the notion which follows from the dissent's view, that modern newspapers, since they are incorporated, have free-speech rights only at the sufferance of Congress, boggles the mind.

In passing, the dissent also claims that the Court's conception of corruption is unhistorical. The Framers "would have been appalled," it says, by the evidence of corruption in the congressional findings supporting the Bipartisan Campaign Reform Act of 2002. For this

> *If speech can be prohibited because, in the view of the Government, it leads to "moral decay" or does not serve "public ends," then there is no limit to the Government's censorship power.*

proposition, the dissent cites a law review article arguing that "corruption" was originally understood to include "moral decay" and even actions taken by citizens in pursuit of private rather than public ends. It is hard to see how this has anything to do with what sort of corruption can be combated by restrictions on political speech. Moreover, if speech can be prohibited because, in the view of the Government, it leads to "moral decay" or does not serve "public ends," then there is no limit to the Government's censorship power.

The dissent says that when the Framers "constitutionalized the right to free speech in the First Amendment, it was the free speech of individual Americans that they had in mind." That is no doubt true. All the provisions of the Bill of Rights set forth the rights of individual men and women—not, for example, of trees or polar bears. But the individual person's right to speak includes the right to speak in association with other individual persons. Surely the dissent does not believe that speech by the Republican Party or the Democratic Party can be censored because it is not the speech of "an individual American." It is the speech of many individual Americans, who have associated in a common cause, giving the leadership of the party the right to speak on their behalf. The association of individuals in a business corporation is no different—or at least it cannot be denied the right to speak on the simplistic ground that it is not "an individual American."

[Footnote] The dissent says that " 'speech' " refers to oral communications of human beings, and since corporations are not human beings they cannot speak. This is sophistry. The authorized spokesman of a corporation is a human being, who speaks on behalf of the human beings who have formed that association—just as the spokesman of an unincorporated association speaks on behalf of its members. The power to publish thoughts, no less than the power to speak thoughts, belongs only to human beings, but the dissent sees no problem with a corporation's enjoying the freedom of the press....

A documentary film critical of a potential Presidential candidate is core political speech, and its nature as such does not change simply because it was funded by a corporation.

But to return to, and summarize, my principal point, which is the conformity of today's opinion with the original meaning of the First Amendment. The Amendment is written in terms of "speech," not speakers. Its text offers no foothold for excluding any category of speaker, from single individuals to partnerships of individuals, to unincorporated associations of individuals, to incorporated associations of individuals—and the dissent offers no evidence about the original meaning of the text to support any such exclusion. We are therefore simply left with the question whether the speech at issue in this case is "speech" covered by the First Amendment. No one says otherwise. A documentary film critical of a potential Presidential candidate is core political speech, and its nature as such does not change simply because it was funded by a corporation. Nor does the character of that funding produce any reduction whatever in the "inherent worth of the speech" and "its capacity for informing the public," *First Nat. Bank of Boston v. Bellotti* (1978). Indeed, to exclude or impede corporate speech is to muzzle the principal agents of the modern free economy. We should celebrate rather than condemn the addition of this speech to the public debate.

CHAPTER FOURTEEN

NON-SPEECH AND UN-FREE SPEECH

~~⚜~~

A S ILLUSTRATED IN THE PREVIOUS CHAPTER, Justice Scalia viewed with suspicion laws that regulate political speech because he viewed protection of such speech to be the main purpose of the First Amendment. He was not sympathetic to free speech claims for pornography and indecency. Scalia's lack of sympathy did not reflect a belief that certain speech or expressive conduct is merely less important, but that the conduct involved was not speech at all. For example, the issue of nude dancing went before the Supreme Court at least twice during Scalia's tenure.[1] In both cases, Scalia voted to uphold local indecency laws from challenge by nude dancers. Scalia argued that public nudity was the object of the law's prohibition, not dancing, and said nudity is not speech. In contrast to the *Eichman* flag-burning case, in which the conduct was banned because of its communicative purpose, the laws in question were not intended to suppress the expressive component of dancing.

Scalia also voted to deny First Amendment protection to artists seeking federal subsidies for their work. Asserting that the issue was government discretion in the exercise of its spending power, Scalia wrote that artists were free to create indecent works but were not entitled to make taxpayers foot the bill. If an artist wishes to accept federal money for his work, he must accept the rules that go with the money—even if they limit his artistic expression.

BARNES v. GLEN THEATRE, INC. (1991)

The State of Indiana enacted a law to combat public indecency, which, among other things, prohibited appearing nude in public. Two strip bars in South Bend and their dancers challenged the law, arguing that the First Amendment's right of free expression prevents enforcement of the public indecency law against nude dancing.

The Supreme Court, in a 5–4 decision, upheld the Indiana law. The majority conceded that nude dancing constitutes expressive conduct, but said the established test for reviewing expression-limiting laws was satisfied. Specifically, the law furthered the state's interest in protecting order and morality. The interest in protecting morality was unrelated to suppressing free expression, since banning public nudity, not expressive dancing, was the object of the law. Finally, the incidental restriction on the dancers' rights— they were forced to wear pasties and G-strings—was no greater than was essential to furthering Indiana's interest.

Justice Scalia concurred with the Court's opinion but wrote separately to state his view that the majority's First Amendment analysis was not appropriate. He wrote that the indecency measure was a general law regulating conduct and was not specifically directed at expression. Thus, the Court need not inquire as to whether the slight limitation on expression was justified by an important government interest. The First Amendment did not apply.

⚜

JUSTICE SCALIA, CONCURRING IN THE JUDGMENT.

I agree that the judgment of the Court of Appeals must be reversed. In my view, however, the challenged regulation must be upheld, not because it survives some lower level of First-Amendment scrutiny, but because, as a general law regulating conduct and not specifically directed at expression, it is not subject to First Amendment scrutiny at all.

I

Indiana's public indecency statute provides:

(a) A person who knowingly or intentionally, in a public place:
   (1) engages in sexual intercourse;
   (2) engages in deviate sexual conduct;
   (3) appears in a state of nudity; or
   (4) fondles the genitals of himself or another person; commits public indecency, a Class A misdemeanor.
(b) "Nudity" means the showing of the human male or female genitals, pubic area, or buttocks with less than a fully opaque covering, the showing of the female breast with less than a fully opaque covering of any part of the nipple, or the showing of covered male genitals in a discernibly turgid state.

INDIANA CODE 35-45-4-1 (1988)

On its face, this law is not directed at expression in particular. As Judge Easterbrook put it in his dissent below: "Indiana does not regulate dancing. It regulates public nudity.... Almost the entire domain of Indiana's statute is unrelated to expression, unless we view nude beaches and topless hot dog vendors as speech." *Miller v. Civil City of South Bend* (CA7 1990). The intent to convey a "message of eroticism" (or any other message) is not a necessary element of the statutory offense of public indecency; nor does one commit that statutory offense by conveying the most explicit "message of eroticism," so long as he does not commit any of the four specified acts in the process.

Indiana's statute is in the line of a long tradition of laws against public nudity, which have never been thought to run afoul of traditional understanding of "the freedom of speech." Public indecency—including public nudity—has long been an offense at common law. Indiana's first public nudity statute predated by many years the appearance of nude barroom dancing. It was general in scope, directed at all public nudity, and not just at public nude expression; and all succeeding statutes, down to the present one, have been the same. Were it the case that Indiana in practice targeted only expressive nudity, while turning a blind eye to nude beaches and unclothed purveyors of hot dogs and machine tools, it might be said that what posed as a regulation of conduct in general was in reality a regulation of only communicative conduct. Respondents have adduced no evidence of that. Indiana officials have brought many public indecency prosecutions for activities having no communicative element.

The dissent confidently asserts that the purpose of restricting nudity in public places in general is to protect nonconsenting parties from offense; and argues that, since only consenting, admission-paying patrons see respondents dance, that purpose cannot apply, and the only remaining purpose must relate to the communicative elements of the performance. Perhaps the dissenters believe that "offense to others" ought to be the only reason for restricting nudity in public places generally, but there is no basis for thinking that our society has ever shared that Thoreauvian "you-may-do-what-you-like-so-long-as-it-does-not-injure-someone-else" beau ideal—much less for thinking that it was written into the Constitution. The purpose of Indiana's nudity law would be violated, I think, if 60,000 fully consenting adults crowded into the Hoosierdome to display their genitals to one another, even if there were not an offended innocent in the crowd. Our society prohibits, and all human societies have prohibited, certain activities not because they harm others but because they are considered, in the traditional phrase, "contra bonos mores," i.e., immoral. In American society, such prohibitions have included, for example, sadomasochism, cockfighting, bestiality, suicide, drug use, prostitution, and sodomy. While there may be great diversity of view on whether various of these prohibitions should exist (though I have found few ready to abandon, in principle, all of them) there is no doubt that, absent specific constitutional protection for the conduct involved, the Constitution does not prohibit them simply because they regulate "morality." The purpose of the Indiana statute, as both its text and the manner of its enforcement demonstrate, is to enforce the traditional moral belief that people should not expose their private parts indiscriminately, regardless of whether those who see them are disedified. Since that is so, the dissent has no basis for positing that, where only thoroughly edified adults are present, the purpose must be repression of communication.

The purpose of Indiana's nudity law would be violated, I think, if 60,000 fully consenting adults crowded into the Hoosierdome to display their genitals to one another, even if there were not an offended innocent in the crowd.

II

Since the Indiana regulation is a general law not specifically targeted at expressive conduct, its application to such conduct does not, in my view, implicate the First Amendment.

The First Amendment explicitly protects "the freedom of speech [and] of the press"—oral and written speech—not "expressive conduct." When any law restricts speech, even for a purpose that has nothing to do with the suppression of communication (for instance, to reduce noise, see *Saia v. New York* (1948), to regulate election campaigns, see *Buckley v. Valeo* (1976), or to prevent littering, see *Schneider v. State* (1939)), we insist that it meet the high First Amendment standard of justification. But virtually every law restricts conduct, and virtually any prohibited conduct can be performed for an expressive purpose—if only expressive of the fact that the actor disagrees with the prohibition. See, e.g., *Florida Free Beaches, Inc. v. Miami*, 734 F.2d 608 (1984) (nude sunbathers challenging public indecency law claimed their "message" was that nudity is not indecent). It cannot reasonably be demanded, therefore, that every restriction of expression incidentally produced by a general law regulating conduct pass normal First Amendment scrutiny, or even—as some of our cases have suggested—that it be justified by an "important or substantial" government interest. Nor do our holdings require such justification: we have never invalidated the application of a general law simply because the conduct that it reached was being engaged in for expressive purposes and the government could not demonstrate a sufficiently important state interest.

This is not to say that the First Amendment affords no protection to expressive conduct. Where the government prohibits conduct precisely because of its communicative attributes, we hold the regulation unconstitutional. See, e.g., *United States v. Eichman* (1990) (burning flag); *Texas v. Johnson* (1989) (same); *Spence v. Washington* (1974) (defacing flag); *Tinker v. Des Moines Independent Community School District* (1969) (wearing black arm bands); *Brown v. Louisiana* (1966) (participating in silent sit-in); *Stromberg v. California* (1931) (flying a red flag). In each of the foregoing cases, we explicitly found that suppressing communication was the object of the regulation of conduct. Where that has not been the case, however—where suppression of communicative use of the conduct was merely the incidental effect of forbidding the conduct for other reasons—we have allowed the regulation to stand. As we clearly expressed the point in *Johnson*:

> The government generally has a freer hand in restricting expressive conduct than it has in restricting the written or spoken word. It may not, however, proscribe particular conduct *because* it has expressive elements. What might be termed the more generalized guarantee of freedom of expression makes the communicative nature of conduct an inadequate *basis* for singling out that conduct for proscription (internal quotations and citations omitted; emphasis in original).

All our holdings (though admittedly not some of our discussion) support the conclusion that "the only First Amendment analysis applicable to laws that do not directly or indirectly impede speech is the threshold inquiry of whether the purpose of the law is to suppress communication. If not, that is the end of the matter so far as First Amendment guarantees are concerned; if so, the court then proceeds to determine whether there is substantial justification for the proscription." *Community for Creative Non-Violence v. Watt*, 703 F.2d 586 (1983) (Scalia, J., dissenting) (footnote omitted; emphasis omitted), rev'd, *Clark v. Community for Creative Non-Violence* (1984). Such a regime ensures that the government does not act to suppress communication, without requiring that all conduct-restricting regulation (which means in effect all regulation) survive an enhanced level of scrutiny.

We have explicitly adopted such a regime in another First Amendment context: that of Free Exercise. In *Employment Division, Oregon
Dept. of Human Resources v. Smith* (1990), we held that general laws not
specifically targeted at religious practices did not require heightened
First Amendment scrutiny even though they diminished some people's
ability to practice their religion. "The government's ability to enforce
generally applicable prohibitions of socially harmful conduct, like its
ability to carry out other aspects of public policy, 'cannot depend on
measuring the effects of a governmental action on a religious objector's
spiritual development.'" *Id.*, quoting *Lyng v. Northwest Indian Ceme-
tery Protective Assn.* (1988). There is even greater reason to apply this
approach to the regulation of expressive conduct. Relatively few can
plausibly assert that their illegal conduct is being engaged in for religious reasons; but almost anyone can violate almost any law as a means
of expression. In the one case, as in the other, if the law is not directed
against the protected value (religion or expression) the law must be
obeyed.

III

While I do not think the plurality's conclusions differ greatly from
my own, I cannot entirely endorse its reasoning. The plurality purports to apply to this general law, insofar as it regulates this allegedly
expressive conduct, an intermediate level of First Amendment scrutiny: the government interest in the regulation must be "'imortant or
substantial,'" quoting *O'Brien*. As I have indicated, I do not believe
such a heightened standard exists. I think we should avoid wherever
possible, moreover, a method of analysis that requires judicial assessment of the "importance" of government interests—and especially of
government interests in various aspects of morality.

Neither of the cases that the plurality cites to support the "importance" of the State's interest here is in point. *Paris Adult Theatre I v. Slaton* and *Bowers v. Hardwick* did uphold laws prohibiting private conduct based on concerns of decency and morality; but neither opinion held that those concerns were particularly "important" or "substantial," or amounted to anything more than a rational basis for regulation. *Slaton* involved an exhibition which, since it was obscene and at least to some extent public, was unprotected by the First Amendment; the State's prohibition could therefore be invalidated only if it had no rational basis. We found that the State's "right...to maintain a decent society" provided a "legitimate" basis for regulation—even as to obscene material viewed by consenting adults. In *Bowers*, we held that, since homosexual behavior is not a fundamental right, a Georgia law prohibiting private homosexual intercourse needed only a rational basis in order to comply with the Due Process Clause. Moral opposition to homosexuality, we said, provided that rational basis. I would uphold the Indiana statute on precisely the same ground: moral opposition to nudity supplies a rational basis for its prohibition, and since the First Amendment has no application to this case, no more than that is needed.

Indiana may constitutionally enforce its prohibition of public nudity even against those who choose to use public nudity as a means of communication. The State is regulating conduct, not expression, and those who choose to employ conduct as a means of expression must make sure that the conduct they select is not generally forbidden. For these reasons, I agree that the judgment should be reversed.

NATIONAL ENDOWMENT FOR THE ARTS
v. FINLEY (1998)

For a small agency of the federal government, the National Endowment for the Arts (NEA) created an enormous controversy in the 1980s and early 1990s. Some of the agency's grants financed "art" that many Americans found objectionable. Perhaps the most infamous award went to Andres Serrano, who created "Piss Christ," a photograph of a crucifix submerged in urine.

While liberals in Congress defended the NEA on First Amendment grounds, conservatives thought the agency was insulting taxpayers by funding patently offensive art with their money. In addition to trying to eliminate the agency's budget, conservatives sought to ensure that no more grants would go to offensive projects or artists.

A compromise was reached in 1990 when Congress directed the chairman of the NEA to establish procedures for judging grant applications. According to the law, "artistic excellence and artistic merit are the criteria by which applications are judged, taking into consideration general standards of decency and respect for the diverse beliefs and values of the American public..." Four performing artists challenged the law, arguing that it violated their First Amendment rights by rejecting their application on political grounds. They also argued that the law was too vague in that it did not give applicants sufficient guidance as to what types of art would be disfavored under the NEA's guidelines.

The Supreme Court, in an opinion written by Justice O'Connor, held that the law did not violate artists' First Amendment rights. O'Connor wrote that while government grants cannot discriminate based on the viewpoint of the recipient, the NEA provision is not viewpoint-based. She said it merely required the NEA to consider "decency and respect" standards when judging applications. In addition, O'Connor and the majority ruled that the law was not impermissibly vague; it simply added some imprecise considerations to an already subjective process for awarding federal grants.

Justice Scalia concurred with the Court's decision to uphold the law, but strongly rejected its reasoning. He conceded that the law discriminates against artists who create works that are indecent or not respectful of the beliefs and values of the American public. However, Scalia said this discrimination is not unconstitutional because it does not abridge the grant applicant's freedom to make indecent art; it merely removes taxpayer funding as the source. The artists could fund their works with private support. "The NEA is far from the sole source of funding for art—even indecent, disrespectful, or just plain bad art," wrote Scalia. Finally, with regard to vagueness, Scalia said that that concern should not apply to funding decisions. He pointed out that the NEA's preexisting standard already was vague, having resulted in grants for "everything from the playing of Beethoven to a depiction of a crucifix immersed in urine."

～✦◦✦◦✦～

JUSTICE SCALIA, WITH WHOM JUSTICE THOMAS JOINS, CONCURRING IN THE JUDGMENT.

The operation was a success, but the patient died. What such a procedure is to medicine, the Court's opinion in this case is to law.

"The operation was a success, but the patient died." What such a procedure is to medicine, the Court's opinion in this case is to law. It sustains the constitutionality of 20 U.S.C. § 954(d) (1) by gutting it. The most avid congressional opponents of the provision could not have asked for more. I write separately because, unlike the Court, I think that § 954(d)(1) must be evaluated as written, rather than as distorted by the agency it was meant to control. By its terms, it establishes content and viewpoint-based criteria upon which grant applications are to be evaluated. And that is perfectly constitutional.

I

THE STATUTE MEANS WHAT IT SAYS

Section 954(d)(1) provides:

> No payment shall be made under this section except upon appli-
> cation therefore which is submitted to the National Endowment
> for the Arts in accordance with regulations issued and procedures
> established by the Chairperson. In establishing such regulations
> and procedures, the Chairperson shall ensure that "(1) artistic
> excellence and artistic merit are the criteria by which applica-
> tions are judged, taking into consideration general standards
> of decency and respect for the diverse beliefs and values of the
> American public."

The phrase "taking into consideration general standards of decency
and respect for the diverse beliefs and values of the American public"
is what my grammar-school teacher would have condemned as a dan-
gling modifier: There is no noun to which the participle is attached
(unless one jumps out of paragraph (1) to press "Chairperson" into
service). Even so, it is clear enough that the phrase is meant to apply
to those who do the judging. The application reviewers must take
into account "general standards of decency" and "respect for the
diverse beliefs and values of the American public" when evaluating
artistic excellence and merit. One can regard this as either suggesting
that decency and respect are elements of what Congress regards as
artistic excellence and merit, or as suggesting that decency and respect
are factors to be taken into account in *addition* to artistic excellence
and merit. But either way, it is entirely, 100% clear that decency and
respect are to be taken into account in evaluating applications.

This is so apparent that I am at a loss to understand what the Court has in mind (other than the gutting of the statute) when it speculates that the statute is merely "advisory." General standards of decency and respect for Americans' beliefs and values *must* (for the statute says that the Chairperson "shall ensure" this result) be taken into account (see, *e.g.*, American Heritage Dictionary (3d ed. 1992): "consider...[t]o take into account; bear in mind") in evaluating all applications. This does not mean that those factors must always be dispositive, but it *does* mean that they must always be considered. The method of compliance proposed by the National Endowment for the Arts (NEA)—selecting diverse review panels of artists and nonartists that reflect a wide range of geographic and cultural perspective—is so obviously inadequate that it insults the intelligence. A diverse panel membership increases the odds that, *if and when* the panel takes the factors into account, it *will* reach an accurate assessment of what they demand. But it in no way increases the odds that the panel will take the factors into consideration—much less *ensures* that the panel will do so, which is the Chairperson's duty under the statute. Moreover, the NEA's fanciful reading of § 954(d)(1) would make it wholly superfluous. Section 959(c) already requires the Chairperson to "issue regulations and establish procedures...to ensure that all panels are composed, to the extent practicable, of individuals reflecting...diverse artistic and cultural points of view."

The statute requires the decency and respect factors to be considered in evaluating *all* applications—not, for example, just those applications relating to educational programs, or intended for a particular audience. Just as it would violate the statute to apply the artistic excellence and merit requirements to only select categories of applications, it would violate the statute to apply the decency and respect factors less than universally. A reviewer may, of course, give varying weight to the factors depending on the context, and in some categories of cases (such as the Court's example of funding for symphony orchestras) the factors may rarely if ever affect the outcome; but § 954(d)(1) requires the factors to be considered in every case.

I agree with the Court that § 954(d)(1) "imposes no categorical requirement," in the sense that it does not require the denial of all applications that violate general standards of decency or exhibit disrespect for the diverse beliefs and values of Americans. . . . But the factors need not be conclusive to be discriminatory. To the extent a particular applicant exhibits disrespect for the diverse beliefs and values of the American public or fails to comport with general standards of decency, the likelihood that he will receive a grant diminishes. In other words, the presence of the "tak[e] into consideration" clause "cannot be regarded as mere surplusage; it means something," *Potter v. United States* (1894). And the "something" is that the decisionmaker, all else being equal, will favor applications that display decency and respect, and disfavor applications that do not.

This unquestionably constitutes viewpoint discrimination. That conclusion is not altered by the fact that the statute does not "compe[l]" the denial of funding any more than a provision imposing a five-point handicap on all black applicants for civil service jobs is saved from being race discrimination by the fact that it does not compel the rejection of black applicants. If viewpoint discrimination in this context is unconstitutional (a point I shall address anon), the law is invalid unless there are some situations in which the decency and respect factors *do not constitute viewpoint discrimination*. And there is none. The applicant who displays "decency," that is, "[c]onformity to prevailing standards of propriety or modesty,"

American Heritage Dictionary 483 (3d ed. 1992) (def. 2), and the applicant who displays "respect," that is, "deferential regard," for the diverse beliefs and values of the American people, *id.*, at 1536 (def. 1), will *always* have an edge over an applicant who displays the opposite. And finally, the conclusion of viewpoint discrimination is not affected by the fact that what constitutes "decency" or "the diverse beliefs and values of the American people" is difficult to pin down—any more than a civil-service preference in favor of those who display "Republican-Party values" would be rendered nondiscriminatory by the fact that there is plenty of room for argument as to what Republican-Party values might be.

The "political context surrounding the adoption of the 'decency and respect' clause," which the Court discusses at some length does not change its meaning or affect its constitutionality. All that is proved by the various statements that the Court quotes from the Report of the Independent Commission and the floor debates is (1) that the provision was not meant categorically to exclude any particular viewpoint (which I have conceded, and which is plain from the text), and (2) that the language was not meant to do anything that is unconstitutional. That in no way propels the Court's leap to the countertextual conclusion that the provision was merely "aimed at reforming procedures," and cannot be "utilized as a tool for invidious viewpoint discrimination." It is evident in the legislative history that § 954(d)(1) was prompted by, and directed at, the public funding of such offensive productions as Serrano's "Piss Christ," the portrayal of a crucifix immersed in urine, and Mapplethorpe's show of lurid homoerotic photographs. Thus, even if one strays beyond the plain text it is perfectly clear that the statute was meant to disfavor—that is, to discriminate against—such productions. Not to ban their funding absolutely, to be sure (though as I shall discuss, that also would not have been unconstitutional); but to make their funding more difficult.

It matters not whether this enactment was the product of the most partisan alignment in history or whether, upon its passage, the Members all linked arms and sang, "The more we get together, the happier we'll be."

More fundamentally, of course, all this legislative history has no valid claim upon our attention at all. It is a virtual certainty that very few of the Members of Congress who voted for this language both (1) knew of, and (2) agreed with, the various statements that the Court has culled from the Report of the Independent Commission and the floor debate (probably conducted on an almost empty floor). And it is wholly irrelevant that the statute was a "bipartisan proposal introduced as a counterweight" to an alternative proposal that would directly restrict funding on the basis of viewpoint. We do not judge statutes as if we are surveying the scene of an accident; each one is reviewed, not on the basis of how much worse it could have been, but on the basis of what it says. It matters not whether this enactment was the product of the most partisan alignment in history or whether, upon its passage, the Members all linked arms and sang, "The more we get together, the happier we'll be." It is "not consonant with our scheme of government for a court to inquire into the motives of legislators." *Tenney v. Brandhove* (1951). The law at issue in this case is to be found in the text of § 954(d)(1), which passed both Houses and was signed by the President, U. S. Const., Art. I, § 7. And that law unquestionably disfavors—discriminates against—indecency and disrespect for the diverse beliefs and values of the American people. I turn, then, to whether such viewpoint discrimination violates the Constitution.

II

WHAT THE STATUTE SAYS IS CONSTITUTIONAL

The Court devotes so much of its opinion to explaining why this statute means something other than what it says that it neglects to cite the constitutional text governing our analysis. The First Amendment reads: "Congress shall make no law . . . *abridging* the freedom of speech." U. S. Const., Amdt. 1 (emphasis added). To abridge is "to contract, to diminish; to deprive of." T. Sheridan, A Complete Dictionary of the English Language (6th ed. 1796). With the enactment of § 954(d)(1), Congress did not *abridge* the speech of those who disdain the beliefs and values of the American public, nor did it abridge indecent speech. Those who wish to create indecent and disrespectful art are as unconstrained now as they were before the enactment of this statute. Avant-garde artistes such as respondents remain entirely free to epater les bourgeois; they are merely deprived of the additional satisfaction of having the bourgeoisie taxed to pay for it. It is preposterous to equate the denial of taxpayer subsidy with measures "'aimed at the *suppression* of dangerous ideas.'" *Regan v. Taxation with Representation of Wash.* (1983) (emphasis added) (quoting *Cammarano v. United States* (1959), in turn quoting *Speiser v . Randall* (1958)). "The reason that denial of participation in a tax exemption or other subsidy scheme does not necessarily 'infringe' a fundamental right is that—unlike direct restriction or prohibition—such a denial does not, as a general rule, have any significant coercive effect." *Arkansas Writers' Project, Inc. v. Ragland* (1987) (Scalia, J., dissenting).

> *Avant-garde artistes such as respondents remain entirely free to epater les bourgeois [to shock the middle classes]; they are merely deprived of the additional satisfaction of having the bourgeoisie taxed to pay for it.*

One might contend, I suppose, that a threat of rejection by the only available source of free money would constitute coercion and hence "abridgment" within the meaning of the First Amendment. I would not agree with such a contention, which would make the NEA the mandatory patron of all art too indecent, too disrespectful, or even too *kitsch* to attract private support. But even if one accepts the contention, it would have no application here. The NEA is far from the sole source of funding for art—even indecent, disrespectful, or just plain bad art. Accordingly, the Government may earmark NEA funds for projects it deems to be in the public interest without thereby abridging speech.

Section 954(d)(1) is no more discriminatory, and no less constitutional, than virtually every other piece of funding legislation enacted by Congress. "The Government can, without violating the Constitution, selectively fund a program to encourage certain activities it believes to be in the public interest, without at the same time funding an alternative program...." *Rust v. Sullivan* (1991). As we noted in *Rust*, when Congress chose to establish the National Endowment for Democracy it was not constitutionally required to fund programs encouraging competing philosophies of government—an example of funding discrimination that cuts much closer than this one to the core of *political* speech which is the primary concern of the First Amendment. It takes a particularly high degree of chutzpah for the NEA to contradict this proposition, since the agency itself discriminates—and is required by law to discriminate—in favor of artistic (as opposed to scientific, or political, or theological) expression. Not all the common folk, or even all great minds, for that matter, think that is a good idea. In 1800, when John Marshall told John Adams that a recent immigration of Frenchmen would include talented artists, "Adams denounced all Frenchmen, but most especially 'schoolmasters, painters, poets, &C.' He warned Marshall that the fine arts were like germs that infected healthy constitutions." J. Ellis, After the Revolution: Profiles of Early American Culture 36 (1979). Surely the NEA itself is nothing less than an institutionalized discrimination against that point of view. Nonetheless, it is constitutional, as is the congressional determination to favor decency and respect for beliefs and values over the opposite because such favoritism does not "abridge" anyone's freedom of speech.

Respondents, relying on *Rosenberger v. Rector and Visitors of Univ. of Va.* (1995), argue that viewpoint-based discrimination is impermissible unless the government is the speaker or the government is "disburs[ing] public funds to private entities to convey a governmental message." It is impossible to imagine why that should be so; one would think that directly involving the government itself in the viewpoint discrimination (if it is unconstitutional) would make the situation even worse. Respondents are mistaken. It is the very business of government to favor and disfavor points of view on (in modern times, at least) innumerable subjects—which is the main reason we have decided to elect those who run the government, rather than save money by making their posts hereditary. And it makes not a bit of difference, insofar as either common sense or the Constitution is concerned, whether these officials further their (and, in a democracy, our) favored point of view by achieving it directly (having government-employed artists paint pictures, for example, or government-employed doctors perform abortions); or by advocating it officially (establishing an Office of Art Appreciation, for example, or an Office of Voluntary Population Control); or by giving money to others who achieve or advocate it (funding private art classes, for example, or Planned Parenthood). None of this has anything to do with abridging anyone's speech. *Rosenberger*, as the Court explains, found the viewpoint discrimination unconstitutional, not because funding of "private" speech was involved, but because the government had established a limited public forum—to which the NEA's granting of highly selective (if not highly discriminating) awards bears no resemblance.

The nub of the difference between me and the Court is that I regard the distinction between "abridging" speech and funding it as a fundamental divide, on this side of which the First Amendment is inapplicable. The Court, by contrast, seems to believe that the First Amendment, despite its words, has some ineffable effect upon funding, imposing constraints of an indeterminate nature which it announces (without troubling to enunciate any particular test) are not violated by the statute here—or, more accurately, are not violated by the quite different, emasculated statute that it imagines. "[T]he Government," it says, "may allocate competitive funding according to criteria that would be impermissible were direct regulation of speech or a criminal penalty at stake." The Government, *I* think, may allocate both competitive and noncompetitive funding *ad libitum*, insofar as the First Amendment is concerned.

Finally, what is true of the First Amendment is also true of the constitutional rule against vague legislation: it has no application to funding. Insofar as it bears upon First Amendment concerns, the vagueness doctrine addresses the problems that arise from government *regulation* of expressive conduct, not government grant programs. In the former context, vagueness produces an abridgment of lawful speech; in the latter it produces, at worst, a waste of money. I cannot refrain from observing, however, that if the vagueness doctrine were applicable, the agency charged with making grants under a statutory standard of "artistic excellence"—and which has itself thought that standard met by everything from the playing of Beethoven to a depiction of a crucifix immersed in urine—would be of more dubious constitutional validity than the "decency" and "respect" limitations that respondents (who demand to be judged on the same strict standard of "artistic excellence") have the humorlessness to call too vague.

In its laudatory description of the accomplishments of the NEA, the Court notes with satisfaction that "only a handful of the agency's roughly 100,000 awards have generated formal complaints." The Congress that felt it necessary to enact § 954(d)(1) evidently thought it much more noteworthy that any money exacted from American taxpayers had been used to produce a crucifix immersed in urine, or a display of homoerotic photographs. It is no secret that the provision was prompted by, and directed at, the funding of such offensive productions. Instead of banning the funding of such productions absolutely, which I think would have been entirely constitutional, Congress took the lesser step of requiring them to be disfavored in the evaluation of grant applications. The Court's opinion today renders even that lesser step a nullity. For that reason, I concur only in the judgment.

CHAPTER FIFTEEN

OBAMACARE

~≈◈✦◈≈~

O N ITS FACE, the Constitution of the United States gives Congress little authority to interfere with the daily lives of American citizens and businesses. The power to regulate conduct and
behavior to promote health, safety, morals, and general welfare—
known as the police power—is left to the states, not the federal government. Congress, of course, has the power to tax the American
people. In addition, the Commerce Clause of the Constitution grants
Congress the authority "to regulate Commerce with foreign Nations,
and among the several States, and with the Indian Tribes."

Beginning in the 1930s, the Supreme Court began sustaining
efforts by Congress to regulate more private and local activities by
interpreting the commerce power expansively. In the (in)famous case
of *Wickard v. Filburn* (1942), the Supreme Court ruled that Congress could dictate how much wheat an individual farmer grew and
sold because his activity (along with that of all other wheat farmers)
affected national wheat prices. Conservatives strongly opposed such
expansions of federal authority on the grounds that they diminished
personal liberty as well as the power of the states.

Justice Scalia at times has played a key role in efforts to scale back the Commerce Clause, twice joining five-to-four majorities to strike down federal laws that sought to expand federal power beyond its constitutional limit. In 1995, for example, Scalia joined the majority in striking down a federal law that prohibited possession of a firearm in a school zone. There the Court reasoned that simply bringing a gun to school does not impact commerce in the way that selling (or not selling) wheat might. Five years later, the same narrow majority invalidated parts of the Violence Against Women Act. In 2005, however, Scalia sided with the Court's liberal justices in holding that Congress had authority under the Commerce Clause to criminalize the production and use of homegrown marijuana, even in a state that had legalized the use of marijuana for medicinal purposes.

Contrasting views about the proper role of the federal government dominated public debate in the wake of Barack Obama's election to the presidency in 2008. Candidate Obama had promised to push legislation to guarantee health insurance for every American. Most Republicans in Congress denounced his proposal as a misguided, ill-conceived, and unconstitutional federal takeover of the nation's healthcare system. In 2010, after a spirited debate in Washington and across the country, Congress passed the Patient Protection and Affordable Care Act, more commonly known as "Obamacare."

As soon as the law was enacted, some of its key provisions were challenged in court. To understand the legal challenges to Obamacare, it is important to understand a few of the law's main provisions:

- The so-called "individual mandate" requires individuals who are not covered by an employer-sponsored health plan or by a government-run health program, such as Medicaid or

Medicare, to purchase an approved private insurance policy. Individuals who fail to buy a health insurance policy are subject to what the law calls a financial "penalty."

- Certain low-income persons are exempt from the individual mandate. To reduce the number of such exemptions, the act calls on states to establish health insurance exchanges—websites where consumers can evaluate and compare qualifying healthcare plans, purchase a policy, and, if they qualify, apply for financial assistance or subsidies. States that agree to set up such exchanges are granted greater discretion over the standards, benefits, and prices of the insurance policies they offer. If states fail to establish exchanges, the secretary of health and human services may establish a federal exchange.

- The act prohibits insurers from denying coverage to individuals because of preexisting medical conditions and requires them to offer the same premium price to all applicants of the same age and geographical location so that poor and sick persons are able to afford policies—the so-called "guaranteed issue" and "partial community rating" requirements.

- Congress's authority to impose the individual mandate, said Obamacare's supporters, rests not only on the Commerce Clause but also on its power to tax. Yet while the bill was working its way through Congress, the president and his supporters insisted that the financial charge imposed on persons not complying with the individual mandate is a "penalty," not a "tax."

Not surprisingly, the first major legal challenge to Obamacare focused on the individual mandate. Conservative legal scholars and

Republican members of Congress had argued that, even under a broad reading of the Commerce Clause, the federal government did not have the authority to compel individual Americans to purchase health insurance policies. *States* can compel individuals to buy insurance, as they do in the case of automobiles, but such a requirement is an exercise of their police power, a power the federal government does not possess.

In *NFIB v. Sebelius* (2012), Chief Justice John Roberts joined the court's liberal justices to uphold the individual mandate as a proper exercise not of Congress's commerce authority but of its taxing power. Justices Scalia, Kennedy, Thomas, and Alito filed a joint dissenting opinion, which was unusual in that none was listed as the main author. Some commentators speculated that the reason the opinion was signed jointly was because it was originally written by Chief Justice Roberts and was intended to be the majority opinion for the court. According to this theory, Roberts changed his mind, so he wrote a new opinion upholding the law under Congress's tax authority, and the four conservative justices simply filed (with edits) his original opinion as their dissenting opinion.

The joint dissent states, "The Court today decides to save a statute Congress did not write. It rules that what the statute declares to be a requirement with a penalty is instead an option subject to a tax." Responding to the majority opinion's claim that saving Obamacare reflected an appropriate deference to Congress, Justice Scalia and his fellow dissenters wrote, "The Court regards its strained statutory interpretation as judicial modesty. It is not. It amounts instead to a vast judicial overreaching. It creates a debilitated, inoperable version of health-care regulation that Congress did not enact and the public does not expect."

Although we might never know for sure who wrote the conclusion of the dissenters' joint opinion, it expresses a keen appreciation for the Constitution's structural arrangements that we find in many of Justice Scalia's other opinions, speeches, and writings:

> The Constitution, though it dates from the founding of the Republic, has powerful meaning and vital relevance to our own times. The constitutional protections that this case involves are protections of structure. Structural protections—notably, the restraints imposed by federalism and separation of powers—are less romantic and have less obvious a connection to personal freedom than the provisions of the Bill of Rights or the Civil War Amendments. Hence they tend to be undervalued or even forgotten by our citizens. It should be the responsibility of the Court to teach otherwise, to remind our people that the Framers considered structural protections of freedom the most important ones, for which reason they alone were embodied in the original Constitution and not left to later amendment. The fragmentation of power produced by the structure of our Government is central to liberty, and when we destroy it, we place liberty at peril. Today's decision should have vindicated, should have taught, this truth; instead, our judgment today has disregarded it.

KING v. BURWELL (2015)

Three years later, another major challenge to Obamacare reached the High Court, this one based on the act's health insurance exchanges. The act provides tax credits for customers who purchase insurance through "exchanges established by the State." No mention is made of tax credits for persons who live in a state that has not set up an exchange. The Internal Revenue Service determined that, despite the language of the statute, tax credits would be available to those enrolled in exchanges established by a state *or* by the federal government. The Obama administration feared that if many states declined to operate exchanges and their residents were not eligible for tax credits, millions of Americans would be exempt from the individual mandate, and the law would not work.

Fortunately for the administration, Chief Justice Roberts joined the liberal justices to beat back this second challenge to Obamacare. Roberts and the majority held that Congress meant for tax credits to be available through both state and federal exchanges. He argued that this meaning was clear when the language was considered in the context of the statute as a whole and that the federally created exchanges were not significantly different from those the states were to create. Finally, Roberts argued that reading "exchange established by the State" to include federally run exchanges advanced the overall purpose of the act, which was to cover as many qualified individuals as possible.

Justice Scalia, joined by Justices Thomas and Alito, dissented. Scalia thought the language chosen by Congress could not have been clearer. "Words no longer have meaning if an Exchange that is *not* established by a State is 'established by the State,'" Scalia wrote. He acknowledged that looking at context is important when interpreting a statute, but it is not appropriate, he argued, to use context to justify a reading that is at odds with the clear meaning of the text. Specifically, Scalia pointed out that Congress referred to both state and federal exchanges in some provisions of the law, while referring only to state exchanges in others.

The ability to distinguish between the two suggested that Congress knew what it was doing when it chose to apply tax credits only to state exchanges.

⤝⧉⤞

Justice Scalia, with whom Justice Thomas and Justice Alito join, dissenting.

The Court holds that when the Patient Protection and Affordable Care Act says "Exchange established by the State" it means "Exchange established by the State or the Federal Government." That is of course quite absurd, and the Court's 21 pages of explanation make it no less so.

I

The Patient Protection and Affordable Care Act makes major reforms to the American health-insurance market. It provides, among other things, that every State "shall... establish an American Health Benefit Exchange"—a marketplace where people can shop for health-insurance plans. And it provides that if a State does not comply with this instruction, the Secretary of Health and Human Services must "establish and operate such Exchange within the State."

A separate part of the Act—housed in § 36B of the Internal Revenue Code—grants "premium tax credits" to subsidize certain purchases of health insurance made on Exchanges. The tax credit consists of "premium assistance amounts" for "coverage months." An individual has a coverage month only when he is covered by an insurance plan "that was enrolled in through an Exchange established by the State under [§ 18031]." And the law ties the size of the premium assistance amount to the premiums for health plans which cover the

individual "and which were enrolled in through an Exchange established by the State under [§ 18031]." The premium assistance amount
further depends on the cost of certain other insurance plans "offered
through the same Exchange."

This case requires us to decide whether someone who buys insurance on an Exchange established by the Secretary gets tax credits.
You would think the answer would be obvious—so obvious there
would hardly be a need for the Supreme Court to hear a case about
it. In order to receive any money under §
36B, an individual must enroll in an insurance
plan through an "Exchange established by the
State." The Secretary of Health and Human
Services is not a State. So an Exchange established by the Secretary is not an Exchange
established by the State—which means people who buy health insurance through such
an Exchange get no money under § 36B.

Words no longer have meaning if an Exchange that is not established by a State is "established by the State."

Words no longer have meaning if an Exchange that is *not* established by a State is "established by the State." It is hard to come up
with a clearer way to limit tax credits to state Exchanges than to use
the words "established by the State." And it is hard to come up with
a reason to include the words "by the State" other than the purpose of limiting credits to state Exchanges. "[T]he plain, obvious, and
rational meaning of a statute is always to be preferred to any curious,
narrow, hidden sense that nothing but the exigency of a hard case
and the ingenuity and study of an acute and powerful intellect would
discover." *Lynch v. Alworth-Stephens Co.* (1925). Under all the usual
rules of interpretation, in short, the Government should lose this
case. But normal rules of interpretation seem always to yield to the

overriding principle of the present Court: The Affordable Care Act must be saved.

II

The Court interprets § 36B to award tax credits on both federal and state Exchanges. It accepts that the "most natural sense" of the phrase "Exchange established by the State" is an Exchange established by a State. (Understatement, thy name is an opinion on the Affordable Care Act!) Yet the opinion continues, with no semblance of shame, that "it is also possible that the phrase refers to *all* Exchanges—both State and Federal." (Impossible possibility, thy name is an opinion on the Affordable Care Act!) The Court claims that "the context and structure of the Act compel [it] to depart from what would otherwise be the most natural reading of the pertinent statutory phrase."

> *Let us not forget, however, why context matters: It is a tool for understanding the terms of the law, not an excuse for rewriting them.*

I wholeheartedly agree with the Court that sound interpretation requires paying attention to the whole law, not homing in on isolated words or even isolated sections. Context always matters. Let us not forget, however, *why* context matters: It is a tool for understanding the terms of the law, not an excuse for rewriting them.

Any effort to understand rather than to rewrite a law must accept and apply the presumption that lawmakers use words in "their natural and ordinary signification." *Pensacola Telegraph Co. v. Western Union Telegraph Co.* (1878). Ordinary connotation does not always prevail, but the more unnatural the proposed interpretation of a law, the more compelling the contextual evidence must be to show that it is correct. Today's interpretation is not merely unnatural; it is unheard of. Who would ever have dreamt that "Exchange established by the State" means "Exchange established by the State *or the Federal Government*"? Little short of an express statutory definition could justify adopting this singular reading. Yet the only pertinent definition here provides that "State" means "each of the 50 States and the District of Columbia." Because the Secretary is neither one of the 50 States nor the District of Columbia, that definition positively contradicts the eccentric theory that an Exchange established by the Secretary has been established by the State.

Far from offering the overwhelming evidence of meaning needed to justify the Court's interpretation, other contextual clues undermine it at every turn. To begin with, other parts of the Act sharply distinguish between the establishment of an Exchange by a State and the establishment of an Exchange by the Federal Government. The States' authority to set up Exchanges comes from one provision; the Secretary's authority comes from an entirely different provision. Funding for States to establish Exchanges comes from one part of the law; funding for the Secretary to establish Exchanges comes from an entirely different part of the law. States generally run state-created Exchanges; the Secretary generally runs federally created Exchanges. And the Secretary's authority to set up an Exchange in a State depends upon the State's "*[f]ailure* to establish [an] Exchange." Provisions such as these destroy any pretense that a federal Exchange is in some sense also established by a State.

Reading the rest of the Act also confirms that, as relevant here, there are *only* two ways to set up an Exchange in a State: establishment by a State and establishment by the Secretary. So saying that an Exchange established by the Federal Government is "established by the

State" goes beyond giving words bizarre meanings; it leaves the limiting phrase "by the State" with no operative effect at all. That is a stark
violation of the elementary principle that requires an interpreter "to
give effect, if possible, to every clause and word of a statute." *Montclair
v. Ramsdell* (1883). In weighing this argument, it is well to remember
the difference between giving a term a meaning that duplicates another
part of the law, and giving a term no meaning at all. Lawmakers sometimes repeat themselves—whether out of a desire to add emphasis, a
sense of belt-and-suspenders caution, or a lawyerly penchant for dou-
blets (aid and abet, cease and desist, null and void). Lawmakers do not,
however, tend to use terms that "have no operation at all." *Marbury v.
Madison* (1803). So while the rule against treating a term as a redun-
dancy is far from categorical, the rule against treating it as a nullity is
as close to absolute as interpretive principles get. The Court's reading
does not merely give "by the State" a duplicative effect; it causes the
phrase to have no effect whatever.

Making matters worse, the reader of the whole Act will come
across a number of provisions beyond § 36B that refer to the establishment of Exchanges by States. Adopting the Court's interpretation
means nullifying the term "by the State" not just once, but again and
again throughout the Act. Consider for the moment only those parts
of the Act that mention an "Exchange established by the State" in
connection with tax credits:

- The formula for calculating the amount of the tax credit,
  as already explained, twice mentions "an Exchange established by the State."
- The Act directs States to screen children for eligibility
  for "[tax credits] under section 36B" and for "any other

assistance or subsidies available for coverage obtained through" an "Exchange established by the State."

- The Act requires "an Exchange established by the State" to use a "secure electronic interface" to determine eligibility for (among other things) tax credits.
- The Act authorizes "an Exchange established by the State" to make arrangements under which other state agencies "determine whether a State resident is eligible for [tax credits] under section 36B."
- The Act directs States to operate Web sites that allow anyone "who is eligible to receive [tax credits] under section 36B" to compare insurance plans offered through "an Exchange established by the State."
- One of the Act's provisions addresses the enrollment of certain children in health plans "offered through an Exchange established by the State" and then discusses the eligibility of these children for tax credits.

It is bad enough for a court to cross out "by the State" once. But seven times?

Congress did not, by the way, repeat "Exchange established by the State under [§ 18031]" by rote throughout the Act. Quite the contrary, clause after clause of the law uses a more general term such as "Exchange" or "Exchange established under [§ 18031]." It is common sense that any speaker who says "Exchange" some of the time, but "Exchange established by the State" the rest of the time, probably means something by the contrast.

Equating establishment "by the State" with establishment by the Federal Government makes nonsense of other parts of the Act. The

Act requires States to ensure (on pain of losing Medicaid funding) that any "Exchange established by the State" uses a "secure
electronic interface" to determine an individual's eligibility for
various benefits (including tax credits). How could a State control
the type of electronic interface used by a federal Exchange? The
Act allows a State to control contracting decisions made by "an
Exchange established by the State." Why would a State get to control the contracting decisions of a federal Exchange? The Act also
provides "Assistance to States to establish American Health Benefit
Exchanges" and directs the Secretary to renew this funding "if the
State... is making progress... toward... establishing an Exchange."
Does a State that refuses to set up an Exchange still receive this
funding, on the premise that Exchanges established by the Federal
Government are really established by States? It is presumably in
order to avoid these questions that the Court concludes that federal
Exchanges count as state Exchanges only "for purposes of the tax
credits." (Contrivance, thy name is an opinion on the Affordable
Care Act!)

It is probably piling on to add that the Congress that wrote the
Affordable Care Act knew how to equate two different types of
Exchanges when it wanted to do so. The Act includes a clause providing that "[a] *territory* that... establishes... an Exchange... shall be
treated as a State" for certain purposes. Tellingly, it does not include
a comparable clause providing that the *Secretary* shall be treated as a
State for purposes of § 36B when *she* establishes an Exchange.

Faced with overwhelming confirmation that "Exchange established by the State" means what it looks like it means, the Court
comes up with argument after feeble argument to support its contrary interpretation. None of its tries comes close to establishing the

implausible conclusion that Congress used "by the State" to mean "by the State or not by the State."

The Court emphasizes that if a State does not set up an Exchange, the Secretary must establish "such Exchange." It claims that the word "such" implies that federal and state Exchanges are "the same." To see the error in this reasoning, one need only consider a parallel provision from our Constitution: "The Times, Places and Manner of holding Elections for Senators and Representatives, shall be prescribed in each State by the Legislature thereof; but the Congress may at any time by Law make or alter *such Regulations*." Just as the Affordable Care Act directs States to establish Exchanges while allowing the Secretary to establish "such Exchange" as a fallback, the Elections Clause directs state legislatures to prescribe election regulations while allowing Congress to make "such Regulations" as a fallback. Would anybody refer to an election regulation made by Congress as a "regulation prescribed by the state legislature"? Would anybody say that a federal election law and a state election law are in all respects equivalent? Of course not. The word "such" does not help the Court one whit. The Court's argument also overlooks the rudimentary principle that a specific provision governs a general one. Even if it were true that the term "such Exchange" in § 18041(c) implies that federal and state Exchanges are the same in general, the term "established by the State" in § 36B makes plain that they differ when it comes to tax credits in particular.

The Court's next bit of interpretive jiggery-pokery involves other parts of the Act that purportedly presuppose the availability of tax credits on both federal and state Exchanges. It is curious that the Court is willing to subordinate the express words of the section that grants tax credits to the mere implications of other provisions with only tangential connections to tax credits. One would think that interpretation would work the other way around. In any event, each of the provisions mentioned by the Court is perfectly consistent with limiting tax credits to state Exchanges. One of them says that the minimum functions of an Exchange include (alongside several tasks that have nothing to do with tax credits) setting up an electronic calculator that shows "the actual cost of coverage after the application of any premium tax credit." What stops a federal Exchange's electronic calculator from telling a customer that his tax credit is zero? Another provision requires an Exchange's outreach program to educate the public about health plans, to facilitate enrollment, and to "distribute fair and impartial information" about enrollment and "the availability of premium tax credits." What stops a federal Exchange's outreach program from fairly and impartially telling customers that no tax credits are available? A third provision requires an Exchange to report information about each insurance plan sold—including level of coverage, premium, name of the insured, and "amount of any advance payment" of the tax credit. What stops a federal Exchange's report from confirming that no tax credits have been paid out?

The Court persists that these provisions "would make little sense" if no tax credits were available on federal Exchanges. Even if that observation were true, it would show only oddity, not ambiguity. Laws often include unusual or mismatched provisions. The Affordable Care Act spans 900 pages; it would be amazing if its provisions all lined up perfectly with each other. This Court "does not revise legislation...just because the text as written creates an apparent anomaly." *Michigan v. Bay Mills Indian Community* (2014). At any rate, the provisions cited by the Court are not particularly unusual. Each requires an Exchange to perform a standardized series of tasks, some aspects of which relate in some way to tax credits. It is entirely natural for slight mismatches to occur when, as here, lawmakers draft "a single statutory provision" to cover "different kinds" of situations. *Robers v. United States* (2014). Lawmakers need not, and often do not, "write extra language specifically exempting, phrase by phrase, applications in respect to which a portion of a phrase is not needed." *Ibid.*

Roaming even farther afield from § 36B, the Court turns to the Act's provisions about "qualified individuals." Qualified individuals receive favored treatment on Exchanges, although customers who are not qualified individuals may also shop there. See *Halbig v. Burwell* (CADC 2014). The Court claims that the Act must equate federal and state establishment of Exchanges when it defines a qualified individual as someone who (among other things) lives in the "State that established the Exchange," Otherwise, the Court says, there would be no qualified individuals on federal Exchanges, contradicting (for example) the provision requiring every Exchange to take the "'interests of qualified individuals'" into account when selecting health plans. Pure applesauce. Imagine that a university sends around a bulletin reminding every professor to take the "interests of graduate students" into account when setting office hours, but that some professors teach only undergraduates. Would anybody reason that the bulletin implicitly presupposes that every professor has "graduate students," so that "graduate students" must really mean "graduate or undergraduate students"? Surely not. Just as one naturally reads instructions about graduate students to be inapplicable to the extent a particular professor has no such students, so too would one naturally read instructions about qualified individuals to be inapplicable to the extent a particular Exchange has no such individuals. There is no need

Pure applesauce.

to rewrite the term "State that established the Exchange" in the definition of "qualified individual," much less a need to rewrite the separate term "Exchange established by the State" in a separate part of the Act.

Least convincing of all, however, is the Court's attempt to uncover support for its interpretation in "the structure of Section 36B itself." The Court finds it strange that Congress limited the tax credit to state Exchanges in the formula for calculating the *amount* of the credit, rather than in the provision defining the range of taxpayers *eligible* for the credit. Had the Court bothered to look at the rest of the Tax Code, it would have seen that the structure it finds strange is in fact quite common. Consider, for example, the many provisions that initially make taxpayers of all incomes eligible for a tax credit, only to provide later that the amount of the credit is zero if the taxpayer's income exceeds a specified threshold. See, *e.g.,* 26 U.S.C. § 24 (child tax credit); § 32 (earned-income tax credit); § 36 (first-time-home-buyer tax credit). Or consider, for an even closer parallel, a neighboring provision that initially makes taxpayers of all States eligible for a credit, only to provide later that the amount of the credit may be zero if the taxpayer's State does not satisfy certain requirements. One begins to get the sense that the Court's insistence on reading things in context applies to "established by the State," but to nothing else.

For what it is worth, lawmakers usually draft tax-credit provisions the way they do—*i.e.,* the way they drafted § 36B—because the mechanics of the credit require it. Many Americans move to new States in the middle of the year. Mentioning state Exchanges in the definition of "coverage month"—rather than (as the Court proposes) in the provisions concerning taxpayers' eligibility for the credit—accounts for taxpayers who live in a State with a state Exchange for a part of the year, but a State with a federal Exchange for the rest of the year. In addition, § 36B awards a credit with respect to insurance plans "which cover the taxpayer, *the taxpayer's spouse, or any dependent...of the taxpayer* and which were enrolled in through an Exchange established by the State." If Congress had mentioned state Exchanges in the provisions discussing taxpayers' eligibility for the credit, a taxpayer who buys insurance from a federal Exchange would get no money, even if he has a spouse or dependent who buys insurance from a state Exchange—say a child attending college in a different State. It thus makes perfect sense for "Exchange established by the State" to appear where it does, rather than where the Court suggests. Even if that were not so, of course, its location would not make it any less clear.

The Court has not come close to presenting the compelling contextual case necessary to justify departing from the ordinary meaning of the terms of the law. Quite the contrary, context only underscores the outlandishness of the Court's interpretation. Reading the Act as a whole leaves no doubt about the matter: "Exchange established by the State" means what it looks like it means.

For its next defense of the indefensible, the Court turns to the Affordable Care Act's design and purposes.

III

For its next defense of the indefensible, the Court turns to the Affordable Care Act's design and purposes. As relevant here, the Act makes three major reforms. The guaranteed-issue and community-rating requirements prohibit insurers from considering a customer's health when deciding whether to sell insurance and how much to charge; its famous individual mandate requires everyone to maintain insurance coverage or to pay what the Act calls a "penalty," and what we have nonetheless called a tax, see

National Federation of Independent Business v. Sebelius (2012); and its tax credits help make insurance more affordable. The Court reasons that Congress intended these three reforms to "work together to expand insurance coverage"; and because the first two apply in every State, so must the third.

This reasoning suffers from no shortage of flaws. To begin with, "even the most formidable argument concerning the statute's purposes could not overcome the clarity [of] the statute's text." *Kloeckner v. Solis* (2012). Statutory design and purpose matter only to the extent they help clarify an otherwise ambiguous provision. Could anyone maintain with a straight face that § 36B is unclear? To mention just the highlights, the Court's interpretation clashes with a statutory definition, renders words inoperative in at least seven separate provisions of the Act, overlooks the contrast between provisions that say "Exchange" and those that say "Exchange established by the State," gives the same phrase one meaning for purposes of tax credits but an entirely different meaning for other purposes, and (let us not forget) contradicts the ordinary meaning of the words Congress used. On the other side of the ledger, the Court has come up with nothing more than a general provision that turns out to be controlled by a specific one, a handful of clauses that are consistent with either understanding of establishment by the State, and a resemblance between the tax-credit provision and the rest of the Tax Code. If that is all it takes to make something ambiguous, everything is ambiguous.

Having gone wrong in consulting statutory purpose at all, the Court goes wrong again in analyzing it. The purposes of a law must be "collected chiefly from its words," not "from extrinsic circumstances." *Sturges v. Crowninshield* (1819). Only by concentrating on the law's terms can a judge hope to uncover the scheme *of the statute,* rather than some other scheme that the judge thinks desirable. Like it or not, the express terms of the Affordable Care Act make only two of the three reforms mentioned by the Court applicable in States that do not establish Exchanges. It is perfectly possible for them to operate independently of tax credits. The guaranteed-issue and communi-ty-rating requirements continue to ensure that insurance companies treat all customers the same no matter their health, and the individual mandate continues to encourage people to maintain coverage, lest they be "taxed."

The Court protests that without the tax credits, the number of people covered by the individual mandate shrinks, and without a broadly applicable individual mandate the guaranteed-issue and community-rating requirements "would destabilize the individual insurance market." If true, these projections would show only that the statutory scheme contains a flaw; they would not show that the statute means the opposite of what it says. Moreover, it is a flaw that appeared as well in other parts of the Act. A different title estab-lished a long-term-care insurance program with guaranteed-issue and community-rating requirements, but without an individual mandate or subsidies. This program never came into effect "only because Congress, in response to actuarial analyses predicting that the [program] would be fiscally unsustainable, repealed the provision in 2013." *Halbig*. How could the Court say that Con-gress would never dream of combining guaranteed-issue and community-rating requirements with a narrow individual mandate, when it combined those requirements with *no* individual mandate in the context of long-term-care insurance?

Similarly, the Department of Health and Human Services originally interpreted the Act to impose guaranteed-issue and community-rating requirements in the Federal Territories, even though the Act plainly does not make the individual mandate applicable there. "This combination, predictably, [threw] individual insurance markets in the territories into turmoil." *Halbig.* Responding to complaints from the Territories, the Department at first insisted that it had "no statutory authority" to address the problem and suggested that the Territories "seek legislative relief from Congress" instead. The Department changed its mind a year later, after what it described as "a careful review of [the] situation and the relevant statutory language." How could the Court pronounce it "implausible" for Congress to have tolerated instability in insurance markets in States with federal Exchanges when even the Government maintained until recently that Congress did exactly that in American Samoa, Guam, the Northern Mariana Islands, Puerto Rico, and the Virgin Islands?

Compounding its errors, the Court forgets that it is no more appropriate to consider one of a statute's purposes in isolation than it is to consider one of its words that way. No law pursues just one purpose at all costs, and no statutory scheme encompasses just one element. Most relevant here, the Affordable Care Act displays a congressional preference for state participation in the establishment of Exchanges: Each State gets the first opportunity to set up its Exchange; States that take up the opportunity receive federal funding for "activities...related to establishing" an Exchange; and the Secretary may establish an Exchange in a State only as a fallback. But setting up and running an Exchange involve significant burdens—meeting strict deadlines, implementing requirements related to the offering of insurance plans, setting up outreach programs, and ensuring that the Exchange is self-sustaining by 2015. A State would have much less reason to take on these burdens if its citizens could receive tax credits no matter who establishes its Exchange. (Now that the Internal

Revenue Service has interpreted § 36B to authorize tax credits every-where, by the way, 34 States have failed to set up their own Exchanges.) So even if making credits available on all Exchanges advances the goal of improving healthcare markets, it frustrates the goal of encouraging state involvement in the implementation of the Act. *This* is what justifies going out of our way to read "established by the State" to mean "estab-lished by the State or not established by the State"?

Worst of all for the repute of today's decision, the Court's rea-soning is largely self-defeating. The Court predicts that making tax credits unavailable in States that do not set up their own Exchanges would cause disastrous economic consequences there. If that is so, however, wouldn't one expect States to react by setting up their own Exchanges? And wouldn't that outcome satisfy two of the Act's goals rather than just one: enabling the Act's reforms to work *and* promoting state involvement in the Act's implementation? The Court protests that the very existence of a federal fallback shows that Congress expected that some States might fail to set up their own Exchanges. So it does. It does not show, however, that Congress expected the number of recalcitrant States to be particularly large. The more accurate the Court's dire eco-nomic predictions, the smaller that number is likely to be. That real-ity destroys the Court's pretense that applying the law as written would imperil "the viability of the entire Affordable Care Act." All in all, the Court's arguments about the law's purpose and design are no more convincing than its arguments about context.

> *Worst of all for the repute of today's decision, the Court's reasoning is largely self-defeating.*

IV

Perhaps sensing the dismal failure of its efforts to show that "established by the State" means "established by the State or the Federal Government," the Court tries to palm off the pertinent statutory phrase as "inartful drafting." This Court, however, has no free-floating power "to rescue Congress from its drafting errors." *Lamie v. United States Trustee* (2004). Only when it is patently obvious to a reasonable reader that a drafting mistake has occurred may a court correct the mistake. The occurrence of a misprint may be apparent from the face of the law, as it is where the Affordable Care Act "creates three separate Section 1563s." But the Court does not pretend that there is any such indication of a drafting error on the face of § 36B. The occurrence of a misprint may also be apparent because a provision decrees an absurd result—a consequence "so monstrous, that all mankind would, without hesitation, unite in rejecting the application." *Sturges*. But § 36B does not come remotely close to satisfying that demanding standard. It is entirely plausible that tax credits were restricted to state Exchanges deliberately—for example, in order to encourage States to establish their own Exchanges. We therefore have no authority to dismiss the terms of the law as a drafting fumble.

Let us not forget that the term "Exchange established by the State" appears twice in § 36B and five more times in other parts of the Act that mention tax credits. What are the odds, do you think, that the same slip of the pen occurred in seven separate places? No provision of the Act—none at all—contradicts the limitation of tax credits to state Exchanges. And as I have already explained, uses of the term "Exchange established by the State" beyond the context of tax credits look anything but accidental. If there was a mistake here, context suggests it was a substantive mistake in designing this part of the law, not a technical mistake in transcribing it.

V

The Court's decision reflects the philosophy that judges should endure whatever interpretive distortions it takes in order to correct a supposed flaw in the statutory machinery. That philosophy ignores the American people's decision to give *Congress* "[a]ll legislative Powers" enumerated in the Constitution. They made Congress, not this Court, responsible for both making laws and mending them. This Court holds only the judicial power—the power to pronounce the law as Congress has enacted it. We lack the prerogative to repair laws that do not work out in practice, just as the people lack the ability to throw us out of office if they dislike the solutions we concoct. We must always remember, therefore, that "[o]ur task is to apply the text, not to improve upon it." *Pavelic & LeFlore v. Marvel Entertainment Group, Div. of Cadence Industries Corp.* (1989).

Trying to make its judge-empowering approach seem respectful of congressional authority, the Court asserts that its decision merely ensures that the Affordable Care Act operates the way Congress "meant [it] to operate." First of all, what makes the Court so sure that Congress "meant" tax credits to be available everywhere? Our only evidence of what Congress meant comes from the terms of the law, and those terms show beyond all question that tax credits are available only on state Exchanges. More importantly, the Court forgets that ours is a government of laws and not of men. That means we are governed by the terms of our laws, not by the unenacted will of our lawmakers. "If Congress enacted into law something different from what it

intended, then it should amend the statute to conform to its intent."
Lamie. In the meantime, this Court "has no roving license... to disregard clear language simply on the view that... Congress 'must have intended' something broader." *Bay Mills.*

Even less defensible, if possible, is the Court's claim that its interpretive approach is justified because this Act "does not reflect the type of care and deliberation that one might expect of such significant legislation." It is not our place to judge the quality of the care and deliberation that went into this or any

Rather than rewriting the law under the pretense of interpreting it, the Court should have left it to Congress to decide what to do about the Act's limitation of tax credits to state Exchanges.

other law. A law enacted by voice vote with no deliberation whatever is fully as binding upon us as one enacted after years of study, months of committee hearings, and weeks of debate. Much less is it our place to make everything come out right when Congress does not do its job properly. It is up to Congress to design its laws with care, and it is up to the people to hold them to account if they fail to carry out that responsibility.

Rather than rewriting the law under the pretense of interpreting it, the Court should have left it to Congress to decide what to do about the Act's limitation of tax credits to state Exchanges. If Congress values above everything else the Act's applicability across the country, it could make tax credits available in every Exchange. If it prizes state involvement in the Act's implementation, it could continue to limit tax credits to state Exchanges while taking other steps to mitigate the economic consequences predicted by the Court. If Congress wants to accommodate both goals, it could make tax credits available everywhere while offering new incentives for States to set up their own Exchanges. And if Congress thinks that the present design of the Act works well enough, it could do nothing. Congress could also do something else altogether, entirely abandoning the structure of the Affordable Care Act. The Court's insistence on making a choice that should be made by Congress both aggrandizes judicial power and encourages congressional lassitude.

Just ponder the significance of the Court's decision to take matters into its own hands. The Court's revision of the law authorizes the Internal Revenue Service to spend tens of billions of dollars every year in tax credits on federal Exchanges. It affects the price of insurance for millions of Americans. It diminishes the participation of the States in the implementation of the Act. It vastly expands the reach of the Act's individual mandate, whose scope depends in part on the availability of credits. What a parody today's decision makes of Hamilton's assurances to the people of New York: "The legislature not only commands the purse but prescribes the rules by which the duties and rights of every citizen are to be regulated. The judiciary, on the contrary, has no influence over... the purse; no direction... of the wealth of society, and can take no active resolution whatever. It may truly be said to have neither force nor will but merely judgment." The Federalist No. 78.

Today's opinion changes the usual rules of statutory interpretation for the sake of the Affordable Care Act. That, alas, is not a novelty. In *National Federation of Independent Business v. Sebelius*, this Court revised major components of the statute in order to save them from unconstitutionality. The Act that Congress passed provides that every individual "shall" maintain insurance or else pay a "penalty." This Court, however, saw that the Commerce Clause does not authorize a federal mandate to buy health insurance. So it rewrote the mandate-cum-penalty as a tax. The Act that Congress passed also requires every State to accept an expansion of its Medicaid program, or else risk losing *all* Medicaid funding. This Court, however, saw that the Spending Clause does not authorize this coercive condition. So it rewrote the law to withhold only the *incremental* funds associated with the Medicaid expansion. Having transformed two major parts of the law, the Court today has turned

> *We should start calling this law SCOTUScare.*

its attention to a third. The Act that Congress passed makes tax credits available only on an "Exchange established by the State." This Court, however, concludes that this limitation would prevent the rest of the Act from working as well as hoped. So it rewrites the law to make tax credits available everywhere. We should start calling this law SCOTUScare.

Perhaps the Patient Protection and Affordable Care Act will attain the enduring status of the Social Security Act or the Taft–Hartley Act; perhaps not. But this Court's two decisions on the Act will surely be remembered through the years. The somersaults of statutory interpretation they have performed ("penalty" means tax, "further [Medicaid] payments to the State" means only incremental Medicaid payments to the State, "established by the State" means not established by the State) will be cited by litigants endlessly, to the confusion of honest jurisprudence. And the cases will publish forever the discouraging truth that the Supreme Court of the United States favors some laws over others, and is prepared to do whatever it takes to uphold and assist its favorites.

I dissent.

CHAPTER SIXTEEN

OTHER "RIGHTS"

❧❦❧

THE SUPREME COURT has occasionally extended constitutional protection to individual freedoms other than those enumerated in the Bill of Rights. Under the theory of "substantive due process," the word "liberty" in the Due Process Clause of the Fourteenth Amendment is deemed to include substantive (and not merely procedural) limitations on a state's power to regulate personal conduct. Courts most commonly use substantive due process to declare certain activities—abortion, child-rearing, marriage, and sodomy, among others—to be "fundamental" rights, even though they are not mentioned specifically or even generally in the Constitution.

When determining whether an asserted right is "fundamental" and therefore constitutionally protected, the Supreme Court will usually look at both the nature of the interest and its historical treatment under the law. If the right asserted involves a highly personal interest, including family or sexual relations, then the Court is likely to deem it a fundamental right. The assertion of a right is also aided by a showing that society has historically accorded strong protection for the activity.

If a right is deemed "fundamental" by the Court, almost any regulation of the activity protected by that right will be invalidated.

Many conservative constitutional scholars, including Justice Scalia, have been highly critical of substantive due process theory. They argue that the lack of textual basis for new rights gives unelected judges too much discretion to give their own preferences the force of law, thereby undermining the rule of law. Scalia wrote succinctly in one case, "The entire practice of using the Due Process Clause to add judicially favored rights to the limitations upon democracy set forth in the Bill of Rights (usually under the rubric of so-called "substantive due process") is in my view judicial usurpation."[1]

Scalia and other critics noted that the Constitution contains procedures for amending it. If additional protections are thought necessary to ward off government interference with personal freedoms, a concerned majority should work to amend the Constitution, as in 1920, when the Nineteenth Amendment, granting women the right to vote, was adopted.

Although some critics accused Scalia of opposing judicial creation of new rights simply because he did not favor the rights being created, the charge does not withstand scrutiny. Scalia opposed the creation of new rights even when he was sympathetic to the claimant. Indeed, he voted against constitutional protection for many freedoms championed by political conservatives, including, among others, the "right" of parents to direct the upbringing of their children and the "right" of companies to avoid having to pay "excessive" punitive damage awards. In another case, a taxpayer asked the Court to strike down on substantive due process grounds a law that increased his taxes retroactively. The Supreme Court rejected that claim in *United States v. Carlton.* In his concurring opinion, Scalia wrote, "I welcome this recognition that the

Due Process Clause does not prevent retroactive taxes, since I believe that the Due Process Clause guarantees no substantive rights, but only (as it says) process."[2]

Scalia went on to note that the Court seemed much more sympathetic to personal rights, such as abortion, than to economic rights, such as that asserted in *Carlton*. He concluded, "The picking and choosing among various rights to be accorded 'substantive due process' protection is alone enough to arouse suspicion; but the categorical and inexplicable exclusion of so-called economic rights (even though the Due Process Clause explicitly applies to property) unquestionably involves policymaking rather than neutral legal analysis. I would follow the text of the Constitution, which sets forth certain substantive rights that cannot be taken away, and adds, beyond that, a right to due process when life, liberty, or property is to be taken away."[3]

The opinions below—involving assertions of a new right to refuse medical treatment and a right of parents to determine who may visit their children—give substance to the view that Scalia was consistent in his opposition to judicially created rights. The Court accepted both into the Constitution; Scalia, neither.

CRUZAN v. MISSOURI DEPARTMENT OF HEALTH (1990)

Nancy Cruzan was involved in an automobile accident and suffered severe brain damage. In a "persistent vegetative state," she had some motor reflexes but was oblivious to her surroundings. She received nutrition through a feeding-and-hydration tube. After it became apparent Cruzan would not regain her mental faculties, her parents sought a court order directing the removal of her feeding-and-hydration tube. It was known to all involved that removal of the tube would result in Cruzan's death. The Supreme Court of Missouri refused to approve the order because it did not find "clear and convincing evidence" that Cruzan would have wanted to withdraw lifesaving equipment under such circumstances.

The Supreme Court, in a closely divided 5–4 decision, held that Cruzan had a "liberty" interest protected by the Fourteenth Amendment to refuse unwanted medical procedures. The majority, however, ruled that the State of Missouri also had an important interest in preserving life. This interest justified a requirement that there is "clear and convincing evidence" of an incompetent patient's wish to decline life-sustaining treatment. Because this level of evidence was not present, the Court agreed with the Missouri Supreme Court's ruling against the Cruzans.

Justice Scalia wrote an opinion agreeing with the Court's decision but disagreeing with its approach. Specifically, Scalia objected to the majority's determination that refusal of medical treatment was constitutionally protected. He argued that the "right" to refuse treatment was equivalent to a right to commit suicide, which had never been recognized by the Court and which was in plain opposition to the nation's legal tradition of prohibiting suicide.

~✦◦✦◦✦~

JUSTICE SCALIA, CONCURRING.

The various opinions in this case portray quite clearly the difficult, indeed agonizing, questions that are presented by the constantly increasing power of science to keep the human body alive for longer than any reasonable person would want to inhabit it. The States have begun to grapple with these problems through legislation. I am concerned, from the tenor of today's opinions, that we are poised to confuse that enterprise as successfully as we have confused the enterprise of legislating concerning abortion—requiring it to be conducted against a background of federal constitutional imperatives that are unknown because they are being newly crafted from Term to Term. That would be a great misfortune.

While I agree with the Court's analysis today, and therefore join in its opinion, I would have preferred that we announce, clearly and promptly, that the federal courts have no business in this field; that American law has always accorded the State the power to prevent, by force if necessary, suicide—including suicide by refusing to take appropriate measures necessary to preserve one's life; that the point at which life becomes "worthless," and the point at which the means necessary to preserve it become "extraordinary" or "inappropriate," are neither set forth in the Constitution nor known to the nine Justices of this Court any better than they are known to nine people picked at random from the Kansas City telephone directory; and hence, that even when it is demonstrated by clear and convincing evidence that a patient no longer wishes certain measures to be taken to preserve her life, it is up to the citizens of Missouri to decide, through their elected representatives, whether that wish will be honored. It is quite impossible (because the Constitution says nothing about the matter) that those citizens will decide upon a line

> *The point at which the means necessary to preserve life become "extraordinary" or "inappropriate," are neither set forth in the Constitution nor known to the nine justices of this Court any better than they are known to nine people picked at random from the Kansas City telephone directory.*

less lawful than the one we would choose; and it is unlikely (because we know no more about "life-and-death" than they do) that they will decide upon a line less reasonable.

The text of the Due Process Clause does not protect individuals against deprivations of liberty *simpliciter.* It protects them against deprivations of liberty "without due process of law." To determine that such a deprivation would not occur if Nancy Cruzan were forced to take nourishment against her will, it is unnecessary to reopen the historically recurrent debate over whether "due process" includes substantive restrictions. It is at least true that no "substantive due process" claim can be maintained unless the claimant demonstrates that the State has deprived him of a right historically and traditionally protected against State interference. That cannot possibly be established here.

At common law in England, a suicide—defined as one who "deliberately puts an end to his own existence, or commits any unlawful malicious act, the consequence of which is his own death," 4 W. Blackstone, Commentaries—was criminally liable. Although the States abolished the penalties imposed by the common law (i.e., forfeiture and ignominious burial), they did so to spare the innocent family, and not to legitimize the act. Case law at the time of the Fourteenth Amendment generally held that assisting suicide was a criminal offense. . . . And most States that did not explicitly prohibit assisted suicide in 1868 recognized, when the issue arose in the 50 years following the Fourteenth Amendment's ratification, that assisted and (in some cases) attempted suicide were unlawful. Thus, "there is no significant support for the claim that a right to suicide is so rooted in our tradition that it may be deemed 'fundamental' or 'implicit in the concept of ordered liberty.'"

Petitioners rely on three distinctions to separate Nancy Cruzan's case from ordinary suicide: (1) that she is permanently incapacitated and in pain; (2) that she would bring on her death not by any affirmative act but by merely declining treatment that provides nourishment; and (3) that preventing her from effectuating her presumed wish to die requires violation of her bodily integrity. None of these suffices. Suicide was not excused even when committed "to avoid those ills which [persons] had not the fortitude to endure." 4 Blackstone. "The life of those to whom life has become a burden—of those who are hopelessly diseased or fatally wounded—nay, even the lives of criminals condemned to death, are under the protection of the law, equally as the lives of those who are in the full tide of life's enjoyment, and anxious to continue to live." *Blackburn v. State*, 23 Ohio St. 146 (1873). Thus, a man who prepared a poison, and placed it within reach of his wife, "to put an end to her suffering" from a terminal illness was convicted of murder, *People v. Roberts*, 211 Mich. 187 (1920); the "incurable suffering of the suicide, as a legal question, could hardly affect the degree of criminality...." Note, 30 Yale L.J. 408 (1921) (discussing *Roberts*). Nor would the imminence of the patient's death have affected liability. "The lives of all are equally under the protection of the law, and under that protection to their last moment.... [Assisted suicide] is declared by the law to be murder, irrespective of the wishes or the condition of the party to whom the poison is administered...." *Blackburn*.

The second asserted distinction—suggested by the recent cases canvassed by the Court concerning the right to refuse treatment—relies on the dichotomy between action and inaction. Suicide, it is said, consists of an affirmative act to end one's life; refusing treatment is not an affirmative act "causing" death, but merely a passive acceptance of the natural

It would not make much sense to say that one may not kill oneself by walking into the sea, but may sit on the beach until submerged by the incoming tide.

process of dying. I readily acknowledge that the distinction between action and inaction has some bearing upon the legislative judgment of what ought to be prevented as suicide—though even there it would seem to me unreasonable to draw the line precisely between action and inaction, rather than between various forms of inaction. It would not make much sense to say that one may not kill oneself by walking into the sea, but may sit on the beach until submerged by the incoming tide; or that one may not intentionally lock oneself into a cold storage locker, but may refrain from coming indoors when the temperature drops below freezing. Even as a legislative matter, in other words, the intelligent line does not fall between action and inaction, but between those forms of inaction that consist of abstaining from "ordinary" care and those that consist of abstaining from "excessive" or "heroic" measures. Unlike action vs. inaction, that is not a line to be discerned by logic or legal analysis, and we should not pretend that it is.

But to return to the principal point for present purposes: the irrelevance of the action-inaction distinction. Starving oneself to death is no different from putting a gun to one's temple as far as the common law definition of suicide is concerned; the cause of death in both cases is the suicide's conscious decision to "pu[t] an end to his own existence." 4 Blackstone. Of course, the common law rejected the action-inaction distinction in other contexts involving the taking of human life as well. In the prosecution of a parent for the starvation death of her infant, it was no defense that the infant's death was "caused" by no action of the parent, but by the natural process of starvation, or by the infant's natural inability to provide for itself. A physician, moreover, could be criminally liable for failure to provide care that could have extended the patient's life, even if death was immediately caused by the underlying disease that the physician failed to treat.

It is not surprising, therefore, that the early cases considering the claimed right to refuse medical treatment dismissed as specious the nice distinction between "passively submitting to death and actively seeking it. The distinction may be merely verbal, as it would be if an adult sought death by starvation instead of a drug. If the State may interrupt one mode of self-destruction, it may with equal authority interfere with the other." *John F. Kennedy Memorial Hosp. v. Heston*, 58 N.J. 576 (1971).

The third asserted basis of distinction—that frustrating Nancy Cruzan's wish to die in the present case requires interference with her bodily integrity—is likewise inadequate, because such interference is impermissible only if one begs the question whether her refusal to undergo the treatment on her own is suicide. It has always been lawful not only for the State, but even for private citizens, to interfere with bodily integrity to prevent a felony. That general rule has of course been applied to suicide. At common law, even a private person's use of force to prevent suicide was privileged. It is not even reasonable, much less required by the Constitution, to maintain that, although the State has the right to prevent a person from slashing his wrists, it does not have the power to apply physical force to prevent him from doing so, nor the power, should he succeed, to apply, coercively if necessary, medical measures to stop the flow of blood. The state-run hospital, I am certain, is not liable under 42 U.S.C. 1983 for violation of constitutional rights, nor the private hospital liable under general tort law, if, in a State where suicide is unlawful, it pumps out the stomach of a person who has intentionally taken an overdose of barbiturates, despite that person's wishes to the contrary.

The dissents of Justices Brennan and Stevens make a plausible case for our intervention here only by embracing—the latter explicitly and the former by implication—a political principle that the States are free to adopt, but that is demonstrably not imposed by the Constitution. "The State," says Justice Brennan, "has no legitimate general interest in someone's life, completely abstracted from the interest of the person living that life, that could outweigh the person's choice *to avoid medical treatment*" (emphasis added). The italicized phrase sounds moderate enough, and is all that is needed to cover the present case—but the proposition cannot logically be so limited. One who accepts it must also accept, I think, that the State has no such legitimate interest that could outweigh "the person's choice to put an end to her life." Similarly, if one agrees with Justice Brennan that "the State's general interest in life must accede to Nancy Cruzan's particularized and intense interest in self-determination *in her choice of medical treatment*" (emphasis added), he must also believe that the State must accede to her "particularized and intense interest in self-determination *in her choice whether to continue living or to die.*" For insofar as balancing the relative interests of the State and the individual is concerned, there is nothing distinctive about accepting death through the refusal of "medical treatment," as opposed to accepting it through the refusal of food, or through the failure to shut off the engine and get out of the car after parking in one's garage after work. Suppose that Nancy Cruzan were in precisely the condition she is in today, except that she could be fed and digest food and water without artificial assistance. How is the State's "interest" in keeping her alive thereby increased, or her interest in deciding whether she wants to continue living reduced?

It seems to me, in other words, that Justice Brennan's position ultimately rests upon the proposition that it is none of the State's business if a person wants to commit suicide. Justice Stevens is explicit on the point: "Choices about death touch the core of liberty.... [N]ot much may be said with confidence about death unless it is said from faith, and that alone is reason enough to protect the freedom to conform choices about death to individual conscience." This is a view that some societies have held, and that our States are free to adopt if they wish. But it is not a view imposed by our constitutional traditions, in which the power of the State to prohibit suicide is unquestionable.

What I have said above is not meant to suggest that I would think it desirable, if we were sure that Nancy Cruzan wanted to die, to keep her alive by the means at issue here. I assert only that the Constitution has nothing to say about the subject. To raise up a constitutional right here, we would have to create out of nothing (for it exists neither in text nor tradition) some constitutional principle whereby, although the State may insist that an individual come in out of the cold and eat food, it may not insist that he take medicine; and although it may pump his stomach empty of poison he has ingested, it may not fill his stomach with food he has failed to ingest. Are there, then, no reasonable and humane limits that ought not to be exceeded in requiring an individual to preserve his own life? There obviously are, but they are not set forth in the Due Process Clause. What assures us that those limits will not be exceeded is the same constitutional guarantee that is the source of most

> *What I have said above is not meant to suggest that I would think it desirable, if we were sure that Nancy Cruzan wanted to die, to keep her alive by the means at issue here. I assert only that the Constitution has nothing to say about the subject.*

of our protection—what protects us, for example, from being assessed a tax of 100% of our income above the subsistence level, from being forbidden to drive cars, or from being required to send our children to school for 10 hours a day, none of which horribles is categorically prohibited by the Constitution. Our salvation is the Equal Protection Clause, which requires the democratic majority to accept for themselves and their loved ones what they impose on you and me. This Court need not, and has no authority to, inject itself into every field of human activity where irrationality and oppression may theoretically occur, and if it tries to do so, it will destroy itself.

TROXEL v. GRANVILLE (2000)

A Washington State law permitted "any person" to petition a court for visitation rights. If a court found that allowing a person—a noncustodial parent or other relative, for instance—to have visitation rights was in "the best interests of the child," the court could authorize the visits.

In *Troxel v. Granville*, grandparents who were estranged from their daughter used the law to petition to gain visitation rights with their granddaughters. The mother objected to the grandparents' proposed visitation schedule. The state supreme court found the law unconstitutional because it violated the substantive due process right of the mother to direct the upbringing of her children.

The Supreme Court of the United States agreed that the law was invalid. A plurality of four justices, relying on a few Court precedents, ruled that the law violated "the fundamental rights of parents to make decisions concerning the care, custody, and control of their children." Two concurring justices (including Justice Clarence Thomas) agreed with the plurality that parental rights are "fundamental" rights guaranteed by the Due Process Clause of the Fourteenth Amendment.

Justice Scalia dissented. Though clearly sympathetic to the idea that parents should be free to raise their children as they see fit, he opposed extension of an unenumerated and judicially created constitutional right. Put simply, he said he did not have authority as a judge to strike down a state law that violates his sense of parental authority but that does not violate a right contained in the Constitution of the United States.

~∽≪◦≫∽~

JUSTICE SCALIA, DISSENTING.

In my view, a right of parents to direct the upbringing of their children is among the "unalienable Rights" with which the Declaration of Independence proclaims "all Men . . . are endowed by their Creator." And in my view that right is also among the "othe[r] [rights] retained by the people" which the Ninth Amendment says the Constitution's enumeration of rights "shall not be construed to deny or disparage." The Declaration of Independence, however, is not a legal prescription conferring powers upon the courts; and the Constitution's refusal to "deny or disparage" other rights is far removed from affirming any one of them, and even farther removed from authorizing judges to identify what they might be, and to enforce the judges' list against laws duly enacted by the people. Consequently, while I would think it entirely compatible

In my view, a right of parents to direct the upbringing of their children is among the "unalienable Rights" with which the Declaration of Independence proclaims "all Men . . . are endowed by their Creator."

with the commitment to representative democracy set forth in the founding documents to argue, in legislative chambers or in electoral campaigns, that the state has *no power* to interfere with parents' authority over the rearing of their children, I do not believe that the power which the Constitution confers upon me *as a judge* entitles me to deny legal effect to laws that (in my view) infringe upon what is (in my view) that unenumerated right.

Only three holdings of this Court rest in whole or in part upon a substantive constitutional right of parents to direct the upbringing of their children—two of them from an era rich in substantive due process holdings that have since been repudiated. The sheer diversity of today's opinions persuades me that the theory of unenumerated parental rights underlying these three cases has small claim to *stare decisis* protection. A legal principle that can be thought to produce such diverse outcomes in the relatively simple case before us here is not a legal principle that has induced substantial reliance. While I would not now overrule those earlier cases (that has not been urged), neither would I extend the theory upon which they rested to this new context.

Judicial vindication of "parental rights" under a Constitution that does not even mention them requires (as Justice Kennedy's opinion rightly points out) not only a judicially crafted definition of parents, but also—unless, as no one believes, the parental rights are to be absolute— judicially approved assessments of "harm to the child" and judicially defined gradations of other persons (grandparents, extended family, adoptive family in an adoption later found to be invalid, long-term guardians, etc.) who may have some claim against the wishes of the parents. If we embrace this unenumerated right, I think it obvious— whether we affirm or reverse the judgment here, or remand as Justice Stevens or Justice Kennedy would do—that we will be ushering in a new regime of judicially prescribed, and federally prescribed, family law. I have no reason to believe that federal judges will be better at this than state legislatures; and state legislatures have the great advantages of doing harm in a more circumscribed area, of being able to correct their mistakes in a flash, and of being removable by the people.

For these reasons, I would reverse the judgment below.

SCALIA'S LEGACY

~◦◦◦~

TRYING TO PREDICT Justice Scalia's legacy so soon after his passing would be futile. Indeed, many public officials like to say that history will judge their influence, though they often add that it depends on who writes the history. So many factors will shape Justice Scalia's legacy, including changes in the Court and country that we cannot possibly foresee today.

Yet any meaningful evaluation of Scalia's legacy must include the views and insights of his peers. For that reason, it seems worthwhile, at the close of this volume of Scalia's greatest opinions, to record some of the opinions of his colleagues and critics, who observed his work during his lifetime.

"Volumes have been written about various courts—the Warren Court, the Rehnquist Court, the Roberts Court. But in many ways the current conservative majority, whose decisions often reflect an originalist view of the Constitution, can be seen as the Scalia Court."
—*New York Times*, editorial, February 13, 2016[1]

"For some 29 years he defended the original meaning of the Constitution against the legal fads and inventions of more political Justices, bequeathing a judicial legacy even in dissent that will carry long into the future.

"Justice Scalia may have been more consequential than any Justice whose jurisprudence so rarely carried a majority of the Court. He was appointed by Ronald Reagan in 1986 when he and we anticipated a conservative restoration on the bench. But mistakes by GOP Presidents and the confirmation defeat of Robert Bork kept Justice Scalia in the minority for too much of his tenure. He also found himself in dissent more often than he would have liked when judicial conservatives like Chief Justices William Rehnquist and John Roberts chose to behave like politicians more than judges."

—*Wall Street Journal*, editorial, February 16, 2016[2]

"If [Justice John] Harlan was 'The Great Dissenter,' then perhaps Scalia was the 'The Unrelenting Provoker.' By forcing his ideological adversaries to engage with his ideas, both through his intellectual rigor and through personal charisma, Scalia reshaped and enriched legal discourse on the court, in the legal academy, and throughout the legal profession. In turn, he won the war even when he lost his hardest-fought battles. As Justice Elena Kagan once said of his approach to statutory interpretation: 'We're all textualists now.'"

—Professor Laurence Tribe, Harvard Law School[3]

"[Justice Scalia] was not only one of the most important justices in the nation's history; he was also among the greatest. With Oliver Wendell Holmes and Robert Jackson, he counts as one of the court's three best writers. Who else would say, in a complex case involving the meaning of a statute, that Congress does not 'hide elephants in mouseholes'?

"But his greatness does not lie solely in his way with words. Nor does it have anything to do with conventional divisions between liberals and conservatives (or abortion, or same-sex marriage). Instead it lies in his abiding commitment to one ideal above any other: the rule of law."

—Professor Cass Sunstein, Harvard Law School[4]

"It was Scalia's constitutional passion, in the end, that made him such a towering figure in 20th-century jurisprudence. His insistence that principled citizens should try to separate their personal convictions from their constitutional conclusions inspired a generation of young lawyers who did not always share his policy views—including me.... [Scalia ranks] among the most influential justices of the 20th century."

—Professor Jeffrey Rosen, George Washington University Law School, President and CEO of the National Constitution Center[5]

"[Justice Scalia and I] disagreed now and then, but when I wrote for the Court and received a Scalia dissent, the opinion ultimately released was notably better than my initial circulation. Justice Scalia nailed all the weak spots—the 'applesauce' and 'argle bargle'—and gave me just what I needed to strengthen the majority opinion. He was a jurist of captivating brilliance and wit, with a rare talent to make even the most sober judge laugh. The press referred to his 'energetic fervor,' 'astringent intellect,' 'peppery prose,' 'acumen,' and 'affability,' all apt descriptions. He was eminently quotable, his pungent opinions so clearly stated that his words never slipped from the reader's grasp."

—Justice Ruth Bader Ginsburg, U.S. Supreme Court

"In years to come any history of the Supreme Court will, and must, recount the wisdom, scholarship, and technical brilliance that Justice Scalia brought to the Court. His insistence on demanding standards shaped the work of the Court in its private discussions, its oral arguments, and its written opinions.

"Yet these historic achievements are all the more impressive and compelling because the foundations of Justice Scalia's jurisprudence, the driving force in all his work, and his powerful personality were shaped by an unyielding commitment to the Constitution of the United States and to the highest ethical and moral standards."

—Justice Anthony Kennedy, U.S. Supreme Court

"Nino Scalia will go down in history as one of the most transformational Supreme Court Justices of our nation. His views on interpreting texts have changed the way all of us think and talk about the law. I admired Nino for his brilliance and erudition, his dedication and energy, and his peerless writing."

—Justice Elena Kagan, U.S. Supreme Court

"[Scalia] was a towering figure who will be remembered as one of the most important figures in the history of the Supreme Court and a scholar who deeply influenced our legal culture."

—Justice Samuel Alito, U.S. Supreme Court

ACKNOWLEDGMENTS

I HAVE TO START BY recognizing Justice Scalia. When I got the news of his passing on February 13, 2016, I was at my computer trying to finish this book. It was a bit eerie sitting alone surrounded by stacks of books and articles about him and by folders filled with his writings.

After all the obvious thoughts and questions bounced through my head—his wife and nine kids must be hurting; had he been ill?—I had a depressing (and self-pitying) thought: I would never get to read another Scalia opinion. For some reason, I had never considered the obvious: that some day these brilliant novellas would cease to be published. And that this gifted judge's body of work was, like life itself, finite. He was a lifelong inspiration.

I want to acknowledge my parents, both of whom passed away between publication of *Scalia Dissents* and this book. Both reveled in my accomplishments and suffered through my setbacks. They inspired me in very different ways.

I also want to recognize the good people of FAMM, especially my boss and friend, Julie Stewart. I shudder to think what might have happened to me if I hadn't joined their team of smart and happy warriors several years ago.

Lastly, I want to thank my family. I happen to not like the increasingly saccharine dedications found these days in the acknowledgment sections of books. Presumably these professions of love and admiration would have greater effect if made in person and in private. Alas, when your children are thirteen and ten, they think it's pretty cool to see their names in print. And I promised them. So, to Kiley and Audrey, you know I love you. Being your dad is the best part of my life. You both are smart, funny, and resilient. You've already been forced to deal with life's unexpected twists and falls, but just like on our trips to Six Flags, there's no one I would rather share this ride with than you.

NOTES

INTRODUCTION

1. Richard H. Pildes, quoted in "How Antonin Scalia Changed America," *Politico Magazine*, February 14, 2016, http://www.politico.com/ magazine/story/2016/02/antonin-scalia-how-he-changed-america– 213631#ixzz40FwY2o95.
2. Frost, 188 (quoting Aristotle, *The Rhetoric of Aristotle* (Lane Cooper trans., 1932).
3. *Romer v. Evans*, 517 U.S. 620, 653 (1996) (Scalia, J., dissenting).
4. *U.S. v. Windsor*, 570 U.S. __ (2013) (Scalia, J., dissenting).
5. *King v. Burwell*, 576 U.S. __ (2015) (Scalia, J., dissenting).
6. *Pope v. Illinois*, 481 U.S. 497, 504 (1987) (Scalia, J., concurring).
7. *Kyles v. Whitley*, 514 U.S. 419, 466–467 (1995) (Scalia, J., dissenting).
8. *MCI Telecommunications v. AT&T*, 512 U.S. 218, 227 (1994).
9. *Lamb's Chapel v. Center Moriches School District*, 508 U.S. 384, 398 (1993) (Scalia, J., concurring).
10. *Webster v. Reproductive Health Services*, 492 U.S. 490, 537 (1989) (Scalia, J., concurring).
11. *Good News Club v. Milford Central School*, 533 U.S. 98, 121 (2001) (Scalia, J., concurring).
12. *Morse v. Republican Party of Virginia*, 517 U.S. 186, 245 (1996) (Scalia, J., dissenting).
13. *Board of Commissioners, Wabaunsee County v. Umbehr*, 518 U.S. 668, 711 (1996) (Scalia, J., dissenting).
14. *Sosa v. Alvarez-Machain*, 124 S.Ct. 2739, 2776 (2004) (Scalia, J., concurring).

15. *Elmbrook School District v. Doe*, 573 U.S. __ (2014) (Scalia, J., dissenting from denial of certiorari).

Chapter One: Scalia's Philosophy

1. Scalia, "The Rule of Law," 1184.
2. Ibid., 1179.
3. Schultz and Smith, 88.
4. *Maryland v. Craig*, 497 U.S. 836 (1990).
5. Scalia, "Originalism," 862.
6. *United States v. Eichman*, 496 U.S. 310 (1990).
7. *Kyollo v. United States*, 533 U.S. 27 (2001).
8. Scalia, *A Matter of Interpretation*, 46.
9. Scalia, "Originalism," 856.
10. Scalia, Remarks at Catholic University.
11. Starr, 25,
12. Zlotnick, 1381,
13. Scalia, *A Matter of Interpretation*, 46.
14. Ibid.
15. Ibid., 37–38.
16. United States Senate, S. Hrg. 99-1064 (statement of Sen. Kennedy).
17. Mauro.
18. Brisbin, 12.
19. Simon, 138.
20. Reid, 146 Cong. Rec., S2653.
21. Reid, 145 Cong. Rec., S1579.
22. See Chemerinksy, 392, and Zlotnick, 1416.
23. Koskela, 32.
24. Zlotnick, 1424.
25. See, e.g., 143 Cong. Rec. H5185 (daily ed. July 15, 1997) (statement of Rep. Barney Frank).
26. Mauro.
27. Schultz and Smith, xvi.
28. *Casey*, 851.
29. See, e.g., Failinger, 471.
30. Benjamin Morris, "How Scalia Became the Most Influential Conservative Jurist since the New Deal," FiveThirtyEight, February 14, 2016, http://

fivethirtyeight.com/features/how-scalia-became-the-most-influential-
conservative-jurist-since-the-new-deal/.

31. Ibid.

32. Schultz and Smith, xiii.

CHAPTER TWO: INTERPRETING LAWS

1. *Smith v. United States*, 508 U.S. 223 (1993).

2. *Wisconsin Public Intervenor v. Mortier*, 501 U.S. 597, 621 (1991) (Scalia, J., concurring in the judgment).

3. *Conroy v. Aniskoff*, 507 U.S. 511, 519 (1993) (Scalia, J., concurring in the judgment).

4. Ibid.

5. *Intel Corp. v. Advanced Micro Devices, Inc.*, 542 U.S. 241, 267 (2004) (Scalia, J., concurring in the judgment).

6. *Nixon v. Missouri Municipal League*, 124 S. Ct. 1555, 1566 (Scalia, J., concurring in the judgment).

CHAPTER THREE: SEPARATION OF POWERS

1. Clark, 754.

2. Fox and McAllister, 244-245.

3. *Mistretta v. United States*, 488 U.S. 361 (1989).

4. Schultz and Smith, 89.

5. *Plaut v. Spendthrift Farm*, 514 U.S. 211, 239 (1995).

CHAPTER FOUR: RACE

1. *Bolling v. Sharpe*, 347 U.S. 497 (1954).

2. *Fullilove v. Klutznick*, 448 U.S. 448, 507) (1980) (Marshall, J., concurring).

CHAPTER FIVE: ABORTION

1. *Griswold v. Connecticut*, 381 U.S. 479 (1965).

2. *Eisenstadt v. Baird*, 405 U.S. 438 (1972).

3. *Hodgson v. Minnesota*, 497 U.S. 417 (1990).

4. Ibid., 480 (Scalia, J., concurring and dissenting)

5. *Akron v. Akron Center for Reproductive Health*, 462 U.S. 416, 458 (1983) (O'Connor, J., dissenting).

Chapter Seven: Death Penalty

1. *Furman v. Georgia*, 408 U.S. 238 (1972).
2. *Rhodes v. Chapman*, 452 U.S. 337, 346 (1981), quoting *Trop v. Dulles*, 356 U.S. 86, 101 (1958) (plurality opinion).
3. *Thompson v. Oklahoma*, 487 U.S. 815, 859 (1988).(Scalia, J., dissenting).
4. *Callins v. Collins*, 510 U.S. 1141 (1994).

Chapter Eight: Rights of the Accused

1. *Sykes v. United States*, 561 U. S. ___ (2010).
2. *Johnson v. United States*, 576 U.S. ___ (2015).

Chapter Nine: Religious Freedom

1. *Everson* v. *Board of Education*, 330 U.S. 1 (1947).
2. Ibid., 15.
3. See, e.g., Carter, 109.
4. Sullivan, 449.
5. *Goldman v. Weinberger*, 475 U.S. 503 (1986).
6. *Sherberg v. Verner*, 374 U.S. 398 (1963).
7. *Employment Division of Oregon v. Smith*, 494 U.S. 872, 890 (1990).
8. *Board of Education of Kiryas Joel v. Grumet*, 512 U.S. 687 (1994) (Scalia, J., dissenting) (quoting *Zorach v. Clauson*, 343 U.S. 306 (1952)).
9. *Durham v. United States*, 94 U.S. App. D.C. 228 (1954).

Chapter Eleven: Homosexuality

1. *Bowers v. Hardwick*, 478 U.S. 186, 191 (1986).
2. 116 U.S. 620 (1996).
3. Ibid., 637 (Scalia, J., dissenting).

Chapter Twelve: Sexual Equality

1. *Craig v. Boren*, 429 U.S. 190 (1976).
2. *Rostker v. Goldberg*, 453 U.S. 57 (1981).
3. *Michael M. v. Superior Court of Sonoma County*, 450 U.S. 464 (1981).

Chapter Thirteen: Free Speech

1. Term comes from Justice Oliver Wendell Holmes in *Abrams v. United States* 250 U.S. 616, 630 (1919) (Holmes, J., dissenting).
2. *McConnell v. Federal Election Commission*, 124 S.Ct. 619 (2003) (Thomas, J., concurring and dissenting).
3. 503 U.S. 703 (2000).
4. Ibid., 742 (Scalia, J., dissenting).
5. Ibid., 749.
6. Ibid., 764.
7. Public Law 107-155 (2002).
8. *FEC v. Wisconsin Right to Life*, 551 U.S. 449.

Chapter Fourteen: Non-Speech and Un-Free Speech

1. *Barnes v. Glen Theater, Inc.*, 501 U.S. 560 (1991) and *City of Erie v. Pap's A.M.*, 529 U.S. 277 (2000).

Chapter Sixteen: Other "Rights"

1. *Chicago v. Morales*, 527 U.S. 41, 85 (1999) (Scalia, J., dissenting).
2. *United States v. Carlton*, 512 U.S. 26, 40 (1994) (Scalia, J., concurring in judgment).
3. Ibid., 41–42.

Epilogue: Scalia's Legacy

1. Editorial Board, "Justice Antonin Scalia's Supreme Court Legacy," *New York Times*, February 13, 2016, http://www.nytimes.com/2016/02/13/opinion/justice-antonin-scalias-supreme-court-legacy.html?_r=0.
2. "Scalia's Legacy and the Court," *Wall Street Journal*, February 16, 2016, http://www.wsj.com/articles/scalias-legacy-and-the-court-1455467765.
3. Laurence H. Tribe, "The Legacy of Antonin Scalia—the Unrelenting Provoker," *Boston Globe*, February 17, 2016, https://www.bostonglobe.com/opinion/2016/02/17/the-legacy-antonin-scalia-unrelenting-provoker/mH40dhHDvEPXCzyXCLfxqI/story.html.

4. Cass Sunstein, "The Antonin Scalia I Knew Will Be Greatly Missed," *Chicago Tribune*, February 15, 2016, http://www.chicagotribune.com/news/sns-wp-blm-scalia-comment-bg-5713e110-d401-11e5-a65b-587e721fb231-20160215-story.html.

5. Jeffrey Rosen, "What Made Antonin Scalia Great," *Atlantic*, February 15, 2016, http://www.theatlantic.com/politics/archive/2016/02/what-made-antonin-scalia-great/462837/.

BIBLIOGRAPHY

❦

Barnett, Randy. "Scalia's Infidelity: A Critique of Faint-Hearted Originalism." http://scholarship.law.georgetown.edu/facpub/841, 2006.

Barron, Jerome A., and C. Thomas Dienes. *Constitutional Law*, 6th ed. West Group, 2003.

Biskupic, Joan. *American Original: The Life and Constitution of Supreme Court Justice Antonin Scalia.* Macmillan, 2009.

Bork, Robert H. *The Tempting of America: The Political Seduction of the Law.* The Free Press, 1990.

Brisbin, Jr., Richard A. *Justice Antonin Scalia and the Conservative Revival.* The Johns Hopkins University Press, 1997.

Burton, Shawn. "Justice Scalia's Methodological Approach to Judicial Decision-Making: Political Actor or Strategic Institutionalist?" *University of Toledo Law Review* 34 (Spring 2003): 575.

Bybee, Jay S. "Printz, The Unitary Executive, and the Fire in the Trash Can: Has Justice Scalia Picked the Court's Pocket?" *Notre Dame Law Review* 77 (November 2001): 269.

Calabresi, Steven G., and Justin Braga. "The Jurisprudence of Justice Antonin Scalia: A Response to Professor Bruce Allen Murphy and Professor Justin Driver." 2015, http://papers.ssrn.com/sol3/papers.cfm?abstract_id=2569336.

Carter, Stephen L. *The Culture of Disbelief: How American Law and Politics Trivialize Religious Devotion.* Basic Books, 1993.

Chemerinsky, Erwin. "The Jurisprudence of Justice Scalia: A Critical Appraisal." *Hawaii Law Review* 22 (Summer 2000): 385.

Clark, Bradford R. "The Constitutional Structure and the Jurisprudence of Justice Scalia." *St. Louis Law Journal* 47(Spring 2003): 753.

Colby, Thomas B. "A Constitutional Hierarchy of Religions? Justice Scalia, The Ten Commandments, and the Future of the Establishment Clause." 100 *Northwestern University Law Review* 1097 (2006).

Driver, Justin. "How Scalia's Beliefs Completely Changed the Supreme Court." *New Republic*, September 9, 2014.

Elsasser, Glen. "No Contest: Top Court's Top Fighter is Scalia, Verbal Combat is Conservative's Forte." *Chicago Tribune*, May 27, 1997.

Eskridge, Jr., William N. "The New Textualism." *UCLA Law Review* 37 (April 1990): 621.

Failinger, Marie A. "Not Mere Rhetoric: On Wasting or Claiming Your Legacy, Justice Scalia." *University of Toledo Law Review* 34 (Spring 2003): 425.

Fox, Autumn, and Stephen R. McAllister. "An Eagle Soaring: The Jurisprudence of Justice Antonin Scalia." *Campbell Law Review* 19 (Spring 1997): 223.

Frank, Barney. Statement. *Congressional Record* 143, daily ed. (July 15, 1997): H 5185.

Friedman, Lawrence M. *American Law: An Introduction.* 2nd ed. W.W. Norton & Company, 1988.

Frost, Michael. "Justice Scalia's Rhetoric of Dissent: A Greco–Roman Analysis of Scalia's Advocacy in the VMI Case." *Kentucky Law Review* 91 (2002 / 2003): 167.

Gerhardt, Michael J. "A Tale of Two Textualists: A Critical Comparison of Justices Black and Scalia." *Boston University Law Review* 74 (January 1994): 25.

Hall, Kermit L., ed. *The Oxford Guide to United States Supreme Court Decisions.* Oxford University Press, 1999.

Kannar, George. "The Constitutional Catechism of Antonin Scalia." *Yale Law Journal* 99 (April 1990): 1297.

Karkkainen, Bradley C. "'Plain Meaning': Justice Scalia's Jurisprudence of Strict Statutory Construction." *Harvard Journal of Law & Public Policy* 17 (Spring 1994). 401.

Kelley, William K. "Justice Antonin Scalia and the Long Game." *George Washington Law Review.* 2012 (found online at: http://papers.ssrn.com/sol3/papers.cfm?abstract_id=2037985).

Koby, Michael H. "The Supreme Court's Declining Reliance on Legislative History: The Impact of Justice Scalia's Critique." *Harvard Journal on Legis.* 36 (Summer 1999): 369.

Koskela, Alice. "Scalia Shows Textualists Have a Sense of Humor." *Advocate* (Idaho) 43 (October 2000): 31.

Lamparello, Adam, and Charles E. MacLean. "It's the People's Constitution, Stupid: Two Liberals Pay Tribute to Antonin Scalia's Legacy." 44 *University of Memphis Law Review*, 2014. http://papers.ssrn.com/sol3/papers.cfm?abstract_id=2436952.

Marquand, Robert. "High Court's Colorful Man in Black." *The Christian Science Monitor*, March 3, 1998.

Mauro, Tony. "High Court Adjourns for the Summer Intact." *Legal Times*, July 9, 1990, 10.

Murphy, Bruce Allen. *Scalia: A Court of One*. Simon & Schuster, 2014.

Public Law 107–155 (2002).

Reid, Harry. Statement. *Congressional Record* 145, daily ed. (February 12, 1999): S 1579.

Reid, Harry. Statement. *Congressional Record* 146, daily ed. (April 13, 2000): S 2653.

Rosen, Jeffrey. *The Supreme Court: The Personalities and Rivalries That Defined America*. Times Books, 2006.

Rossum, Ralph A. *Antonin Scalia's Jurisprudence: Text and Tradition*. University Press of Kansas, 2006.

Scalia, Antonin. *A Matter of Interpretation: Federal Courts and the Law*. Edited by Amy Grutman. Princeton U. Press, 1997.

Scalia, Antonin. "Originalism: The Lesser Evil." *University of Cincinnati Law Review*. 57(1989): 849.

Scalia, Antonin. Remarks at the Catholic University of America, Washington, D.C., October 18, 1996. http://www.courttv.com/archive/legaldocs/rights/scalia.html.

Scalia, Antonin. "The Rule of Law as a Law of Rules." *University of Chicago Law Review* 56 (Fall 1989): 1175.

Scalia, Antonin, and Bryan Garner. *Reading Law: The Interpretation of Legal Texts*. Thomson West, 2012.

Schultz, David A., and Christopher E. Smith. *The Jurisprudential Vision of Justice Antonin Scalia*. Rowman & Littlefield Publishers, Inc., 1996.

Simon, James F. *The Center Holds: The Power Struggle Inside the Rehnquist Court*. Simon & Schuster, 1995.

Smith, Christopher E., and Madhavi McCall. "Justice Scalia's Influence on Criminal Justice." *University of Toledo Law Review* 34
(Spring 2003): 535.

Starr, Kenneth W. *First Among Equals: The Supreme Court in American Life.* Warner Books, 2002.

Sullivan, Kathleen M. "Justice Scalia and the Religion Clauses."
Hawaii Law Review 22 (Summer 2000): 449.

Sunstein, Cass R. "Justice Scalia's Democratic Formalism." *Yale Law
Journal.* 107 (November 1997): 529.

Thro, William E. "Limiting Judges: A Review of Ralph A. Rossum's Antonin Scalia's Jurisprudence." 33 *Journal of College & University Law* (2006): 169.

Tribe, Laurence, and Joshua Matz. *Uncertain Justice: The Roberts
Court and the Constitution.* Henry Holt and Company, 2014.

Tushnet, Mark. *A Court Divided: The Rehnquist Court and the Future
of Constitutional Law.* W.W. Norton, 2006.

U.S. Congress. Senate. Committee on the Judiciary. *Nomination of
Judge Antonin Scalia to be Associate Justice of the Supreme Court of the
U.S.: Hearing 99-1064 before the Committee on the Judiciary.* 99th
Congress, 2nd sess., 1986.

Zlotnick, David M. "Justice Scalia and His Critics: An Exploration
of Scalia's Fidelity to His Constitutional Methodology." *Emory
Law Journal* 48 (Fall 1999): 1377.

CASES

Adarand Constructors, Inc. v. Pena, 515 U.S. 200 (1995).

Agostini v. Felton, 521 U.S. 203 (1997).

Akron v. Akron Center for Reprod. Health, 462 U.S. 416 (1983).

Atkins v. Virginia, 535 U.S. 304 (2002).

558 *Bibliography*

Arizona v. United States, 132 S. Ct. 2492 (2012).

Austin v. Michigan Chamber of Commerce, 494 U.S. 652 (1990).

Barnes v. Glen Theater, Inc., 501 U.S. 560 (1991).

Bd. of Comm'r, Wabaunsee County v. Umbehr, 518 U.S. 668 (1996).

Bd. of Educ. of Kiryas Joel v. Grumet, 512 U.S. 687 (1994).

Bolling v. Sharpe, 347 U.S. 497 (1954).

Boumediene v. Bush, 553 U.S. 723 (2008).

Bowers v. Hardwick, 478 U.S. 186 (1986).

Buckley v. Valeo, 424 U.S. 1 (1976).

Callins v. Collins, 510 U.S. 1141 (1994).

Chicago v. Morales, 527 U.S. 41 (1999).

Citizens United v. FEC, 558 U.S. 310 (2010).

City of Erie v. Pap's A.M., 529 U.S. 277 (2000).

Comm. for Public Educ. and Religious Liberty v. Regan, 444 U.S. 646
   (1980).

Conroy v. Aniskoff, 507 U.S. 511 (1993).

Craig v. Boren, 429 U.S. 190 (1976).

Cruzan v. Dir., Mo. Dep't. of Health, 497 U.S. 261 (1990).

District of Columbia v. Heller, 554 U.S. 570 (2008).

Durham v. United States, 94 U.S. App. D.C. 228 (1954).

Eisenstadt v. Baird, 405 U.S. 438 (1972).

Employment Division of Oregon v. Smith, 494 U.S. 872 (1990).

FEC v. Wisconsin Right to Life, Inc., 551 U.S. 449 (2007).

Fullilove v. Klutznick, 448 U.S. 448 (1980).

Furman v. Georgia, 408 U.S. 238 (1972).

Glossip v. Gross, 576 U.S. __ (2015).

Goldman v. Weinberger, 475 U.S. 503 (1986).

Gonzalez v. Carhart, 550 U.S. 124 (2007).

Good News Club v. Milford Central School, 533 U.S. 98 (2001).

Gratz v. Bollinger, 123 S. Ct. 2411 (2003).

Griswold v. Connecticut, 381 U.S. 479 (1965).

Grutter v. Bollinger, 123 S. Ct. 2325 (2003).

Hill v. Colorado, 503 U.S. 703 (2000).

Hodgson v. Minnesota, 497 U.S. 417 (1990).

Intel Corp. v. Advanced Micro Devices, Inc., 542 U.S. 241 (2004).

Intervenor v. Mortier, 501U.S. 597 (1991).

Johnson v. United States, 576 U.S. __ (2015).

King v. Burwell, 135 S.Ct. 475 (2014).

Korematsu v. United States, 323 U.S. 214 (1944).

Kyollo v. United States, 533 U.S. 27 (2001).

Lamb's Chapel v. Center Moriches School District, 508 U.S. 384 (1993).

Lawrence v. Texas, 123 S. Ct. 2472 (2003).

Lee v. Weisman, 505 U.S. 577 (1992).

Lemon v. Kurtzman, 403 U.S. 602 (1971).

Marbury v. Madison, 5 U.S. 137 (1803).

Martin v. PGA Tour, Inc., 532 U.S. 661 (1991).

Maryland v. Craig, 497 U.S. 836 (1990).

Maryland v. King, 133 S. Ct. 1958 (2013).

McConnell v. FEC, 124 S. Ct. 619 (2003).

MCI Telecomm. v. AT&T, 512 U.S. 218 (1994).

Michael M. v. Superior Court of Sonoma County, 450 U.S. 464 (1981).

Mistretta v. United States, 488 U.S. 361 (1989).

Morrison v. Olsen, 487 U.S. 654 (1988).

Morse v. Republican Party of Virginia, 517 U.S. 186 (1996).

National Endowment for the Arts v. Finley, 524 U.S. 569 (1998).

National Federation of Independent Business v. Sebelius, 132 S. Ct. 2566 (2012).

Obergefell v. Hodges, 135 S. Ct. 2071 (2015).

Penry v. Lynaugh, 492 U.S. 302 (1989).

Planned Parenthood of Southeastern Pennsylvania v. Casey, 505 U.S. 833 (1992).

Plaut v. Spendthrift Farm, 514 U.S. 211 (1995).

Pope v. Illinois, 481 U.S. 497 (1987).

Rasul v. Bush, 542 U.S. 466 (2004).

Rhodes v. Chapman, 452 U.S. 337 (1981).

Richmond v. J.A. Croson Co., 488 U.S. 469 (1989).

Roe v. Wade, 410 U.S. 113 (1973).

Romer v. Evans, 116 U.S. 1620 (1996).

Roper v. Simmons, 543 U.S. 551 (2005).

Rostker v. Goldberg, 453 U.S. 57 (1981).

Scott v. Sanford (Dred Scott), 60 U.S. 393 (1956).

Sherbert v. Verner, 374 U.S. 398 (1963).

Smith v. United States, 508 U.S. 223 (1993).

Stanford v. Kentucky, 492 U.S. 361 (1989).

Stenberg v. Carhart, 530 U.S. 914 (2000).

Sykes v. United States, 131 S. Ct. 2267 (2011).

Thompson v. Oklahoma, 487 U.S. 815 (1988).

Troxel v. Granville, 530 U.S. 57 (2000).

United States v. Carlton, 512 U.S. 26 (1994).

United States v. Eichman, 496 U.S. 310 (1990).

United States v. Va., 518 U.S. 515 (1996).

United States v. Windsor, 133 S. Ct. 2675 (2013).

Wallace v. Jaffree, 472 U.S. 38 (1985).

Webster v. Reproductive Health Services, 492 U.S. 490 (1989).

Wickard v. Filburn, 317 U.S. 111 (1942).

Wisconsin Public Intervenor v. Mortier, 501U.S. 597 (1991).

Zelman v. Simmons-Harris, 536 U.S. 639 (2002).

Zorach v. Clauson, 343 U.S. 306 (1952).

INDEX

A

abortion, xi, xiii, 2, 15, 18, 43, 91–130, 196, 204, 207, 212, 353, 359–60, 362, 365, 444–45, 493, 525, 527, 529
anti-abortion protest and, 444–45
fundamental right and, 2, 91–92, 102, 110, 360, 365, 525. See also *Roe v. Wade*
partial-birth, 18, 124–25, 130, 445
Scalia on, 92–93, 91–130
"undue burden" standard and, 95, 99–100, 102, 108–16, 119, 128
Acton, John E. E. D. (Lord Acton), 104–5
ADA (Americans with Disabilities Act), 24–28, 31–32, 39–40, 84
Adams, John, 305, 311, 492–93
Adarand Constructors, Inc. v. Pena, 84–85
affirmative action, 12, 84–87
AFL-CIO, 448
Aguilar v. Fenton, 299
Akron v. Akron Center for Reproductive Health, Inc. (Akron I), 99–100, 108, 111

Alito, Samuel, 130, 394
joining Scalia's opinion in *Boumediene v. Bush,* 248
joining Scalia's opinion in *Citizens United v. Federal Election Commission,* 468–74
joining Scalia's opinion in *District of Columbia v. Heller,* 134–73
joining Scalia's opinion in *King v. Burwell,* 501–23
joint dissent in *NFIB v. Sebelius,* 500
Allegheny, County of v. American Civil Liberties Union, Greater Pittsburgh Chapter, 281, 319, 323
American Association of Mental Retardation, 193
American Civil Liberties Union, 281, 301, 459
American flag, 4, 14, 342, 443–44, 475, 480
burning of, 4, 14, 443, 475, 480
American Psychiatric Association, 193
American Psychological Association, 204

Americans with Disabilities Act (ADA). *See* ADA (Americans with Disabilities ACT)

Appointments Clause, 44, 52

Aristotle, x, 221

Arizona, 328–30, 337–51

Armed Career Criminal Act, 228

artists
federal subsidies sought by, 475–76, 484–87, 491–95

Atkins v. Virginia, 176–79, 194, 197, 200, 204

Austin v. Michigan Chamber of Commerce, 446, 459, 465–67

B

Barnes v. Glen Theatre, Inc., 361, 476

Barnette (West Virginia State Board of Education v. Barnette), 288, 289, 293

BCRA (Bipartisan Campaign Finance Reform Act), 448–50, 466–67

Beethoven, Ludwig van, 485, 495

Bell, Griffin B., 69

Bickel, Alexander, 77, 82

Bill of Rights, 3, 42, 46–47, 91, 137, 147–48, 151, 153, 157–58, 180, 275, 304, 318, 336, 364–66, 397, 409, 443, 446, 457, 461, 472, 501, 525–26. *See also individual amendments*
federalism and, 3, 501
importance of separation of powers and, 3, 42, 501
premise of, 446, 460
ratification of, 153, 163, 170, 304, 397
Scalia and, 3, 42

Bipartisan Campaign Finance Reform Act (BCRA). *See* BCRA

Blackmun, Harry, 96, 114, 217

Blackstone, Sir William, 140, 147–48, 156, 159, 169, 180–81, 251–53, 257–58, 292, 530–32

BMW v. Gore, 16

Boumediene v. Bush, 247–48

Bowers v. Hardwick, 353–70, 483

Brandeis, Louis D., 380, 399, 439

Brennan, William J., Jr., 17, 282, 534–35

Breyer, Stephen, 125, 133, 217–18, 220–25

Buckley v. Valeo, 447, 452, 455, 457, 459, 465, 480

Burger, Warren, 183

Bush, George H. W., 10, 45, 101, 284

Bush, George W., 125, 247, 249

C

capital punishment, 6, 175–77, 180–81, 183–84, 191, 193–95, 197–98, 200–1, 208–9, 217–18, 220, 222–25. *See also* death penalty

Carlton, United States v., 526–27

Casey (Planned Parenthood of Southeastern Pennsylvania v. Casey), xiii, 10, 126–30, 356–62, 365

Center Moriches Union Free School District, xi, 297–99

Charles I (king), 162, 253

Charles II (king), 146

Citadel, The, 410

Citizens United v. Federal Election Commission, 466–68

Civil Rights Act (1871), 165

Civil Rights Act (1964), 26, 31, 59, 416

Clinton, Bill, 10, 45, 125, 376

Clinton, Hillary, 467

Commerce Clause, 497–500, 522

Cruzan v. Missouri Department of Health, 527–35

D

death penalty, 6–7, 43, 117, 129, 175–225, 227, 336. *See also* capital punishment

  age of convicted criminals and, 176

  contemplated by Constitution, 6, 176

  "living" Constitution and, 6–7

  mentally retarded convicted criminals and, 176–82, 184, 186, 188–92, 194, 200

Declaration of Independence, 282, 291, 296, 301, 318–19, 395, 456, 537

Defense of Marriage Act (DOMA), 376–77, 383–84, 386–92

disability, 24, 27, 34, 38, 40

discrimination, 24, 26–28, 73–90, 97, 308, 328, 370, 372–73, 408, 413, 420, 438, 455, 485, 488–90, 492–94

  on basis of disability, 24, 27, 34, 38, 40

  on basis of gender, 408, 413–14, 420, 422, 425, 437

  on basis of homosexual behavior, 370–73

  on basis of race, 74–90, 97, 328, 438, 488

  employment, 26–27

  by government entities, 26

  by places of public accommodation, 26, 28

  reverse, 75, 86

  viewpoint, 488–90, 493–94

District of Columbia v. Heller, xiii, 132

DNA, 229–46

Dobson, James, 297

Douglas, William O., 82

Dred Scott v. Sandford, 108, 120, 123–24, 126

Due Process Clause, 73, 175, 228, 249, 252, 268–69, 361, 363–65, 383, 393–94, 401, 483, 525–27, 530, 535, 537

  judicial creation of new fundamental rights and, 526, 535–37

  Scalia on, 13, 526–27

  substantive due process and, 13, 91, 105, 120, 356, 360, 363–65, 384, 401, 525–27, 530, 536, 538

Durham v. United States, 280–81

E

Easterbrook, Frank H., 286, 292, 477

education, 80, 86–90, 212, 294, 299–300, 304, 349, 374, 404–8, 410–11, 416, 425–42, 444, 457, 463, 470, 487

  "school prayer" cases and, 293–94

  single-sex, 406, 409–11, 413, 416–18, 422, 425–27, 429, 432–41

Education Amendments (1972), 416

Eichman, United States v., 14, 444, 475, 480

Eighth Amendment, 18, 175–78, 180–81, 185, 187–88, 192, 196–

98, 203, 213, 215–17, 219–20, 224

Cruel and Unusual Clause of, 6, 17, 175–77, 180, 182, 192, 194, 197, 218–19

Eisenstadt v. Baird, 364–65

Elkhart County, IN, 322

Employment Division of Oregon v. Smith, 13, 277, 482

Equal Protection Clause, 5, 12–13, 73–74, 84, 86, 354, 356–57, 365, 369–71, 375, 383–84, 397, 401, 403–5, 408–9, 427, 433, 438, 536

application of tests and, 408–11

distribution of contraceptives to unmarried persons and, 91, 365

gender and, 73, 403–5, 408, 427, 433, 438

homosexuals and, 73, 354, 356–57, 369–71, 375, 383–84, 401

race and, 12, 73–74, 86

Scalia's interpretation of, 5, 12–13

Establishment Clause, xi, 8, 11, 212, 275, 277–82, 285–86, 289, 291–92, 296, 298–302, 304, 307, 310, 312–16, 322

Ethics in Government Act (1978), 43, 64, 71

Ex parte Milligan, 262–64, 266–6

Ex parte Quirin, 256, 265–67

F

Federal Election Campaign Act (1971), 447

Federal Election Commission, 447, 466–67

federalism, 3, 41, 382, 384, 389, 501

Feingold, Russell, 465

Fifth Amendment, 73, 175, 218–19, 228, 249, 383–84

Due Process Clause of. *See* Due Process Clause

Grand Jury Clause of, 175, 220

fingerprinting, 229, 230, 235–36, 240–45

First Amendment, xi, 4, 8–9, 11, 14, 110, 133, 137, 139, 145, 148, 156, 275, 277–79, 284, 297–301, 304, 306, 313–14, 316, 332, 338, 407, 443–50, 452–53, 455–60, 465, 467–73, 475–77, 479–84, 491–92, 494

anti-abortion protest and, 444

artists seeking federal subsidies and, 475–76, 485

drafting, 300

election-related speech and, 444, 446

Establishment Clause of. *See* Establishment Clause

extension of, 443

Free Exercise Clause of, 275, 277, 300, 309, 316, 396, 482

Free Speech Clause of, 14, 300. *See also* free speech indecency laws and, 361, 475–80

political speech and, 4, 18, 443, 446, 490, 460, 465–68, 472–73, 475, 492

right to criticize government and, 4, 449–50, 467

Flag Protection Act (1989), 4

Fourteenth Amendment, 7, 12–13, 73, 76–77, 80, 86, 91, 104, 165–66, 175, 285, 315, 354, 356, 363, 365–66, 383, 393, 396–97, 399,

403–4, 409, 457, 459, 525, 528, 530, 537

Due Process Clause of. *See* Due Process Clause

Equal Protection Clause of. *See* Equal Protection Clause

ratification of, 7, 73, 104, 153, 231, 285, 366, 397, 399

Fourth Amendment, 2, 5, 18, 137–39, 146, 227–33, 241–43, 245–47, 339

freedom, xi, 2–4, 13–14, 18, 64, 91, 104, 124, 128, 131, 168, 214, 249, 251, 272, 279, 312, 329, 360, 374, 395–97, 401, 405, 443, 445, 447, 449–50, 453–57, 461–62, 467–68, 471, 473, 478, 480–81, 385, 491, 493, 501, 525–26, 535

of expression, 4, 476, 481

of political association, xi, 457

of the press, 453–54, 471, 473

of religion. *See* religion, freedom of

of speech. *See* free speech; Free Speech Clause

Free Exercise Clause, 275–77, 300, 309, 316, 396, 482

free speech, 4, 14, 148, 168, 297–98, 300, 396, 443–95. *See also* Free Speech Clause

anti-abortion protest and, 444

Free Speech Clause, 14, 300

Fullilove v. Klutznick, 77–78

fundamental right(s), 7, 91–92, 102, 110, 147, 214, 354–56, 358, 360, 363–65, 367–68, 375, 399, 408, 483, 525, 536–37

abortion and, 91–92, 360, 365, 525

certain "private" activities as, 91

classifications affecting, 408

contraceptive use as, 91, 353, 365

"heightened scrutiny protection" and, 363

history and tradition and, 360, 363–68, 384

homosexual behavior held not to be, 364–68, 375, 483

judicial creation of, 526

marriage as, 7, 399

nature of interest and, 525

parents, raising children and, 525, 536–37

privacy and, 102, 355–56, 364–65

sodomy and, 354–56, 358, 364–65, 375, 525

suicide and, 107, 528–33, 535

"undue burden" and, 110

Furman v. Georgia, 192

G

gender, 407, 414, 416, 422, 425, 437

classifications and, 414

discrimination on basis of, 403–22. *See also Virginia, United States v.*

equality and, 403–22

Equal Protection Clause and, 5, 383, 403–4, 427, 438

intermediate scrutiny standard and, 439

single-sex education and, 406, 410–11, 418, 426, 432–33, 436–39, 441

strict scrutiny standard and, 109, 403

Glossip v. Gross, 216–18

Grand Jury Clause, 175

Gratz v. Bollinger, 86, 89

Griswold v. Connecticut, 353, 355, 364–65

Grutter v. Bollinger, 85, 89–90

gun rights. See *District of Columbia v. Heller*

H

habeas corpus, 193, 247–73

Hamdi v. Rumsfeld, 247, 249, 251–54, 257–62, 266–70

Hamilton, Alexander, 47, 66, 150, 196, 252, 254, 265, 272, 522

Harlan, John, 77, 399

Harmelin v. Michigan, 188, 213

Hill v. Colorado, 444–45

Holmes, Oliver Wendell, ix, 282, 399

homosexuality, 353–402, 483

classifications based on, 353, 371, 384, 403, 407

discrimination based upon, 370–73

Equal Protection Clause and, 354, 356, 383

fundamental right and, 354–56, 358, 364–68, 375, 483, 525

sodomy and. *See* sodomy

I

immigration, 327–29, 332

federal regulation of, 329, 332, 334–41, 344–45, 348–51

illegal, 327–51

indecency laws, 475–76, 480

Independent Counsel law, 10–11, 44–45

expiration of, 11, 45

Supreme Court's upholding constitutionality of, 10, 45

intermediate scrutiny, 403–6, 408–9, 411–14, 420, 435, 439

expressive conduct and, 482, 494

gender cases and, 403–4, 435

redefined, 405, 435

strict scrutiny versus, 405, 408–9, 414, 435

Islam, 248, 310, 314, 323

J

James II (king of Scotland), 35, 146

Jefferson, Thomas, 149, 154, 258, 260–61, 275, 283, 305, 311–12, 333, 425, 470

Johnson, Samuel, 139

Johnson v. United States, 228

Judaism, 310, 314, 319, 323

judicial activism, 5, 9, 12, 15–17

judicial conservative, 7–8

political conservative versus, 13–14

K

Kagan, Elena, 19, 328

joining Scalia's opinion in *Maryland v. King*, 229–73

Kennedy, Anthony, 18, 94, 101, 126, 128, 195, 229, 279–81, 323, 329, 376, 393–94, 462, 467, 500, 538

joining Scalia's opinion in *District of Columbia v. Heller*, 134

joining Scalia's opinion in *McCreary County vs. ACLU*, 303

Kennedy, Ted, 9

Kentucky, 301–25

Kerry, John, 463
Korematsu v. United States, 126

L

Lamb's Chapel v. Center Moriches Union Free School District, 276, 297
Lawrence v. Texas, 11, 355, 375–76, 383, 389–90
Lee, Robert E., 290
Lee v. Weisman, 11, 279
legislative intent, 23
Lemon v. Kurtzman, 276, 298
Lincoln, Abraham, 119, 258, 262, 292

M

Madison, James, 8, 41–42, 46–48, 52–53, 78, 144–45, 231, 260, 264, 284, 306, 311–12, 331, 333, 379
Mapplethorpe, Robert, 489
Marbury v. Madison, 15, 21, 115, 507
marriage
  as fundamental right, 7, 374–75, 525
  preserving traditional institution of, 357, 361, 371
  same-sex, 7, 11, 357, 370, 375–401
Marshall, John, 285, 304–5, 400, 492–93
Marsh v. Chambers, 304
Martin, Casey, 24–25
Martin v. PGA Tour, Inc., 24
Mary Baldwin College, 430, 437
Maryland v. King, 229–30
Matter of Interpretation, A, 131
McCain, John, 462

McConnell v. Federal Election Commission, 447
McCreary County v. ACLU, 301, 303
mental retardation, 179–80
  death penalty and, 186–88, 193
Mercer County, KY, 322
Metro Broadcasting, Inc. v. FCC, 414
Michael H. v. Gerald D., 104, 408
money. *See under* speech
Morrison v. Olson, 10–11, 43
Murray, Patty, 462

N

National Conference of Christians and Jews, 279, 290
National Endowment for the Arts v. Finley, 483
National Guard, 132
national origin
  classifications based on, 59, 74, 408, 414
National Rifle Association, 448, 459
Naval Academy (Annapolis), 410, 420
NEA (National Endowment for the Arts), 484–87, 492–95
Nicklaus, Jack, 37
Nineteenth Amendment, 5, 526
Ninth Amendment, 120, 122, 137–38, 537
Nixon v. Shrink Missouri Government PAC, 452
Northwest Territory Ordinance, 300, 304, 311

O

Obama, Barack, 498

administration of, 328, 376, 501–2
Obamacare, 498–502. *See also*
  Patient Protection and Affordable
  Care Act
Obergefell v. Hodges, 7, 393–94
O'Connor, Sandra Day, 75–77, 86,
  94–101, 108, 110–11, 130, 184,
  200, 249, 255, 356–57, 369–72,
  411, 484
*Ohio v. Akron Center for Reproductive
  Health*, 103
Olson, Theodore B., 49–51
originalism, 8–9, 12, 19, 23, 468

P

parents
  rights to raise children, 14, 526–27,
    536–38
"partial-birth abortion," 18, 124–25,
  130, 445
Partial-Birth Abortion Ban Act, 130
Patient Protection and Affordable
  Care Act, 498–523
Penry v. Lynaugh, 180–81, 200
PGA TOUR, Inc., 24–25, 30–31,
  33–37, 39
*Planned Parenthood of Southeastern
  Pennsylvania v. Casey*, xiii, 101,
  126–30, 356–362, 365
Pledge of Allegiance, 11, 280, 293,
  306–7, 315
political conservative, 277, 526
  judicial conservative versus, 13–14
political speech. *See under* speech
Powell, Lewis F., Jr., 411, 440
press
  freedom of, 4, 8–9, 154, 168, 453–
    54, 471, 473, 480

privacy
  right to, 91, 102, 355–56, 364–65
Pulaski County Courthouse, 303,
  318, 321

R

race
  classifications based on, 73–76, 79,
    82
  discrimination on basis of. *See under*
    discrimination
  Equal Protection Clause and. *See
    under* Equal Protection Clause
  strict scrutiny standard and. *See
    under* strict scrutiny
"rational basis" scrutiny, 74, 105,
  353–61, 364, 368–71, 374, 384,
  408–9, 411, 415, 418, 483
Reagan, Ronald, 94
"reasoned judgment," 105–7, 122,
  397, 400, 402
Rehnquist, William, 406
  joining Scalia's opinion in *Atkins v.
    Virginia*, 178
  joining Scalia's opinion in *Lawrence
    v. Texas*, 357
  joining Scalia's opinion in *Lee v.
    Weisman*, 280
  joining Scalia's opinion in *Planned
    Parenthood of Southeastern Penn-
    sylvania v. Casey*, 103
Reid, Harry, 10
religion
  freedom of, 13, 18, 279, 312, 405
  "school prayer" cases and, 293–94
religious accommodations, 13
reverse discrimination, 75, 86
Richmond v. J.A. Croson Co., 74–75

right(s)
  fundamental. *See* fundamental right(s)
  "to die," 2. *See also* suicide
Roberts, John, 389, 394, 500, 502
  joining Scalia's opinion in *Boumedi-
    ene v. Bush*, 248
  joining Scalia's opinion in *District of
    Columbia v. Heller*, 134
  joining Scalia's opinion in *Roper v.
    Simmons*, 196
  joining Scalia's opinion in *United
    States v. Windsor*, 377
Roe v. Wade, xi, 91–92, 94–102,
  105–6, 109–11, 114–17, 119–21,
  129, 213, 353, 356–57, 359–62,
  365
Rome, 303
Romer v. Evans, 354–56, 383
Roosevelt, Franklin D., 15, 65
Roper v. Simmons, 194–96, 216
Rostker v. Goldberg, 414
Rutan v. Republican Party of Ill., 409
Rutherford County, TN, 321

S

same-sex marriage, 7, 11, 357, 361,
  365–66, 371, 375–78, 383–99
S.B. 1070, 328–29, 337–39, 342,
  345
Schlesinger, Arthur M., 454
"school prayer" cases, 293–95
schools. *See* education
Second Amendment, 131–73
seizures and searches, 2
  constitutional prohibition of. *See
    under* United States Constitution
  unreasonable, 227–29, 231, 233,
    396

separation of powers, 41, 247, 378,
  501
  importance of, 3, 41–43
  importance of Bill of Rights versus,
    3, 47
  Scalia on, 3, 42–43
Serrano, Andres, 484, 489
Seventeenth Amendment, 5
single-sex education, 406, 409–11,
  416–18, 420, 422, 425–29, 432–
  41
Sixth Amendment, 3, 18, 97
  Confrontation Clause of, 3, 227
Smith, William French, 69
sodomy, 388
  as criminal offense, 353–57, 362–
    65, 368, 371, 375
  fundamental right and, 355–58,
    364, 367, 375, 525
  homosexuality and. *See* homosex-
    uality
Sotomayor, Sonya
  joining Scalia's opinion in *Maryland
    v. King*, 229–73
Souter, David, 101, 133, 301
Soviet Union, 42
speech
  by corporations, 445–50, 458–59,
    462, 466
  election-related, 444, 446, 465–73
  free. *See* free speech; Free Speech
    Clause
  money and, 452–66
  political, 4, 18, 443, 446, 449, 460,
    465–68, 472–73, 475, 492
  protected, 4
Speech or Debate Clause, 62
stare decisis, 15, 101–2, 106, 114–15,
  358–59, 362, 538

Starr, Kenneth, 10, 45
statutory interpretation
  judicial conservatives' approach to, 7–8, 22
  legislative history and, 23
  Scalia's method and, 7–9, 22–24
Stenberg v. Carhart, 124, 126, 130
Stevens, John Paul, 133–34, 142–45, 155, 158, 311–16, 369, 452, 467–68, 534–35, 538
  joining Scalia's decision in *Hamdi v. Rumsfeld*, 249–50
Stewart, Potter, 78
"strict constructionists," 8–9, 94
strict scrutiny, 74
  intermediate scrutiny versus, 403, 405, 408, 435
  race cases and, 74–76, 84–85, 403
  sex and, 412, 414–15, 420
  sodomy and, 355, 358, 364, 360, 384
substantive due process, 13, 91, 105, 120, 356, 360, 363–65, 384, 401, 525, 527, 530, 536. *See also* Due Process Clause
suicide
  assisted, 530–31
  attempted, 530
  defined, 530
  power of State to prevent, 479, 528–29, 532–35
  rights and, 107
Sykes v. United States, 227–28

T

Taft, William Howard, 399
Taney, Roger Brooke, 123

Ten Commandments, 301–25
Texas v. Johnson, 480
textualism, ix, 1–3, 5, 7, 9, 12–13, 15, 19, 22
Thomas, Clarence, 9, 101, 126, 128, 368, 404
  joining Scalia's opinion in *Atkins v. Virginia*, 178
  joining Scalia's opinion in *Boumediene v. Bush*, 248
  joining Scalia's opinion in *Citizens United v. Federal Election Commission*, 468
  joining Scalia's opinion in *District of Columbia v. Heller*, 134
  joining Scalia's opinion in *Glossip v. Gross*, 218
  joining Scalia's opinion *in Grutter v. Bollinger*, 87
  joining Scalia's opinion in *King v. Burwell*, 502–3
  joining Scalia's opinion in *Lamb's Chapel v. Center Moriches Union Free School District*, 298
  joining Scalia's opinion in *Lawrence v. Texas*, 357
  joining Scalia's opinion in *Lee v. Weisman*, 280
  joining Scalia's opinion in *Martin v. PGA Tour, Inc.*, 25–26
  joining Scalia's opinion in *McCreary County v. ACLU*, 303
  joining Scalia's opinion in *National Endowment for the Arts v. Finley*, 485
  joining Scalia's opinion in *Obergefell v. Hodges*, 394

joining Scalia's opinion in *Planned Parenthood of Southeastern Pennsylvania v. Casey*, 103
joining Scalia's opinion in *Roper v. Simmons*, 196
joining Scalia's opinion in *United States v. Windsor*, 377
joint dissenting opinion in *NFIB v. Sebelius*, 500
Troxel v. Granville, 14, 536
Twain, Mark, 36

U

"undue burden" standard, 95, 99–100, 105, 108–16, 119, 128
United States Air Force Academy, 410
United States Catholic Conference, 186–87
United States Constitution. *See also individual clauses*
amendments to. *See* Bill of Rights
capital punishment and death penalty contemplated by, 6, 176, 187, 218–19
"living," theory regarding, 6–7
"original intent" of Framers and, 8. *See also* originalism
Scalia's method of interpreting, 1–11
"strict constructionists" and, 8–9, 94
unreasonable searches and seizures prohibited under, 2, 5, 18, 227–29, 231–33, 396
United States Naval Academy (Annapolis), 410, 420

United States Supreme Court
cases of. *See individual cases*
justices of. *See individual justices*
life tenure of, 4, 24, 68, 71, 97, 98, 118, 196
Scalia's appointment to, 9
Scalia's influence on, 17–19
unreasonable searches and seizures. *See under* United States Constitution

V

Van Orden v. Perry, 304
Violence Against Women Act (1994), 416, 498
Virginia, United States v., 403–4
Virginia Military Institute (VMI), 404–42
Virginia Women's Institute for Leadership (VWIL), 430–31, 437

W

Walsh, Lawrence, 10, 45
Washington, George, 283, 292, 304, 310, 314
Webster v. Reproductive Health Services, 93–95
Weinberger, Caspar, 45
West Point (United States Military Academy), 410, 420
West Virginia State Board of Education v. Barnette, 288–89, 293
White, Byron, 353
joining Scalia's opinion in *Lee v. Weisman*, 280

joining Scalia's opinion in *Planned Parenthood of Southeastern Pennsylvania v. Casey*, 103
Wickard v. Filburn, 497
Wilson, Charles, 141
Windsor, United States v., 375–77
Woods, Tiger, 37